Cisco Networking Academy Program
CCNA 1 and 2 Lab Companion
Revised Third Edition

Cisco Systems, Inc.

Cisco Networking Academy Program

Cisco Press

800 East 96th Street

Indianapolis, IN 46240 USA

Cisco Networking Academy Program
CCNA 1 and 2 Lab Companion

Revised Third Edition

Cisco Systems, Inc.

Cisco Networking Academy Program

Copyright © 2005 Cisco Systems, Inc.

Published by:

Cisco Press

800 East 96th Street

Indianapolis, IN 46240 USA

Printed in the United States of America   1 2 3 4 5 6 7 8 9 0

First Printing   August 2004

ISBN: 1-58713-149-8

Warning and Disclaimer

This book is designed to provide information on *CCNA 1: Networking Basics* and *CCNA 2: Routers and Routing Basics* of the Cisco Networking Academy Program CCNA course. Every effort has been made to make this book as complete and as accurate as possible, but no warranty or fitness is implied.

The information is provided on an "as is" basis. The author, Cisco Press, and Cisco Systems, Inc., shall have neither liability nor responsibility to any person or entity with respect to any loss or damages arising from the information contained in this book or from the use of the programs that may accompany it.

The opinions expressed in this book belong to the author and are not necessarily those of Cisco Systems, Inc.

This book is part of the Cisco Networking Academy® Program series from Cisco Press. The products in this series support and complement the Cisco Networking Academy Program curriculum. If you are using this book outside the Networking Academy program, then you are not preparing with a Cisco trained and authorized Networking Academy provider.

For information on the Cisco Networking Academy Program or to locate a Networking Academy, please visit www.cisco.com/edu.

Trademark Acknowledgments

All terms mentioned in this book that are known to be trademarks or service marks have been appropriately capitalized. Cisco Press or Cisco Systems, Inc., cannot attest to the accuracy of this information. Use of a term in this book should not be regarded as affecting the validity of any trademark or service mark.

Corporate and Government Sales

Cisco Press offers excellent discounts on this book when ordered in quantity for bulk purchases or special sales. For more information, please contact: **U.S. Corporate and Government Sales** 1-800-328-3419 corpsales@pearsontechgroup.com

For sales outside of the U.S., please contact: **International Sales** international@pearsontechgroup.com.

Feedback Information

At Cisco Press, our goal is to create in-depth technical books of the highest quality and value. Each book is crafted with care and precision, undergoing rigorous development that involves the unique expertise of members of the professional technical community.

Readers' feedback is a natural continuation of this process. If you have any comments regarding how we could improve the quality of this book, or otherwise alter it to better suit your needs, you can contact us at networkingacademy@ciscopress.com. Please be sure to include the book title and ISBN in your message.

We greatly appreciate your assistance.

Publisher	John Wait
Editor-in-Chief	John Kane
Executive Editor	Mary Beth Ray
Cisco Systems Representative	Anthony Wolfenden
Cisco Press Program Manager	Nannette M. Noble
Production Manager	Patrick Kanouse
Technical Editor	Jim Lorenz
Compositor	Mark Shirar
Cover and Interior Designer	Louisa Adair

CISCO SYSTEMS

Corporate Headquarters	**European Headquarters**	**Americas Headquarters**	**Asia Pacific Headquarters**
Cisco Systems, Inc.	Cisco Systems International BV	Cisco Systems, Inc.	Cisco Systems, Inc.
170 West Tasman Drive	Haarlerbergpark	170 West Tasman Drive	Capital Tower
San Jose, CA 95134-1706	Haarlerbergweg 13-19	San Jose, CA 95134-1706	168 Robinson Road
USA	1101 CH Amsterdam	USA	#22-01 to #29-01
www.cisco.com	The Netherlands	www.cisco.com	Singapore 068912
Tel: 408 526-4000	www-europe.cisco.com	Tel: 408 526-7660	www.cisco.com
800 553-NETS (6387)	Tel: 31 0 20 357 1000	Fax: 408 527-0883	Tel: +65 6317 7777
Fax: 408 526-4100	Fax: 31 0 20 357 1100		Fax: +65 6317 7799

Cisco Systems has more than 200 offices in the following countries and regions. Addresses, phone numbers, and fax numbers are listed on the
Cisco.com Web site at www.cisco.com/go/offices.

Argentina • Australia • Austria • Belgium • Brazil • Bulgaria • Canada • Chile • China PRC • Colombia • Costa Rica • Croatia • Czech Republic
Denmark • Dubai, UAE • Finland • France • Germany • Greece • Hong Kong SAR • Hungary • India • Indonesia • Ireland • Israel • Italy
Japan • Korea • Luxembourg • Malaysia • Mexico • The Netherlands • New Zealand • Norway • Peru • Philippines • Poland • Portugal
Puerto Rico • Romania • Russia • Saudi Arabia • Scotland • Singapore • Slovakia • Slovenia • South Africa • Spain • Sweden
Switzerland • Taiwan • Thailand • Turkey • Ukraine • United Kingdom • United States • Venezuela • Vietnam • Zimbabwe

Contributing Author

Jim Lorenz is an instructor and curriculum developer for the Cisco Networking Academy Program. He has more than 20 years of experience in information systems and has held various IT positions in Fortune 500 companies, including Honeywell and Motorola. Jim has developed and taught computer and networking courses for both public and private institutions for more than 15 years. He is coauthor of the Cisco Networking Academy Program Fundamentals of UNIX course, contributing author for the CCNA Lab Companion manuals and technical editor for the Companion Guides. Jim is a Cisco Certified Academy Instructor (CCAI) for CCNA and CCNP courses. He has a bachelor''s degree in computer information systems and is currently working on his master's degree in telecommunications. Jim and his wife Mary have two daughters, Jessica and Natasha.

Table of Contents

Chapter 4 Cable Testing 59

Chapter 5 Cabling LANs and WANs 77

Part III   Appendixes   397

Appendix A   Structured Cabling Case Study Labs   399

Appendix B   Router Interface Summary   429

Appendix C   Erasing and Reloading the Router   431

Foreword

Throughout the world, the Internet has brought tremendous new opportunities for individuals and their employers. Companies and other organizations are seeing dramatic increases in productivity by investing in robust networking capabilities. Some studies have shown measurable productivity improvements in entire economies. The promise of enhanced efficiency, profitability, and standard of living is real and growing.

Such productivity gains aren't achieved by simply purchasing networking equipment. Skilled professionals are needed to plan, design, install, deploy, configure, operate, maintain, and troubleshoot today's networks. Network managers must assure that they have planned for network security and for continued operation. They need to design for the required performance level in their organization. They must implement new capabilities as the demands of their organization, and its reliance on the network, expands.

To meet the many educational needs of the internetworking community, Cisco Systems established the Cisco Networking Academy Program. The Networking Academy is a comprehensive learning program that provides students with the Internet technology skills essential in a global economy. The Networking Academy integrates face-to-face teaching, web-based content, online assessment, student performance tracking, hands-on labs, instructor training and support, and preparation for industry-standard certifications.

The Networking Academy continually raises the bar on blended learning and educational processes. The Internet-based assessment and instructor support systems are some of the most extensive and validated ever developed, including a 24/7 customer service system for Networking Academy instructors. Through community feedback and electronic assessment, the Networking Academy adapts the curriculum to improve outcomes and student achievement. The Cisco Global Learning Network infrastructure designed for the Networking Academy delivers a rich, interactive, and personalized curriculum to students worldwide. The Internet has the power to change the way people work, live, play, and learn, and the Cisco Networking Academy Program is in the forefront of this transformation.

This Cisco Press title is one of a series of best-selling companion titles for the Cisco Networking Academy Program. Designed by Cisco Worldwide Education and Cisco Press, these books provide integrated support for the online learning content that is made available to Academies all over the world. These Cisco Press books are the only authorized books for the Networking Academy by Cisco Systems, and provide print and CD-ROM materials that ensure the greatest possible learning experience for Networking Academy students.

I hope you are successful as you embark on your learning path with Cisco Systems and the Internet. I also hope that you will choose to continue your learning after you complete the Networking Academy curriculum. In addition to

its Cisco Networking Academy Program titles, Cisco Press also publishes an extensive list of networking technology and certification publications that provide a wide range of resources. Cisco Systems has also established a network of professional training companies—the Cisco Learning Partners—who provide a full range of Cisco training courses. They offer training in many formats, including e-learning, self-paced, and instructor-led classes. Their instructors are Cisco certified, and Cisco creates their materials. When you are ready, please visit the Learning & Events area on Cisco.com to learn about all the educational support that Cisco and its partners have to offer.

Thank you for choosing this book and the Cisco Networking Academy Program.

Kevin Warner
Senior Director, Marketing
Worldwide Education
Cisco Systems, Inc.

Introduction

CCNA 1 and 2 Lab Companion, Revised Third Edition, is the complete collection of labs for the CCNA 1 and 2 online curriculum in the Cisco Networking Academy Program.

There are over 100 labs in this volume all designed to provide you hands-on experience in practicing the skills learned in these courses. The material begins to prepare you to take the Cisco Certified Network Associate (CCNA) certification exam.

The Audience of This Book

This book is written for anyone who wants to learn about networking technologies. The main audience is students enrolled in an educational program like the Cisco Networking Academy Program CCNA 1 and CCNA 2 courses that focus on the topics covered in these labs.

How This Book is Organized

Table I-1 outlines all the labs in this book, the corresponding Target Indicator (TI) in the online curriculum, and the time it should take to do the lab.

Table I-1 Master Lab Overview

Lab TI	Title	Estimated Time (Minutes)
Part I CCNA 1: Networking Basics Labs Chapter 1: Introduction to Networking		
1.1.2	PC Hardware	15
1.1.6	PC Network TCP/IP Configuration	15
1.1.7	Using ping and tracert from a Workstation	20
1.1.8	Web Browser Basics	15
1.1.9	Basic PC/Network Troubleshooting Process	15
1.2.5	Decimal to Binary Conversion	15
1.2.6	Binary to Decimal Conversion	15
1.2.8	Hexadecimal Conversions	20
Chapter 2: Networking Fundamentals		
2.3.6	OSI Model and TCP/IP Model	15
2.3.7	OSI Model Characteristics and Devices	15
Chapter 3: Networking Media		
3.1.1	Safe Handling and User of a Multimeter	15
3.1.2	Voltage Measurement	15
3.1.3	Resistance Measurement	15
3.1.5	Series Circuits	15
3.1.9a	Communications Circuits	30

Table I-1 Master Lab Overview (Continued)

Lab TI	Title	Estimated Time (Minutes)
3.1.9b	Fluke 620 Basic Cable Testing	30
3.1.9c	Straight-Through Cable Construction	20
3.1.9d	Rollover Cable Construction	20
3.1.9e	Crossover Cable Construction	20
3.1.9f	UTP Cable Purchase	20
3.2.8	Fiber-Optic Cable Purchase	20
Chapter 4: Cabling Testing		
4.2.9a	Fluke 620 Cable Tester – Wire Map	20
4.2.9b	Fluke 620 Cable Tester – Faults	20
4.2.9c	Fluke 620 Cable Tester – Length	20
4.2.9d	Fluke LinkRunner – LAN Tests	20
4.2.9e	Fluke LinkRunner – Cable and NIC Tests	20
Chapter 5: Cabling LANs and WANs		
5.1.5	RJ-45 Jack Punch Down	20
5.1.7	Hub and NIC Purchase	20
5.1.10	Purchasing LAN Switches	20
5.1.12	Building a Peer-to-Peer Network	20
5.1.13a	Building a Hub-Based Network	20
5.1.13b	Building a Switch-Based Network	20
5.2.3a	Connecting Router LAN Interfaces	15
5.2.3b	Building a Basic Routed WAN	30
5.2.3c	Troubleshooting Interconnected Devices	30
5.2.7	Establishing a Console Connection to a Router or Switch	20
Chapter 6: Ethernet Fundamentals		
	There are no labs in this module.	
Chapter 7: Ethernet Technologies		
7.1.2	Waveform Decoding	60+
7.1.9a	Introduction to Fluke Network Inspector	60+
7.1.9b	Introduction to Fluke Protocol Inspector	60+
Chapter 8: Ethernet Switching		
	There are no labs in this module.	

Table I-1 Master Lab Overview (Continued)

Lab TI	Title	Estimated Time (Minutes)
Chapter 9: TCP/IP Protocol Suite and IP Addressing		
9.2.7	IP Addressing Basics	30
9.3.5	DHCP Client Setup	20
9.3.7	Workstation ARP	15
Chapter 10: Routing Fundamentals and Subnets		
10.2.9	Small Router Purchase	20
10.3.5a	Basic Subnetting	30
10.3.5b	Subnetting a Class A Network	20
10.3.5c	Subnetting a Class B Network	20
10.3.5d	Subnetting a Class C Network	20
Chapter 11: TCP/IP Transport and Application Layers		
11.2.4	Protocol Inspector, TCP, and HTTP	30
Part II CCNA 2: Routers and Routing Basics Labs Chapter 1: WANs and Routers		
1.2.5	Connecting Console Interfaces	15
1.2.6	Connecting Router LAN Interfaces	15
1.2.7	Connecting WAN Interfaces	20
Chapter 2: Introduction to Routers		
2.2.1	Router Configuration Using Setup	20
2.2.4	Establishing a Console Session with HyperTerminal	20
2.2.9	Command-Line Fundamentals	20
Chapter 3: Configuring a Router		
3.1.2	Command Modes and Router Identification	20
3.1.3	Configuring Router Passwords	20
3.1.4	Using Router show Commands	20
3.1.5	Configuring a Serial Interface	20
3.1.6	Making Configuration Changes	30
3.1.7	Configuring an Ethernet Interface	20
3.2.3	Configuring Interface Descriptions	20

Table I-1 Master Lab Overview (Continued)

Lab TI	Title	Estimated Time (Minutes)
3.2.5	Configuring Message-of-the-Day (MOTD)	20
3.2.7	Configuring Host Tables	20
3.2.9	Backing Up Configuration Files	30
Chapter 4: Learning about Other Devices		
4.1.4	Creating a Network Map Using CDP	20
4.1.6	Using CDP Commands	20
4.2.2	Establishing and Verifying a Telnet Connection	20
4.2.3	Suspending and Disconnecting Telnet Sessions	20
4.2.4	Advanced Telnet Operations	20
4.2.5a	Connectivity Tests – Ping	20
4.2.5b	Connectivity Tests – Traceroute	20
4.2.6	Troubleshooting IP Address Issues	30
Chapter 5: Managing Cisco IOS Software		
5.1.3	Using the Boot System Command	20
5.1.5	Troubleshooting Configuration Register Boot Problems	20
5.2.3	Managing Configuration Files with TFTP	30
5.2.5	Managing IOS Images with TFTP	30
5.2.6a	Password Recovery Procedures	30
5.2.6b	Managing IOS Images with ROMmon and Xmodem	30
Chapter 6: Routing and Routing Protocols		
6.1.6	Configuring Static Routes	20
Chapter 7: Distance Vector Routing Protocols		
7.2.2	Configuring RIP	20
7.2.6	Troubleshooting RIP	30
7.2.7	Preventing Routing Updates Through an Interface	20
7.2.9	Load Balancing Across Multiple Paths	30
7.3.5	Configuring IGRP	20
7.3.6	Default Routing with RIP and IGRP	30
7.3.8	Unequal Cost Load Balancing with IGRP	30

Table I-1 Master Lab Overview (Continued)

Lab TI	Title	Estimated Time (Minutes)
Chapter 8: TCP/IP Suite Error and Control Messages		
	There are no labs in this module.	
Chapter 9: Basic Router Troubleshooting		
9.1.1	Using **show ip route** to Examine Routing Tables	20
9.1.2	Gateway of Last Resort	20
9.1.8	Last Route Update	20
9.2.6	Troubleshooting Using Ping and Telnet	30
9.3.4	Troubleshooting using Traceroute	30
9.3.5	Troubleshooting Routing Issues with **show ip route** and **show ip protocols**	30
9.3.7	Troubleshooting Routing Issues with **debug**	30
Chapter 10: Intermediate TCP/IP		
10.1.6	Multiple Active Host Sessions	20
10.2.5	Well-Known Port Numbers and Multiple Sessions	20
Chapter 11: Access Control Lists (ACLs)		
11.2.1a	Configuring Standard Access Lists	30
11.2.1b	Standard ACLs	30
11.2.2a	Configuring Extended Access Lists	30
11.2.2b	Simple Extended Access Lists	45
11.2.3a	Configuring a Named Access List	30
11.2.3b	Simple DMZ Extended Access Lists	45
11.2.3c	Multiple Access Lists Functions (Challenge Lab)	45
11.2.6	VTY Restriction	45
Part III Appendix A: Structured Cabling Case Study Labs		
Lab A-1	Examination of Termination Types	45
Lab A-2	Terminating a Category 5e Cable on a Category 5e Patch Panel	30
Lab A-3	Tool Usage and Safety	20
Lab A-4	Identification of Cables	30
Lab A-5	Category 5e Outlet Termination	30
Lab A-6	Terminating Category 5e to a 110 Block	30
Lab A-7	Category 6 Jack Termination	30

This Book's Features

Many of the book's features will help facilitate your full understanding of the networking and routing topics covered in the labs:

- **Objective**—Identifies the goal or goals that are to be accomplished in the lab.

- **Background/Preparation**—Provides a list of the equipment to be used to run the lab.

- **Reflection Question**—As appropriate, labs include questions that are designed to elicit particular points of understanding. These questions help verify your comprehension of the technology being implemented.

The conventions used to present command syntax in this book are the same conventions used in the *Cisco IOS Command Reference*:

- **Bold** indicates commands and keywords that are entered literally as shown. In examples (not syntax), bold indicates user input (for example, a **show** command).

- *Italic* indicates arguments for which you supply values.

- Braces ({ }) indicate a required element.

- Square brackets ([ ]) indicate an optional element.

- Vertical bars (|) separate alternative, mutually exclusive elements.

- Braces and vertical bars within square brackets (such as [x {y | z}]) indicate a required choice within an optional element. You do not need to enter what is in the brackets, but if you do, you have some required choices in the braces.

PART I

CCNA 1: Networking Basics Labs

Chapter 1: Introduction to Networking

Chapter 2: Networking Fundamentals

Chapter 3: Networking Media

Chapter 4: Cabling Testing

Chapter 5: Cabling LANs and WANs

Chapter 6: Ethernet Fundamentals

Chapter 7: Ethernet Technologies

Chapter 8: Ethernet Switching

Chapter 9: TCP/IP Protocol Suite and IP Addressing

Chapter 10: Routing Fundamentals and Subnets

Chapter 11: TCP/IP Transport and Application Layers

Introduction to Networking

The following labs are in this chapter:

Lab TI	Title
1.1.2	PC Hardware
1.1.6	PC Network TCP/IP Configuration
1.1.7	Using **ping** and **tracert** from a Workstation
1.1.8	Web Browser Basics
1.1.9	Basic PC/Network Troubleshooting Process
1.2.5	Decimal to Binary Conversion
1.2.6	Binary to Decimal Conversion
1.2.8	Hexadecimal Conversions

Lab 1.1.2: PC Hardware

Objectives

- Become familiar with the basic peripheral components of a PC system.
- Identify PC connections, including network attachments.
- Examine the internal PC configuration and identify major components.
- Observe the boot process for the Windows operating system.
- Use the Control panel to find out information about the PC.

Background/Preparation

Knowing the components of a PC is valuable when troubleshooting and important to your success in the networking field. Before you begin, the instructor or lab assistant should have a typical desktop PC available with all peripherals, such as keyboard, monitor, mouse, speakers or headphones, a network interface card (NIC), and network cable. The system unit cover should be removed, or you should have tools to remove it. You can work individually or in teams. In addition, the instructor needs to identify the location of the A+ or PC hardware training materials.

Step 1. Examine the computer and peripheral components both front and back.

Note: The components and configuration of the PC you are working with might vary.

a. What are the manufacturer and model number of this computer?

Manufacturer	
Model Number	

b. What are the major external components of the PC, including the peripherals?

Component Name	Manufacturer/Description/Characteristics
1.	
2.	
3.	
4.	
5.	

Step 2. Remove the PC system unit cover and examine the internal components.

a. List at least eight major internal components inside the system unit. (Use the procedure in Step 4 to find the CPU and amount of RAM.)

Component Name	Manufacturer/Description/Characteristics
1.	
2.	
3.	
4.	
5.	
6.	
7.	
8.	
9.	
10.	

Step 3. Assemble the PC components and observe the boot process.

a. Assemble the PC components, attach all peripherals, and boot the PC. Observe the boot process. The computer should boot to the Windows operating system. If the computer does not boot, contact the lab assistant.

b. Did the Windows operating system boot okay? _____

c. Could you see the memory amount as the system was booting? _____

Step 4. Gather basic information about the computer's CPU and RAM.

a. Click **Start > Settings > Control Panel**. Click the **System** icon and then the **General** tab. You are viewing information about the computer using the operating system.

b. What is the CPU? _____

c. What is the speed in MHz of the CPU? _____

d. How much RAM is installed? _____

Lab 1.1.6: PC Network TCP/IP Configuration

Objectives

- Identify tools used for discovering a computer's network configuration with various operating systems.

- Gather information, including the connection, host name, MAC (Layer 2) address, and TCP/IP network (Layer 3) address information.

- Compare the network information to that of other PCs on the network.

Background/Preparation

This lab assumes that you are using any version of Windows. This is a nondestructive lab that you can perform on any machine without changing the system configuration.

Ideally, you perform this lab in a LAN environment that connects to the Internet. You can use a single remote connection via a modem or DSL-type connection. You will need the IP address information which the instructor should provide.

The following instructions run the lab twice reflecting the operating-system differences between Windows 95/98/Me systems and Windows NT/2000/XP systems. You should perform the lab on both types of systems if possible.

Note: All users complete Step 1.

Step 1. Connect to the Internet.

Establish and verify connectivity to the Internet. This step ensures the computer has an IP address.

Note: Windows 95/98/Me users complete Steps 2 through 6.

Step 2. Gather basic TCP/IP configuration information.

a. Using the taskbar, choose **Start > Run** to open the dialog box in Figure 1-1. Type **winipcfg** and press **Enter**. The spelling of **winipcfg** is critical, but the case is not. It is short for Windows IP configuration.

Figure 1-1 Run Dialog Box

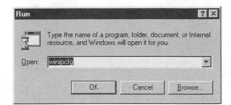

b. This first screen shows the adapter address (or MAC address), IP address, subnet mask, and default gateway.
Figure 1-2 shows the basic IP configuration screen. Select the correct adapter if the list contains more than one.

Figure 1-2 Basic IP Configuration Screen

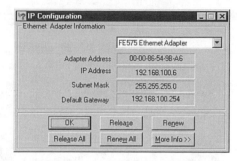

c. The IP address and default gateway should be in the same network or subnet; otherwise, this host wouldn't be able to communicate outside the network. In Figure 1-2, the subnet mask reveals that the first three octets must be the same number in the same network.

Note: If this computer is on a LAN, you might not see the default gateway if it is running behind a proxy server. Record the following information for this computer:

d. IP address: _____

e. Subnet mask: _____

f. Default gateway: _____

Step 3. Compare this computer's TCP/IP configuration to that of others on the LAN.

If this computer is on a LAN, compare the information on several machines.

a. Are there any similarities? _____

b. What is similar about the IP addresses? _____

c. What is similar about the default gateways? _____

d. What is similar about the adapter (MAC) addresses? _____

e. The IP addresses should share the same network portion. All machines in the LAN should share the same default gateway. Although it is not a requirement, most LAN administrators standardize components such as NICs, so it would not be surprising to find that all machines share the first three hexadecimal (hex) pairs in the adapter address. These three pairs identify the manufacturer of the adapter.

f. Record a couple of the IP addresses.

_____

Step 4. Verify the selection of a network adapter.

a. The box at the top of the screen should display this computer's adapter model. Use the drop-down arrow in that box to see any other configurations for this adapter (such as PPP). You might see configurations for a modem if this computer connects to the Internet with a dial-up account. On a server, it is possible to find another NIC in this list, or a machine with both a NIC and a modem could include both configurations in this list. Figure 1-3 shows an AOL modem IP configuration screen. Notice that the figure shows no IP address. This configuration is what a home system could have if the user does not log on to the Internet.

Figure 1-3 AOL Modem IP Configuration Screen

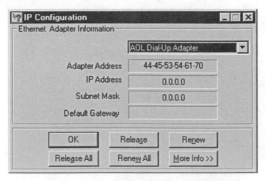

b. Return to the adapter that displays the NIC or modem data with an IP address.

Step 5. Check additional TCP/IP configuration information.

a. Click the **More Info** button. Figure 1-4 shows the detailed IP configuration screen.

Figure 1-4 Detailed IP Configuration Screen

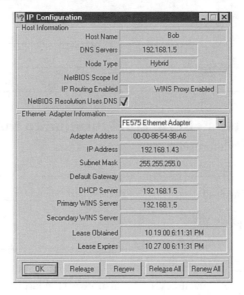

b. You should see the following information: the host name (computer name, NetBIOS name); the Dynamic Host Config-uration Protocol (DHCP) server's address, if used; and the date the IP lease starts and ends. Look over the remaining information. You might also see entries for Domain Name System (DNS) and Windows Internet Name Service (WINS) servers, which are used in name resolution.

c. Write down the IP addresses of any servers listed:

_____

_____

d. Write down the computer's host name:

_____

e. Write down the host names of a couple of other computers:

_____

Step 4. Type in another web URL.

To load a new page, type in a new URL, such as http://www.cnn.com. Notice the status on the bottom bar of your browser. What do you see? _____

Step 5. Use the browser management buttons.

a. Each of the buttons on top of your browser has a function. If you position the mouse over a button, a box will appear identifying the button.

b. Click the **Back** button. What did it do? _____

c. Click the **Forward** button. Does it return you to the CNN website? _____

d. Click the **Reload** or **Refresh** button. What do you think it does?

_____

e. Type **http://www.microsoft.com** and press **Enter**. Click on the **Stop** button as the window is loading. What happens?

_____

Step 6. Use a search engine.

Type the URL for a search engine such as http://www.google.com. Search for the word **browser**. What is the result?

_____

Step 7. Access networking terms definitions websites.

a. Enter the URL for **http://www.webopedia.com**. Enter the keyword **browser**. What is the result?

_____

b. What hyperlinks are available? _____

c. Enter the URL for **http://www.whatis.com**. Look up the keyword **DNS**. Click on **Exact Match for DNS** under **whatis.com terms**. What does it say about DNS?

_____

Reflection

Identify a way in which you can navigate from one site to another.

If you see the same graphics or text the next time you go to the NBA site, what should you do to ensure that you can see updated news? _____

_____

_____

_____

Lab 1.1.9: Basic PC/Network Troubleshooting

Objectives

- Learn the proper sequence for troubleshooting computer and network problems.
- Become familiar with the more common hardware and software problems.
- Given a basic problem situation, be able to troubleshoot and resolve the problem.

Background/Preparation

The ability to effectively troubleshoot computer problems is an important skill. The process of identifying the problem and trying to solve it requires a systematic, step-by-step approach. This lab will introduce some basic hardware and software problems to solve and will help you become more familiar with PC components and the software required to use the Cisco curriculum. The process of trying to solve a problem is fairly straightforward. Some of the suggestions here are more than you will need to solve basic hardware and software problems, but they will provide a framework and guidelines to use when more complex problems arise. The instructor's version of the lab provides a list of sample problems that the instructor can introduce.

The Seven Basic Steps for PC and Network Troubleshooting

Step 1. Define the problem.

Describe what is happening or not happening using proper terminology. For example, the PC can't get to the Internet or the PC cannot print.

Step 2. Gather the facts.

Observe the symptoms and characterize or identify the source of the problem:

- Is it hardware (check for lights and noises) or software (errors on screen) related?
- Does it affect only this computer or user or are others also impacted?
- Does it affect only this software or more than one application?
- Is this the first time it has happened, or has it happened before?
- Did someone recently change anything on the PC?
- Get the opinions of others who might have more experience.
- Check websites and troubleshooting knowledge databases.

Step 3. Consider the possibilities.

Using the facts you gathered, identify one or more possible causes and potential solutions. Rank the solutions in order of the most likely to the least likely cause.

Step 4. Create an action plan.

Develop a plan that involves the single most likely solution. You can try the other options if the original solution fails. Consider the following in developing your plan:

Check the simplest possible causes first. Is the power turned on or plugged in?

Verify hardware first and then software. (Do any lights come on?)

If it is a network problem, start at Layer 1 of the Open System Interconnection (OSI) model and work your way up. Studies show the majority of problems occur at Layer 1.

Can you use substitution to isolate the problem? If the monitor does not work, the problem could be the monitor, video adapter, or cables. Try another monitor to see whether that corrects the problem.

Step 5. Implement the plan.

Make changes from your plan to test the first possible solution.

Step 6. Observe the results.

a. If the problem is solved, document the solution. Double-check to make sure everything still works.

b. If the problem is not resolved, restore the changes and return to your plan to try the next solution. If you do not reverse this change, you will never know whether the solution was a later change or a combination of two changes.

Step 7. Document the results.

You should always document your results to assist in solving similar problems as well as developing a documentation history for each device. If you are going to replace part of the devices, it might be nice to know if any are frequent sources of trouble or if they have recently been reconditioned.

Step 8. Introduce problems and troubleshoot.

a. Work in teams of two. Team Member A (or the instructor) will select two problems from a list of common hardware and software problems and introduce the problems into the computer. The desired goal is to run one of the videos or movies from the online curriculum or the CD.

b. Team Member A (or the instructor) should create the hardware or software problems with the computer while the other team member is out of the room and then turn off the computer and monitor.

c. After Team Member B identifies the problems and corrects them, switch places and let the other introduce some new problems.

d. Each team member solving a problem should fill in the table based on the symptoms observed, problems identified, and solutions.

Team Member A

	Symptom Observed	Problem Identified	Solution	
Problem 1				
Problem 2				

Team Member B

	Symptom Observed	Problem Identified	Solution	
Problem 1				
Problem 2				

Lab 1.2.5: Decimal to Binary Conversion

Objectives

- Learn the process for converting decimal values to binary values.
- Practice converting decimal values to binary values.

Background/Preparation

Knowing how to covert decimal values to binary values is valuable when converting human readable IP addresses in dotted-decimal format to machine-readable binary format. This is normally done for calculation of subnet masks and other tasks.

The following is an example of an IP address in 32-bit binary form and dotted-decimal form:

Binary IP address: 11000000.10101000.00101101.011110001

Decimal IP address: 192.168.45.121

Table 1-1 provides a simple tool for easily converting binary values to decimal values. You create the first row by counting right to left from one to eight for the basic eight bit positions (although it would work for any size binary value). The value row starts with one and doubles (base 2) for each position to the left.

Table 1-2 Converting Binary to Decimal Values

Position	8	7	6	5	4	3	2	1
Value	128	64	32	16	8	4	2	1

You can use the same conversion table and simple division to convert decimal values to binary. To convert the decimal number 207 to binary, start with 128 (2^7) and divide by each lesser power of 2 until the number remaining is either a 0 or 1. Refer to the following division example and the steps list that follow.

```
128 ⌐207
        128
        ‾‾‾
   64   79
        64
        ‾‾‾
    8   15
         8
        ‾‾‾
    4    7
         4
        ‾‾‾
    2    3
         2
        ‾‾‾
         1
```

Networking Media

The following labs are in this chapter:

Lab TI	Title
3.1.1	Safe Handling and Use of a Multimeter
3.1.2	Voltage Measurement
3.1.3	Resistance Measurement
3.1.5	Series Circuits
3.1.9a	Communications Circuits
3.1.9b	Fluke 620 Basic Cable Testing
3.1.9c	Straight-Through Cable Construction
3.1.9d	Rollover Cable Construction
3.1.9e	Crossover Cable Construction
3.1.9f	UTP Cable Purchase
3.2.8	Fiber-Optic Cable Purchase

Lab 3.1.1: Safe Handling and Use of a Multimeter

Figure 3-1 Fluke 110 Series Multimeter

Objective

■ Learn how to use or handle a multimeter correctly.

Background/Preparation

A multimeter is a powerful electrical testing tool that can detect voltage levels, resistance levels, and open and closed circuits. It can check both alternating current (AC) and direct current (DC) voltage. Open and closed circuits are indicated by resistance measurements in ohms. Each computer and networking device consists of millions of circuits and small electrical components. You can use a multimeter to debug electrical problems within a computer or networking device or with the media between networking devices.

Prior to starting the lab, the teacher or lab assistant should have several multimeters available (one for each team of two students) and various batteries for testing. Work in teams of two. You need the following resources:

■ A digital multimeter (Fluke 110 Series, 12B or similar) for each team

■ A manual for the multimeter

■ A battery (for example, a 9V, 1.5V, or lantern; it doesn't matter) for each team to test

---

Caution: The multimeter is a sensitive piece of electronic testing equipment. Be sure that you do not drop it or handle it carelessly. Be careful not to accidentally nick or cut the red or black wire leads (probes). Because it is possible to check high voltages, you should take extra care when doing so to avoid electrical shock.

Perform the following steps to become familiar with the handling of the multimeter.

Step 1. Insert the red and black leads (probes) into the proper jacks on the meter.

The black probe should go in the COM jack, and the red probe should go in the + (plus or positive) jack.

Step 2. Turn on the multimeter. (Click or turn the on button.)

a. What model of multimeter are you working with?

_____

b. What action must you take to turn on the meter?

_____

Step 3. Switch or turn to different measurements (for example, voltage, ohms, and so on).

a. How many different switch positions does the multimeter have?

_____

b. What are they?

_____

_____

Step 4. Switch or turn the multimeter to the voltage measurement.

What is the symbol for this? _____

Step 5. Put the tip of the red (positive) lead on one end of a battery (the + side), and put the tip of the black (negative) lead on the other end of a battery.

Is any number showing up on the multimeter? _____

If not, make sure you switch to the correct type of measurement (Vol, voltage, or V). If the voltage is negative, reverse your leads.

Reflection

1. Name one thing that you should not do to a multimeter.

   _____

2. Name one important function of a multimeter.

   _____

3. Why would you get a negative voltage when measuring a battery?

   _____

Lab 3.1.2: Voltage Measurement

Figure 3-2 Fluke 110 Series Multimeter-AC Voltage Scale

Objective

- Demonstrate the ability to measure voltage safely with the multimeter.

Background/Preparation

The digital multimeter is a versatile testing and troubleshooting device. This lab covers both DC and AC voltage measurements. Voltage is measured in either AC or DC volts (indicated by a V). *Voltage* is the pressure that moves electrons through a circuit from one place to another. Voltage differential is essential to the flow of electricity. The voltage differential between a cloud in the sky and the earth is what causes lightning to strike.

Warning: It is important to be careful when taking voltage measurements because it is possible to receive an electrical shock.

DC: DC voltage rises to a set level and then stays at that level and flows in one direction (positive or negative). Batteries produce DC voltage and are commonly rated at 1.5V or 9V (flashlight batteries) and 6V (lantern and vehicle batteries). Typically, the battery in your car or truck is a 12V battery. When you place an electrical "load" such as a light bulb or motor between the positive (+) and negative (-) terminals of a battery, electricity flows.

AC: AC voltage rises above zero (positive) and then falls below zero (negative) and actually changes direction very rapidly. The most common example of AC voltage is the wall outlet in your home or business. In North America, these outlets provide approximately 120 volts of AC directly to any electrical appliance that is plugged in, such as a computer, toaster, or television. Some devices, such as small printers and laptop computers, have a transformer (small black box) that plugs into a 120V AC wall outlet and then converts the AC voltage to DC voltage for use by the device. Some AC outlets can provide a higher voltage of 220V for use by devices and equipment with heavier requirements, such as clothes dryers and arc welders.

Prior to starting the lab, the teacher or lab assistant should have several multimeters available (one for each team of students) and various items for testing voltage. Work in teams of two. You need the following resources:

- Fluke 110 or 12B multimeter (or equivalent)
- An assortment of batteries: A cell, C cell, D cell, 9 volts, 6V lantern

- Duplex wall outlet (typically 120V)
- Power supply (for laptop or other networking electrical device)

The following resources are optional:

- A lemon with a galvanized nail stuck in one side and a piece of uninsulated copper wire stuck in the opposite side
- Solar cell with leads attached
- Homemade generator (wire wound around a pencil 50 times and a magnet)

Step 1. Select the proper voltage scale.

a. The method of selecting the voltage scale will vary, depending on the type of meter. The Fluke 110 has two separate positions for voltage: a letter V with a wave over it for AC and a V with a solid and a dashed line above it for DC. With the Fluke 12B, move the rotary selector to the V symbol for voltage (black V) to be able to measure voltage. Press the button that has the VDC and VAC symbol to select between DC and AC measurements.

DC measurements: The screen will show a V (voltage) with a series of dots and a line over the top. The available scales depend on the voltage to be measured. They start from millivolts (abbreviated mV, 1000th of a volt) to voltages up to hundreds of volts. Use the Range button to change the range of DC voltage to be measured based on what voltage you expect to measure. You can typically measure batteries (less than 15V) accurately with the VDC scale and 0.0 range. You can use DC voltage measurements to determine whether batteries are good or whether there is voltage coming out of an AC adapter (transformer or converter). AC adapters are common; you use them with hubs, modems, laptops, printers, and other peripherals. These adapters can take wall-outlet AC voltage and step it down to lower AC voltages for the device, or they can convert the AC voltage to DC and step it down. Check the back of the adapter to see what the input (AC) and output voltages (AC or DC) should be.

AC measurements: The screen will show a V (voltage) with a tilde (~) after it. This symbol represents alternating current. There available scales depend on the voltage to be measured. They start from millivolts (abbreviated mV, 1000th of a volt) to voltage up to hundreds of volts. Use the Range button to change the range of AC voltage to be measured based on what voltage you expect to measure. You can typically measure voltage from power outlets (120V or greater) accurately with the VAC scale and 0.0 range. AC voltage measurements are useful in determining whether there is adequate voltage coming from an AC outlet to power equipment.

b. Use a Fluke 110 or 12B multimeter (or equivalent) to measure the voltage of the items in Step 2.

Step 2. Check the voltages of the items in Table 3-1. Be sure to turn off the meter when finished.

Table 3-1 Taking Voltage Measurements

Item to Measure the Voltage Of	Set Selector and Range Scale To	Voltage Reading
Batteries: A cell (AA, AAA), C cell, D cell, 9V, 6V lantern		
Duplex wall outlet (typically 120V)		
Power supply (converts AC to lower AC or DC) for laptop, mobile phone, or other networking electrical device		
(Optional) A lemon with a galvanized nail stuck in one side and a piece of uninsulated copper wire stuck in the opposite side		

Reflection

Why might you want to measure voltage when troubleshooting a network?

_____

_____

_____

Lab 3.1.3: Resistance Measurement

Figure 3-3 Fluke 110 Series Multimeter-Resistance Scale

Objective

- Demonstrate the ability to measure resistance and continuity with the multimeter.

Background/Preparation

The digital multimeter is a versatile testing and troubleshooting device. This lab covers resistance measurements and related measurements called *continuity*. Resistance is measured in ohms (indicated by the Greek letter Omega or Ω). Copper wires (conductors), such as those commonly used in network cabling (unshielded twisted-pair (UTP) and coaxial), normally have very low resistance or "good" continuity (the wire is continuous) if you check them from end to end. If the wire has a break, it is called "open," which creates very high resistance. (Air has nearly infinite resistance, indicated by the infinity symbol, or ∞, a sideways 8.)

The multimeter has a battery in it, which it uses to test the resistance of a conductor (wire) or insulator (wire sheathing). When you apply the probes to the ends of a conductor, the battery current flows and the meter measures the resistance it encounters. If the battery in the multimeter is low or dead, you must replace it or you will not be able to take resistance measurements.

With this lab, you test common networking materials so that you can become familiar with them and their resistance characteristics. You first learn to use the resistance setting on the multimeter. As you measure small resistances, you should also note the continuity feature. The instructions apply to the Fluke 110 and 12B. Other meters function in a similar way.

Prior to starting the lab, the teacher or lab assistant should have several multimeters available (one for each team of two students) and various networking items for testing resistance. Work in teams of two. You need the following resources:

- Fluke 110 Series or 12B multimeter (or equivalent)
- 1000 ohm resistor
- 10,000 ohm resistor
- Pencil for creating graphite paths on paper
- Category 5 jack
- Small section (0.2 m or approximately 6 to 8 inches) of CAT 5 UTP solid cable
- BNC terminated coaxial cable
- Unconnected DB9 to RJ-45 adapter
- Terminated Category 5 UTP patch cable

Step 1. Select the resistance scale on the multimeter.

Fluke 110:

Resistance measurements: Move the rotary selector to the omega symbol for ohms (Ω) to measure resistance. Use the Range button to change the range of resistance to be measured based on what resistance you expect to get. The screen will show Ω (ohms), KΩ (kilohms, thousands of ohms), or MΩ (megohms, millions of ohms).

Continuity measurements: Move the rotary selector to the Beeper Sound symbol to the left of the ohms symbol to measure continuity. When there is good continuity (less than 20ohms), the beep will sound. You use the continuity setting when you just want to know whether there is a good path for electricity and you don't care about the exact amount of resistance.

Fluke 12B:

Resistance measurements: Move the rotary selector to the omega symbol for ohms (Ω) to measure resistance. Press the button with the ohms symbol on it to select resistance mode instead of continuity. The screen should not show a diode symbol, which is a small black triangle pointing to a vertical bar. Use the Range button to change the range of resistance to be measured based on what resistance you expect to get.

Continuity measurements: Move the rotary selector to the omega symbol for ohms (Ω)to measure resistance. Press the button that has the ohms symbol on it to select continuity mode. The screen will show a diode symbol, which is a small black triangle pointing to a vertical bar. A *diode* is an electronic device that either passes or blocks electrical current. When there is good continuity (low resistance), the beep will sound. You use the continuity setting when you just want to know whether there is a good path for electricity and you don't care about the exact amount of resistance.

Step 2. Check the resistances in Table 3-2. Turn off the meter when finished or battery will drain.

Table 3-2 Taking Resistance Measurements

Item to Measure the Resistance Of	Set Selector and Range Scale To	Resistance Reading
1000Ω resistor		
10kΩ resistor		
Graphite marking from a pencil on a piece of paper		
Category 5 jack		
0.2 m section of Category 5 UTP solid cable		
Touch red and black probe contacts together.		
Your own body (Touch the tips of the probes with your fingers.)		
BNC terminated coaxial cable		
Unconnected DB9 to RJ-45 adapter		
Terminated Category 5 UTP patch cable		

Reflection

What purpose might the multimeter serve in maintaining and troubleshooting a computer network?

_____

_____

_____

Lab 3.1.5: Series Circuits

Figure 3-4 Series Circuit

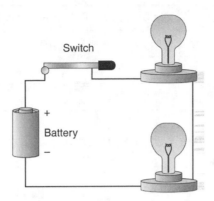

Objective

■ Build series circuits and explore their basic properties.

Background/Preparation

One of the most basic concepts in electronics is that of a continuous loop through which electrons flow, which is called a *circuit*. Throughout networking materials are references to ground loop circuit, circuit versus packet switching, and virtual circuits, in addition to all the real circuits formed by networking media and networking devices. One of the fundamental electrical circuits is the *series circuit*. Although most networking devices and networks are built from very complex circuits that are beyond the scope of the lessons in this course, the process of building some series circuits will help you with some of the terminology and concepts of networking. This lab also helps increase your overall understanding of some of the most basic electrical-circuit building blocks.

Prior to starting the lab, the teacher or lab assistant should have several multimeters available (one for each team of students) and various items to create circuits. Work in teams of two. You need the following resources:

■ Fluke 110 Series or 12B multimeter (or equivalent)

■ Light switch

■ Wire cutters and stripper

■ Copper wire

■ Two light bulbs (6V) with bulb bases

■ 6V lantern battery

Step 1. Measure the resistance of all devices.

a. Measure the resistances of all devices and components except the battery. All resistances should be less than 1Ω (ohm), except the light bulbs. All the devices except the battery should register continuity (with the tone), indicating a short circuit or a conducting path.

b. Check the resistance of the items in Table 3-3. Turn off the meter when finished, or it will drain the battery.

Table 3-3 Measuring Device Resistance

Item to Measure the Resistance Of	Set Selector and Range Scale To	Resistance Reading
Pieces of wire to connect components		
Light switch		
Light bulbs		

Step 2. Measure the voltage of the battery, unloaded (with nothing attached to it), filling in the information in Table 3-4.

Table 3-4 Measuring Battery Voltage

Item to Measure the Voltage Of	Set Selector and Range Scale To	Voltage Reading
Lantern battery (6V) with no load		

Step 3. Build a series circuit, one device at a time.

a. Use one battery, one switch, one bulb, and connecting wires.

b. Connect the battery's positive lead to the end of one wire, and connect the negative lead to the other wire. If you turn on the switch, the bulb should light.

c. Disconnect one item, and see that the circuit is broken. Did the bulb go out? _____

Step 4. Measure the battery voltage while the circuit is running.

a. The switch should be turned on and the light bulb should be lit.

b. What is the voltage of the battery with the light bulb on? _____

Step 5. Add the second bulb to the series and measure the battery voltage again.

a. What is the voltage of the battery with the light bulbs on? _____

Reflection

How do series circuits apply to networking?

_____

_____

Lab 3.1.9a: Communications Circuits

Objective

■ Design, build, and test a simple, complete, fast, and reliable communications system, using common materials.

Background/Preparation

For reliable communications to take place on a network, you must define many things ahead of time, including the physical method of signaling and the meaning of each signal or series of signals. With this lab, you create a simple physical network and agree on some basic rules for communication to send and receive data. You will base this digital network on the American Standard Code for Information Interchange (ASCII). It will be somewhat similar to the old telegraph Morse-code systems, where the only means of communicating over long distances was by sending a series of dots and dashes as electrical signals over wires between locations. Although the technology will be simpler than that of real systems, you will learn many of the key concepts of data communications between computers. This lab also helps to clarify the functions of the layers of the Open System Interconnection (OSI) model.

Prior to starting the lab, the teacher or lab assistant should have several multimeters available (one for each team of students) and various items for the construction of a simple communication network. Work in teams of two to four.

Table 3-5 lists the required resources. Review the purpose of each of the required items because it will help in designing your network.

Table 3-5 Required Network Construction Items

Network Construction Item Required	Purpose
Fluke 110 or 12B multimeter (or equivalent)	For testing communications connections
20' CAT 5 UTP cable	For the physical communications lines (the cabling medium)
ASCII chart	To help with coding and interpretation of signals (If you do not have a hard copy of the 7-bit ASCII code chart, search the Internet for the words "ACSII chart," and you will find several.)
Light switch	To activate the signaling device to create the digital on/off (binary) signals
Light bulbs (6V) with bulb bases	To act as the signaling device
6V lantern battery	To power the signaling device
Wire cutters and stripper	To adjust the length and prepare the ends of the communication lines

Lab Goals

Your group must design, build, and test a communications circuit with another team. You must communicate as much data as possible, as quickly and as error-free as possible. Spoken, written, or miscellaneous nonverbal communication of any kind is forbidden; you communicate only over the wire. You will agree as a team on the physical connections and on the coding you will use. One of the main goals is to send a message to the other team and have it interpret what you intended without it knowing the message ahead of time. Keep the OSI model in mind as you design your system.

- **Layer 1 issues:** You must connect two pairs of wire to have communication in both directions (half or full duplex).

- **Layer 2 issues:** You must communicate some sort of frame start and stop sequence. This sequence of bits is different from the character and number bits you will be transmitting.

- **Layer 3 issues:** You must invent an addressing scheme (for hosts and networks) if it is more than point-to-point communication.

- **Layer 4 issues:** You must include some form of control to regulate quality of service (QoS) (such as error correction, acknowledgment, windowing, flow controls, and so on).

- **Layer 5 issues:** You must implement some way of synchronizing or pausing long conversations.

- **Layer 6 issues:** You must use some means of data representation (for example, ASCII encoded as optical bits).

- **Layer 7 issues:** You must be able to communicate an idea supplied by your instructor or come up with a message on your own.

Reflection

1. What issues arose as you built your communications system that you think apply to data communications between computers?

_____

_____

_____

2. Analyze your communications system in terms of the OSI layers.

_____

_____

_____

_____

_____

Lab 3.1.9b: Fluke 620 Basic Cable Testing

Figure 3-5 Fluke 620 LAN CableMeter

Objectives

- Use a simple cable tester to verify whether a straight-through or crossover cable is good or bad.
- Use the Fluke 620 advanced cable tester to test cables for length and connectivity.

Background/Preparation

In this lab, you work with several prepared cables and test them for basic continuity (breaks in wires) and shorts (two or more wires touching) using a basic cable tester. You will create similar cables in the future labs.

Simple cable testers: There are a number of simple and inexpensive basic cable testers available (less than $100). They usually consist of one or two small boxes with RJ-45 jacks to plug the cables into. Many models test only Ethernet UTP cable.

Plug both ends of the cable into the proper jacks; the tester will test all eight wires and indicate whether the cable is good or bad. Simple testers might just have a single light to indicate the cable is good or bad; others might have eight lights to tell you which wire is bad. These testers, which have internal batteries, are performing continuity checks on the wires.

Advanced cable testers: Advanced cable testers, such as the Fluke 620 LAN CableMeter, perform basic cable-testing functions and much more. The Fluke 620 advanced cable testers can cost from hundreds to thousands of dollars. You will use an advanced cable tester in future labs to do wire maps and so on. The 620 LAN CableMeter verifies connectivity for all LAN cable types. This rugged tester can measure cable length; test for faults such as opens, shorts, reversed, crossed, or split pairs; and show the distance to the defect. Each 620 LAN CableMeter comes with one cable identifier.

The Fluke 620 has the following characteristics:

- Only requires single-person verification
- Tests all LAN cable types: UTP, shielded twisted-pair (STP), FTP, and coaxial
- Detects a multitude of wiring problems: open, short, crossed, reversed, and split pair
- Locates wiring and connection errors (distance to the open or short)
- Measures cable length

Prior to starting the lab, the teacher or lab assistant should have several basic cable testers or several Fluke CableMeters and various lengths of wire with induced problems. Work in teams of two. You need the following resources:

- Basic cable tester
- Advanced cable tester (Fluke 620 or equivalent)
- Two good Category 5 or higher cables— one crossover and one straight-through
- Two bad Category 5 or higher cables—one with a break and one with a short (Use different colors or labels.)

Step 1. Test the cables.

Simple cable tester: Refer to the instructions from the manufacturer, and insert the ends of the cable to be tested into the jacks accordingly.

Fluke 620: Insert the RJ-45 from one end of the cable into the UTP/FTP jack on the tester, and turn the dial to test. You will test all conductors to verify they are not broken or shorted. (*Note*: This test does not verify that the pins are connected correctly from one end to the other.)

For each test, insert the cable into the RJ-45 jacks of the cable tester and record your results in Table 3-6.

Table 3-6 Cable Test Results

	Color or Cable Number	Category Type	Straight-Through or Crossover?	Length of Cable	Test Results Pass/Fail
Cable #1					
Cable #2					
Cable #3					
Cable #4					

Lab 3.1.9c: Straight-Through Cable Construction

Figure 3-6 Straight-Through Cable

Objective

- Build a Category 5 or Category 5e (CAT 5 or 5e) UTP Ethernet network patch cable (or patch cord).
- Test the cable for good connections (continuity) and correct pinouts (correct color of wire on the right pin).

Background/Preparation

The cable constructed will be a four-pair (eight-wire) straight-through cable, which means that the color of wire on Pin 1 on one end of the cable will be the same as that of Pin 1 on the other end. Pin 2 will be the same as Pin 2, and so on. You will wire the cable to either TIA/EIA-568B or A standards for 10BASE-T Ethernet, which determines what color wire is on each pin. T568B (also called AT&T specification) is more common in the U.S., but many installations are also wired to T568A (also called ISDN).

Prior to starting the lab, the teacher or lab assistant should have a spool of CAT 5 UTP cable, RJ-45 (8-pin) connectors, an RJ-45 crimping tool, and an Ethernet/RJ-45 continuity tester available. Work individually or in teams. You need the following resources:

- Two- to three-foot length of CAT 5 cabling (one per person or one per team)
- Four RJ-45 connectors (two extra for spares)
- RJ-45 crimping tools to attach the RJ-45 connectors to the cable ends
- Ethernet cabling continuity tester that can test straight-through or crossover cables (T568A or T568B).
- Wire cutters

Figure 3-7 shows the wire color scheme for both the T568A and T568B wiring standards. Table 3-7 provides the cabling pinout information for the T568B wiring standard.

Figure 3-7 T568A and T568B Wire Colors

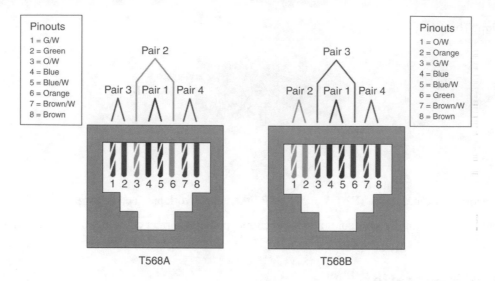

Table 3-7 T568B Cabling Pinout

Pin #	Pair #	Function	Color	Used with 10/100 BASE-T Ethernet?	Used with 100 BASE-T4 and 1000 BASE-T4 Ethernet?
1	2	Transmit	White/orange	Yes	Yes
2	2	Transmit	Orange	Yes	Yes
3	3	Receive	White/green	Yes	Yes
4	1	Not used	Blue	No	Yes
5	1	Not used	White/blue	No	Yes
6	3	Receive	Green	Yes	Yes
7	4	Not used	White/brown	No	Yes
8	4	Not used	Brown	No	Yes

Steps

Use Figure 3-7 and Table 3-7 to create a T568B patch panel cable. You should wire both cable ends the same when looking at the conductors.

Step 1 Determine the distance between devices, or device and plug, and then add at least 12" to it. The maximum length for this cable according to TIA/EIA structured wiring standards is 3 meters, although it can vary somewhat. Standard lengths are 6' and 10'.

Step 2 Cut a piece of stranded CAT 5 UTP cable to the desired length. You should use stranded cable for patch cables because it is more durable when bent repeatedly. Solid wire is fine for cable runs that are punched down into jacks.

Step 3 Strip 2" of the jacket off of one end of the cable.

Step 4   Hold the four pairs of twisted cables tightly where jacket was cut away and then reorganize the cable pairs into the order of the T568B wiring standard. Take care to maintain as much of the twist as possible because it provides noise cancellation.

Step 5   Holding the jacket and cable in one hand, untwist a short length of the green and blue pairs and reorder them to reflect the T568B wiring color scheme. Untwist and order the rest of the wire pairs according to the color scheme.

Step 6   Flatten, straighten, and line up the wires and then trim them in a straight line to within 1/2" to 3/4" from the edge of the jacket. Be sure not to let go of the jacket and the wires, which are now in the proper order! You should minimize the length of untwisted wires because overly long sections near connectors are a primary source of electrical noise.

Step 7   Place an RJ-45 plug on the end of the cable, with the prong (clip) on the underside and the orange pair to the left side of the connector.

Step 8   Gently push the plug onto wires until you can see the copper ends of the wires through the end of the plug. Make sure that the end of the jacket is inside the plug (to provide for stress relief) and that all wires are in the correct order. If the jacket is not inside the plug, it will not be properly gripped and will eventually cause problems. If everything is correct, crimp the plug hard enough to force the contacts through the insulation on the wires as shown in Figure 3-8, thus completing the conducting path.

Figure 3-8 Crimping the Wires

Step 9   Repeat Steps 3 through 8 to terminate the other end of the cable, using the same scheme to finish the straight-through cable.

Step 10   Test the finished cable and have the instructor check it. How can you tell whether your cable is functioning properly?

Lab 3.1.9d: Rollover Cable Construction

Objectives

- Build a Category 5 or Category 5e (CAT 5 or 5e) UTP console rollover cable.

- Test the cable for good connections (continuity) and correct pinouts (correct wire on the right pin).

Background/Preparation

This cable will be a four-pair (eight-wire) *rollover* cable. This type of cable is typically 10 feet long but can be as long as 25 feet. You can use it to connect a workstation or dumb terminal to the console port on the back of a Cisco router or switch. Both ends of the cable you build will have RJ-45 connectors on them. One end plugs directly into the RJ-45 console-management port on the back of the router or switch, and the other end plugs into an RJ-45-to-DB9 terminal adapter. This adapter converts the RJ 45 to a 9-pin female D connector for attachment to the PC or dumb-terminal serial (COM) port. A DB25 terminal adapter is also available to connect with a PC or dumb terminal, which uses a 25-pin connector. Figure 3-9 shows a (rollover) console cable kit that ships with most Cisco devices.

Figure 3-9 Rollover Console Cable Kit

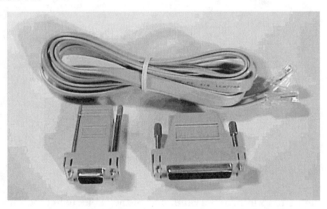

For all practical purposes, if you put the second RJ-45 on upside-down when you build a straight-through jumper, you have a rollover cable. It's called a rollover because the pins on one end are all reversed on the other end, as if you rotated or rolled over one end of the cable.

Prior to starting the lab, the teacher or lab assistant should have a spool of CAT 5 or CAT 5e UTP cable, RJ-45 (8-pin) connectors, an RJ-45 crimping tool, and a continuity tester. Work individually or in teams. You need the following resources:

- 10- to 20-foot length of CAT 5 cabling (one per person or one per team)

- Four RJ-45 connectors (two extra for spares)

- RJ-45 crimping tools to attach the RJ-45 connectors to the cable ends

- An RJ-45 to DB9 female terminal adapter (available from Cisco)

- Cabling continuity tester

- Wire cutters

Steps

1. Use Table 3-8 as a reference to help you create a rollover console cable.

Table 3-8 Rollover Console Cable Information

Router or Switch Console Port (DTE)	RJ-45 to RJ-45 Rollover Cable (Left End)	RJ-45 to RJ-45 Rollover Cable (Right End)	RJ-45 to DB9 Adapter	Console Device (PC Workstation Serial Port)
Signal	From RJ-45 Pin Number	To RJ-45 Pin Number	DB9 Pin Number	Signal
RTS	1	8	8	CTS
DTR	2	7	6	DSR
TxD	3	6	2	RxD
GND	4	5	5	GND
GND	5	4	5	GND
RxD	6	3	3	TxD
DSR	7	2	4	DTR
CTS	8	1	7	RTS

Signal legend: RTS = Request to Send, DTR = Data Terminal Ready, TxD = Transmit Data, GND = Ground (one for TxD and one for RxD), RxD = Receive Data, DSR = Data Set Ready, CTS = Clear to Send.

2. Determine the distance between devices and then add at least 12" to it. Make your cable about 10" unless you are connecting to a router or switch from a greater distance. The maximum length for this cable is about 8m (approximately 25").

3. Strip 2" of the jacket off of one end of the cable.

4. Hold the four pairs of twisted cables tightly where jacket was cut away and then reorganize the cable pairs and wires into the order of the T568B wiring standard. You can order them in any sequence, but use the T568B sequence to become more familiar with it.

5. Flatten, straighten, and line up the wires and then trim them in a straight line to within 1/2" to 3/4" from the edge of the jacket. Be sure not to let go of the jacket and the wires, which are now in order!

6. Place an RJ-45 plug on the end of the cable, with the prong on the underside and the orange pair to the left side of the connector.

7. Gently push the plug onto wires until you can see the copper ends of the wires through the end of the plug. Make sure that the end of the jacket is inside the plug and that all the wires are in the correct order. If the jacket is not inside the plug, it will not be properly protected from stress and will eventually cause problems.

8. If everything is correct, crimp the plug hard enough to force the contacts through the insulation on the wires, thus completing the conducting path.

9. Repeat Steps 2 through 6 to terminate the other end of the cable but reversing every wire as indicated in the preceding table. (Pin 1 to Pin 8, Pin 2 to Pin 7, Pin 3 to Pin 6 and so on).

   Alternate method: Arrange the wires into the order of the T568B wiring standard. Place a RJ-45 plug on the end with the prong on the top side of the connector. This method will achieve the proper reversing of every pair of wires.

10. Test the finished cable and have the instructor check it. How can you tell whether your cable is functioning properly?

Lab 3.1.9e: Crossover Cable Construction

Objectives

- Build a Category 5 or Category 5e (CAT 5 or 5e) UTP Ethernet crossover cable to T568B and T568A standards.

- Test the cable for good connections (continuity) and correct pinouts (correct wire on the right pin).

Background/Preparation

This cable will be a four-pair (eight-wire) crossover cable, which means that Pairs 2 and 3 on one end of the cable will be reversed on the other end. The pinouts will be T568A on one end and T568B on the other end. You should terminate all eight conductors (wires) with RJ-45 modular connectors.

This patch cable will conform to the structured cabling standards. If you use it between hubs or switches, it is part of the "vertical" cabling, also know as backbone cable. You can use a crossover cable as a backbone cable to connect two or more hubs or switches in a LAN or to connect two isolated workstations to create a mini-LAN. This setup will allow you to connect two workstations or a server and a workstation without the need for a hub between them. Such a connection can be helpful for training and testing. If you want to connect more than two workstations, you will need a hub or a switch.

Prior to starting the lab, the teacher or lab assistant should have a spool of CAT 5 or CAT 5e UTP cable, RJ-45 (8-pin) connectors, an RJ-45 crimping tool, and an Ethernet/RJ-45 continuity tester. Work individually or in teams. You need the following resources:

- Two- to three-foot length of CAT 5 cabling (one per person or one per team)

- Four RJ-45 connectors (two extra for spares)

- RJ-45 crimping tools to attach the RJ-45 connectors to the cable ends

- Ethernet cabling continuity tester that can test crossover cables (T568A to T568B)

- Wire cutters

Steps

1. Refer to Tables 3-9 and 3-10 as well as Figure 3-10 and follow the steps to create a crossover cable. You should wire one end of the cable to the T568A standard and the other end to the T568B standard. This setup crosses the transmit and receive pairs (2 and 3) to allow communication to take place.

   You use only four wires with 10BASE-T or 100BASE-TX Ethernet.

Table 3-9 T568A Cabling Pinout

Pin #	Pair #	Function	Color	Used with 10/100 BASE-T Ethernet?	Used with 100 BASE-T4 and 1000 BASE-T4 Ethernet?
1	3	Transmit	White/green	Yes	Yes
2	3	Transmit	Green	Yes	Yes
3	2	Receive	White/orange	Yes	Yes
4	1	Not used	Blue	No	Yes

Table 3-9 T568A Cabling Pinout (Continued)

Pin #	Pair #	Function	Color	Used with 10/100 BASE-T Ethernet?	Used with 100 BASE-T4 and 1000 BASE-T4 Ethernet?
5	1	Not used	White/blue	No	Yes
6	2	Receive	Orange	Yes	Yes
7	4	Not used	White/brown	No	Yes
8	4	Not used	Brown	No	Yes

Table 3-10 T568B Cabling Pinout

Pin #	Pair #	Function	Color	Used with 10/100 BASE-T Ethernet?	Used with 100 BASE-T4 and 1000 BASE-T4 Ethernet?
1	2	Transmit	White/orange	Yes	Yes
2	2	Transmit	Orange	Yes	Yes
3	3	Receive	White/green	Yes	Yes
4	1	Not used	Blue	No	Yes
5	1	Not used	White/blue	No	Yes
6	3	Receive	Green	Yes	Yes
7	4	Not used	White/brown	No	Yes
8	4	Not used	Brown	No	Yes

Figure 3-10 T568A and T568B Wire Colors

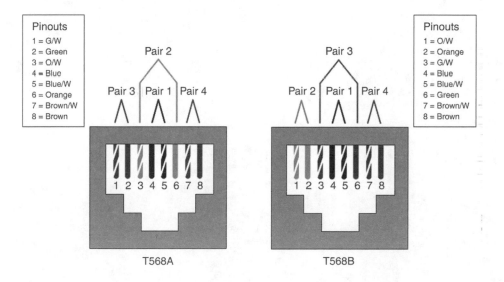

2. Determine the distance between devices, or between device and plug, and then add at least 12" to it. Standard lengths for this cable are 6' and 10'.

3. Cut a piece of stranded UTP cable to the desired length. You will use stranded cable for patch cables because it is more durable when bent repeatedly. Solid wire is fine for cable runs that are punched down into jacks.

4. Strip 2" of the jacket off one end of the cable.

5. Hold the four pairs of twisted cables tightly where jacket was cut away and then reorganize the cable pairs into the order of the T568B wiring standard. Take care to maintain the twist because it provides noise cancellation.

6. Hold the jacket and cable in one hand, untwist a short length of the green and blue pairs, and reorder them to reflect the T568B wiring color scheme. Untwist and order the rest of the wire pairs according to the color scheme.

7. Flatten, straighten, and line up the wires and then trim them in a straight line to within 1/2" to 3/4" from the edge of the jacket. Be sure not to let go of the jacket and the wires, which are now in order! Minimize the length of untwisted wires because overly long sections near connectors are a primary source of electrical noise.

8. Place an RJ-45 plug, prong down, on the end of the cable with the green pair on the left side of the T568A end and the orange pair on the left side of the T568B end.

9. Gently push the plug onto wires until you can see the copper ends of the wires through the end of the plug. Make sure that the end of the jacket is inside the plug and that all wires are in the correct order. If the jacket is not inside the plug, it will not be protected from stress and will eventually cause problems.

10. If everything is correct, crimp the plug hard enough to force the contacts through the insulation on the wires, thus completing the conducting path.

11. Repeat Steps 4 through 8 to terminate the other end of the cable, using the T568A scheme to finish the crossover cable.

12. Test the finished cable and have the instructor check it. How can you tell whether your cable is functioning properly?

Lab 3.1.9f: UTP Cable Purchase

Objectives

- Introduce the variety and prices of network cabling and components in the market.
- Gather pricing information for UTP patch cables and bulk cable.

Background/Preparation

You are asked to put together a price list for an upcoming cabling project. You need to gather pricing information for the horizontal (UTP) cabling. If your area does not use UTP, substitute shielded products. The items include the following:

- Twenty-four 1m (3 feet) CAT 5 or higher UTP patch cables
- Twenty-four 3m (10 feet) CAT 5 or higher UTP patch cables
- Two 15m (50 feet) CAT 5 or higher UTP patch cables
- 500 feet of UTP (Compare the price to STP.)
- 500 feet of UTP plenum

Step 1. Research cable pricing.

Use at least three sources for pricing. If you do web searches, try **http://www.cdw.com** and **http://www.google.com**, plus any others you prefer. Perform searches from those sites looking for **CAT 5 jumpers**, **CAT 5 patch**, and **CAT 5 bulk**. Although the CDW site will give you prices quickly, the Google search will turn up many interesting sites, from custom cable-building firms to instructions for building your own cables. You might also refer to networking equipment and supplies catalogs.

Step 2. Compile your results in Table 3-11.

Table 3-11 UTP Cable Pricing Results

Site, Catalog, or Store			
Twenty-four 1m (3 feet) CAT 5 or higher			
Twenty-four 3m (10 feet) CAT 5 or higher			
Two 15m (50 feet) CAT 5 or higher			
500 feet of UTP			
500 feet of STP			
500 feet of UTP plenum			

Lab 3.2.8: Fiber-Optic Cable Purchase

Objectives

- Introduce the variety and prices of network cabling and components in the market.
- Gather pricing information for fiber patch cables and fiber bulk cable.

Background/Preparation

You are asked to put together a price list for an upcoming cabling project. You need to gather pricing information for the vertical or fiber cabling. You will be using multimode (MM) fiber. The items include the following:

- Twenty-four 2m (6 feet) MM patch cables
- Twenty-four 5m (15 feet) MM patch cables
- Two 15m (50 feet) MM patch cables
- 1000 feet of MM fiber-optic bulk cable

Step 1. Research cable pricing.

Use at least three sources for pricing. If you do Web searches, try **http://www.cdw.com** and **http://www.google.com**, plus any others you prefer. Perform searches from those sites looking for **fiber optic jumpers**, **fiber optic patch**, and **fiber optic bulk**. Although the CDW site will give you prices quickly, a Google search will turn up many interesting sites, from custom cable-building firms to instructions for building your own cables. You can also refer to networking equipment and supplies catalogs.

Step 2. Compile your results in Table 3-12.

Table 3-12 Fiber-Optic Cable Pricing Results

Site, Catalog, or Store			
Twenty-four 2m (6 feet) MM patch cables			
Twenty-four 5m (15 feet) MM patch cables			
Two 15m (50 feet) MM patch cables			
1000 feet of MM fiber-optic cable			

Cable Testing

The following labs are in this chapter:

Lab TI	Title
4.2.9a	Fluke 620 Cable Tester – Wire Map
4.2.9b	Fluke 620 Cable Tester – Faults
4.2.9c	Fluke 620 Cable Tester – Length
4.2.9d	Fluke LinkRunner – LAN Tests
4.2.9e	Fluke LinkRunner – Cable and NIC Tests

Lab 4.2.9a: Fluke 620 Cable Tester—Wire Map

Figure 4-1 Fluke 620 LAN CableMeter

Objectives

- Learn the wire-mapping features of the Fluke 620 LAN CableMeter (or its equivalent).

- Learn how to use a cable tester to check for the proper installation of unshielded twisted-pair (UTP) Category 5 (CAT 5) cable according to Telecommunications Industry Association/Electronic Industries Association (TIA/EIA)-568 cabling standards in an Ethernet network.

Background/Preparation

Wire maps can be helpful in troubleshooting cabling problems with UTP cable. A wire map allows the network technician to verify which pins on one end of the cable are connected to which pins on the other end.

Prior to starting the lab, the teacher or lab assistant should have several correctly wired CAT 5 cables (both straight-through and crossover) to test. Several CAT 5 cables should have problems to test, such as poor connections and split pairs. The teacher or lab assistant should number the cables to simplify the testing process and to maintain consistency. You should have access to a cable tester that can test at least continuity, cable length, and wire maps. Work individually or in teams.

You need the following resources:

- CAT 5 straight-wired cables of different colors

- CAT 5 crossover-wired cable (T-568A on one end and T-568B on the other)

- CAT 5 straight-wired cables of different colors and different lengths with open-wire connections in the middle or one or more conductors shorted at one end

- CAT 5 straight-wired cable with a split-pair miswire

- Fluke 620 LAN CableMeter or similar to test cable length, continuity, and wire maps

Steps

1. Turn the rotary switch selector on the tester to the **Wire Map** position. Press the **Setup** button to enter the setup mode, and observe the LCD screen on the tester. The first option should be Cable: Press the **Up/Down** arrows until you select the cable type **UTP**. Press **Enter** to accept that setting, and go to the next one. Continue pressing the **Up/Down** arrows and pressing **Enter** until the tester is set to the cabling characteristics in Table 4-1. Once you have completed setting up the meter, press the **Setup** button to exit setup mode.

Table 4-1 Fluke 620 Cabling Characteristic Settings

Tester Option	Desired Setting—UTP
Cable:	UTP
Wiring:	10BASE-T or EIA/TIA 4PR
Category:	CAT 5
Wire Size:	American wire gauge (AWG) 24
Cal to Cable:	No
Beeping:	On or Off
LCD Contrast:	From 1 through 10 (brightest)

2. For each cable, use the procedure that follows, placing the near end of the cable into the RJ-45 jack labeled UTP/FTP on the tester. Place the RJ-45-to-RJ-45 female coupler on the far end of the cable and then insert the cable identifier into the other side of the coupler. The coupler and the cable identifier, shown in Figure 4-2, are accessories that come with the Fluke 620 LAN CableMeter.

Figure 4-2 Coupler and Cable Identifier Tools

3. Using the tester Wire Map function and a cable ID unit, you can determine the wiring of both the near and far ends of the cable. The top set of numbers on the LCD screen is the near end, and the bottom set is the far end. Perform a wire-map test on each of the cables, and fill in the following table based on the result for each CAT 5 cable. Write down the number and color, whether the cable is straight-through or crossover, the tester screen test results, and what you think the problem is. Use Table 4-2 to record your results.

Table 4-2 Cable Test Results

Cable Number	Cable Color	How Cable Is Wired (Straight-Through or Crossover)	Tester Displayed Test Results*	Problem Description
1			Top: Bot:	
2			Top: Bot:	
3			Top: Bot:	
4			Top: Bot:	
5			Top: Bot:	

*Refer to the Fluke manual for a detailed description of test results for wire maps.

Lab 4.2.9b: Fluke 620 Cable Tester—Faults

Figure 4-3 Fluke 620 LAN CableMeter

Objectives

- Learn the cable test pass/fail features of the Fluke 620 LAN CableMeter (or its equivalent).

- Learn how to use a cable tester to check for the proper installation of UTP for an Ethernet network.

- Test different cables to determine some problems that can occur from incorrect cabling installation and termination.

Background/Preparation

Basic cable tests can be helpful in troubleshooting cabling problems with UTP. The cabling infrastructure (or cable plant) in a building is expected to last at least 10 years. Cabling-related problems are one of the most common causes of network failure. The quality of cabling components, the routing and installation of the cable, and the quality of the connector terminations are the main factors in determining how trouble-free the cabling will be.

Prior to starting the lab, the teacher or lab assistant should have several correctly wired CAT 5 cables (both straight-through and crossover) to test. Several CAT 5 cables should have problems to test. The teacher or lab assistant should number the cables to simplify the testing process and to maintain consistency. You need the following resources:

- CAT 5 straight-through and crossover wired cables of different colors (some good and some bad)

- CAT 5 straight-through and crossover wired cables of different colors and different lengths with open-wire connections in the middle or one or more conductors shorted at one end

- Cable tester (Fluke 620 LAN CableMeter or similar) to test cable length

Steps

1. Turn the rotary switch selector on the tester to the **Test** position. Press the **Setup** button to enter the setup mode, and observe the LCD screen on the tester. The first option should be Cable: Press the **Up/Down** arrows until you select the cable type **UTP**. Press **Enter** to accept that setting and go to the next one. Continue pressing the **Up/Down** arrows and pressing **Enter** until the tester is set to the cabling characteristics in Table 4-3. Once the options have been properly selected, press the **Setup** button to exit setup mode.

Table 4-3 Fluke 620 Cabling Characteristic Settings

Tester Option	Desired Setting—UTP
Cable:	UTP
Wiring:	10BASE-T or EIA/TIA 4PR
Category:	CAT 5
Wire Size:	AWG 24
Cal to Cable:	No
Beeping:	On or Off
LCD Contrast:	From 1 through 10 (brightest)

2. For each cable, use the procedure that follows, placing the near end of the cable into the RJ-45 jack labeled UTP/FTP on the tester. Place the RJ-45-to-RJ-45 female coupler on the far end of the cable, and then insert the cable identifier into the other side of the coupler. The coupler and the cable identifier are accessories that come with the Fluke 620 LAN CableMeter (see Figure 4-4).

3. Using the tester **Test** function and a cable ID unit (for UTP), you can determine the functionality of the cable. Perform a basic cable test on each of the cables, and fill in Table 4-4 based on the result for each CAT 5 cable. Write down the number and color, whether the cable is straight-through or crossover or coaxial, the tester screen test results, and what you think the problem is. For UTP cables, press the **Up/Down** arrows to see all pairs.

Figure 4-4 Coupler and Cable Identifier Tools

Table 4-4 Cable Test Results

Cable Number	Cable Color	Tester Test Results	Problem
1			
2			
3			
4			

Lab 4.2.9c: Fluke 620 Cable Tester—Length

Figure 4-5 Fluke 620 LAN CableMeter

Objectives

- Learn the cable-length feature of the Fluke 620 LAN CableMeter (or its equivalent).
- Learn how to use a cable tester to check the length of Ethernet cabling to verify that it is within the standards specified and that the wires inside are the same length.

Background/Preparation

Cable-length tests can be helpful in troubleshooting cabling problems with UTP. The cabling infrastructure (or cable plant) in a building is expected to last at least 10 years. Cabling-related problems are one of the most common causes of network failure. The quality of cabling components, the routing and installation of the cable, and the quality of the connector terminations are the main factors in determining how trouble-free the cabling will be.

Prior to starting the lab, the teacher or lab assistant should have several correctly wired CAT 5 cables (both straight-through and crossover) to test. The teacher or lab assistant should number the cables to simplify the testing process and to maintain consistency. You should have access to a cable tester that can do cable-length tests for UTP. Work individually or in teams. You need the following resources:

- CAT 5 straight or crossover cables of different colors (some good and some bad)
- Cable tester (Fluke 620 LAN CableMeter or similar) to test cable length

Steps

1. Turn the rotary switch selector on the tester to the **Length** position. Press the **Setup** button to enter the setup mode, and observe the LCD screen on the tester. The first option should be Cable: Press the **Up/Down** arrows until you select the cable type **UTP**. Press Enter to accept that setting and go to the next one. Continue pressing the **Up/Down** arrows and pressing **Enter** until the tester is set to the cabling characteristics in Table 4-5. Once the options have been properly selected, press the **Setup** button to exit setup mode.

Table 4-5 Fluke 620 Cabling Characteristic Settings

Tester Option	Desired Setting—UTP
Cable:	UTP
Wiring:	10BASE-T or EIA/TIA 4PR
Category:	CAT 5
Wire Size:	AWG 24
Cal to Cable:	No
Beeping:	On or Off
LCD Contrast:	From 1 through 10 (brightest)

2. For each cable, use the procedure that follows, placing the near end of the cable into the RJ-45 jack labeled UTP/FTP on the tester. Place the RJ-45-to-RJ-45 female coupler on the far end of the cable and then insert the cable identifier into the other side of the coupler. The coupler and the cable identifier are accessories that come with the Fluke 620 LAN CableMeter (see Figure 4-6).

Figure 4-6 Coupler and Cable Identifier Tools

3. Using the tester **Length** function and a UTP cable ID unit, you can determine the length of the cable. Perform a basic cable test on each of the cables, and fill in Table 4-6 based on the result for each cable. Write down the number and color, the cable length, the tester screen test results, and what you think the problem is (if there is a problem). For UTP cables, press the **Up/Down** arrows to see all pairs.

Table 4-6 Cable Test Results

Cable Number	Cable Color	Tester Test Results	Problem
1			
2			
3			
4			

Lab 4.2.9d: Fluke LinkRunner—LAN Tests

Figure 4-7 Fluke LinkRunner

Objectives

- Become familiar with the capabilities of the Fluke LinkRunner.
- Determine whether a cable drop is active.
- Identify the cable drop speed, duplex capabilities, and service type.
- Verify network layer connectivity with ping.

Background/Preparation

In this lab, you work with Ethernet cable drops that are attached to networking devices such as hubs and switches to determine the characteristics and cabling of the devices and identify potential networking problems. You will use some of the key capabilities of the Fluke LinkRunner, such as drop activity, and ping to perform the analysis.

As networks run faster and become more complex, infrastructure cabling and devices must operate to precise levels in a tighter performance window. As a result, nearly 80 percent of network problems stem from simple wiring and connection problems. You need the following resources:

- Ethernet hub and switch
- Several Ethernet straight-through patch cables
- Cable run from a wall plate to a switch through a patch panel

The following URLs provide information on the Fluke LinkRunner. The first one is a virtual demo of LinkRunner capabilities, and the second is a link to the downloadable *LinkRunner Quick Reference Guide* in various languages:

- http://www.flukenetworks.com/us/LAN/Handheld+Testers/LinkRunner/_see+it+live.htm#
- http://www.flukenetworks.com/us/LAN/Handheld+Testers/LinkRunner/_manuals.htm

Step 1. Become familiar with the capabilities of the Fluke LinkRunner.

Access the virtual demo of the LinkRunner using the first URL. You can try different tests to become familiar with its capabilities.

Step 2. Obtain access to the *LinkRunner Quick Reference Guide.*

You can directly access the quick reference guide online or download it to your PC using the link provided. Your instructor might also have a copy of the quick reference guide. This lab reproduces selected pages of the quick reference guide. Figure 4-8 shows the connectors and buttons on the LinkRunner.

Figure 4-8 LinkRunner Connectors and Buttons

1. RJ-45 LAN port
2. RJ-45 MAP port
   (cable testing)
3. Selection buttons
   Left – Highlight
   Right – Action
4. Power Button

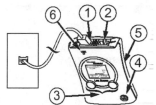

Power off - press and hold
Backlight – press once briefly

5. Batteries (2) AA
6. Link indicator light

Step 3. Configure the LinkRunner.

a. From any screen, you can access the main configuration by pressing both buttons simultaneously. You have the option to configure LinkRunner or go into the ping configuration.

b. Pressing the left button takes you to the LinkRunner configuration, where you can find the MAC address of the Link-Runner and toggle between feet and meters.

   What is the Layer 2 MAC address? _____

c. Pressing the right button takes you to the ping configuration, which is covered later.

Step 4. Test active workstation links to a switch.

a. LinkRunner allows you to determine what type of service users are connected to (e.g. Ethernet, Token Ring, Telco). On Ethernet segments, you can determine whether the drop is active and identify its speed, duplex capabilities, and auto-negotiation settings.

b. This test will determine whether the cable drop is active while identifying its speed, duplex, and service type. (10 or 10/100 indicates Ethernet.)

c. Turn on the LinkRunner by pressing the small button in the lower-right corner.

d. Disconnect a functioning LAN patch cable from a workstation and plug it into the RJ-45 LAN port on the LinkRunner. You can perform this nondestructive test on a live network. The cable should be attached to a wall plate, which then attaches to a switch through a patch panel in a wiring closet. Cabling should be in accordance with current structured-cabling standards.

e. Observe the display on the LinkRunner and record the information for Drop #1 in Table 4-7. Figure 4-9 provides a sample display from the quick reference guide.

f. Obtain another patch cable of any length and plug one end directly into the switch. Plug the other end into the Link-Runner LAN port. Record the information for Drop #2 in Table 4-7.

Table 4-7 LinkRunner Cable Test Results

	Link Active ?	Cable Type/Link Status	Advertised Speed/Duplex	Actual Link Speed/Duplex	Network Utilization
Drop #1					
Drop #2					

Figure 4-9 LinkRunner Sample Display

Is this an active Ethernet port?

1. Activity indicator
2. Cable/Link Status:
   ═══ Straight patch
   ⋊⋉ Crossover patch

   ⠶⤬⠶ Unknown patch (Auto-MDIX port on hub or switch)
   ⠸⤮！ Link Level (displays when low)
3. Advertised speed/duplex
4. Actual link speed/duplex

5. Softkeys (correspond to L/R selection buttons).
   ▯ Battery Low Indicator: displays when low.
6. Network utilization

g. Disconnect the end of the cable from the switch and observe the display. What was the result?

_____

Step 5. Test a direct link to a hub.

a. Obtain another patch cable of any length and plug one end directly into an active regular hub port. Plug the other end into the LinkRunner LAN port. Described the results. _____

b. How does this display differ from that of a cable drop attached to a switch?

_____

c. Disconnect the power from the hub and described the display now.

_____

d. Plug the hub back in.

e. Move the cable from one of the regular ports on the hub to the uplink port on the hub. Make sure the uplink is not active. (The button is not pushed in.) Describe the results.

_____

f. Activate the uplink port. (Push in the button.) What happened to the wires in the display?

_____

g. Why did this occur? _____

Step 6. Use the Dynamic Host Configuration Protocol (DHCP) ping function to verify network layer connectivity.

If you connect the LAN port in a DHCP network environment, LinkRunner acts as a DHCP client. It acquires an IP address and verifies basic connectivity to key devices by pinging the default gateway (router) and Domain Name System (DNS) server. See Figure 4-10 for a sample of the screen display.

Figure 4-10 LinkRunner Ping Capabilities

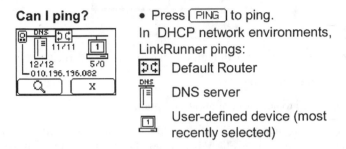

a. Turn on the LinkRunner by pressing the small button in the lower-right corner.

b. Obtain a patch cable of any length and plug one end directly into the switch on a LAN with a DHCP server available. Plug the other end into the LinkRunner LAN port.

c. The LinkRunner must be in DHCP mode to perform this test. Press the right softkey (Ping) once to see if the DHCP magnifying glass appears. If not, press the left softkey twice and place a checkmark in the DHCP option box. Allow time for the LinkRunner to obtain an IP address from the DHCP server and then press the right softkey (Ping).

Note: If the LinkRunner fails to obtain an IP address, verify that the DHCP option box is checked and that there is a DHCP server active on the network.

---

d. What IP address did the LinkRunner obtain? _____

e. Press the left softkey (magnifying glass), which provides ping details.

f. What is the IP address of the default router (gateway)?

g. What is round-trip time for the ping to the default router? _____

h. What is the IP address of the DNS server?

i. What is round-trip time for the ping to the DNS server? _____

j. If one response time is slower than the other, why do you think that it is?

Step 7. Ping a user-defined IP address.

You can use the LinkRunner to ping user-defined IP addresses (up to four common IP address ping targets). See Figure 4-11 for a sample of the screen display used to edit the IP address for Computer Target 1.

Figure 4-11 LinkRunner Ping Target

a. Turn on the LinkRunner by pressing the small button in the lower-right corner.

b. Disconnect any cables from the LinkRunner.

c. Press the right softkey (wrench) to access configuration options.

d. Press the right softkey again (ping and wrench). If you will be working on a network with a DHCP server, turn off the LinkRunner DHCP client by removing the checkmark from the DHCP checkbox. Press the right softkey (checkmark) to uncheck it.

e. Press the left softkey (down arrow) to get to the computer icon and then press the right softkey (computer, IP, and wrench) to access the IP address configuration function.

f. Press the right softkey (down arrow and computer) to cycle through the four IP targets. Zero indicates no ping for the computer target. Select IP Target 1.

g. Press the left softkey (down arrow) to access the IP address, and press the right softkey (IP x.x.x.x) to begin configuring the IP address for Target Computer 1 (see Figure 4-11).

h. Identify the IP address of a lab server or a partner's workstation and record it here.

_____

i. Press the left softkey (right arrow) to advance the cursor from one number to the next in the IP address. Press the right softkey (IP and up arrow) to change the value of the number. You must account for all 12 decimal digits, including zeros. While working with the first digit of any of the four octets, press the up arrow four or five times. What is the maximum number that the LinkRunner lets you set for the first number of an octet?

_____

j. After you finish with the last digit, the left softkey becomes a down arrow. Press the left softkey until you get to the X (exit) and then press the right softkey (X). Press the left softkey (down arrow) again until you get to the X, and press the right softkey again to exit the configuration function.

k. Once you set the IP address to be pinged and exit the configuration function, connect a patch cable from the LAN port on the LinkRunner to a wall-plate jack, hub, or switch on the network you will be pinging. What does the cable display look like? _____

_____

l. Press the right softkey (PING) to start the ping function. You should see a workstation icon with a target number 1 on the screen. Does the workstation have a solid lines or dashed lines?_____

_____ What do you think this means?_____

_____

m. Press the left softkey (magnifying glass) to see the IP addresses of all the devices being pinged and the round-trip time for each in milliseconds.

n. Which devices did you ping, and what were the round-trip times for each?

_____

o. Press the right softkey (X) twice to exit the detailed view and ping function.

Step 8. Disconnect the equipment and store the cabling and devices.

Lab 4.2.9e: Fluke LinkRunner—Cable and NIC Tests

Figure 4-12 Fluke LinkRunner

Objectives

- Become familiar with the capabilities of the Fluke LinkRunner.
- Verify cable length and integrity.
- Determine where a cable terminates.
- Verify PC NIC functionality.

Background/Preparation

In this lab, you will work with Ethernet cables to determine their characteristics and identify potential problems. You will use some of the key capabilities of the Fluke LinkRunner, such as cable mapping and NIC testing.

As networks run faster and become more complex, infrastructure cabling and devices must operate to precise levels in a tighter performance window. As a result, nearly 80 percent of network problems stem from simple wiring and connection problems. You need the following resources:

- Ethernet straight-through patch cables (good and bad)
- Ethernet crossover cables
- An Ethernet cable from a wall-plate RJ-45 jack through a patch panel
- A hub or switch
- A computer with a NIC

The following URLs provide information on the Fluke LinkRunner. The first one is a virtual demo of LinkRunner capabilities, and the second is a link to the downloadable *LinkRunner Quick Reference Guide* in various languages:

- http://www.flukenetworks.com/us/LAN/Handheld+Testers/LinkRunner/_see+it+live.htm#
- http://www.flukenetworks.com/us/LAN/Handheld+Testers/LinkRunner/_manuals.htm

Step 1. Become familiar with the capabilities of the Fluke LinkRunner.

Access the virtual demo of the LinkRunner using the first URL. You can try different tests to become familiar with its capabilities.

Step 2. Obtain access to the *LinkRunner Quick Reference Guide*.

You can directly access the quick reference guide online or download it to your PC using the link provided. Your instructor might also have a copy of the quick reference guide. This lab reproduces selected pages of the quick reference guide. Figure 4-13 shows the connectors and buttons on the LinkRunner.

Figure 4-13 LinkRunner Connectors and Buttons

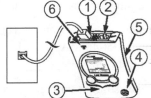

1. RJ-45 LAN port
2. RJ-45 MAP port
   (cable testing)
3. Selection buttons
   Left – Highlight
   Right – Action
4. Power Button

Power off - press and hold
Backlight – press once briefly

5. Batteries (2) AA
6. Link indicator light

Step 3. Configure the LinkRunner.

a. From any screen, you can access the main configuration by pressing both buttons simultaneously. You have the option to configure LinkRunner or go into the ping configuration.

b. Pressing the left button takes you to the LinkRunner configuration, where you can find the MAC address of the LinkRunner and toggle between feet and meters.

What is the Layer 2 MAC address? _____

c. Pressing the right button takes you to the ping configuration, which is covered in the preceding lab.

Step 4. Test the length and continuity for a long cable run.

LinkRunner's cable-test function helps you determine whether the cable length is within specification. This basic test determines that all four pairs of wires are intact and have the same length. Figure 4-14 shows a good cable test.

Figure 4-14 LinkRunner Cable Test Display

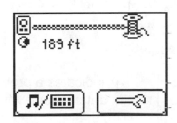

a. Turn on the LinkRunner by pressing the small button in the lower-right corner. What does the display look like now?

_____

b. Use a long straight-through cable drop that is not connected to a patch panel, hub, or switch at the other end. Plug one end of the cable into the RJ-45 LAN port on the LinkRunner. What does the display look like now?

_____

c. What is the length of the cable being tested?

_____

Step 5. Test the length and wire map for good and bad patch cables.

The cable-test function helps you determine whether the cable length is within specification, whether it is a straight or crossover cable, and whether it has any faults. These tests work for both structured and patch cables. You will test cable integrity for excessive length, opens, shorts, crossed wires, and split pairs.

a. Turn on the LinkRunner by pressing the small button in the lower-right corner.

b. Use a good straight-through patch cable. Plug one end of the cable into the RJ-45 LAN port on the LinkRunner and the other end into the LinkRunner RJ-45 MAP port. Figure 4-15 shows the result of testing a good straight-through cable. What is the length of the cable? _____

How can you tell whether this is a straight-through or crossover cable?_____

_____

c. Use a good crossover cable. Plug one end of the cable into the RJ-45 LAN port on the LinkRunner and the other end into the LinkRunner RJ-45 MAP port. What is the length of the cable?

_____

How can you tell whether this is a straight-through or crossover cable?

_____

Figure 4-15 LinkRunner Straight-Through Cable Test Results

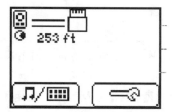

d. Use a bad straight-through patch cable that is improperly wired or that has some faults in the wires. Plug one end of the cable into the RJ-45 LAN port on the LinkRunner and the other end into the RJ-45 MAP port. Figure 4-16 shows a problem cable with symbols indicating the type of problems. What problem did you encounter?_____

_____

Figure 4-16 LinkRunner Cable Test Problem Results

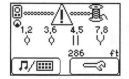

⚠ indicates a problem cable and details display below.

|| Good Ỵ Short

⚠ Unknown ◊ Split

⥮ Open (wiremap or cable ID)

Step 6. Test the length and wire map for long cable runs.

a. Turn on the LinkRunner by pressing the small button in the lower-right corner.

b. Use a good workstation patch cable drop to a wall-plate that is connected to a patch panel at the other end (but not to a hub or switch). Plug the cable into the RJ-45 LAN port on the LinkRunner. Plug the wire-map adapter into the associated patch panel port on the opposite end. You will test the cable run from the patch cable in the work area through all horizontal cabling to the patch panel in the wiring closet.

c. What is the length of the cable? _____

d. Does the cable test okay? _____

e. If not, indicate problems you encountered.

_____

Step 7. Use Link Pulse to test the connection to a hub or switch and identify the cable location.

Link Pulse blinks the hub or switch port-link light while simultaneously sending a tone on the wire to aid in cable location. You can use the optional Microprobe Tone Receiver to pick up the tone and audibly locate cables. You can use the optional cable ID kit to identify unmarked segments.

a. Obtain a good patch cable of any length. Plug one end directly into an active regular hub or switch port. Plug the other end into the LinkRunner LAN port. _____

b. Press the left softkey (musical note and hub symbol). What does this cause the link light on the hub or switch port to do? _____

c. What does this test do and how could it be useful in locating or identifying where cables terminate?

_____

Step 8. Test PC NIC functionality.

a. Turn on the LinkRunner by pressing the small button in the lower-right corner.

b. Plug one end of a patch cable into the RJ-45 LAN port on the LinkRunner and the other end into the PC NIC. If the PC NIC link light comes on, then the NIC is good. Did the NIC test okay?

_____

Step 9. Disconnect the equipment and store the cabling and devices.

Cabling LANs and WANs

The following labs are in this chapter:

Lab TI	Title
5.1.5	RJ-45 Jack Punch Down
5.1.7	Hub and NIC Purchase
5.1.10	Purchasing LAN Switches
5.1.12	Building a Peer-to-Peer Network
5.1.13a	Building a Hub-Based Network
5.1.13b	Building a Switch-Based Network
5.2.3a	Connecting Router LAN Interfaces
5.2.3b	Building a Basic Routed WAN
5.2.3c	Troubleshooting Interconnected Devices
5.2.7	Establishing a Console Connection to a Router or Switch

Lab 5.1.5: RJ-45 Jack Punch Down

Objectives

- Learn the correct process for terminating (punching down) an RJ-45 jack.
- Learn the correct procedure for installing the jack in a wall plate.

Background/Preparation

In this lab, you will learn to wire an RJ-45 data jack for installation in a wall plate using a punch-down tool. These skills are useful when you must install a small amount of cabling in an office or residence. A *punch tool* is a device that uses spring-loaded action to push wires between metal pins while at the same time skinning the sheath away from the wire. This process ensures that the wire makes a good electrical connection with the pins inside the jack. The punch tool also cuts off any extra wire.

You will work with CAT 5 or CAT 5e cabling and CAT 5 or 5e T568-B jacks. You normally plug a CAT 5/5e straight-wired patch cable with an RJ-45 connector into the data jack (or outlet) to connect a PC in a work area to the network. It is important that you use CAT 5 or 5e jacks and patch panels with CAT 5 or 5e cabling to support FastEthernet (100 Mbps) and Gigabit Ethernet (1000 Mbps). The process of punching down wires into a data jack in an office area is the same as punching them down in a patch panel in a wiring closet. You need the following resources:

- Two- to three-foot length of CAT 5/5e cabling (one per person or one per team).
- Two CAT 5/5e RJ-45 data jacks (one extra for spare). If both ends of the cable have RJ-45 data jacks, you can test the installation by inserting cable with RJ-45 connectors and a simple cable continuity tester.
- CAT 5/5e wall plate.
- 110 type punch-down tool.
- Wire cutters.

Use the following procedure to punch down the wires into the RJ-45 jack and install the jack into the wall plate:

Step 1   Remove the jacket 1" from the end of the cable.

Step 2   Hold the jack with the 8-pin jack receptacle (the part that the RJ-45 connector goes into) facing up or away from you while looking at the wire channels or slots. There should be four wire channels on each side. Match the wiring colors to the codes on the jack. Position wires in the proper channels on the jack, maintaining the twists as close as possible. Most jacks have the channels color-coded to indicate where the wires go. Jacks are typically stamped to indicate whether they are T-568A or T-568B, as shown in Figure 5-1.

Figure 5-1 RJ-45 Jack

Step 3   Use the 110 punch-down tool (see Figure 5-2) to push conductors into the channels.

Make sure that you position the cut side of the punch-down tool so that it faces the outside of the jack, or you will cut the wire you are trying to punch down. (*Note*: If you tilt the handle of the punch tool a little to the outside, it will cut better.) If any wire remains attached after you use the punch tool, simply twist the ends gently to remove them, and then place the clips on the jack and tighten them.

Note: Make sure that no more than .5" of untwisted wire is between the end of the cable jacket and the channels on the jack.

Figure 5-2 Single-Wire Punch Tool

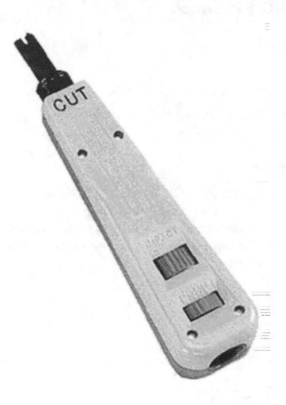

Step 4   Snap the jack into its faceplate by pushing it in from the back side. Make sure, when you do this, that the jack is right-side up. (The clip faces down when the wall plate is mounted.)

Step 5   Use the screws to attach the faceplate to either the box or the bracket. If you surface-mount the box, keep in mind that it might hold 1' or 2' of excess cable. Then, you need to either slide the cable through its tie-wraps or pull back the raceway that covers it to push the rest of the excess cable back into the wall. If you flush-mount the jack, all you need to do is push the excess cable back into the wall.

Lab 5.1.7: Hub and NIC Purchase

Objectives

- Introduce the variety and prices of network components in the market.
- Gather pricing information for hubs and Ethernet NICs for a small network.

Background/Preparation

A friend has asked you to help him put together a price list for a small LAN to set up in his very small business. Rapid growth is not really a concern. He has the computers but has not networked them together. He is getting a DSL connection so that he can access the Internet, and all he needs is a small hub and connections to each computer to complete the project. Each machine is running a version of Windows that will work on a peer-to-peer network. You can use any local source, catalog, or website. The requirements include the following:

- Ethernet hub
- Ethernet NICs for existing laptop PCs
- Ethernet NICs for existing desktop PCs
- Each computer will be close enough so that a 20' jumper would reach the hub. Price the CAT 5 jumpers as well.

Step 1. Research equipment prices.

Start by going to http://www.cisco.com, selecting **Products & Services**, and following the links to **Hubs and Concentrators** to gather basic information. The small list of choices should indicate something.

Use at least three other sources for technologies and pricing. If you do web searches, use http://www.cdw.com and http://www.google.com, plus any others you prefer. As you look at the prices for small hubs, how much more would it cost to use a small switch? Compare the cost to a wireless implementation.

Step 2. Compile a one-page summary of your results.

Use Microsoft Excel or Word (or any comparable products) to compile a one-page summary of your results. Use a table to show the choices and the features or factors that you compared (number of ports, features, price, performance, etc.).

Lab 5.1.10: Purchasing LAN Switches

Figure 5-3 Cisco Catalyst 2900 and 3550 Series Switches

Objectives

- Introduce the variety and prices of network components in the market.
- Gather pricing information for Ethernet switches and NICs for a network.

Background/Preparation

You have been asked to put together a proposal for replacing a branch office's hubs with switches. You will research at least two different solutions and develop a proposal. The project details follow:

Your company has a branch location using an Ethernet hub network. Congestion issues are becoming a serious problem as the company adds more services to the network. Currently, each of the four floors has one or more hubs in a wiring closet supporting 30-35 computers except the ground floor, which has 65 computers.

The four floors plug into an 8-port 10 Mbps switch that the company added earlier to reduce the congestion problems. Although that solution was a major improvement, it can't keep up all of the time. The two servers and router to the Internet also connect to the 8-port switch.

The branch cabling is relatively new and certified to CAT 5 standards. The company is not interested in any major cabling changes at this time.

At least 75 percent of the 160 current workstations have NICs with 10/100, full-duplex capabilities. All laptop computers have the newer NICs. All new machines include similar NICs.

The requirements include the following:

- Replace all hubs with switches.
- Replace the 10 Mbps NICs for existing desktop PCs.
- Each host connection should be 10/100 Mbps minimum.

What should you do with the existing switch? Are there higher bandwidth options for connecting the two servers?

Step 1. Research equipment prices.

Start by going to http://www.cisco.com, selecting **Products & Solutions**, and following the links to **Switches** to gather basic information. Look specifically at the Catalyst 29xx and 35xx models.

Use at least three other sources for technologies and pricing. If you do web searches, use http://www.cdw.com and http://www.google.com, plus any others you prefer.

Step 2. Compile a table of your results.

Use Microsoft Excel or Word (or any comparable products) to compile a table of your results as well as the following:

Page 1—An executive summary, where you recommend your choice of products and the total cost. Include a short reason (8-15 lines) why you selected this implementation.

Page 2—A comparison table showing the choices you worked from and the features or factors that you compared (price, performance, etc.).

Page 3—A bulleted list of any security concerns you discovered. Summarize whether you think the concerns are serious and whether you can overcome them.

Optional Step 2. Create a four- to eight-slide PowerPoint presentation.

Instead of creating the Excel or Word docments, create a four- to eight-slide PowerPoint presentation covering the same requirements.

Assume that you will present the material.

If time allows, do both Step 2s, which is often the norm.

Lab 5.1.13a: Building a Hub-Based Network

Figure 5-7 Hub-Based Network Topology

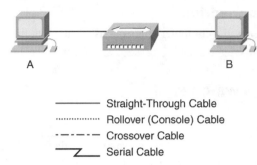

——————— Straight-Through Cable
················ Rollover (Console) Cable
–·–·–·– Crossover Cable
——⤸—— Serial Cable

Objective

- Create a simple network with two PCs using a hub.
- Identify the proper cable to connect the PCs to the hub.
- Configure workstation IP address information.
- Test connectivity using the ping command.

Background/Preparation

This lab will focus on the ability to connect two PCs to create a simple two-workstation, hub-based Ethernet LAN. A hub is a networking concentration device sometimes referred to as a *multiport repeater*. Hubs are inexpensive and easy to install, but they permit collisions to occur. They are appropriate for a small LAN with light traffic.

In addition to the physical and data link (layers 1 and 2) connections, you must also configure the computers with the correct IP network settings (layer 3) so that they can communicate. Because this lab uses a hub, you need a basic CAT 5/5e UTP straight-through cable to connect each PC to the hub. This *patch cable* or horizontal cabling connects workstations and a typical LAN. Start this lab with the equipment turned off and with cabling disconnected. Work in teams of two (one person per PC). You need the following resources:

- Two workstations with an Ethernet 10/100 NIC installed
- An Ethernet 10BASE-T or FastEthernet hub
- Several Ethernet cables (straight-through and crossover) for connecting the two workstations

Step 1. Identify the proper Ethernet cable and connect the two PCs to the hub.

a. You make the connection between the two PCs and the hub using a CAT 5 or 5e straight-through patch cable. Locate two cables that are long enough to reach from each PC to the hub. Attach one end to the NIC and the other end to a port on the hub. Be sure to examine the cable ends carefully and select only a straight-through cable.

b. What kind of cable do you need to connect from NIC to hub?

_____

c. What is the category rating of the cable?

_____

d. What is the AWG wire-size designation of the cable?

_____

Step 2. Verify the physical connection.

Plug in and turn on the computers. To verify the computer connections, ensure that the link lights on the both PC NICs and the hub interfaces are lit. Are all link lights lit? _____

Step 3. Access the IP settings window.

_____

Note: Be sure to write down the existing IP settings so that you can restore them at the end of the lab. These settings include the IP address, subnet mask, default gateway, and DNS servers. If the workstation is a DHCP client, it is not necessary to record this information.

Windows 95/98/Me users:

Click **Start > Settings > Control Panel > Network**.

Select the **TCP/IP protocol** icon that is associated with the NIC in this PC and click on **Properties.** Click the **IP Address** tab and the **Gateway tab.**

Windows NT/2000 users:

Click **Start > Settings > Control Panel > Network**.

Click the **Protocols** tab and select the **TCP/IP protocol** icon that is associated with the NIC in this PC. Click **Properties** and click **Specify an IP Address**.

Windows XP users:

Click **Start > Control Panel > Network Connection**.

Select the **Local Area Network Connection** and click **Change Settings of This Connection** (see Figure 5-8).

Step 4. Configure the TCP/IP settings for the two PCs.

a. Set the IP address information for each PC according to the information in Table 5-2.

b. Note that you do not need the default gateway IP address because these computers are directly connected. You only need the default gateway on LANs that are connected to a router.

Figure 5-8 TCP/IP Properties

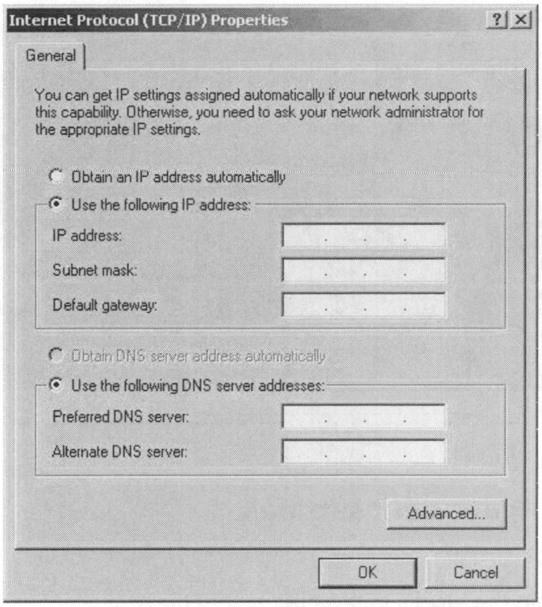

Table 5-2 IP Address Settings for PCs in a Hub-Based Network

Computer	IP Address	Subnet Mask	Default Gateway
PC A	192.168.1.1	255.255.255.0	Not required
PC B	192.168.1.2	255.255.255.0	Not required

Step 5. Access the command or MS-DOS prompt.

Use the Start menu to open the command prompt (MS-DOS-like) window.

Windows 95/98/Me users:

> **Start > Programs > MS-DOS Prompt**

Windows NT/2000 users:

> **Start > Programs > Command Prompt**

Windows XP users:

> **Start > Programs > Accessories > Command Prompt**

Step 6. Verify that PCs can communicate.

a. Test connectivity from one PC to the other through the hub by pinging the IP address of the opposite computer. Enter the following command at the command prompt:

C:>**ping 192.168.1.1** (or 192.168.1.2)

b. You should get results similar to those in Figure 5-9. If not, check your PC connections and network TCP/IP settings for both PCs. What is the ping result?

Figure 5-9 Ping Results from PC B to PC A

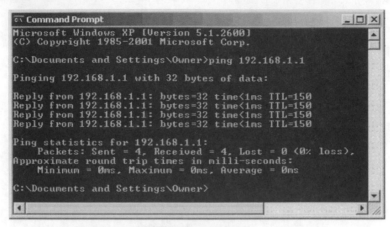

Step 7. Confirm your TCP/IP network settings.

Windows 95/98/Me users:

Run the **winipcfg** command from the MS-DOS prompt. Record the results:

Windows NT/2000/XP users:

Run the **ipconfig** command from the command prompt. Record the results:

Step 8. Restore the PCs to their original IP settings, disconnect the PCs from the hub, and store the hub and cables.

■ Several straight-through, crossover, and improperly wired or bad cables for connecting the workstations and routers to the hub or switch

■ One female (DCE) and one male (DTE) V.35 cable for interconnecting the routers

Step 1. Set up the lab configuration (Team Member A).

a. Set up the lab according to the specifications of Lab 5.2.3b.

b. As you connect the components, use a variety of CAT 5 cables, including at least one crossover cable and a cable that is improperly wired.

c. When configuring the workstations, introduce at least one misconfiguration of IP address information per PC.

d. Record the problems in Table 5-10. The table provides space for up to three cabling problems and three IP problems. For a cabling problem, indicate the location of the problem (e.g. PC A to Switch A). For an IP-related problem, indicate which PC has the problem. In the third column, describe the problem you introduced (such as a crossover cable, incorrect IP address, or incorrect default gateway).

Table 5-10 Network Cabling Problems (Team A)

Type of Problem	Location of Problem	Problem Introduced
Cabling related		
Cabling related		
Cabling related		
IP related		
IP related		
IP related		

Step 2. Troubleshoot the lab configuration (Team Member B).

a. Check workstation to workstation connectivity.

Ping from the command prompt on Workstation A to the IP address of Workstation B. If the first team member introduced problems, the ping attempt should fail.

b. Check physical layer integrity.

Start with Layer 1 issues and check cabling between the PCs and the switch. Check for the proper type of cable as well as good connections. Check the cabling between the routers and the switches for connections. Replace cables and ensure good connections as necessary.

c. Check network layer integrity.

Check for Layer 3 configuration problems with the workstations. (Note that the router should be preconfigured and should not have problems.) Use the command prompt or the **run** command to check the IP configuration of each workstation. You can also use the Control Panel network application to check IP settings. Verify the IP address, subnet mask, and default gateway for each workstation.

Step 3. Record the problems found in Table 5-11 (Team Member B).

Table 5-11 Network Cabling Problems (Team B)

Type of Problem	Location of Problem	Corrective Action Taken
Cabling related		
Cabling related		
Cabling related		
IP related		
IP related		
IP related		

Step 4. Team Members A and B switch rolls and repeat lab.

Step 5. Restore the PCs to their original IP settings, disconnect the equipment, and store the cables.

Lab 5.2.7: Establishing a Console Connection to a Router or Switch

Figure 5-22 Console Connection to Router or Switch

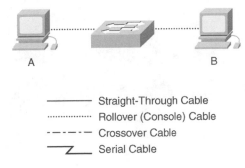

————— Straight-Through Cable
·············· Rollover (Console) Cable
–—–—–— Crossover Cable
⌐_ Serial Cable

Objectives

- Create a console connection from a PC to a router and switch using the proper cable.
- Configure HyperTerminal on the PC.
- Observe the router and switch user interface.

Background/Preparation

This lab will focus on the ability to connect a PC to a router or a switch so you can establish a console session and observe the user interface. A console session lets you check or change the configuration of the switch or router; it is the simplest method of connecting to one of these devices.

You should perform this lab twice, once with a router and once with a switch, to see the differences between the user interfaces. Start this lab with the equipment turned off and with cabling disconnected. Work in teams of two (one for the router and one for the switch). You need the following resources:

- A workstation with a serial interface and HyperTerminal installed
- An Ethernet 10BASE-T or Fast Ethernet switch
- A Cisco router
- Crossover (console) cable for connecting the workstation to the router or switch

Step 1. Identify the router and switch console connectors.

Examine the router or switch and locate the RJ-45 connector labeled "Console," as indicated in Figure 5-23.

Figure 5-23 Router Console RJ-45 Connector

Step 2. Identify the computer serial interface (COM 1 or 2).

It should be a 9- or 25-pin male connector labeled "serial" or "COM1." It might not have a label (see Figure 5-24).

Figure 5-24 9-Pin Serial Port

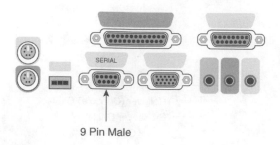

9 Pin Male

Step 3. Locate the RJ-45–to-DB9 adapter.

One side of the adapter connects to the PC's serial interface and the other to the RJ-45 rollover cable connector. If the serial interface on the PC or dumb terminal is a DB25, you need an RJ-45-to-DB25 adapter. Both the RJ-45-to-DB9 and RJ-45-to-DB25 adapters typically come with a Cisco router or switch.

Figure 5-25 RJ-45–to-DB9 Female Adapter

Step 4. Locate or build a rollover cable.

Use a rollover cable of adequate length, making one if necessary, to connect the router or switch to a workstation.

Step 5. Connect cabling components.

Connect the rollover cable to the router or switch console port RJ-45 connector. Next, connect the other end of the rollover cable to the RJ-45-to-DB9 or -DB25 adapter. Attach the adapter to a PC serial port, either DB9 or DB25, depending on the computer (see Figure 5-26).

Figure 5-26 Router to PC Connection

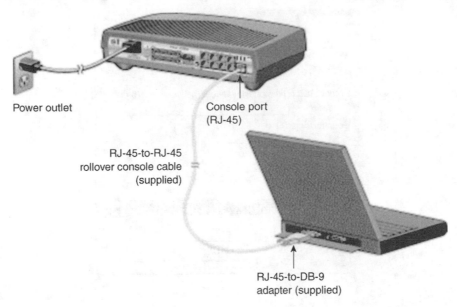

Power outlet

Console port
(RJ-45)

RJ-45-to-RJ-45
rollover console cable
(supplied)

RJ-45-to-DB-9
adapter (supplied)

Step 6. Start the PC HyperTerminal program.

a. Turn on the computer.

b. From the Windows taskbar, locate the **HyperTerminal** program (**Start > Programs > Accessories > Communications > HyperTerminal**).

Step 7. Name the HyperTerminal session.

In the Connection Description window, enter a name in the connection **Name** field and click **OK** (see Figure 5-27).

Figure 5-27 HyperTerminal Connection Description

Step 8. Specify the computer's connecting interface.

In the Connect To window (see Figure 5-28), use the drop-down arrow in the **Connect Using** field to select **COM1** and click **OK. Note:** Depending on which serial port you used on the PC, it might be necessary to set this to **COM2**.

Figure 5-28 HyperTerminal Connect To Dialog Box

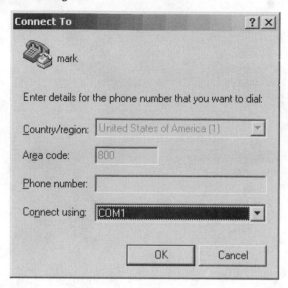

Step 9. Specify the interface connection properties.

 a. In the COM1 Properties window (see Figure 5-29), use the drop-down arrows to select the following:

  Bits per second = **9600**

  Data Bits = **8**

  Parity = **None**

  Stop bits = **1**

  Flow control = **none**

 b. Click **OK**.

Figure 5-29 HyperTerminal COM1 Properties

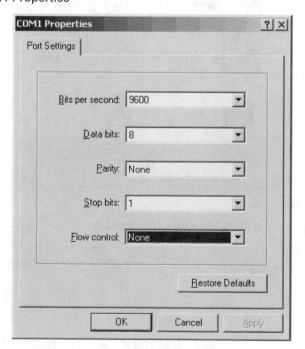

c. When the HyperTerminal session window opens, turn on the router or switch. If router or switch is already on, press **Enter**. You should see a response from the router or switch. If you do, then you successfully completed the connection.

Step 10. Observe the router or switch user interface.

a. Observe the user interface.

b. If this is a router, what is the prompt? _____

c. If this is a switch, what is the prompt? _____

Step 11. Closing the session.

a. To end the console session from a HyperTerminal session, select **File > Exit**.

b. When the HyperTerminal disconnect warning window appears (see Figure 5-30), select **Yes**.

Figure 5-30 Closing a HyperTerminal Session

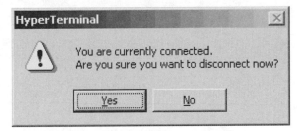

c. The computer will then ask whether you want to save the session. Select **No**.

Step 12. Shut down the router or switch and store the cables.

Ethernet Fundamentals

There are no labs in this module. Please review the information in Chapter 6 of CCNA1 in the *Cisco Networking Program CCNA 1 and 2 Companion Guide*, Revised Third Edition, to ensure that you can answer the following questions:

- What are the IEEE naming standards?
- In which layers of the OSI model does Ethernet operate?
- What are the 802.3 frame formats?
- What is Media Access Control (MAC)?
- What is the CSMA/CD process?
- What is link establishment
- What is full duplex?

Ethernet Technologies

The following labs are in this chapter:

Lab TI	Title
7.1.2	Waveform Decoding
7.1.9a	Introduction to Fluke Network Inspector
7.1.9b	Introduction to Fluke Protocol Inspector

Lab 7.1.2: Waveform Decoding

Objective

The purpose of this lab is to integrate knowledge of networking media; Open System Interconnection (OSI) Layers 1, 2, and 3; and Ethernet by taking a digital waveform of an Ethernet frame and decoding it. Specifically, you will do the following:

- Review numbering systems, OSI concepts, and encoding methods as background (Module 1).

- Learn to decode the waveform into binary, reorder the binary, and identify Ethernet field boundaries (Module 2).

- Decode the Ethernet Length/Type field, locate and read RFCs, and decode Layer 3 of the waveform (Module 3).

- Use a protocol analyzer (Module 4).

Background/Preparation

As a student of networking, you are learning about many new concepts: the OSI model, networking media and signals, Ethernet, and the TCP/IP protocols. Network administrators, technicians, and engineers study and troubleshoot a network using protocol-analysis software. Protocol-analysis software facilitates the capture and interpretation of frame-level data, which is crucial for understanding what is happening on a live (and perhaps troublesome) network. Hand-decoding the signal gives you more insight into what the software is doing automatically for you. This lab will provide an important foundation for future network troubleshooting.

A digital oscilloscope was attached to an Ethernet 10BASE2 coaxial cable to capture actual Ethernet waveforms. Although it is possible to capture waveforms on 10BASE-T and 100BASE-TX twisted-pair media, the coaxial cable gives the cleanest and most readable waveform data. This data is available from your instructor. Decoding the waveform is a crucial step in understanding how networks operate.

For the first part of the lab, all that you need is this lab companion and the printout of the waveform to "mark up" as you decode. The last task of the lab will involve using a protocol analyzer such as Fluke Protocol Inspector or the equivalent.

Module 1

Review numbering systems, OSI concepts, and encoding methods as background.

Counting Systems

Computers rely upon the concept of *on* and *off* to perform any action. On and off is the equivalent of the *binary* counting system, which uses only the digits 0 and 1. Before describing how the binary counting system works, let's first review the decimal counting system that we use every day. The review will provide a reference for the other counting systems.

Decimal

The *decimal* counting system is based on the numbers zero through nine. You depict decimal by writing the number 10 in subscript immediately after the number. For example, you can clearly express the number 22_{10} as decimal in this way.

A single decimal digit can represent any quantity between zero and nine. If the current number were nine, adding one changes the number from a single digit to two digits. Thus, groupings are based on sets of ten. You show a complete set of ten by a change in columns, moving one column to the left.

A counting sequence follows:

0

1

2

3

4

5

6

7

8

9

10

11

12

Figure 7-1 provides a graphical representation of the placeholders represented by each digit in a given number. Because of size limitations, the figure depicts only the grouping increments of 1s, 10s, and 100s. If it helps, look upon the placeholder graphic as a method of counting beans, one bean per placeholder circle.

Notice how Figure 7-1 shows a placeholder for nine sets in each column. Zero is represented by a lack of any populated placeholder in that column. Populating more than nine placeholders in any column is not possible, because no placeholder is offered. To increase the number of placeholders, it is necessary to change columns. All the placeholders, plus the placeholder that forced the change in columns, move to the next column to the left as a single entry. The second column, the 10s column, is populated by completed sets of the 1s column. The 100s column is likewise populated with completed sets of the 10s column, and so on.

Figure 7-1 Set Groupings in the Decimal Counting System

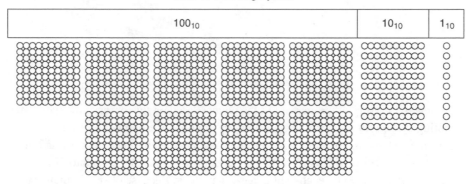

Populate the placeholders with values using the decimal number 275. As indicated by the number itself, you have two populated placeholders in the 100s column, seven in the 10s column, and five in the 1s column. Although this result appears obvious because of your familiarity with the decimal counting system, try calculating the number of placeholders required, as shown in Figure 7-2. Again, this math is simple because you use the same counting system for the original number and the placeholders. This figure illustrates the concept that you will use shortly.

Figure 7-2 The Required Number of Decimal Counting-System Placeholders Populated by the Decimal Number 275

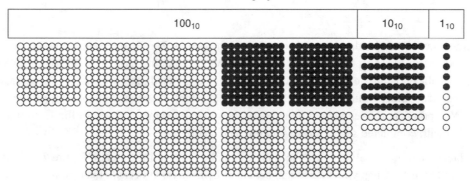

The largest column required to hold the current number is the 100s column. Thus, subtract 100 from the number until it no longer fits. This subtraction is possible twice, so you populate two placeholders in the 100s column. Subtract the next placeholder value from the number until that is no longer possible. It is possible seven times, so you populate seven placeholders. Repeating the process for the 1s column yields five populated placeholders.

Now that you have reviewed counting in decimal graphically, try the binary system using the same format.

Binary

The binary counting system is based on the numbers 0 and 1. You depict binary by writing the number 2 in subscript immediately after the number. For example, you can clearly express the number 1011_2 as binary in this way.

A single binary digit can represent zero or one. If the current number were one, adding one changes the number from a single digit to two digits. Thus, groupings are based on sets of two. You show a complete set of two by a change in columns, moving one column to the left.

A counting sequence follows:

0

1

10

11

100

Notice that the column changes for every other increase in the count. Based on this observation, you can calculate the column values in the binary counting system for the decimal equivalent by doubling the number repeatedly. The first column is 1, so the second column is 2, followed by 4, 8, 16, and so on. Writing these doubled numbers in a row and using subtraction and addition as appropriate to make the conversion can create a quick conversion manual calculator. Figure 7-3 is a graphical representation of the placeholders represented by each digit in a given number. Because of size limitations, the figure depicts only the first eight grouping increments. The decimal equivalent of each column value appears in the lower-left corner.

Figure 7-3 Set Groupings in the Binary Counting System

Base 2 Counting System

10000000_2 128_{10}	1000000_2 64_{10}	100000_2 32_{10}	10000_2 16_{10}	1000_2 8_{10}	100_2 4_{10}	10_2 2_{10}	1_2 1_{10}

Notice how the figure shows a placeholder for only one set in each column. Zero is represented by the lack of a populated placeholder in that column, and the only other value permitted is one. Populating more than one placeholder in any column is not possible, because no placeholder is offered. To increase the number of used placeholders, it is necessary to change columns. You move all the placeholders, plus the extra placeholder that forced the change in columns, to the next column to the left as a single entry. You populate the second column, the 2s column, with completed sets of the 1s column. You likewise populate the 4s column with completed sets of the 2s column, and so on.

Next, populate the placeholders with values using the decimal number 157 as illustrated in Figure 7-4. Deciding which columns to populate is a little harder when you change numbering systems in the process. This example uses the process outlined in the decimal counting-system example.

Figure 7-4 The Required Number of Binary Counting System Placeholders Populated by the Decimal Number 157 (10011101)

Base 2 Counting System

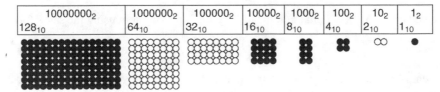

10000000_2 128_{10}	1000000_2 64_{10}	100000_2 32_{10}	10000_2 16_{10}	1000_2 8_{10}	100_2 4_{10}	10_2 2_{10}	1_2 1_{10}

The largest column required to hold the current number is the 128s column. Thus, subtract 128 from the number until it no longer fits. This subtraction is possible once, so you populate the 128s column placeholder. The remainder is 29, which is already smaller than the next column to the right and the column after that. Both of those columns will have unpopulated placeholders representing zero. Subtract the next placeholder value from the number until that is no longer possible. It is possible once, so you populate the 16s column placeholder. The remainder is 13. Repeating the process for the remaining columns results in a placeholder populated in the 8s, 4s, and 1s columns.

Most people prefer the decimal counting system because we grew up working in that system. Computers will continue to operate on the binary counting system until quantum physics finds a way to cheaply build computers that can store more than *on* or *off* in a single location. Trying to count in binary or to write long strings of binary numbers would be tedious at best, so we use hexadecimal notation to reduce the number of digits required for many computer-related activities.

Hexadecimal

The *hexadecimal* counting system is based on the numbers 0 through 15. Unfortunately, the numeric representation of 15 in decimal requires numbers in two columns, and those values all represent values in only a single hexadecimal column. For numbers larger than nine, you use the alphabetic characters of A through F so that only a single "digit" is present as a placeholder. You depict hexadecimal by writing the number 16 in subscript immediately after the number. For example, you can clearly express the number $6D_{16}$ as hexadecimal in this way.

As indicated, a single decimal digit can represent any quantity between 0 and F. If the current number were F, adding one changes the number from a single digit to two digits. Thus, groupings are based on sets of sixteen . You show a complete set of sixteen by a change in columns, moving one column to the left.

A counting sequence follows:

0
1
2
3
4
5
6
7
8
9
A
B
C
D
E
F

Figure 7-5 shows a graphical representation of the placeholders represented by each digit in a given number. Because of size limitations, the figure depicts only the first three grouping increments.

The most obvious difference between hexadecimal and either binary or decimal is the quantity of placeholders represented in each column. Until you see it represented graphically, you cannot appreciate the significance of a few extra placeholders per set.

Notice how Figure 7-5 shows a placeholder for 15 sets in each column. Zero is represented by a lack of any populated placeholder in that column. Populating more than 16 (F_{16}) placeholders in any column is not possible, because no additional placeholder are offered. To increase the number of used placeholders, it is necessary to change columns. You move all the placeholders, plus the placeholder that forced the change in used columns, to the next column to the left as a single entry. You populate the second column, the 16s column, with completed sets of the 1s column. You likewise populate the 256s column with completed sets of the 16s column, and so on.

Figure 7-5 Set Groupings in the Hexadecimal Counting System

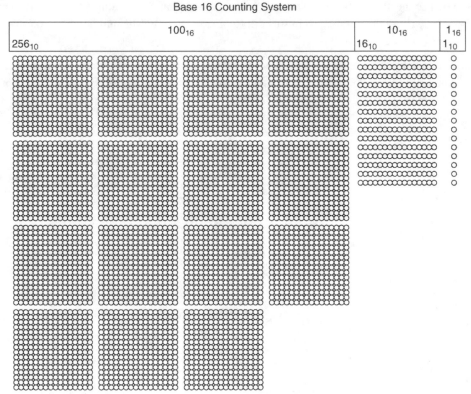

Base 16 Counting System

Populate the placeholders with values using the decimal number 157, as demonstrated in Figure 7-6. Deciding which columns you should populate is somewhat difficult because you are once more changing numbering systems in the process. Repeat the process outlined in the decimal counting system.

Figure 7-6 The Required Number of Hexadecimal Counting System Placeholders Populated by the Decimal Number 157 (Binary 10011101_2 and Hexadecimal $9D_{16}$)

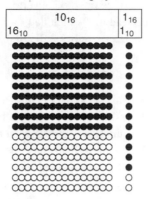

The largest column required to hold the current number is the 16s column because the number is less than the number of place-holders in the 256s column. Thus, subtract 16 from the number until it no longer fits. This subtraction is possible nine times, so you populate nine placeholders in the 16s column. The remainder is 13. The next column is the 1s column, and you use the entire remainder to populate placeholders.

That is a fast tour through counting systems, so look Table 7-1 to help with the conversions. First, be aware that computer-related use of hexadecimal numbers virtually always represents octets, or groups of eight binary digits. That means that you will virtually never use the 256s column with hexadecimal conversions. Here is almost everything you need in one table.

Table 7-1 Conversion Between Hexadecimal, Decimal, and Binary Counting Systems

Hexadecimal	Decimal	Binary	Four-Digit Binary
0	0	0	0000
1	1	1	0001
2	2	10	0010
3	3	11	0011
4	4	100	0100
5	5	101	0101
6	6	110	0110
7	7	111	0111
8	8	1000	1000
9	9	1001	1001
A	10	1010	1010
B	11	1011	1011
C	12	1100	1100
D	13	1101	1101
E	14	1110	1110
F	15	1111	1111

Also, compare the calculation performed to obtain the binary conversion and the hexadecimal conversion in their respective sections. Notice especially that the left four binary digits convert to a hexadecimal nine and the right four binary digits convert to a hexadecimal D. This conversion is always true: The left group of four binary digits converts to one hexadecimal number and the right to another. Thus, you only have to memorize how to convert the 1s column of hexadecimal. To simplify memorization, Table 7-1 shows a fourth column, which has leading 0s included for a total of four binary digits. That is how you usually see the binary when you are converting. After a surprisingly small number of calculations, converting between binary and hexadecimal becomes easy.

OSI Seven-Layer Model

You can best understand most issues related to networking when you align them with the OSI model for network communications. The International Organization for Standardization (ISO) created the OSI seven-layer basic reference model as standard ISO/IEC 7498. At the time of its creation, the various networking protocols available were proprietary and offered little or no interoperability. The OSI model, as outlined in Table 7-2, has since become the most common reference point for discussing network protocols, features, and hardware. For complete description of each layer in the OSI model, see ISO/IEC 7498-1 or ITU-T X.200.

Table 7-2 Simple OSI Seven-Layer Model Description

Layer	Name	Purpose
7	Application	Provides interface with network users
6	Presentation	Performs format and code conversion
5	Session	Manages connections for application programs
4	Transport	Ensures error-free, end-to-end delivery
3	Network	Handles internetwork addressing and routing
2	Data Link	Performs local addressing and error detection
1	Physical	Includes physical signaling and interfaces

Figure 7-7 provides a chart to aid in understanding the various concepts and relationships between the OSI reference model and internetworking devices. This chart condenses as much information as possible to provide a visual reference. This basic information should become second nature to any networking professional for that person to be effective.

Each layer (except the physical layer) relies on the next lower layer to provide services as specified but to perform these services in a manner that is transparent to the next higher layer. Imagine a higher layer opening a trap door and dropping a request in the form of a package with a note attached into a dark hole. The higher layer neither knows nor cares how the needed services are accomplished, only that if it waits at the trap door long enough a response will usually appear.

As you can see in Figure 7-8, each layer adds a bit of header information as it handles the request from the next higher layer. The added information is intended for the corresponding layer in the receiving station and is removed by that layer before it hands the data payload to the next higher layer. Almost everything received from or handed to the next higher layer is considered part of the data payload and holds no special meaning to the current layer. As mentioned before, there is some interaction between adjacent layers, but most of the information is typically intended for the corresponding layer in the receiving station.

Figure 7-7 OSI Model Compared to Various Device Functions and Protocols

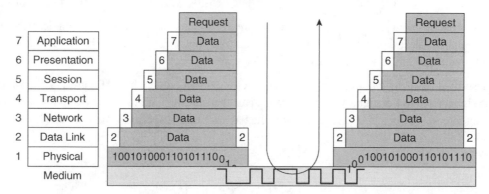

Even in the simplified conceptual depiction in Figure 7-8, it should be evident that a small request from the user grows in size as each layer adds a little handling information to the request. Each layer adds the same amount of overhead to the message whether it is large or small. The efficiency of a network is not good for small frames but improves considerably as the message approaches the maximum size.

OSI Layers 5 through 7 tend to be interested in handling the request, whereas Layers 4 and below are more interested in delivering the request across the network. Not indicated in the graphic is the fact that each higher layer is usually able to work with a larger portion of a given request. The higher layer parcels out pieces of a request to the lower layer and reassembles the pieces upon reception. The data link layer is the only layer that places both a header and a trailer on the request, effectively framing it. The header includes addressing information for proper delivery, and the trailer holds error-checking information to ensure that the request arrives undamaged. Higher layers include any error-checking information in the header. The physical layer takes the binary string that results from the framed request from the data link layer and encodes it for transmission on the specified medium. The specified medium might be expecting light pulses, rising and falling electrical voltages, or radio waves.

For the receiving station to decode the request, it must be using the same encoding scheme and the same medium. This requirement might be fairly obvious. Not so obvious is the fact that Ethernet uses signaling from one scheme to communicate link-partner capabilities before potentially switching to another encoding scheme. The 10BASE-T link pulse was adapted for use in auto-negotiation between link partners on unshielded twisted-pair (UTP) cable. By transmitting coded groups of link pulses, the two link partners negotiate which is the fastest encoding scheme that both can support. Then they switch to that scheme and proceed.

Once linked at the same speed and using the same encoding scheme, the two link partners are ready to service the user's requests. They do so using the process described earlier and shown in Figure 7-8.

To decode a received request, each header includes a code that lets the next higher layer know how to decode the request. For example, in the Ethernet header is a field called Length/Type. If the value in that field is at least 0600_{16}, then the data payload is interpreted according to the indicated EtherType. RFC 1700 includes a partial list of EtherType codes. In the header for Layer 3 is another protocol code, and so on.

If you were to hand-decode a single frame, you would need to manually repeat this process of identifying which code is in the header for each layer and finding the instructions for how to decode the protocol indicated by that code. In a computer, you install software drivers for the particular software you are using. The driver software has the encoding and decoding instructions for a limited set of protocols. If the received frame is not one of those known protocols, the first layer that cannot decode it discards the frame.

Signaling and Encoding Methods

Networking protocols use a considerable number of encoding and signaling schemes. The intent of a signaling scheme is to convey information across a given medium at the highest possible density, with the lowest acceptable error rate and cost.

Because computers operate in binary, the signaling scheme represents binary information. You can describe this scheme electrically as *on* or *off* in the simplest terms. For an electrical signal to convey an alternating series of 1s and 0s, varying the voltage over time might produce the following signal.

Signals are often described by their *frequency*, or how many cycles per second they have. Figure 7-9 shows one cycle. In a complete cycle, the signal rises to the highest point, descends past the starting point to the lowest point, and returns to the starting point. This timing interval is one cycle period, and it is the basis for one bit-period with a number of networking protocols.

Figure 7-9 One-Cycle Period

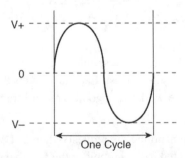

For most of the slower signaling schemes used in networking, one cycle also represents the time duration or interval for one bit period. For a few signaling schemes, the signal holds at a constant voltage for the duration of one period and then changes to the next voltage between periods if necessary.

The form of signaling in Figure 7-10 would be adequate for any networking need, except that electrical behavior and the laws of physics start interfering. Transmitting signals involves a variety of problems. One obvious problem is that the interface components must be able to turn on and off or to transition fast enough to represent the signal. At lower speeds, this transition is not a problem. Another problem is that as the frequency of the signal (the number of cycles per second) increases, the maximum distance from the transmitter that you can reliably recover data decreases. Yet a third problem is that if the signal were to represent a single binary value for a length of time, say a long string of 1s, the interface electronics in the receiver sometimes begins to lose track of what voltage it is seeing. This loss is called *baseline wander*. In fiber optic cables, the signals tend to spread out over distance due to the way they reflect down the fiber so that high-frequency pulses start blurring together. A fourth problem is how to synchronize the clock at both ends of a link so that the signal is sampled at the right times to allow reliable recovery of the data.

Figure 7-10 Simple Signaling Technique, Known as Nonreturn to Zero (NRZ), Where Zero Volts Equals a Binary 0 and V+ Equals a Binary 1

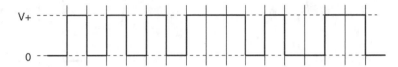

Networks must address two issues at the same time. First, methods for reducing the frequency are helpful to increase the maximum transmission distance (and usually the amount of information contained in a single cycle at the same time). Second, transitions must be regular enough to establish and maintain clock synchronization (and avoid baseline wander).

In Figure 7-11, the signaling is called *level sensitive*. As long as the signal remains at V+, it is sampled as a binary 1. When it is sampled at zero volts, it is a binary 0. Another way that signals are often sampled is on an edge. If the signal is rising or falling at the moment it is sampled, it is interpreted according to the edge direction or the mere presence of an edge. For example, a rising edge might indicate a binary 1. This system requires very good clocking and extremely small amounts of variation in the signal timing. If a transition takes place but not at the exact moment when the signal is sampled, it does not produce the desired result. Variations in the timing, usually seen as oscillations between slightly too soon and slightly too late, are called *jitter*.

Figure 7-11 How Signal Jitter Causes Inaccurate Sampling of the Data (with X Indicating a Failure to Properly Sample the Edge-Sensitive Signal)

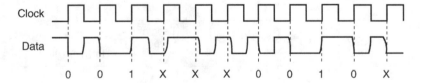

As suggested by Figure 7-12, other systems rely on the presence or absence of an edge transition instead of the direction the signal is headed during the transition.

Figure 7-12 Encoding Example Where a Transition in the Center of the Timing Window Represents a Binary 1 and the Absence of a Transition Indicates a Binary 0 (Nonreturn to Zero, Inverting on Ones [NRZI])

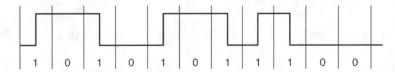

The example in Figure 7-13 shows the signaling system for FastEthernet, called Multilevel Transmit - 3 (MLT-3), which only transitions the signal for a binary 1 but uses +1, 0, and -1 volts for signaling. Each transition carries only the signal half of the peak-to-peak distance. This system allows for the highest information density so far for a single cycle. Transmitting four consecutive 1s would occupy only a single cycle.

Figure 7-13 Encoding example Where a Transition in the Center of the Timing Window Represents a Binary 1 and the Absence of a Transition Indicates a Binary 0

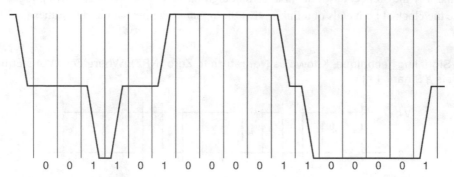

Many other and more complex signaling systems exist. However, this discussion is adequate for a simple overview of the process and some of the reasons for encoding the signal differently.

Module 2

Decode the waveform into binary, reorder the binary, and identify Ethernet field boundaries.

10Mbps Transmission Process

First, here is a quick description of the process used by the 10Mbps versions of Ethernet to transmit a frame. Figure 7-14 shows the fields present in a simple 802.3 Ethernet frame.

Figure 7-14 Basic 802.3 Ethernet Frame Fields

Preamble 7	SFD 1	Destination 6	Source 6	Length Type 2	Data : Pad 46 to 1500	FCS 4

Sample data for the first few fields in a frame might appear as in Figure 7-15. Each field is delineated above the sample hexadecimal data for that field and appears as it might appear at the MAC layer.

Figure 7-15 802.3 Ethernet Frame Fields with Sample Data

```
|      Preamble      | SFD |  Destination  |     Source    | Length/Type | ...
 55 55 55 55 55 55 55  D5    00 C0 17 A0 02 35 00 80 20 56 33 D4   08 06      ...
```

Using the hexadecimal-to-binary conversion process described in Module 1, Figure 7-16 demonstrates converting the hexadecimal data for the first two fields in the Ethernet frame to binary.

Figure 7-16 Converting the Hexadecimal Data in an Ethernet Frame to Binary

```
|                              Preamble                     |  SFD  |...
01010101  01010101  01010101  01010101  01010101  01010101  01010101  11010101 ...
```

Transmitting the frame involves passing it from the MAC layer to the physical layer. Ethernet encoding rules specify that each octet is transferred least-significant bit (LSB) first from the MAC layer to the physical layer, so the bits are reordered on a per-octet basis (see Figure 7-17). The frame check sequence (FCS) field is not reordered.

Figure 7-17 Ethernet Requires that Each Octet Be Transferred LSB First, so the Order Is Reversed

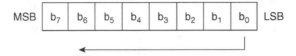

This concept is easiest to grasp as simply turning over each octet, as shown in Figure 7-18. The change is most identifiable in the start of frame delimiter (SFD) octet.

Figure 7-18 Reinterpretation of Figure 7-17

```
|                              Preamble                     |  SFD  |...
10101010  10101010  10101010  10101010  10101010  10101010  10101010  10101011 ...


01010101  01010101  01010101  01010101  01010101  01010101  01010101  11010101 ...
```

Following the LSB reordering of each octet by the MAC layer, the octets are transferred to the physical layer. LSB-ordered octets received from the MAC layer are serialized from left-to-right using Manchester encoding rules.

Manchester encoding relies on the direction of the edge transition in the *middle* of the timing window to determine the binary value for that bit period.

The encoding example in Figure 7-19 has one timing window highlighted vertically through all four waveform examples; it is labeled as *one bit period*. The top waveform has a falling edge in the center of the timing window, so it is interpreted as a binary 0.

Figure 7-19 Manchester Encoding

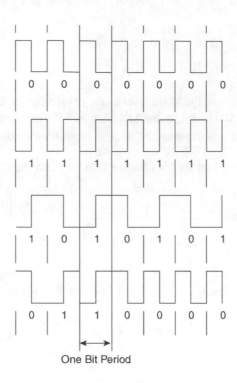

One Bit Period

Depending on how you view it, the second waveform is 180 degrees out of phase, or it is shifted half of one bit period to the side. It is otherwise identical. The result is that the center of the timing window for the second waveform has a rising edge, which is interpreted as a binary 1.

Instead of a repeating sequence of the same binary value, the third waveform example has an alternating binary sequence. In the first two examples, the signal must transition back between each bit period so that it can make the same-direction transition each time in the center of the timing window. With alternating binary data, there is no need to return to the previous voltage level in preparation for the next edge in the center of the timing window. Thus, any time there is a long separation between one edge and the next, you can be certain that *both edges represent the middle of a timing window*. This tip will be useful later.

The fourth waveform example (see Figure 7-20) is random data, which allows you to verify that whenever there is a wide separation between two transitions, both edges are in the center of a timing window and represent the binary value for that timing window.

After encoding the binary into Manchester, the physical layer transmits the resulting signal onto the attached medium.

Figure 7-20 shows two vertical lines clearly delineating the timing windows. In the center of both marked timing windows is an edge transition. The figure shows black dots at the boundaries of some other timing windows to aid in decoding the binary data. The decoded binary appears below the waveform along with the Ethernet field boundaries as appropriate.

Figure 7-20 Actual 10BASE5 Signal Decoded

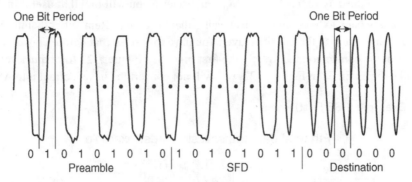

One Bit Period   One Bit Period

0 1 0 1 0 1 0 1 0 | 1 0 1 0 1 0 1 1 | 0 0 0 0 0 0
          Preamble   SFD   Destination

Now that you know the basic process, take out the lab sheet bearing the undecoded waveform.

Decoding the Waveform – Part A

Step 1   Locate the boundaries of the timing windows. Your lab sheet has faint timing marks placed appropriately. Compare the locations of those timing marks with the Manchester-encoding examples in Figure 7-19 and the section of decoded waveform in Figure 7-20. Study the waveform and the examples until you feel that you could correctly annotate another sheet that did not have those timing marks. Remember the tip given earlier: Whenever there are widely spaced edges in the waveform, both edges (rising and falling) represent the center of a timing window. It is not possible to locate the timing boundaries in areas where the waveform has closely spaced edges. In those areas is a consecutive pattern of the same binary value, but you have to look forward or backward along the waveform to find a widely spaced edge to determine which it is.

Step 2   This step is only possible after you find and mark some of the timing-window boundaries. Using a pencil (almost everyone makes mistakes), mark the direction of the edge in the center of the timing window, as shown in Step 3. After a short time, lean back and look at the spacing of the arrows you are using to mark the direction of the edge. Notice that despite how the waveform has narrow and wide spaced sections, your arrows are all evenly spaced.

Step 3   Go back and write the binary value below each arrow, as in Figure 7-21, but only after you mark several feet of waveform in that manner. Do not mark the binary values as you go; you will make mistakes if you are not watching the waveform closely.

Figure 7-21 Appearance of the Waveform After Step 2 and During Step 3

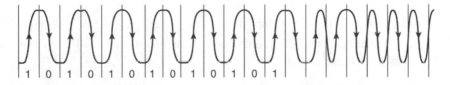

1 0 1 0 1 0 1 0 1 0 1 0 1

Step 4   Look for the SFD, which appears at the end of the initial stretch of widely spaced waveform edges. You see a change in the pattern, and you should decode a binary 11_2 right where the waveform pattern changes. Draw a vertical line through the waveform along the timing mark to the right of the binary 11_2 pattern and before the next timing window. That line separates the end of the SFD from the beginning of the destination address. Count back to the left eight bits, and draw another vertical line on the left clocking line for the eighth bit. That line marks the end of the SFD (including the binary 11_2) and the beginning of the next field. Refer to Figure 7-14 to obtain the number of octets required for each Ethernet field. For example, the SFD in Figure 7-14 appears with the number 1 below it. That indicates one octet, or eight binary bits. Count bits as indicated by Figure 7-17 until you draw vertical lines between each of the Ethernet fields leading up to the Data field. You might want to make small marks along the way for each octet division, because you will find that useful in the next step.

Step 5   Convert the binary back to hexadecimal. But wait—there is a trick! Remember that the MAC layer reordered the bits before handing them to the physical layer. You have to reverse that before converting back to binary. Most people perform the conversion incorrectly the first time. See Figure 7-22 for a quick refresher on what happened. Unlike the example in Figure 7-22, you will not convert the hexadecimal into ASCII.

Figure 7-22 Reordering Example (LSB First)

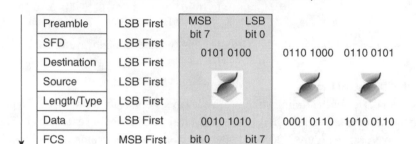

This example converts the word "The" from the appropriate ASCII hexadecimal codes into binary. The binary is then LSB reordered before passing from the MAC layer to the physical layer Ethernet implementation for transmission as follows:

$$T = 54_{16} = 0101\ 0100_2$$

$$h = 68_{16} = 0110\ 1000_2$$

$$e = 65_{16} = 0110\ 0101_2$$

Step 6   Identify the Layer 3 protocol contained in the Length/Type field. You perform this step after you mark all the Ethernet header information into the correct fields and convert it into hexadecimal. If you do not perform the conversion correctly, the next operation results in the wrong answer for Module 3.

If the value in the Length/Type field is less than 0600_{16} (1536 in decimal), then in most cases the contents of the Data field are decoded according to the 802.2 protocol. If the value is less than 0600_{16}, then the field indicates length.

If the value in the Length/Type field is equal to or greater than 0600_{16} (1536 in decimal), then in most cases the contents of the Data field are decoded according to the Ethernet II protocol. If the value is equal to or greater than 0600_{16}, then the field indicates type.

If your Length/Type field indicated a type, then you can look up the value in a table to learn which protocol is next in the Data field.

Module 3

Decode the Ethernet Length/Type field, locate and read RFCs, and decode Layer 3 of the waveform.

Standards and RFCs

There are two processes in use for determining the structure and specifications of various aspects of networking. One process is to go through the formal standards bodies, which produce documents such as the 802.3 Ethernet specifications and the ISO/IEC 7498 OSI basic model. These standards and RFC-issuing bodies include the ISO, the Institute of Electrical and Electronics Engineers (IEEE), the Internet Engineering Task Force (IETF), and the American National Standards Institute (ANSI).

The IETF publishes the specification documents of the Internet protocol suite as RFCs, but they can originate from anyone with a good idea. Read RFC 2223 for instructions on how to submit one. The RFC documents are subject to nearly the same level of scrutiny as the standards process before they are published, but they used to be more casual.

In 1969, when the RFC process started, the idea was to put a good proposal together, post it on the fledgling Internet, and wait to see what your peers thought of the idea. After the idea was vetted in this manner, your peers either implemented the proposal or not. No standards organization behind the proposal insisted that it be done in the prescribed manner, universally across all platforms. That is perhaps the single greatest difference between what is published as a standard and what is published as an RFC. Everyone must comply with the standards, but there is no obligation (except pressure from your customers and your peers) for compliance with an RFC.

As the RFC process becomes more structured, and more customers come to rely on the information available through compliance with published RFCs, the difference between being required by the standard and being pressured by your customer is growing narrower. To learn more about the standards development process, read RFC 2026.

RFCs are available from many sites on the Internet. The best site so far for obtaining published RFCs, as well as work in progress, is probably the RFC Editor site. Start at the URL http://www.rfc-editor.org/rfc.html.

Download the RFC index and save it on your local drive. It is really handy to have around (http://www.rfc-editor.org/rfc-index.html).

In the index, each entry has some valuable information. Here is a sample entry:

> 0760 **DoD standard Internet Protocol** J. Postel [Jan-01-1980] (TXT = 81507 bytes)(Obsoletes IEN 123) (Obsoleted by RFC0791) (Updated by RFC0777)

The most important information in this entry is that RFC 760 has been "obsoleted" and that the replacement is RFC 791. Other good information to know is in RFC 777, which in this case is related to the Internet Control Message Protocol (ICMP) error-messaging protocol for TCP/IP at Layer 3.

Decoding the Waveform – Part B

Step 1   To proceed with the waveform-decoding exercise, search the RFC index for the phrase *Assigned Numbers*. Make sure that you find the RFC number for the latest version of that document and then download it.

Step 2   Search through the RFC until you locate the section on *EtherTypes*. Once you find that section, take the value that you decoded in Step 6 of Module 2 and find it in the list.

Step 3   Go back to the RFC index and search on the protocol name that you found. Be sure to use the full name and not an acronym because the RFC you want defines that protocol and does not mention the acronym in the title.

Step 4   Download the appropriate RFC for the protocol. Sometimes it is necessary to check several RFCs for the information you are seeking. If you download the correct RFC, in Section 3 you find a table or chart that looks similar to Figure 7-23.

Figure 7-23 Data Field as Shown in RFCs

```
 0                   1                   2                   3
 0 1 2 3 4 5 6 7 8 9 0 1 2 3 4 5 6 7 8 9 0 1 2 3 4 5 6 7 8 9 0 1
+-+-+-+-+-+-+-+-+-+-+-+-+-+-+-+-+-+-+-+-+-+-+-+-+-+-+-+-+-+-+-+-+
|Version|  IHL  |Type of Service|          Total Length         |
+-+-+-+-+-+-+-+-+-+-+-+-+-+-+-+-+-+-+-+-+-+-+-+-+-+-+-+-+-+-+-+-+
```

This exact field listing shows you how to interpret the first part of the Data field. This document guides you through decoding Layer 3 of your waveform. The format in Figure 7-23 is common to the RFC documents. The numbers across the top represent bits. The 32 bits form four octets; you will often see fields aligning on the octet boundaries but not always.

Protocol-related RFCs typically provide a table or chart of the fields in a particular frame followed by a definition for and description of how to use each field depicted in the chart.

Step 5 Take the information from Step 4 and decode Layer 3 in your waveform. The portion of the table corresponds to the 32 bits immediately following the end of the MAC layer Length/Type field. The information appears in the order you see it in your waveform. The Version field follows as the next four bits after the Length/Type field.

Step 6 Find and decode the Protocol field from Layer 3. You will use this value to find the field definitions for Layer 4. Be very careful; there is another trick. Your clue is that when you look it up in the table of protocols, don't use the raw hexadecimal number.

Module 4

Use a protocol analyzer. Protocol analyzers let you view the contents of individual frames from the medium and offer functionality from Layer 2 up through Layer 7. They typically have a variety of built-in summary features that allow you to see who is talking to whom, by which protocol, and how much.

Protocol analyzers come in two general configurations: software based and hardware based. The software protocol analyzer is usually unable to detect or report upon MAC layer errors because it relies upon a standard network adapter. Software protocol analyzers tend to be somewhat limited in the amount of traffic that you can capture for the same reason. A typical network adapter is not well suited to capturing traffic at line rates because the typical workstation cannot process traffic at those rates. Dropped frames are not reported, and you cannot determine when a frame was missed. Hardware-based protocol analyzers usually have some level of integration to the front-end electronics and can show some or all the errors on a link. The level of error detection is often related to the price. Hardware protocol analyzers are more likely to be able to capture at line rates without dropping frames.

Both categories of protocol analyzer usually have several software modules that you can add for a price. These modules range from support for multiple network access protocols (Ethernet, Token Ring, Frame Relay, Wireless, etc.) to an integrated *Expert System* that compares the contents of a captured trace file against libraries of common symptoms related to specific faults or causes. Once beyond the built-in or automated test summary functions, the ability to obtain useful information from a protocol analyzer is directly related to the user's knowledge about the inner workings of the protocol in question. Protocol analysis is usually the domain of the senior network support staff for that reason.

Using a protocol analyzer as part of the instructional process will greatly enhance the clarity of the topic of discussion. It is one thing to sit back and listen about a particular protocol or process, but it is quite another to take apart that process bit-by-bit at the same time.

The software protocol analyzer in the CCNA curriculum is the Protocol Inspector (Educational Version), or PI-EDV. Following is a quick way to begin exploring with a protocol analyzer, without having to learn all the different functions.

Protocol Inspector in Five Buttons

This section provides a five-button quick start for PI. Figure 7-24 shows the PI startup screen.

Figure 7-24 PI Startup Screen

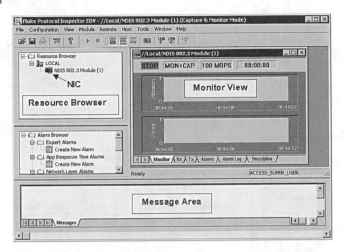

 1. Launch the application. Press the **Start** button, which appears on the toolbar at the top of the screen. One of the buttons looks like this and causes PI to begin capturing everything detected on the attached network adapter. If multiple network adapters are present, it might be necessary to select one from the Resource Browser first.

2. Click the **Detail View** button in the toolbar or double-click anywhere on the Monitor View chart. This action opens another window and allows you to see what sort of traffic you have captured so far.

3. To open an individual frame, you must first stop the capture. Press the **Stop** button.

 4. To open the captured trace file, press the **Capture View** button. With the educational version, a message box appears telling you that the capture is limited to 250 packets. Just click OK. You see a three-window screen similar to Figure 7-25. The top window shows a summary of all the captured frames. The middle window shows a field-by-field breakdown of the frame highlighted in the top window. And the bottom windows show the raw, uninterpreted hexadecimal for the highlighted frame.

Figure 7-25 PI Decode Screen

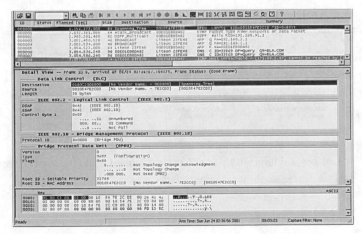

This screen shows a lot of information to absorb on the first visit.

5. Press the **Expert View** button on the toolbar at the top of the screen to examine the entire trace file for possible problems and warnings.

Congratulations! You have successfully used a protocol analyzer. For further exploration, Figure 7-26 and Figure 7-27 provide a quick summary of what some of the other toolbar buttons do.

Figure 7-26 shows the functionality of all the buttons on the toolbar for the first screen you see after launching the application.

Figure 7-26 Detail View Toolbar Menu Buttons

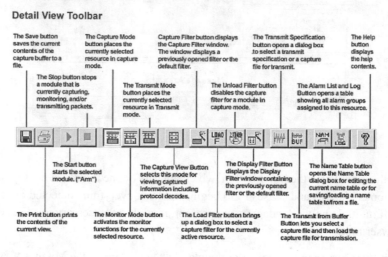

Figure 7-27 shows the functionality of all the buttons on the second screen, which is available after you press the **Capture View** button. Press each of these buttons to learn how each of these built-in summary tests operate and how you can view the contents of the capture file in different ways.

Figure 7-27 Data View Toolbar Menu Buttons

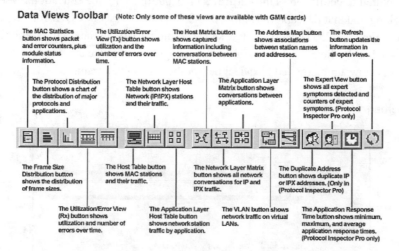

The Cisco Academy website contains several labs, and you can use the linked Fluke Networks website to further explore PI in the classroom. Additional labs will be posted as they are completed.

Protocol Inspector Lab

As part of this lab, you can open the frame used to create the waveform lab on the linked Fluke Networks website. You can also capture a similar frame from the classroom network to use in this lab.

Step 1 Open the PI application. Either open the trace file containing the frame used to create the waveform lab or capture a new trace file.

Step 2 Press the **Capture View** button to open the Detail View window. If you capture a new trace file, look through the trace file for a frame of the same Layer 3 protocol as the Ethernet Length/Type field indicated at the end of Module 2 and highlight it. Click on the middle window to freeze the top window on the frame you are interested in. This step also allows you to scroll the middle window. Compare the decoded waveform field-by-field with the information in the middle window of the Detail View. Also compare the hexadecimal data from the bottom window with the hexadecimal that you decoded from the waveform.

Step 3 Compare the information in the middle window with the field descriptions in the RFC you used to decode Layer 3 of the waveform in Module 3. Having first hand-decoded this frame, you should be intimately familiar with the structure and contents of the frame. Comparing this new knowledge against what the protocol analyzer shows you about the same frame will usually take all the fear and mystery about a protocol analyzer.

Congratulations! You now have a good understanding of what a protocol analyzer does! You should never have to hand-decode another frame—ever.

Use the protocol analyzer to capture each type of frame discussed in the lecture from this point forward. Compare the captured sample with the lecture material and the appropriate RFC for a better understanding of what is presented. The experience you gain from examining the behavior of a protocol using a protocol analyzer will place you several years ahead of your competition in the job market. Many networking professionals never master the protocol analyzer.

Lab 7.1.9a: Introduction to Fluke Network Inspector

Figure 7-28 Topology for Lab 7.1.9a

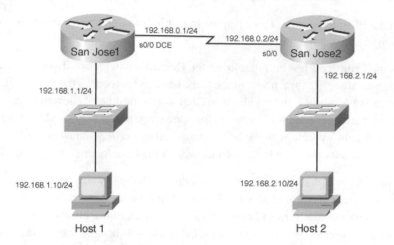

Objective

This lab is a tutorial demonstrating how to use the Fluke Networks *Network Inspector (NI)* to discover and analyze network devices within a broadcast domain. This lab will demonstrate the key features of the tool that you can incorporate into various troubleshooting efforts in the remaining labs.

Background/Preparation

The Network Inspector software can distinguish workstations, servers, network printers, switches, and managed hubs, if they have been assigned a network address.

Options for conducting this lab.

You may use Network Inspector in a small controlled LAN that is configured by the instructor in a closed lab environment as shown in Figure 7-28. The minimum equipment should include a workstation, a switch and a router.

You might also perform the steps in a larger environment such as the classroom or the school network to see more variety. Before attempting to run NI on the school LAN, check with your instructor and the network administrator.

The following are some points to consider:

- NI detects the devices within a network subnet or VLAN. It does not search beyond a router. It will not inventory the school's entire network unless it is all on one subnet.

- NI is not a Cisco product nor is it limited to detecting just Cisco devices.

- NI is a detection tool, but it is not a configuration tool. You cannot use it to reconfigure any devices.

The output in this lab is representative only, and output will vary depending on the number of devices, device MAC addresses, device host names, and LAN.

This lab introduces the Fluke Networks Network Inspector software, which can be useful in later troubleshooting labs and in the field. Although the NI software is a valuable part of the Academy program, it is also representative of features available on other products in the market.

At least one host must have the NI software installed. If you perform the lab in pairs, having the software installed on both machines means that each person can run the lab steps. Be sure to select both the Network Inspector and the Network Inspector Agent during installation.

The console can be anywhere that has a valid IP path and security to allow the connection to an agent. In fact, it might be an interesting exercise to have the console reach across the serial link to load the database from the other agent. You can have the console reading from a different database than the one that is currently in use by the agent on the same PC.

Step 1. Configure the lab or attach the workstation to the school LAN.

Option 1. If you select the closed lab environment, cable the equipment as shown in Figure 7-28 and load the configuration files into the appropriate routers. These files might already be pre-loaded. If not, you can obtain them from your instructor. These files should support the IP addressing scheme as shown in Figure 7-28 and Table 7-3.

Configure the workstations according to the specifications in Table 7-3.

Table 7-3 Workstation Configuration Settings

	Host #1	Host #2
IP Address	192.168.1.10	192.168.2.10
Subnet Mask	255.255.255.0	255.255.255.0
Default Gateway	192.168.1.1	192.168.2.1

Because the software discovers devices on the network, using additional devices provides a better demonstration.

If available, add additional hosts to both LANs.

Option 2. If you select option 2 (connect to school LAN), simply connect the workstation, with Protocol Inspector or Protocol Expert installed, directly to a classroom switch or to a data jack connected to the school LAN.

Step 2. Start NI and the agent.

From the Start menu, choose **Network Inspector > Console**.

Click the **Agent** button at the left end of the toolbar (see Figure 7-29) to start the agent.

Figure 7-29 Launching the NI Agent

If necessary, select the Agent tab in the window, click the **Start** button, and watch the **Status** box until it shows that the agent is running (see Figure 7-30). This process might take several minutes to start.

Figure 7-30 NI Agent Status

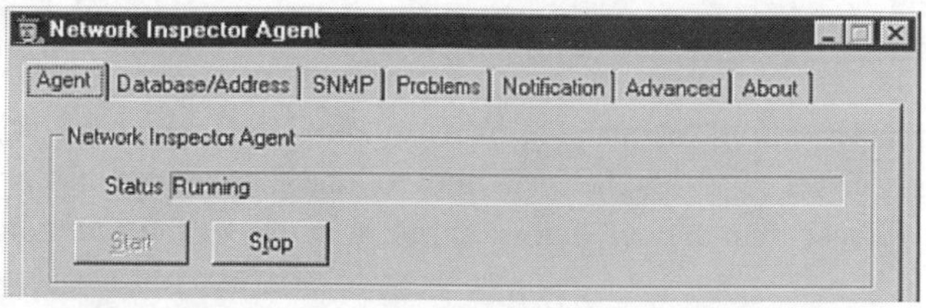

Step 3. Allow network discovery to occur.

The NI software is designed to quietly (passively and actively) collect network data. As such, it takes time for devices to appear. NI should discover this small network in a minute or two. The active collection of statistical data is delayed for the first 10 minutes. An actual production network might take 30 minutes or more before NI discovers most data.

Notice the agent status on the bottom of the console window in Figure 7-31. If you look closely, you will notice that the agent has been running since 9:57 PM.

After a few minutes, the console window should start showing information about the network. The example in Figure 7-31 added two workstations.

Figure 7-31 NI Active Session

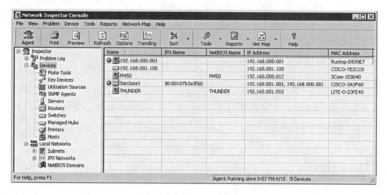

Use the **Close** button in the lower-right corner of the agent window to send the agent away. (Some versions might have a Hide button.) Do not use the **Stop** button, or the discovery process will cease.

Note: You might see entries from previous sessions. It takes a few minutes for the entries to match the network. In the Agent window, under the **Database/Address** tab is a checkbox for **Overwrite** (see Figure 7-32). If that box is checked, NI discards the current database content and loads a fresh data set as it is discovered when the agent starts. Otherwise, NI integrates any new data with the existing database as it is discovered.

Figure 7-32 Overwriting Previous NI Session Entries

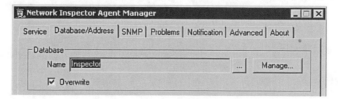

Notice the host names (M450, SanJose1, and THUNDER--PC host names will be different in student output), IP addresses, and MAC addresses for each discovered device in Figure 7-30. It should be obvious that both SanJose1 and SanJose2 have two IP addresses assigned to the LAN interface.

Notice that NI does not investigate beyond the router interface. It collects information only on the devices that share the same broadcast domain as the computer's NIC.

Step 4. Investigate device properties.

Double-click the router device's name and look over the available device properties, as in Figure 7-33. Remember that results depend on the devices included in the LAN's subnet.

The **Overview** tab in Figure 7-33 shows IP addresses, the Internetwork Packet Exchange (IPX) address, the IPX networks, the IPX data frame (802.3 here), and the MAC address. Notice that the organizational unique identifier (OUI) was converted to identify the manufacturer in this example.

Closest switches only appear if NI was provided a valid Simple Network Management Protocol (SNMP) community string for them.

The **Problems** tab in Figure 7-34 reveals that one of the IP addresses is duplicated within the network. This duplication occurs if the student configured an optional host as defined in Step 1. The red ball to the left of the description indicates a problem.

Figure 7-33 Analyzing Router Properties

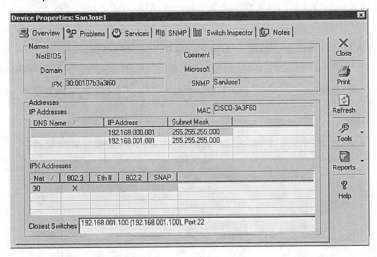

Figure 7-34 NI Problems Tab

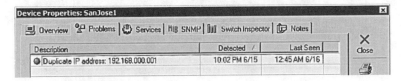

The **Services** tab in Figure 7-35 reveals the IP and IPX services running on the routers.

Figure 7-35 NI Services Tab

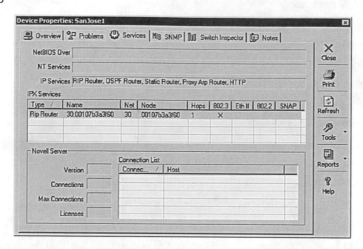

The IP Services field in Figure 7-36 reveals that the **IP HTTP Server** service is turned on, meaning that you can access the router via a web browser.

The IPX Services shows the IPX network ID (30), the node address (MAC), the frame type, and the fact that IPX Routing Information Protocol (RIP) is running.

The bottom third of the window shows the information that would have been revealed if the device had been a Novell server. A multihomed server, one with more than one NIC (connection) in separate networks, is working as a router or bridge.

The **MIB SNMP** tab in Figure 7-36 reveals SNMP information as well as the router Cisco IOS Software information.

Figure 7-36 NI MIB SNMP Tab

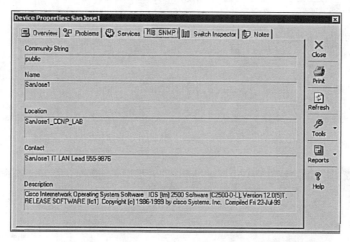

The **Switch Inspector** tab creates a variety of charts of the switch interface data for the selected device. This data is not collected during the initial 10-minute period.

 The Switch Inspector test provides basic utilization graphs for any SNMP-enabled device. The level of information depends on which management information bases (MIBs) are supported by the selected device. For example, because SanJose1 is a router, you cannot display the address of any directly connected devices for a highlighted port. The buttons on the left side of the window change the chart format. The **Graph Legend** button at the bottom-left corner displays the floating legend in Figure 7-37.

The second button is the **Tabular View**; selecting it details each interface on the device, including whether the interface is up or down (see Figure 7-38). The checkbox at the left of each line determines whether statistics are gathered for trending on that interface. Scrolling to the right reveals maximum transmission unit (MTU) and description (FastEthernet0/0 or Token-Ring 0/1) details.

The two clock-like buttons switch between a one-hour or 24-hour history, which can create an interesting comparison if the NI has been running for an extended time. The results will be the same in this short exercise.

Figure 7-37 NI Switch Inspector Tab: Graph Legend

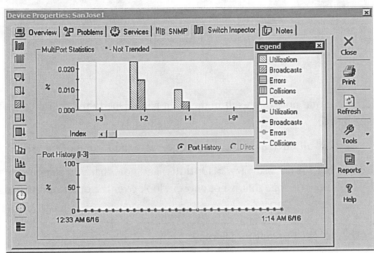

Figure 7-38 NI Switch Inspector Tab: Tabular View

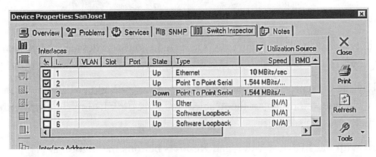

While in the Switch Inspector, the **Reports** button on the right side of the screen expands to show two options (see Figure 7-38). Select the **Switch Performance**, and a multipage report with various charts appears on the screen. Look over the results.

The **Switch Detail** option only works with a switch.

Figure 7-39 NI Switch Inspector Tab: Reports Options

After looking over the Device Properties window, click the **Close** button in the upper-right corner to return to the NI console.

Step 5. Explore left panel options.

At the NI console, experiment with expanding and contracting the choices in the left pane. As with the Explorer, if you select an item on the left side, the right side shows the details. In Figure 7-40, expanding the Problems Log and selecting **Errors** shows the devices on the right side with errors making it easy to spot the duplicate IP address device.

Figure 7-40 Navigating the NI Console

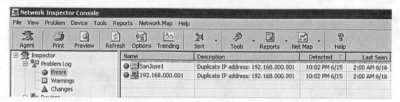

Try different options on the left pane, and note the result in the right pane. Due to the limited number of devices, some will be empty. Try it later with a larger sample.

In the left pane, select **Devices** to show all devices in the right pane. Note the format of the MAC address.

Click the **Options** button in the toolbar (or choose **View > Options**) and note that you can choose between **Manufacturer Prefix** and **Hex** (see Figure 7-41). Select the one that is not chosen, look over the other options, and then click **OK**. Note the result.

Figure 7-41 Selecting the MAC Address Format for Display

In the Console main screen, check that the **Problems Log** is selected and that a device in the detail window is highlighted. Press the F1 (Help) function key to show a list of problems by category, as demonstrated in Figure 7-42.

One of the problems created by the current lab configuration is a duplicate IP address. To learn about duplicate IP addresses, what the symptoms are, and what you can do about them, select the hyperlink listing for **Duplicate IP Address**. There is a wealth of information in the help for this software.

Take a minute and experiment with the **Preview**, **Sort**, and **Reports** buttons in the toolbar. The features should be obvious. Look particularly at the troubleshooting and documentation possibilities of the reports.

Select a host, open the **Tools** button in the toolbar, and pick **Ping**.

Figure 7-42 NI Help

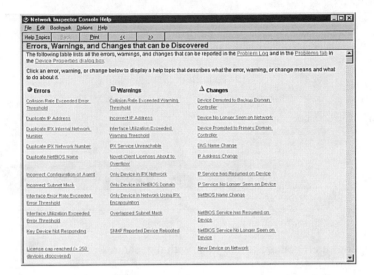

The Select Parameter box (see Figure 7-43) includes the LAN IP addresses that you can ping. Select one and click **OK**.

A command (MS-DOS) window appears to show the results.

Type **exit** to close the new window when finished.

Figure 7-43 Selecting Parameters to Ping

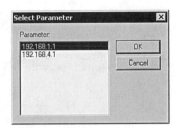

Use the **Telnet** and **Traceroute** options. Select a router or switch in the console display, choose **Tools > Telnet**, and a window with a Telnet session open appears. Trace works the same way.

The **Web** option on the **Tools** button opens a web session with a device if the IP HTTP server feature is turned on. If you want to try it, the username is the host name (**SanJose1** or **SanJose2**), and the password is **cisco**.

In this lab, the switch is a Catalyst 1924 with an IP address assigned, so the screen in Figure 7-44 appears if you select the **Web** choice while the switch is highlighted.

Figure 7-44 Opening a Web Session

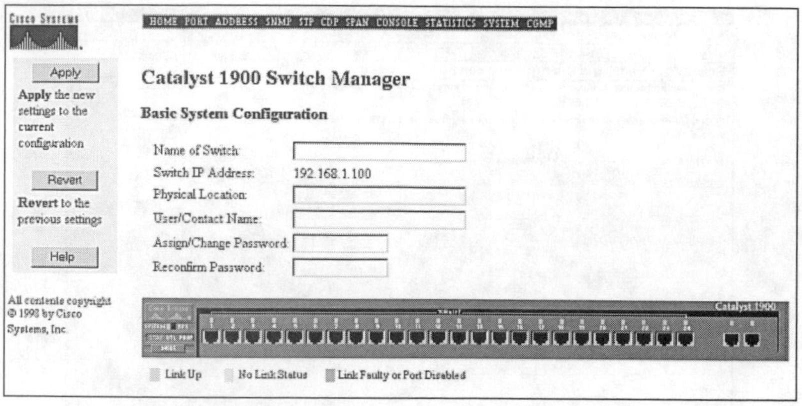

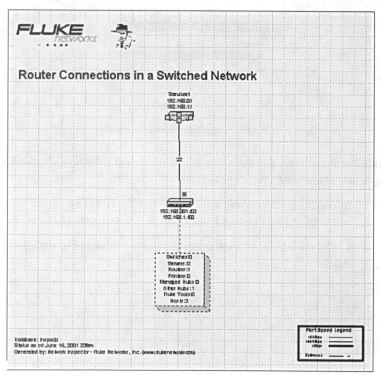

Experiment with the toolbar options until you are comfortable with the features.

Step 6. Use Net Map and Visio to diagram the network.

If Visio is installed on the workstation, the **Net Map** button on the toolbar activates Visio and creates a network map of the broadcast domain. Figure 7-45 uses "Router Connections in a Switched Network" on the Net Map button. It draws the network whether or not it includes a switch.

Figure 7-45 Creating a Network Map with Visio

Visio is fully integrated into NI, meaning that double-clicking one of the devices in the drawing calls up the Device Properties window that you used in Step 4.

Step 7. Document router information.

Using the skills covered earlier, select the router and document the following information where available:

a.What is the name of the device? _____

b.What IP services is the device running?

_____

c. What IPX services is the device running?

_____

d. What is the SNMP community string?

_____

e. What is the location? _____

f. Who is the contact? _____

g. Which interfaces are available? _____

h. Which interfaces are up? _____

i. List here any problem that the software has discovered:

_____

Step 8. Observe device discovery.

If possible, connect the two switches with a crossover cable and watch the NI output as it discovers new devices. If a crossover cable is unavailable, remove one of the switches and plug the hosts and router into the second switch. Although you would not normally do this step in a production environment, do it now just to see how NI responds.

New devices should show up initially with blue triangles indicating they are newly discovered. Many should eventually get a yellow warning rectangle indicating a potential problem. Remember that this process could take 10 or more minutes.

Eventually, NI will show the other subnets and the second router.

Step 9. Stop the capture and access the Problems and Notification tabs.

Click the **Agent** button in the toolbar. The agent has been collecting data all this time. Click the **Stop** button and then confirm your intentions when prompted.

Look over the tabs to see the database options that you can set. Note the **Problems** tab and the choices for focusing the investigation (see Figure 7-46).

Figure 7-46 NI Agent Manager: Problems Tab

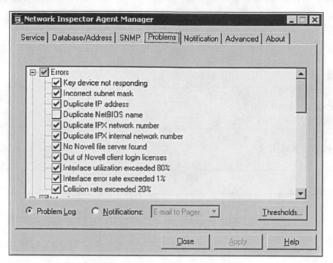

On the **Notification** tab (see Figure 7-47) notice that you can send out e-mail notifications. To use this feature, you need the same information as that required to set up an Internet e-mail account or Outlook e-mail account.

Figure 7-47 NI Agent Manager: Notification Tab

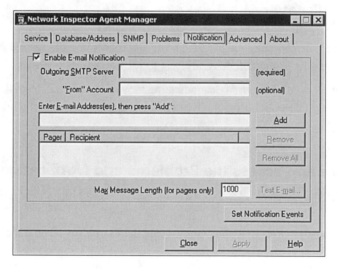

If you start the agent again, it might take a few minutes to detect any changes that occurred while the agent was off.

Step 10. Experiment with NI.

Experiment with the NI tool by looking at the different devices.

If NI is installed on the classroom computers, investigate the devices on that larger network.

Reflection

a. How might you use this information in troubleshooting?

b. What advantages over HyperTerminal might NI have for troubleshooting documentation?

Lab 7.1.9b: Introduction to Fluke Protocol Inspector

Figure 7-48 Topology for Lab 7.1.9b

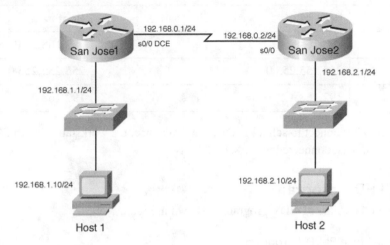

Objective

This lab is a tutorial demonstrating how to use the Fluke Networks Protocol Inpsector (PI) to analyze network traffic and data frames. Fluke OptiView Protocol Expert (PE) can also be used with this lab. Examples and screens shown in this lab are from Protocol Inspector. This lab will demonstrate key features of the tool that you can incorporate into various troubleshooting efforts in the remaining labs.

Background/Preparation

The output in this lab is representative only, and output will vary depending on the number of devices, device MAC addresses, device host names, the LAN, and so on.

This lab will be useful in later troubleshooting labs as well as in the field. Although the PI software is a valuable part of the Academy program, it is also representative of features available on other products in the market.

Options for conducting this lab.

You can use Protocol Inspector or Protocol Expert in a small controlled LAN that is configured by the instructor in a closed lab environment as shown in Figure 7-48. The minimum equipment should include a workstation, a switch, and a router.

You can also perform the steps in a larger environment such as the classroom or the school network to see more variety. Before attempting to run PI or PE on the school LAN, check with your instructor and the network administrator.

At least one the hosts must have the PI software installed. If you perform the lab in pairs, having the software installed on both machines means that each person can run the lab steps, although each host can display slightly different results.

Step 1. Configure the lab or attach a workstation to the school LAN.

Option 1. If you select the closed lab environment, cable the equipment as shown in Figure 7-48 and load the configuration files into the appropriate routers. These files might be preloaded. If not, you can obtain them from your instructor. These files should support the IP addressing scheme as shown in Figure 7-48 and Table 7-4.

Configure the workstations according to the specifications as shown in Figure 7-48 and Table 7-4 (the same as those for Lab 7.1.9a).

Table 7-4 Workstation Configuration Settings

	Host #1	**Host #2**
IP Address	192.168.1.10	192.168.2.10
Subnet Mask	255.255.255.0	255.255.255.0
Default Gateway	192.168.1.1	192.168.2.1

Option 2. If you select option 2 (connect to school LAN), simply connect the workstation, with PI or PE installed, directly to a classroom switch or to a data jack connected to the school LAN.

Step 2. Start the PI EDV program.

From the Start menu, launch the Fluke PI-EDV program as shown in Figure 7-49.

Figure 7-49 Launching the Fluke PI-EDV Program

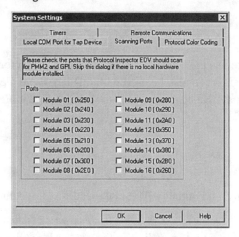

Note: The first time the program runs, a message appears: Do you have any Fluke analyzer cards or Fluke taps in your local system?

If you are using the educational version, click **No**. If you answer, yes or if the following screen appears, just click **OK** without selecting any ports.

The four main PI views are the following:

- Summary View
- Detail View
- Capture View of Capture Buffers
- Capture View of Capture Files

The program opens in the **Summary View**. This view shows several windows used by the tool. The **Resource Browser** window in the upper-left corner shows the only monitoring device that you have: the Network Driver Interface Specification

(NDIS) 802.3 Module (NIC) of the host. If there were protocol media monitors, they would appear with the associated host devices. You will cover the **Alarm Browser** (left side) and **Message Area** (bottom) later.

The **Monitor View** (upper right in the main window) monitors one resource per window in a variety of viewing options. Figure 7-50 and probably the startup screen show no information in the Monitor View window. (The **Stop** in the upper-left corner of the Monitor View window confirms that no monitoring is occurring.)

Figure 7-50 Monitor View Window in PI

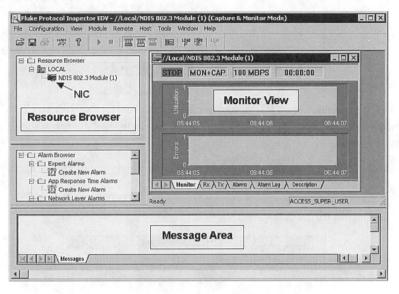

Step 3. Start the monitor and capture process.

 To start the monitoring and capturing process, use the **Start** button or select **Module > Start**. The Utilization chart should start showing activity, as in Figure 7-51.

Figure 7-51 Activity in the Utilization Chart

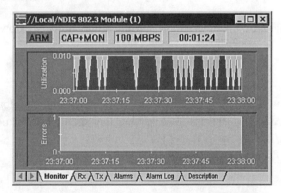

The word **Arm** should appear where Stop was before. If you open the **Module** menu, notice that Stop is an option, but Start is muted. Do not stop the process yet, or at least restart it again if it is stopped.

The tabs at the bottom of the window (see Figure 7-51) show the resulting data in a variety of forms. Click each and note the results. (Transmit (**Tx**), **Alarms**, and **Alarm Log** will be blank.) Figure 7-52 shows the Received (**Rx**) frames, which indicates that **Broadcast** and **Multicast** frames are being received, but might not show any **Unicasts**.

Figure 7-52 Tab Options for Data Reports

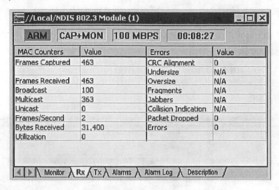

Using the console connection to the router, ping the monitoring host (192.168.1.10 or 192.168.2.10) and notice that **Unicast** frames appear. Unfortunately, the errors in the third column will not appear in the lab exercise unless you have a traffic generator such as Fluke Networks OptiView.

The **Description** tab (see Figure 7-53) reveals the MAC address, manufacturer, and model of the NIC. It also shows which error counters are on.

Figure 7-53 Description Tab Option for Data Reports

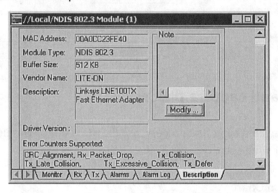

Take a few minutes to become familiar with the tabs and the scroll features of the window.

Step 4. View details.

To go to the **Detail View** window, click on the **Detail View** button in the toolbar or double-click anywhere on the Monitor View chart. This action opens a second window that should look something like Figure 7-54 after you maximize the **Utilization/Errors Strip Chart (RX)** window.

Figure 7-54 Detail View Window

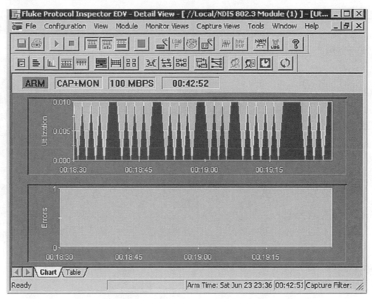

Note: If necessary, activate all toolbars on the View menu.

Initially, the chart output is the same as before, but there are more toolbar and menu options than in the Summary View. Before looking at these features, confirm that the Chart and Table tabs show the same information you saw earlier.

Like all Windows-compliant programs, placing the mouse over a button brings up a screen tip briefly identifying the button's purpose. As the mouse moves over the buttons, notice that some are muted, meaning that the feature is not appropriate under current circumstances or, in some cases, not supported in the educational version.

Note: The Lab 7.1.9b Appendix, "PI Toolbars," at the end of this lab provides a complete display of the toolbars and what they do.

 Click the **Mac Statistics** button to see the Rx frame table data in another format. The result should be obvious. Maximize the resulting window. The one piece of new information is the **Speed** showing the NIC transmission rate.

 Click the **Frame Size Distribution** button to see a distribution of the size frames received by the NIC. Placing the mouse over any bar displays a small summary like the one in Figure 7-55. Maximize the resulting window.

Figure 7-55 Frame Size Distribution Window

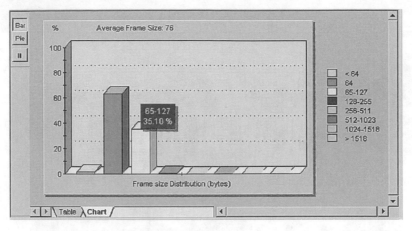

  Click the **Pie**, **Bar**, and **Pause** buttons in the upper-left corner.

Note: Pause stops the capture, so click on it again to resume the capture. Look at both the Table and Chart tab displays as well.

With the sample configurations, you should be getting mainly small frames because the only thing happening is routing updates. Use the extended ping feature from the router console connection, and specify 100 pings with a larger packet size.

If you are maximizing each new display, return to any previous view by using the Window menu. You can also **Tile** the windows. Experiment with the Window menu features and then close any unwanted views.

  Click the **Protocol Distribution** button to see a distribution of the protocols received by the NIC. Placing the mouse over any bar displays a small summary panel. Maximize the resulting window, as in Figure 7-56.

Figure 7-56 Protocol Distribution Window

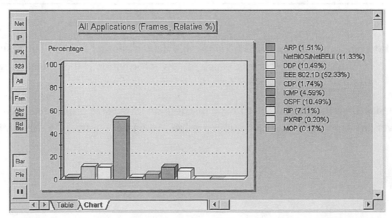

Click each of the buttons and tabs to see the results. The **Net** button shows only network protocols. The **323** button refers to the H323 voiceover IP protocols. This button may also be labeled VoIP instead of 323. Look at **Frm** (frame), **Abs Bts** (absolute bytes), and **Rel Bts** (relative bytes) to see the results. Remember that the **Pause** button stops the capture.

Click the **Host Table** button to see the MAC stations and related traffic, as in Figure 7-57.

Figure 7-57 Viewing MAC Stations and Related Traffic

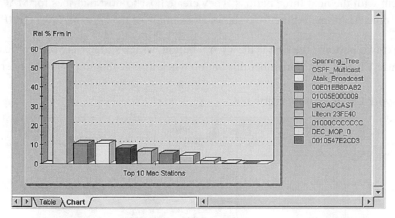

Notice the Spanning Tree, AppleTalk, and Open Shortest Path First (OSPF) protocol traffic. Be sure to look at the Table tab to see the actual values.

Click the **Network Layer Host Table** button to see the network (IP/IPX) stations and related traffic, as in Figure 7-58.

Figure 7-58 Viewing IP/IPX Stations and Related Traffic

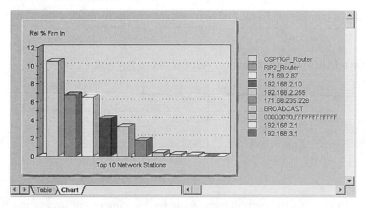

Any pings and any additional hosts that might have added to the configuration impact the actual addresses that appear on the right.

Click the **Application Layer Host Table** button to see the network station traffic by application, as in Figure 7-59.

Figure 7-59 Viewing Network Station Traffic by Application

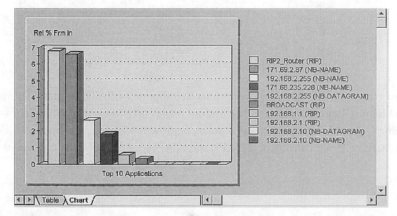

Experiment with the next three buttons. They create host-to-host matrices for MAC, network, and application layer conversations. Figure 7-60 shows an example of the network layer (IP/IPX) conversations.

Of the next two buttons, the first is the VLAN button, which shows network traffic on VLANs. This sample does not use VLANs, but remember this button when troubleshooting VLANs later.

Figure 7-60 Viewing Network Layer Conversations

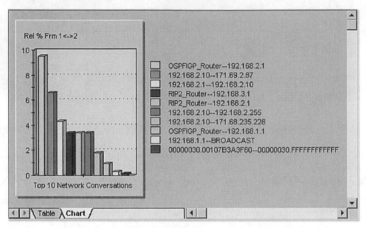

The second button creates a matrix comparing MAC and network station addresses to names. In Figure 7-61, the second row is a Novell station.

Figure 7-61 Matrix to Compare MAC/Network Station Addresses to Names

MAC Station Name	MAC Station Address	Network Station Name	Network Station Address
00107B3A3F60	00107B3A3F60	192.168.1.1	192.168.1.1
00107B3A3F60	00107B3A3F60	00000030.00107B3A3F60	00000030.00107B3A3F60
Liteon 23FE40	00A0CC23FE40	192.168.2.10	192.168.2.10
00E01EB8DA82	00E01EB8DA82	192.168.2.1	192.168.2.1
00E01EB8DA82	00E01EB8DA82	192.168.3.1	192.168.3.1

 The **Name Table** button opens the current name table for viewing or editing, as in Figure 7-62.

Figure 7-62 Name Table Window for Viewing and Editing

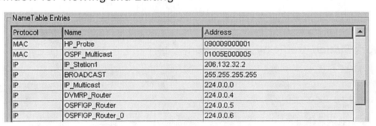

 The **Expert View** button shows the expert symptoms (see Figure 7-63). These statistics are PI's way of pointing out potential problems. Clicking the underlined options brings up additional detail windows if there are any values recorded. The sample for this lab will not show much, but it will look over the options for debugging Inter-Switch Link (ISL), Hot Standby Router Protocol (HSRP), and other types of problems that you will see in later labs.

Figure 7-63 Expert View Window

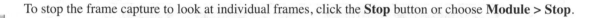

Expert Category	Value	Expert Category	Value
ICMP All Errors	368	Duplicate Network Address	0
ICMP Destination Unreachable	368	Unstable MST	0
ICMP Redirects	0	SAP Broadcast	0
Excessive Bootp	0	OSPF Broadcast	923
Excessive ARP	0	RIP Broadcast	25
NFS Retransmissions	0	ISL Illegal VLAN ID	0
TCP/IP SYN Attack	0	ISL BPDU/CDP Packets	0
TCP/IP RST Packets	0	IP Time to Live Expiring	0
TCP/IP Retransmissions	0	IP Checksum Errors	0
TCP/IP Zero Window	0	Illegal Network Source Address	0
TCP/IP Long Acks	0	Illegal MAC Source Address	0
TCP/IP Frozen Window	0	Total MAC Stations	11
Network Overload	0	Broadcast/Multicast Storm	0
Non Responsive Stations	0	Physical Errors	0
		HSRP Errors	0
		TCP Checksum Errors	0

Step 5. Stop the capture process.

To stop the frame capture to look at individual frames, click the **Stop** button or choose **Module > Stop**.

Once you stop the capture, click the **Capture View** button. With the education version, a message box announces that the capture is limited to 250 packets. Just click **OK**.

The resulting window in Figure 7-64 can be a little overwhelming at first. Maximize the window to hide any other windows open in the background.

Figure 7-64 Capture View Window

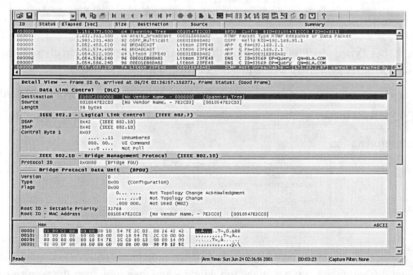

In the results, note that three horizontal windows are open. The top window lists the captured packets. The middle window shows the detail of the selected packet in the top window, and the bottom window shows the hex values for the packet.

If you position the mouse over the borders between the three windows, a "line mover" (two-headed arrow) will appear, letting you change the distribution of space for each window. It might be advantageous to make the middle window as large as possible, leaving five or six rows in each of the other two, as shown in the figure.

Look over the packets in the top window. You should see Domain Name System (DNS), Address Resolution Protocol (ARP), Routing Table Maintenance Protocol (RTMP), and other types of packets. If you are using a switch, you should see Cisco Discovery Protocol (CDP) and Spanning Tree packets. Notice that as you select rows in the top window, the contents of the other two windows change.

Select information in the middle window, and notice that the hex display in the bottom window changes to show where that specific information is stored. In Figure 7-65, selecting the Source Address (IP) shows hex values from the packet.

Figure 7-65 Viewing Hexadecimal Values from a Packet

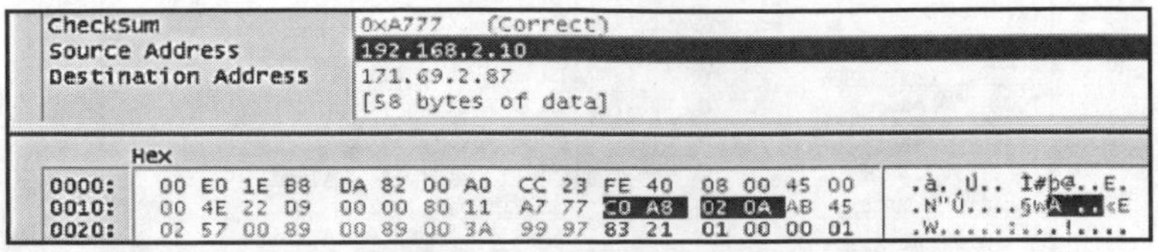

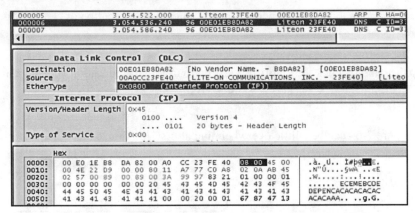

The color coding makes it easier to locate information from the middle window in the hex window. In Figure 7-66 with a DNS packet, the data in the Data Link Control (DLC) section of middle window is purple, whereas the IP section is green. The corresponding hex values are the same colors.

Figure 7-66 Color-Coded Packets and Hexadecimal Values

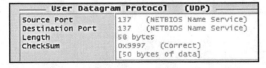

Notice in Figure 7-66, the **EtherType** is **0x0800**, indicating that it is an IP packet. You can also notice the MAC addresses for both the destination and source hosts as well as where that data is stored in the hex display.

In the same example, the next section in the middle window is the **User Datagram Protocol (UDP)** information, including the UDP port numbers (see Figure 7-67).

Figure 7-67 Viewing UDP Information

The structure of the middle window changes for each type of packet.

Take a few minutes to select different packet types in the top window and then look over the resulting display in the other two windows. Pay particular attention to the EtherType, any port numbers, and source and destination addresses (both MAC and network layer). You should see RIP, OSPF, and RTMP (AppleTalk) packets in the capture. Make sure that you can locate and interpret the important data. In the RIP capture in Figure 7-68, notice that it is a RIP Version 2 packet; the multicast destination address is 224.0.0.9 (what would it be in Version 1?); and that you can see the actual route table entries.

Figure 7-68 RIP Packet Information

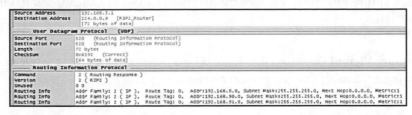

If you see any CDP packets, figure out the platform. Figure 7-69 is from a Catalyst 1900 switch.

Figure 7-69 Determining the Networking Device Platform Based on CDP Packet Information

Experiment until you are comfortable with the tools.

Step 6. Save the captured data.

 Depending on the version of Protocol Expert\Inspector, **File > Save Capture** may be **File > Save Current Section**. To save captured data, click the **Save Capture** button or choose **File > Save Capture** to open the dialog box in Figure 7-70. Accept the **All** option by clicking the **Continue** button. You can save just a range of captured frames with this window.

Figure 7-70 Captured Data Save Options

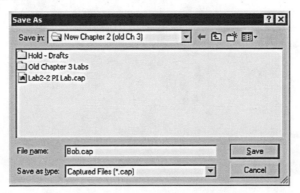

Use a proper filename and store the file on the appropriate disk. If the CAP extension is showing when the window in Figure 7-71 opens, make sure it remains after you type the name.

Figure 7-71 Saving Captured Data to File

Click the **Open Capture File** button and open the file called Lab3-2 PI Lab.cap, or if it is not available, open the file that you just saved.

You are now using the **Capture View of Capture Files**. There is no difference in tools, but the title bar at the top of the screen indicates that you are viewing a file rather than a capture in memory.

Step 7. Examine frames.

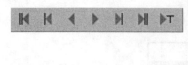 Select a frame in the top window and click the buttons. The arrows by themselves move up or down one frame. The arrow with single line jumps to the top or bottom of the current window, whereas the arrow with two arrows jumps to the top or bottom of the entire list. The arrow with the T also moves to the top of the list.

 Click the **Search** buttons to perform searches. Type text such as OSPF in the list box, click the binoculars, and you can move from one OSPF entry to the next.

Experiment until you are comfortable with the tools.

Reflection

a. How might you use this tool in troubleshooting?

_____

b. Is PI analyzing all the data on the network? _____

c. What is the impact of being connected to a switch?

_____

Lab 7.1.9b: Appendix: Protocol Inspector Toolbars

Figure 7-72 PI Toolbar

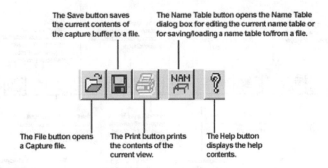

The Save button saves the current contents of the capture buffer to a file.

The Name Table button opens the Name Table dialog box for editing the current name table or for saving/loading a name table to/from a file.

The File button opens a Capture file.

The Print button prints the contents of the current view.

The Help button displays the help contents.

Figure 7-73 Module Toolbar (Summary View)

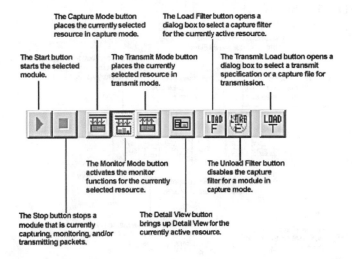

The Capture Mode button places the currently selected resource in capture mode.

The Load Filter button opens a dialog box to select a capture filter for the currently active resource.

The Start button starts the selected module.

The Transmit Mode button places the currently selected resource in transmit mode.

The Transmit Load button opens a dialog box to select a transmit specification or a capture file for transmission.

The Monitor Mode button activates the monitor functions for the currently selected resource.

The Unload Filter button disables the capture filter for a module in capture mode.

The Stop button stops a module that is currently capturing, monitoring, and/or transmitting packets.

The Detail View button brings up Detail View for the currently active resource.

Figure 7-74 Detail View Toolbar

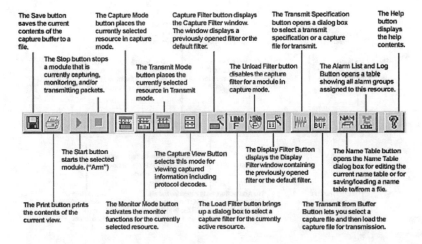

The Save button saves the current contents of the capture buffer to a file.

The Capture Mode button places the currently selected resource in capture mode.

Capture Filter button displays the Capture Filter window. The window displays a previously opened filter or the default filter.

The Transmit Specification button opens a dialog box to select a transmit specification or a capture file for transmit.

The Help button displays the help contents.

The Stop button stops a module that is currently capturing, monitoring, and/or transmitting packets.

The Transmit Mode button places the currently selected resource in Transmit mode.

The Unload Filter button disables the capture filter for a module in capture mode.

The Alarm List and Log Button opens a table showing all alarm groups assigned to this resource.

The Start button starts the selected module. ("Arm")

The Capture View Button selects this mode for viewing captured information including protocol decodes.

The Display Filter Button displays the Display Filter window containing the previously opened filter or the default filter.

The Name Table button opens the Name Table dialog box for editing the current name table or for saving/loading a name table to/from a file.

The Print button prints the contents of the current view.

The Monitor Mode button activates the monitor functions for the currently selected resource.

The Load Filter button brings up a dialog box to select a capture filter for the currently active resource.

The Transmit from Buffer Button lets you select a capture file and then load the capture file for transmission.

Figure 7-75 Data Views Toolbar (Note that Only Some of These Views Are Available with GMM Cards)

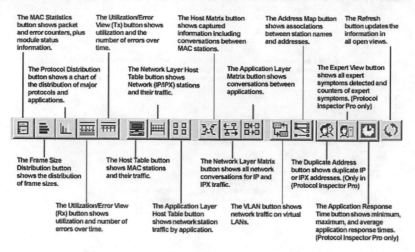

Figure 7-76 Create/Modify Filter Toolbar

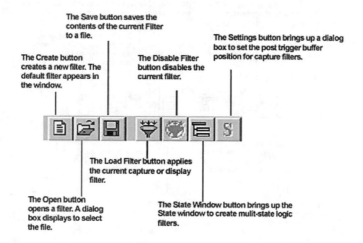

Figure 7-77 State Toolbar

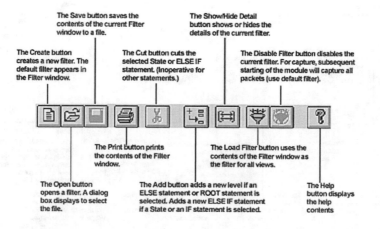

Figure 7-78 Capture View Toolbar

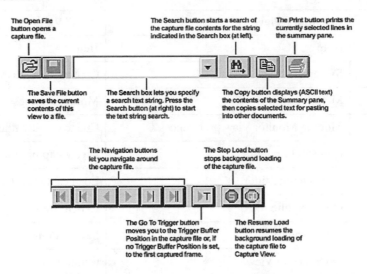

Figure 7-79 Capture View Toolbar, *continued*

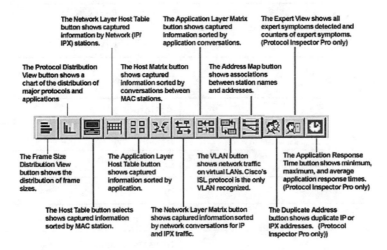

Table 7-5 Protocol Inspector Function Keys

Function Key	Summary View	Detail View
F1	Help	Help
F2	System settings	Capture View display options
F3	Module settings	Module settings
F4	Module Monitor View preferences	Create display filter
F5	Connect to remote	Create capture filter
F6	Load capture filter	Load capture filter
F7	Open capture file	Expert Summary view
F8	Save capture	Save capture
F9	Go to Detail View	Capture View
F10	Start/Stop	Start/Stop
F11	N/A	N/A
F12	N/A	N/A

Table 7-6 PI Keyboard Shortcuts

Key Combination	Action
Alt-F4	Close window
Ctrl-O	Open
Ctrl-S	Save
Ctrl-T	Start module
Ctrl-P	Stop module

Ethernet Switching

There are no labs in this module. Please review the information in Chapter 8 of CCNA 1 in the *Cisco Networking Program CCNA 1 and 2 Companion Guide*, Revised Third Edition, to ensure that you can answer the following questions:

- What is Layer 2 bridging?
- How does a LAN switch operate?
- What is latency?
- What are the differences among common switching methods such as cut-through switching, store-and-forward switching, and fragment-free switching?
- What are the functions and features of the Spanning Tree Protocol (STP)?
- How does STP work?
- What is the difference between a collision domain and broadcast domain?
- Which Layer 1, 2, and 3 devices are used to create collision domains and broadcast domains.
- What is segmentation?
- What is a broadcast?
- How does data flow through a network?
- What is network segmentation and which devices are used to create segments?

TCP/IP Protocol Suite and IP Addressing

The following labs are in this chapter:

Lab TI	Title
9.2.7	IP Addressing Basics
9.3.5	DHCP Client Setup
9.3.7	Workstation ARP

Lab 9.2.7: IP Addressing Basics

Objectives

- Name the five different classes of IP addresses.

- Describe the characteristics and use of the different IP address classes.

- Identify the class of an IP address based on the network number.

- Determine which part (octet) of an IP address is the network ID and which part is the host ID.

- Identify valid and invalid IP host addresses based on the rules of IP addressing.

- Define the range of addresses and default subnet mask for each class.

Background/Preparation

This lab helps you develop an understanding of IP addresses and how TCP/IP networks operate. It is primarily a written exercise, but it would be worthwhile to review some real network IP addresses using the command-line utilities **ipcconfig** (Windows NT/2000/XP) or **winipcfg** (Windows 9x/Me). IP addresses uniquely identify individual TCP/IP networks and hosts (computers and printers) on those networks so devices can communicate. Workstations and servers on a TCP/IP network are called *hosts*, and each has a unique IP address, which is its *host address*. TCP/IP is the most widely used protocol in the world. The Internet, or World Wide Web, uses only IP addressing. For a host to access the Internet, it must have an IP address.

In its basic form, the IP address has two parts: a network address and a host address. The network portion of the IP address is assigned to a company or organization by the Internet Network Information Center (InterNIC). Routers use the IP address to move data packets between networks. IP addresses are 32 bits long (with the current version, IPv4) and have 4 octets of 8 bits each. They operate at the network Layer 3 of the OSI model (the internetwork layer of the TCP/IP model) and are assigned statically (manually) by a network administrator or dynamically (automatically) by a Dynamic Host Configuration Protocol (DHCP) server. The IP address of a workstation (host) is a *logical address*, meaning it can change. The MAC address of the workstation is a 48-bit *physical address*, which is burned into the NIC and cannot change unless you replace the NIC. The combination of the logical IP address and the physical MAC address helps route packets to their proper destinations.

There are five different classes of IP addresses, and depending on the class, the network and host part of the address will use a different number of bits. In this lab, you work with the different classes of IP addresses and become familiar with the characteristics of each. Understanding IP addresses is critical to understanding TCP/IP and internetworks in general. This lab requires a PC workstation with Windows 9x/NT/2000/XP and access to the Windows calculator.

Step 1. Review IP address classes and their characteristics.

a. Address Classes

There are five classes of IP addresses (A through E). Only the first three classes are used commercially use. Table 9-1 starts with a Class A network address. The first column is the class of IP address. The second column is the first octet, which must fall within the range shown for a given class of address. The Class A address must start with a number between 1 and 126. The first bit of a Class A address is always a zero, meaning that you cannot use the High Order Bit (HOB), or the 128 bit. The 127 bit is reserved for loopback testing. The first octet alone defines the network ID for a Class A network address.

b. Default Subnet Mask

The default subnet mask uses all binary 1s (decimal 255) to mask the first 8 bits of the Class A address. The default subnet mask helps routers and hosts determine whether the destination host is on this network or another one. Because there are only 126 Class A networks, you can use the remaining 24 bits (3 octets) for hosts. Each Class A network can have 2^{24} (2 to the 24th power) or more than 16 million hosts. It is common to subdivide the network into smaller groupings called *subnets* by using a custom subnet mask, which is discussed in the next lab.

c. Network and Host Address

The network or host portion of the address cannot be all 1s or all 0s. For example, the Class A address of 118.0.0.5 is a valid IP address because the network portion (the first 8 bits, equal to 118) is not all 0s, and the host portion (the last 24 bits) is not all 0s or all 1s. If the host portion were all 0s, it would be the network address itself. If the host portion were all 1s, it would be a broadcast for the network address. The value of any octet can never be greater than decimal 255 or binary 11111111. Table 9-1 shows the information you should know about the five classes of IP addresses.

Table 9-1 IP Address Class Information

Class	1st Octet Decimal Range	1st Octet HOBs	Network/Host ID (N=Network, H=Host)	Default Subnet Mask	Number of Networks	Hosts per Network (Usable Addresses)
A	1–126*	0	N.H.H.H	255.0.0.0	126 ($2^7 - 2$)	16,777,214 ($2^{24} - 2$)
B	128–191	1 0	N.N.H.H	255.255.0.0	16,382 ($2^{14} - 2$)	65,534 ($2^{16} - 2$)
C	192–223	1 1 0	N.N.N.H	255.255.255.0	2,097,150 ($2^{21} - 2$)	254 ($2^8 - 2$)

Table 9-1 IP Address Class Information (Continued)

Class	1st Octet Decimal Range	1st Octet HOBs	Network/Host ID (N=Network, H=Host)	Default Subnet Mask	Number of Networks	Hosts per Network (Usable Addresses)
D	224–239	1 1 1 0	Reserved for multicasting Experimental; used for research			
E	240–254	1 1 1 1 0				

* You cannot use Class A address 127, which is reserved for loopback and diagnostic functions.

Step 2. Determine basic IP addressing.

Use the IP address chart in Table 9-1 and your knowledge of IP address classes to answer the following questions.

  a. What is the decimal and binary range of the first octet of all possible Class B IP addresses?

  Decimal:From: _____ To: _____

  Binary:From: _____ To: _____

  b. Which octets represent the network portion of a Class C IP address?

  _____

  c. Which octets represent the host portion of a Class A IP address?

  _____

  d. What is the maximum number of hosts you can have with a Class C network address?

  _____

  e. How many Class B networks are there? _____

  f. How many hosts can each Class B network have? _____

  g. How many octets does an IP address have? _____ How many bits per octet?

  _____

Step 3. Determine the host and network portions of the IP address.

  a. With the following IP host addresses, indicate the class of each address, the network address or ID, the host portion, the broadcast address for this network, and the default subnet mask. The host portion will be all 0s for the network ID. Enter only the octets that make up the host. The host portion will be all 1s for a broadcast. The network portion of the address will be all 1s for the subnet mask. Fill in Table 9-2.

Table 9-2 Determining IP Address Network and Host Portions

Host IP Address	Address Class	Network Address	Host Address	Network Broadcast Address	Default Subnet Mask
216.14.55.137					
123.1.1.15					
150.127.221.244					
194.125.35.199					
175.12.239.244					

Step 4. Given an IP address of 142.226.0.15, answer the following questions.

a. What is the binary equivalent of the second octet? _____

b. What is the class of the address? _____

c. What is the network address of this IP address? _____

d. Is this a valid IP host address (Yes/No)? _____

e. Why or why not? _____

_____

_____

_____

Step 5. Determine which IP host addresses are valid for commercial networks.

a. For the following IP host addresses, determine which are valid for commercial networks and indicate why or why not. *Valid* means you could assign it to a workstation, server, printer, router interface, and so on. Fill in Table 9-3.

Table 9-3 Determining Valid IP Host Addresses for Commercial Networks

IP Host Address	Valid Address? (Yes/No)	Why or Why Not?
150.100.255.255		
175.100.255.18		
195.234.253.0		
100.0.0.23		
188.258.221.176		
127.34.25.189		
224.156.217.73		

Lab 9.3.5: DHCP Client Setup

Objective

- The purpose of this lab to introduce DHCP and the process for setting up a network computer as a DHCP client to use DHCP services.

Background/Preparation

Dynamic Host Configuration Protocol (DHCP) provides a mechanism for dynamically assigning IP addresses and other information. Instead of configuring a static IP address, subnet mask, default gateway, Domain Name System (DNS) server, and other resource addresses to each host, a DHCP server device located on the LAN or at the Internet service provider (ISP) can respond to a host request and furnish the required information. The DHCP device is typically a network server.

In small networks, including many home networks with DSL, cable, or wireless connections, a small router can provide DHCP services. Cisco and many other manufacturers offer small routers that include an Internet (WAN) connection, a small built-in hub or switch, and DHCP server service. This lab focuses on setting up a computer to use the DHCP services provided.

This lab assumes the PC is running any version of Windows. Ideally, you will perform this lab in a classroom or other LAN connected to the Internet. You can also perform it from a single remote connection via a modem or DSL-type connection.

Important Note: If the network connecting the computer uses static addressing, follow the lab and view the various screens. Do not change these machines to DHCP usage because you will lose the static settings and a network administrator will need to reconfigure them.

Step 1. Establish a network connection.

If the connection to the Internet is dial-up, connect to the ISP to ensure that the computer has an IP address. In a TCP/IP LAN with a DHCP server, it shouldn't be necessary to do this step.

Step 2. Access a command prompt.

Windows NT / 2000 / XP users: Use the Start menu to open the command prompt (MS-DOS-like) window (**Start > Programs > Accessories > Command Prompt** or **Start > Programs > Command Prompt**).

Windows 95 / 98 / Me users: Use the Start menu to open the MS-DOS prompt window (**Start > Programs > Accessories > MS-DOS Prompt** or **Start > Programs > MS-DOS Prompt**).

Step 3. Display IP settings to determine whether the network is using DHCP.

Windows 95 / 98 / Me users: Type **winipcfg** and press **Enter**.

Then click the **More Info** button.

    a. The example in Figure 9-1 indicates that DHCP is in use with the entries in the DHCP Server IP Address, Lease Obtained, and Lease Expires boxes. These entries would be blank in a "static" configured device. DHCP also supplied the DHCP and WINS server addresses. The missing default gateway indicates a proxy server.

Figure 9-1 IP Configuration Settings Help Determine DHCP Information

Windows NT / 2000 / XP users: Type **ipconfig /all** and press Enter.

b. The Windows NT / 2000 / XP example in Figure 9-2 indicates that DHCP is in use with the **DHCP Enabled** entry. The entries for **DHCP Server**, **Lease Obtained**, and **Lease Expires** confirm this fact. These last three entries would not exist in a "static" configured device, and **DHCP Enabled** would say **No**.

Figure 9-2 IP Configuration Settings Determine Whether DHCP is Enabled

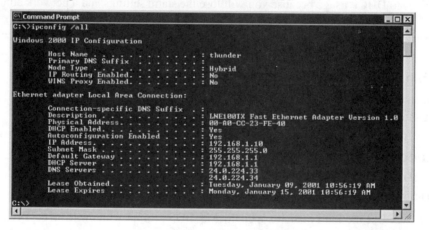

Very Important: Look over the results.

c. Is DHCP running on the network? _____

   Confirm this with a teacher or lab assistant if you are not sure.

d. What is the length of the DHCP lease? _____

   DHCP servers provide IP addresses for a limited time, in the same way a library checks out books. The network administrator can configure the actual length of time, but often it is several days. If a lease expires, the IP address returns to the pool to be used by others. This process allows DHCP to recapture inactive IP addresses without humans updating the records. An organization that lacks enough IP addresses for every user might use very short lease durations so that the addresses are reused even during brief periods of inactivity.

The computer has an automatic method for requesting that the lease be extended, often avoiding an expired lease as long as the computer is used regularly.

e. Releasing and Renewing the DHCP Lease

If you move a computer from one network to another (a different network portion of the IP address), it might still retain its settings from the old network and be unable to connect to the new network. One solution is to release and renew the lease. Statically configured computers can do this, but there will be no change to the IP address. Computers connected directly to an ISP might lose connections and have to replace their calls, but no permanent changes occur. Follow the steps to release and renew the DHCP lease.

Windows NT / 2000 / XP users

Type **ipconfig/release** and press **Enter**. Look over the results and then type **. ipconfig/renew**. You will probably get the same settings as before; had you changed networks, you would get new settings.

Windows 95 / 98 / Me users

f. Click the **Release All** button. Look over the results and then click the **Renew All** button. You will probably get the same settings as before; had you changed networks, you would get new settings.

Step 4. Accessing the network configuration window.

a. On your desktop, right-click the Network Neighborhood or **My Network Places** icon and choose **Properties**. If you do not have either icon on this machine, use the Start button (**Start > Settings > Control Panel**) and then double-click on the **Network** icon.

Some users will see a screen like the Network Properties dialog box shown in Figure 9-3.

Figure 9-3 Network Properties Dialog Box

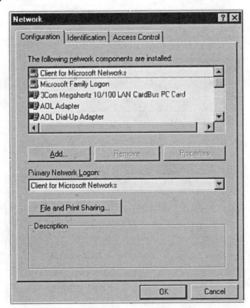

b. Different versions of Windows will have slightly different tabs, and the computer's current configuration will determine the items included in the Network Components box—but it should still look basically like Figure 9-3.

Most Windows 95, 98, and Me systems should see the network properties at this point. If you have a Network window similar to the one shown, skip to the next numbered step.

Windows 2000 and XP users need to do two more things.

In the window, double-click your **Local Area Connection**. When the **Local Area Connection Status** window appears, click on the **Properties** button. That opens a **Local Area Connection Properties** dialog box similar to the one shown in Figure 9-4.

Figure 9-4 Local Area Connection Properties Window

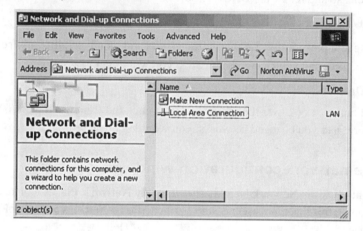

d. In the Network Properties dialog box, scroll through the listed components until you find TCP/IP. If you see more than one (older Windows), find the one for your current network connection, NIC or modem. In Windows 2000 and XP, it will look like Figure 9-5.

Figure 9-5 Local Area Connection Properties Dialog Box: Network Connection Component

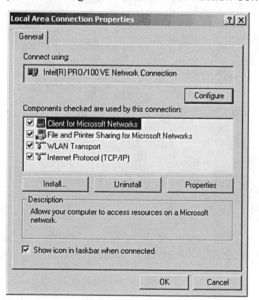

e. Either select the appropriate TCP/IP entry and click the **Properties** button, or just double-click directly on the TCP/IP entry. The screen that appears next depends again on the version of Windows you are using, but the process and concepts are the same. The screen in Figure 9-6 should look similar to what Windows 2000 / XP users are seeing. The first thing you notice in the sample computer is that it is configured for static addressing.

Figure 9-6 TCP/IP Properties

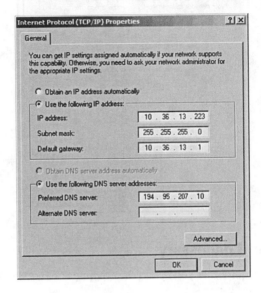

Step 5. Enable DHCP.

a. To enable DHCP, select **Obtain an IP Address Automatically** and typically select **Obtain DNS Server Address Automatically.** You see the various settings blank out as you select those options. If your computer had static addressing as in Figure 9-7, and you want it restored, you click the **Cancel** button. To keep the changed settings, you click **OK**.

Older versions of Windows had multiple tabs and required that you select **Obtain an IP Address Automatically** on this tab, go to the **DNS Configuration** tab, and select **Obtain DNS Server Address Automatically**.

b. If you were really converting this computer from static to DHCP, you should also go to the **Gateway** and **WINS Configuration** tabs and remove any entries.

c. If your computer had static addressing and you want it restored, you click the **Cancel** button.

d. To keep the settings, you click **OK**.

Figure 9-7 TCP/IP Properties: Static Addressing

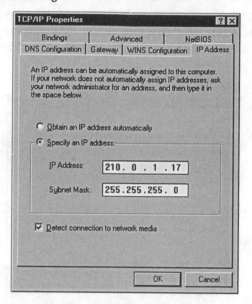

Step 6. Restart the computer if necessary.

a. All older versions of Windows require that you restart the computer. Windows 2000 and XP typically do not require a restart.

On some old versions (Windows 95), you might even be asked for the installation CD-ROM to complete the process.

b. If you were really changing over to DHCP, you would repeat Step 3 to confirm that you now have a valid set of configurations.

Reflection

a. As a network administrator, why might you prefer to use network profiles that hide the preceding options and screens, thereby preventing users from making these changes?_____

_____

b. As a network administrator, what are some of the potential benefits of using a DHCP server within your network?

_____

_____

Note to home or small network users: Many small routers supplied for cable, DSL, or ISDN connections have DHCP configured by default. This configuration allows you to use the hub or switch ports (or add either device) so that additional computers can share the connection. You would configure each computer as you did in this lab. Typically, DHCP assigns addresses using one of the "private" networks (such as 192.168.1.0) that are set aside for this purpose. Although it is common to change these settings, read and understand the book first; learn the location of the **Reset Defaults** button.

Routing Fundamentals and Subnets

The following labs are in this chapter:

Lab TI	Title
10.2.9	Small Router Purchase
10.3.5a	Basic Subnetting
10.3.5b	Subnetting a Class A Network
10.3.5c	Subnetting a Class B Network
10.3.5d	Subnetting a Class C Network

Lab 10.2.9: Small Router Purchase

Figure 10-1 806 Router Components and Connections

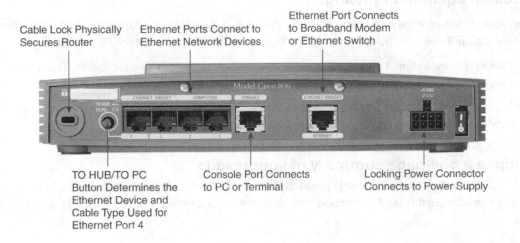

Objective

- The purpose of this lab is to introduce the variety and prices of network components in the market. This lab looks specifically at small routers that telecommuters use when working from home. The lab uses the website http://www.cdw.com, but you can use any local source, catalog, or website.

Background/Preparation

You are asked to put together a proposal for purchasing small routers that company executives will use for more secure connections when working with cable and DSL connections from home. You have been asked to research at least two different solutions and develop a proposal. The project details follow:

The company IT department is interested in reliability and concerned about working with and supporting too many models of devices. The company uses Cisco routers throughout the corporate network and wants to extend Cisco IOS Software features, such as virtual private networks (VPNs) and firewalls to these remote users.

From talking to the executives and support personnel, you know that some live-in areas do not support either DSL or cable service, so you want to see if any models also support ISDN.

The requirements include the following:

- Twelve routers supporting DSL or cable connections
- Three routers supporting ISDN connections
- Support for IOS features
- The assumptions that the service provider will supply any required "modem" device and that the router will connect to it via an Ethernet interface

Several executives expressed an interest in connecting two or three computers to the same link. Assume this setup will be the norm.

Step 1. Research equipment pricing.

a. Start by going to **http://www.cisco.com**, selecting **Products & Services**, and following the links to **Routers** to gather basic information. Look specifically at the 700, 800, and small office, home office (SOHO) models.

b. Look at the Overview option, particularly any white papers, presentations, and brochures. These documents might provide useful data and graphics for your final presentation.

c. Use at least three other sources for technologies and pricing. If you do web searches, use http://www.cdw.com and http://www.google.com, plus any others you prefer.

Step 2. Compile a one-page summary of your results.

Use Microsoft Excel or Word (or any comparable products) to compile a summary of your results. Include a short explanation (8-15 lines) of why you selected this implementation. Include a simple diagram showing the router, PCs, power cord, and cable or DSL modem.

Optional Step 2

Instead of creating the Excel/Word documents, create a four- to eight-slide PowerPoint presentation covering the same requirements.

Assume that you will be asked to present the material.

If time allows, perform both Step 2s, which would often be the norm.

Lab 10.3.5a: Basic Subnetting

Objectives

- Identify the reasons to use a subnet mask.

- Distinguish between a default subnet mask and a custom subnet mask.

- Given the requirements, determine the subnet mask, number of subnets, and hosts per subnet.

- Understand usable subnets and usable number of hosts.

- Use the ANDing process to determine whether a destination IP address is local or remote.

- Identify valid and invalid IP host addresses based on a network number and subnet mask.

Background/Preparation

This lab helps you understand the basics of IP subnet masks and their use with TCP/IP networks. You can use the subnet mask to split up an existing network into subnetworks or *subnets*. Some of the primary reasons for subnetting follow:

- Reduce the size of the broadcast domains. (Create smaller networks with less traffic.)

- Allow LANs in different geographical locations to communicate through routers.

- Provide improved security by separating one LAN from another.

Routers separate subnets, and the router determines when a packet can go from one subnet to another. Each router a packet goes through is considered a *hop*. Subnet masks help workstations, servers, and routers in an IP network determine whether the destination host for the packet they want to send is on their own network or another network. This lab reviews the default subnet mask and then focuses on custom subnet masks, which uses more bits than the default subnet mask by "borrowing" these bits from the host portion of the IP address. This
process creates a three-part address:

- The original network address

- The subnet address consisting of the bits borrowed

- The host address consisting of the bits left after borrowing some for subnets.

Step 1. Review IP address basics and default subnet masks.

a. If your organization has a Class A IP network address, the first octet (8 bits) is assigned and does not change. Your organization can use the remaining 24 bits to define up to 16,777,214 hosts on your network. That is a lot of hosts! It is not possible to put all of these hosts on one physical network without separating them with routers and subnets.

b. It is common for a workstation to be on one network or subnet and a server to be on another. When the workstation needs to retrieve a file from the server, it must use its subnet mask to determine the network or subnet that the server is on. The purpose of a subnet mask is to help hosts and routers determine the network location where a destination host appears. Refer to Table 10-1 to review IP address classes, default subnet masks, and the number of networks and hosts that you can create with each class of network address.

Table 10-1 IP Address Classes and Information

Address Class	1st Octet Decimal Range	1st Octet High Order Bits	Network/Host ID (N = Network, H=Host)	Default Subnet Mask	Number of Networks	Hosts per Network (Usable Addresses)
A	1–126*	0	N.H.H.H	255.0.0.0	126 $(2^7 - 2)$	16,777,214 $(2^{24} - 2)$
B	128–191	1 0	N.N.H.H	255.255.0.0	16,382 $(2^{14} - 2)$	65,534 $(2^{16} - 2)$
C	192–223	1 1 0	N.N.N.H	255.255.255.0	2,097,150 $(2^{21} - 2)$	254 $(2^8 - 2)$
D	224–239	1 1 1 0	Reserved for multicasting			
E	240–254	1 1 1 1 0	Experimental; used for research			

* You cannot use Class A address 127 because it is reserved for loopback and diagnostic functions.

Step 2. Review the ANDing process.

Hosts and routers use the ANDing process to determine whether a destination host is on the same network. The ANDing process happens each time a host wants to send a packet to another host on an IP network. To connect to a server, the host must know the IP address of the server or the host name (for example, http://www.cisco.com). If the host uses the host name, a Domain Name System (DNS) server converts it to an IP address.

First, the source host compares (ANDs) its own IP address to its own subnet mask. The result of the ANDing is to identify the network where the source host resides. It then compares the destination IP address to its own subnet mask. The result of the second ANDing is the network that the destination host is on. If the source network address and the destination network address are the same, they can communicate directly. If the results are different, they are on different networks or subnets, and they need to communicate through routers, or they might not be able to communicate at all.

ANDing depends on the subnet mask. The subnet mask always uses all 1s to represent the network, or network plus subnet, portion of the IP address. A default subnet mask for a Class C network is 255.255.255.0 or 11111111.11111111.11111111.00000000. The host compares this mask to the source IP address bit for bit. It compares the first bit of the IP address to the first bit of the subnet mask, the second bit to the second, and so on. If the two bits are both 1s, the ANDing result is a 1. If the two bits are a 0 and a 1 or two 0s, the ANDing result is a 0. Basically, this rule means that a combination of two 1s results in a 1, but anything else is a 0. The result of the ANDing process is the network or subnet number that the source or destination address is on.

Step 3. Determine a host network using two Class C default subnet masks.

This example in Figure 10-2 shows how you can use a Class C default subnet mask to determine which network a host is on. A default subnet mask does not break an address into subnets. If you use the default subnet mask, the network is not being *subnetted*. Host X (source) on network 200.1.1.0 has an IP address of 200.1.1.5 and wants to send a packet to Host Z (destination) on network 200.1.2.0, which has an IP address of 200.1.2.8. All hosts on each network are connected to hubs or switches and then to a router. Remember that with a Class C network address, the first three octets (24 bits) are assigned as the network address, so these are two different Class C networks. This requirement leaves one octet (8 bits) for hosts, so each Class C network can have up to 254 hosts $(2^8 = 256 - 2 = 254)$.

Figure 10-2 Using a Class C Default Subnet Mask to Determine a Host's Network

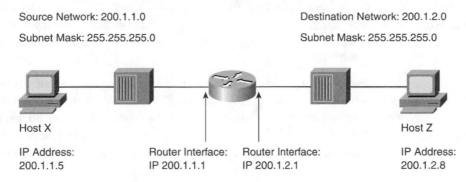

Source Network: 200.1.1.0

Subnet Mask: 255.255.255.0

Destination Network: 200.1.2.0

Subnet Mask: 255.255.255.0

Host X

IP Address:
200.1.1.5

Router Interface:
IP 200.1.1.1

Router Interface:
IP 200.1.2.1

Host Z

IP Address:
200.1.2.8

The ANDing process helps the packet get from Host 200.1.1.5 on network 200.1.1.0 to Host 200.1.2.8 on network 200.1.2.0 by using the following steps:

Host X compares its own IP address to its own subnet mask using the ANDing process.

Host X IP address 200.1.1.5: 11001000.00000001.00000001.00000101

Subnet Mask 255.255.255.0: 11111111.11111111.11111111.00000000

ANDing Result (200.1.1.0): 11001000.00000001.00000001.00000000

Note: The result of Step 3a of the ANDing process is the network address of Host X, which is 200.1.1.0.

Next, Host X compares the IP address of the Host Z destination to its own subnet mask using the ANDing process.

Host Z IP address 200.1.2.8: 11001000.00000001.00000010.00001000

Subnet Mask 255.255.255.0: 11111111.11111111.11111111.00000000

ANDing Result (200.1.2.0): 11001000.00000001.00000010.00000000

Note: The result of Step 3b of the ANDing process is the network address of Host Z, which is 200.1.2.0.

Host X compares the ANDing results from Step A and the ANDing results from Step B, and they are different. Host X now knows that Host Z is not in its LAN, and it must send the packet to its default gateway, which is the IP address of the router interface of 200.1.1.1 on network 200.1.1.0. The router then repeats the ANDing process to determine which router interface to send the packet out.

Step 4. Determine the host subnet using a Class C network custom subnet mask.

This example uses a single Class C network address (200.1.1.0) and shows how you can use a Class C custom subnet mask to determine which subnetwork (or subnet) a host is on and to route packets from one subnetwork to another. Remember that, with a Class C network address, the first three octets (24 bits) are assigned as the network address. This requirement leaves 8 bits (one octet) for hosts, so each Class C network can have up to 254 hosts ($2^8 = 256 - 2 = 254$).

Perhaps you want less than 254 hosts (workstations and servers) all on one network, and you want to create two subnetworks and separate them with a router for security reasons or to reduce traffic. This setup creates smaller independent broadcast domains and can improve network performance and increase security because one or more routers will separate these subnetworks. Assume you need at least two subnetworks and at least 50 hosts per subnetwork. Because you have only one Class C network address, you have only 8 bits in the fourth octet available for a total of 254 possible hosts, so you must create a custom subnet mask. You use the custom subnet mask to "borrow" bits from the host portion of the address. Perform the following steps:

The first step to subnetting is to determine how many subnets you need. In this case, you need two subnetworks. To see how many bits you should borrow from the host portion of the network address, add the bit values from right to left until the total is equal to or greater than the number of subnets you need. Because you need two subnets, add the one bit and the two bit, which equals three. This number is greater than the number of subnets you need, so you need to borrow at least two bits from the host address starting from the left side of the octet that contains the host address. Table 10-2 provides this information.

Table 10-2 Calculating Subnet Bits to Be Borrowed

4ᵗʰ Octet Host Address Bits	1	1	1	1	1	1	1	1
Host Address Bit Values (from Right)	128	64	32	16	8	4	2	1

(Add bits starting from the right side [the 1 and the 2] until you get more than the number of subnets you need.)

Note: An alternate way to calculate the number of bits to borrow for subnets is to take the number of bits borrowed to the power of 2. The result must be greater than the number of subnets you need. For example, if you borrow 2 bits, the calculation is 2 to the second power, which equals 4. Because the number of subnets you need is two, this result should be adequate.

After you know how many bits to borrow, you take them from the left side of the host address (the fourth octet). Every bit you borrow leaves fewer bits for the hosts. Even though you increase the number of subnets, you decrease the number of hosts per subnet. Because you need to borrow two bits from the left side, you must show that new value in the subnet mask. The existing default subnet mask was 255.255.255.0, and the new, "custom" subnet mask is 255.255.255.192. As Table 10-3 indicates, the 192 results from adding the first two bits from the left (128 + 64 = 192). These bits now become 1s and are part of the overall subnet mask. This change leaves 6 bits for host IP addresses, or $2^6 = 64$ hosts per subnet.

Table 10-3 Determining the "Custom" Subnet Mask

4ᵗʰ Octet Borrowed Bits for Subnet	1	1	0	0	0	0	0	0
Subnet Bit Values (from Left Side)	128	64	32	16	8	4	2	1

With this information, you can build Table 10-4. The first two bits are the subnet binary value. The last six bits are the host bits. By borrowing 2 bits from the 8 bits of the host address, you can create 4 subnets (2^2) with 64 hosts each. The 4 networks created are the 0 net, the 64 net, the 128 net, and the 192 net. The 0 net and the 192 net are unusable—because the 0 net has all zeros in the host portion of the address and the 192 net has all 1s in the host portion of the address.

Table 10-4 Determining the Usable Subnets

Subnet Number	Subnet Bits Borrowed Binary Value	Subnet Bits Decimal Value	Host Bits Possible Binary Values (Range) (6 Bits)	Subnet/Host Decimal Range	Usable?
0 Subnet	00	0	000000–111111	0–63	No
1st Subnet	01	64	000000–111111	64–127	Yes
2nd Subnet	10	128	000000–111111	128–191	Yes
3rd Subnet	11	192	000000–111111	192–254	No

Notice that the first subnet always starts at 0 and, in this case, increases by 64, which is the number of hosts on each subnet. One way to determine the number of hosts on each subnet or the start of each subnet is to take the remaining host bits to the power of 2. Because you borrowed 2 of the 8 bits for subnets and you have 6 bits left, the number of hosts per subnet is 2^6 or 64. Another way to figure the number of hosts per subnet or the "increment" from one subnet to the next is to subtract the subnet mask value in decimal (192 in the fourth octet) from 256 (which is the maximum number of possible combinations of 8 bits), which equals 64. This result means you start at 0 for the first network and add 64 for each additional subnetwork. If you take the second subnet (the 64 net) as an example, you cannot use the IP address of 200.1.1.64 for a host ID because it is the network ID of the 64 subnet. (The host portion is all 0s.) You cannot use the IP address of 200.1.1.127 because it is the broadcast address for the 64 net. (The host portion is all 1s.)

Another common way to represent a subnet mask is the use of the "slash/number" (/#) where the # following the slash is the number of bits used in the mask (network and subnet combined). As an example, a Class C network address such as 200.1.1.0 with a standard subnet mask (255.255.255.0) would be written as 200.1.1.0 /24, indicating that 24 bits are used for the mask. The same network, when subnetted by using two host bits for subnets, would be written as 200.1.1.0 /26. This indicates that 24 bits are used for the network and 2 bits for the subnet. This would represent a custom subnet mask of 255.255.255.192 in dotted decimal format.

A Class A network of 10.0.0.0 with a standard mask (255.0.0.0) would be written as 10.0.0.0 /8. If 8 bits (the next octet) were being used for subnets it would be written as 10.0.0.0 /16. This would represent a custom subnet mask of 255.255.0.0 in dotted decimal format. The "slash" number after the network number is an abbreviated method of indicating the subnet mask being used.

Step 5. Use the following information and the previous examples to answer the following subnet-related questions.

Your company has applied for and received a Class C network address of 197.15.22.0. You want to subdivide your physical network into four subnets, which will be interconnected by routers. You need at least 25 hosts per subnet. You need to use a Class C custom subnet mask and a router between the subnets to route packets from one subnet to another. Determine the number of bits you need to borrow from the host portion of the network address and then the number of bits left for host addresses. (*Hint*: There will be eight possible subnets, of which six can be used.)

Fill in Table 10-5 and answer the questions that follow.

Table 10-5 Creating a Class C Custom Subnet Mask to Support at Least 25 Hosts per Subnet

Subnet Number	Subnet Bits Borrowed Binary Value	Subnet Bits Decimal and Subnet Number	Host Bits Possible Binary Values (Range) (5 Bits)	Subnet/Host Decimal Range	Use?
0 Subnet					
1st Subnet					
2nd Subnet					
3rd Subnet					
4th Subnet					
5th Subnet					
6th Subnet					
7th Subnet					

Notes

_____

_____

_____

_____

_____

Use the information in Table 10-5 you just developed to help answer the following questions.

1. Which octets represent the network portion of a Class C IP address?

   _____

2. Which octets represent the host portion of a Class C IP address?

   _____

3. What is the binary equivalent of the Class C network address in the scenario (**197.15.22.0**)?

   Decimal network address: _____ . _____ . _____ . _____

   Binary network address: _____ . _____ . _____ . _____

4. How many high-order bits did you borrow from the host bits in the fourth octet? _____

5. What subnet mask must you use? (Show the subnet mask in decimal and binary.)

Decimal subnet mask: _____ . _____ . _____ . _____

Binary subnet mask: _____ . _____ . _____ . _____

6. What is the maximum number of subnets that you can create with this subnet mask?

_____

7. What is the maximum number of usable subnets that you can create with this mask?

_____

8. How many bits were left in the fourth octet for host IDs?

_____

9. How many hosts per subnet can you define with this subnet mask?

_____

10. What is the maximum number of hosts that you can define for all subnets with this scenario (assuming you cannot use the lowest and highest subnet numbers and cannot use the lowest and highest host ID on each subnet)?

_____

11. Is 197.15.22.63 a valid host IP address with this scenario?

_____

12. Why or why not? _____

13. Is 197.15.22.160 a valid host IP address with this scenario?

_____

14. Why or why not? _____

15. Host A has an IP address of 197.15.22.126. Host B has an IP address of 197.15.22.129. Are these hosts on the same subnet? _____ Why?

_____

_____

Lab 10.3.5b: Subnetting a Class A Network

Objective

■ Analyze a Class A network address with the number of network bits specified to determine the subnet mask, number of subnets, hosts per subnet, and information about specific subnets.

Background/Preparation

You should perform this written lab *without* the aid of an electronic calculator.

Step 1. Given a Class A network address of 10.0.0.0 /24, answer the following questions.

a. How many bits were borrowed from the host portion of this address? _____

b. What is the subnet mask for this network?

    1. Dotted decimal: _____

    2. Binary: _____ . _____ . _____ . _____

c. How many usable subnetworks? _____

d. How many usable hosts per subnet? _____

e. What is the host range for usable Subnet 16? _____

f. What is the network address for usable Subnet 16? _____

g. What is the broadcast address for usable Subnet 16? _____

h. What is the broadcast address for the last usable subnet? _____

i. What is the broadcast address for the major network? _____

Lab 10.3.5c: Subnetting a Class B Network

Objective

- Provide a subnetting scheme using a Class B network.

Background/Preparation

You should perform this written lab *without* the aid of an electronic calculator.

ABC Manufacturing has acquired a Class B address, 172.16.0.0, and needs to create a subnetting scheme to provide 36 subnets with at least 100 hosts, 24 subnets with at least 255 hosts, and 10 subnets with at least 50 hosts. It is not necessary to supply an address for the WAN connection because the Internet service provider supplies it.

Step 1. Given this Class A network address and these requirements, answer the following questions.

a. How many subnets do you need for this network? _____

b. What is the minimum number of bits that you can borrow? _____

c. What is the subnet mask for this network?

   1. Dotted decimal: _____

   2. Binary: _____ . _____ . _____ . _____

   3. Slash format: _____

d. How many usable subnetworks? _____

e. How many usable hosts per subnet? _____

Step 2. Complete the chart in Table 10-6 listing the first three subnets and the last four subnets.

Table 10-6 Subnetwork Chart

Subnetwork #	Subnetwork ID	Host Range	Broadcast ID

a. What is the host range for Subnet 2? _____

b. What is the broadcast address for the 126th subnet? _____

c. What is the broadcast address for the major network? _____

Lab 10.3.5d: Subnetting a Class C Network

Objective

■ Provide a subnetting scheme using a Class C network.

Background/Preparation

You should perform this written lab *without* the aid of an electronic calculator.

The Classical Academy has acquired a Class C address, 192.168.1.0, and needs to create subnets to provide low-level security and broadcast control on the LAN. It is not necessary to supply an address for the WAN connection because the Internet service provider supplies it.

The LAN consists of the following, each of which will require its own subnet:

■ Classroom #1: 28 nodes

■ Classroom #2: 22 nodes

■ Computer lab: 30 nodes

■ Instructors: 12 nodes

■ Administration: 8 nodes

Step 1. Given this Class C network address and these requirements, answer the following questions.

a. How many subnets do you need for this network? _____

b. What is the subnet mask for this network?

    1. Dotted decimal: _____

    2. Binary: _____ . _____ . _____ . _____

    3. Slash format: _____

c. How many usable hosts per subnet? _____

Step 2. Complete the chart in Table 10-7.

Table 10-7 Subnetwork Chart

Subnetwork #	Subnetwork IP	Host Range	Broadcast ID

a. What is the host range for Subnet 6? _____

b. What is the broadcast address for the third subnet?

_____

c. What is the broadcast address for the major network?

_____

TCP/IP Transport and Application Layer

The following labs are in this chapter:

Lab TI	Title
11.2.4	Protocol Inspector, TCP, and HTTP

Lab 11.2.4: Protocol Inspector, TCP, and HTTP

Objective

- Use Fluke Protocol Inspector (PI), Optiview Protocol Expert (OPE) or equivalent protocol analysis software to view dynamic TCP operations and HTTP while accessing a web page.

Background/Preparation

Protocol analysis software has a feature called *capture*. This feature lets you capture all the frames through an interface. With this feature, you can see how TCP moves segments filled with user data across the network. You might find TCP to be a bit abstract, but with the protocol analyzer, you can see just how important TCP is to network processes (such as e-mail and web browsing).

At least one of the hosts must have the Protocol Inspector software installed. If you do the lab in pairs, installing the software on both machines means that each person can run the lab steps, although each host might display slightly different results.

Step 1. Start Protocol Inspector and your browser.

Step 2. Go to detail view.

Step 3. Start a capture.

Step 4. Request a web page.

Step 5. Watch the monitor view while the web page is requested and delivered.

Step 6. Stop the capture.

Step 7. Study the TCP frames, HTTP frames, and statistics using various views, especially the detail view.

Step 8. Using the detail view, explain what evidence it provides about the following:

a. TCP handshakes

_____

b. TCP acknowledgments

_____

c. TCP segmentation and segment size

_____

d. TCP sequence numbers

_____

e. TCP sliding windows

_____

f. HTTP protocol

_____

Reflection

How did this lab help you visualize TCP in action?

_____

_____

CCNA 2: Routers and Routing Basics Labs

WANs and Routers

The following labs are in this chapter:

Lab 1.2.5: Connecting Console Interfaces

Figure 1-1 Topology for Lab 1.2.5

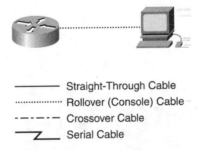

——————— Straight-Through Cable
················· Rollover (Console) Cable
– – – – – Crossover Cable
——Z—— Serial Cable

Objective

- Connect a PC to a router using a console or rollover cable.

Background/Preparation

A console cable is necessary to establish a console session so you can check or change the configuration of the router. You need the following resources:

- Workstation with a serial interface
- Cisco router
- Console rollover cable for connecting the workstation to the router

Step 1. Identify connectors and components.

Examine the router and locate the RJ-45 connector labeled "Console," as shown in Figure 1-2.

Figure 1-2 Locating the RJ-45 Console Connector on a Router

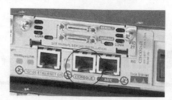

Step 2. Identify the computer serial interface (COM 1 or 2).

Examine the computer and locate a 9- or 25-pin male connector labeled "serial," as shown in Figure 1-3. It might not have a label.

Step 3. Locate the RJ-45–to-DB9 adapter, which looks like Figure 1-4.

Figure 1-3 Locating the COM Port on a PC

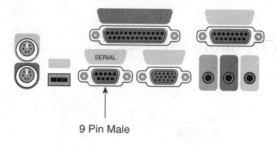

9 Pin Male

Figure 1-4 RJ-45–to-DB9 Female Adapter

Step 4. Locate or build a rollover cable.

Use a console or rollover cable of adequate length (see Figure 1-5), making one if necessary, to connect the router to one of the workstations.

Figure 1-5 Using a Rollover Cable

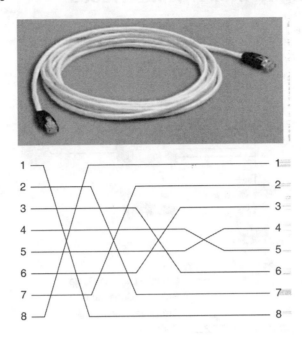

Step 5. Connect cabling components.

a. Connect the console or rollover cable to the router console port using an RJ-45 connector. Next, connect the other end of the console or rollover cable to the RJ-45-to-DB9 or the RJ-45-to-DB25 adapter depending on the available PC serial port.

b. Attach the adapter to a PC serial port, either DB9 or DB25, depending on the computer. Figure 1-6 illustrates the necessary connections.

Figure 1-6 Connecting the Router to the PC

Console port
(RJ-45)

RJ-45-to-DB-9 or
RJ-45-to-DB-25
adapter

Lab 1.2.6: Connecting Router LAN Interfaces

Figure 1-7 Topology for Lab 1.2.6

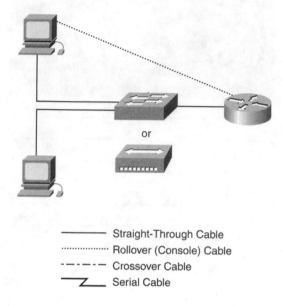

————— Straight-Through Cable
.... Rollover (Console) Cable
—·—·—·— Crossover Cable
——Z— Serial Cable

Objectives

- Identify the Ethernet or FastEthernet interfaces on the router.
- Identify and locate the proper cables to connect the router and PC to a hub or switch.
- Use the cables to connect the router and PC to the hub or switch.

Background/Preparation

This lab focuses on the ability to connect the physical cabling between Ethernet LAN devices such as hubs and switches and the appropriate Ethernet interface on a router. The computers and router should already have the correct IP network settings. Start this lab with the computers, router, and hub or switch turned off and unplugged. You need the following resources:

- At least one workstation with an Ethernet 10/100 NIC installed
- One Ethernet switch or hub
- One router with an RJ-45 Ethernet or FastEthernet interface (or an attachment unit interface (AUI))
- One 10BASE-T AUI transceiver (DB15 to RJ-45) for a router with an AUI Ethernet interface (2500 series)
- Several Ethernet cables (straight-through and crossover) for connecting the workstation and router to the hub or switch

Step 1. Identify the Ethernet or FastEthernet interfaces on the router.

a. Examine the router.

b. What is the model number of the router? _____

c. Locate one or more RJ-45 connectors on the router labeled "10/100 Ethernet" (see Figure 1-8). This identifier can vary depending on the type of router. A 2500 series router has an AUI DB15 Ethernet port labeled AUI 0. This port requires a 10BASE-T transceiver to connect to the RJ-45 cable.

Figure 1-8 RJ-45 Ethernet Connectors on the Router

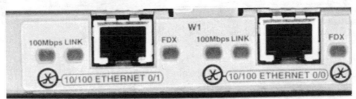

d. Identify the Ethernet ports that you could use for connecting the routers. Record the information in the following table. Record the AUI port numbers if you are working with a Cisco 2500 series router.

Router	Port	Port

Step 2. Identify the proper cables and connect the router to a hub or switch.

a. You will make the connection between the router and the hub using a Category 5 (CAT 5), or better, straight-through patch cable. Locate a patch cable that is long enough to reach from the router to the hub. Be sure to examine the cable ends carefully and select only straight-through cables.

b. Use a cable to connect the Ethernet interface that uses the 0 (zero) designation on the router to a port on the hub or switch. Also use the 10BASE-T AUI transceiver for the 2500 series.

Step 3. Connect the workstation Ethernet cabling.

a. The computers will also connect to the hub using a straight-through patch cable. Run CAT 5 patch cables from each PC to where the switch or hub is located. Connect one end of these cables to the RJ-45 connector on the computer NIC, and connect the other end to a port on the hub or switch. Be sure to examine the cable ends carefully and select only straight-through cables.

Step 4. Verify the connection.

a. Plug in and turn on the routers, computers, and hub or switch.

b. To verify the router connections, ensure that the link lights on the router interface and the hub or switch interface are both lit.

c. To verify the computer connections, ensure that the link lights on the NIC and the hub interface are both lit.

Lab 1.2.7: Connecting WAN Interfaces

Figure 1-9 Topology for Lab 1.2.7

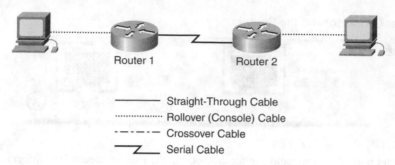

```
──────── Straight-Through Cable
············ Rollover (Console) Cable
─ ─ ─ ─ ─ Crossover Cable
───Z─── Serial Cable
```

Objectives

- Identify the serial interfaces on the router.
- Identify and locate the proper cables to connect the routers.
- Use the cables to connect the routers.

Background/Preparation

This lab will connect two routers using directly attached cables to simulate a WAN link. This setup lets you configure and test the routers as though they were geographically separated. You can consider this simulated WAN link, which takes the place of the service provider's network, a CSU/DSU eliminator. The first steps will involve finding out the kinds of connections on the router and the kinds of cables you need.

Step 1. Identify the serial interfaces on the router.

a. Examine the routers.

b. What is the model number of the first router? _____

c. What is the model number of the second router? _____

d. How many serial ports are there on each router that could be used for connecting the routers? Record the information in Table 1-1.

Table 1-1 Router Serial Port Information

Router Name	Serial Port	Serial Port	Serial Port
Router 1			
Router 2			

Step 2. Identify and locate the proper cables.

a. Inspect the serial cables available in the lab. Depending on the type of router and serial card, the router might have different connectors. The two most common types are the DB60 and the smart serial connectors, as shown in Figure 1-10.

Figure 1-10 Smart Serial and DB60 Connectors

Indicate which type of interfaces the routers have in Table 1-2.

Table 1-2 Router Serial Interface Connector Types

Router	Smart Serial	DB60
1		
2		

b. Since this lab will not be connected to a live leased line, one of the routers must provide the clocking for the circuit. The service provider normally provides the clocking signal to each of the routers. To provide this clocking signal in the lab, one of the routers needs a DCE cable instead of the DTE cable used on the other router.

In this lab, the connection between routers uses one DCE cable and one DTE cable. The DCE-DTE connection between routers is a *null serial cable*. This lab uses one V.35 DCE cable and one V.35 DTE cable to simulate the WAN connection.

The V.35 DCE connector is usually a female V.35 (34-pin) connector. The DTE cable has a male V.35 connector. Figure 1-11 shows the male and female V.35 connectors. The cables are also labeled as DCE or DTE on the router end. Using the chart in Table 1-3, identify the V.35 cable that you will use on each router by placing a checkmark in the appropriate column.

Figure 1-11 V.35 Male and Female Connectors

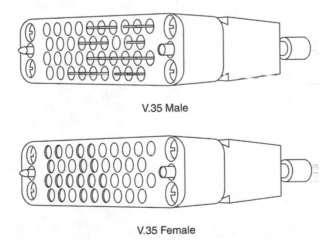

V.35 Male

V.35 Female

Table 1-3 Router DTE/DCE Connector Identification

Router	DTE (V.35 Male)	DCE (V.35 Female)
Router 1		
Router 2		

c. After indicating the cables required to interconnect the router, locate them in the equipment inventory.

Step 3. Cable the routers.

a. You must now join the DTE and DCE V.35 cables. Holding the V.35 ends in each hand, examine the pins and sockets as well as the threaded connectors. Note that there is only one proper way for the cables to fit together. Align the pins on the male cable with the sockets on the female cable and gently couple them. It should require very little effort. Turn the thumbscrews (clockwise) and secure the connectors.

b. Before making the connection to one of the routers, examine the connector on the router and the cable. Note that the connectors are tapered to help prevent improper connection. Holding the connector in one hand, orient the cable and router connecters so that the tapers match. Now, push the cable connector partially into the router connector. It probably will not go on all the way because you must tighten the threaded connectors to completely insert the cable. While holding the cable in one hand and gently pushing the cable toward the router, turn one of the thumbscrews clockwise, three or four rounds to start the screws. Now, turn the other thumbscrew clockwise, three or four rounds to get it started. At this point, the cable should be attached enough that you can use both hands to advance each thumbscrew at the same rate until the cable is fully inserted. Do not over-tighten these connectors.

Introduction to Routers

The following labs are in this chapter:

Lab TI	Title
2.2.1	Router Configuration Using Setup
2.2.4	Establishing a Console Session with HyperTerminal
2.2.9	Command-Line Fundamentals

Lab 2.2.1: Router Configuration Using Setup

Figure 2-1 Topology for Lab 2.2.1

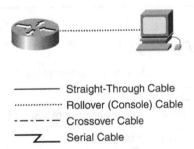

— Straight-Through Cable
············ Rollover (Console) Cable
– · — · – Crossover Cable
Serial Cable

Objectives

- Use the system configuration dialog (**setup**).
- Establish some basic router configuration parameters.

Background/Preparation

A new router will not find its configuration file when started, so it should automatically enter the setup dialog. If the router has already been configured, you can use the **setup** command at the command line while in privileged mode. The setup dialog prompts for basic setup options, such as protocols and the IP address and subnet mask for each interface. The setup dialog provides default values for most of the configurable options. You can either accept them or enter your own. If setup does not provide a prompted entry for specific interface information, you must enter it manually at a later time. (In this lab, you run the setup utility but not save the configuration.)

Cable a network as in Figure 2-1. You can use any router that meets the interface requirements (that is, 800, 1600, 1700, 2500, and 2600 routers or a combination). You need the following resources:

This lab assumes that the HyperTerminal console session to the router has already been established by the instructor. You need the following resources:

- A PC with HyperTerminal configured
- One console (rollover) cable and DB9-to-RJ-45 adapter
- A Cisco router

Step 1. Start the router and begin setup mode.

Option 1—If the router starts without a configuration file, it automatically enters setup mode without requiring a password. A new router starts in this way.

Option 2—If the router was previously configured but you want to see and change existing settings, you must log in and provide a password of **cisco**. Type **enable** at the command prompt to enter privileged mode, and enter the password **class**. Enter **setup** at the router prompt to open the system configuration dialog.

Option 3—If the router was previously configured, you can simulate a new router setup by removing the configuration file from nonvolatile RAM (NVRAM) using the **erase startup-config** command in privileged mode. Use the **reload** command to restart the router and enter setup mode.

Note: The order of the messages displayed during setup may vary depending on the Cisco IOS Software release and feature set on the router. Therefore, the following prompts may not exactly reflect the messages on your screen.

Step 2. Continue with the setup dialog.

a. The router prompts, "Would you like to enter the initial configuration dialog? [yes/no]:". Enter **yes** to continue with the setup dialog.

b. The router prompts "Would you like to enter basic management setup? [yes/no]:". Enter **no** and press **Enter**.

c. What is the importance of the words in square brackets?

Step 3. Show the current interface summary.

a. The router prompts, "First, would you like to see the current interface summary?" Type **yes** or press **Enter** to accept the default answer.

b. Fill in Table 2-1 with the information displayed.

Table 2-1 Router Interface Summary Information

Interface	IP Address	OK	Method	Status	Protocol

Step 4. Configure the global parameters.

a. Configure the router using the default settings for any questions the router asks if it has already been configured. Enter parameters such as router name, privileged level passwords, and virtual terminal password. Answer the prompts as follows: Router name = **Central**, enable secret password = **class**, enable password = **cisco**, virtual password = **cisco**.

Note: At any point in the setup dialog process, press **Ctrl-C** to abort and start over.

---

b. You are now prompted to enter various parameters, including SNMP settings and routed and routing protocol settings. Answer **no** to these prompts, except for the "Configure IP?" prompt.

Step 5. Configure the interface parameters.

a. From this point on, the prompts vary depending on the available router interfaces. Complete the setup steps as appropriate.

Step 6. Specifying whether to use the configuration command script.

a. The router displays the configuration command script that you created and then asks whether you want to save this configuration.

b. Answer **no** to the question, "Use this configuration?" If prompted with the selection menu shown below, select [**0**].

```
[0] Go to the IOS command prompt without saving this config
[1] Return back to the setup without saving this config and
[2] Save this configuration to nvram and exit.
```

c. If you had opted to save the configuration, where would the router save this information?

Note: Remember that setup does not let you enter key information such as clock rate for DCE interfaces. You must enter it later.

When you finish the preceding steps, log off (by typing **exit**) and turn off the router.

Lab 2.2.4: Establishing a Console Session with HyperTerminal

Figure 2-2 Topology for Lab 2.2.4

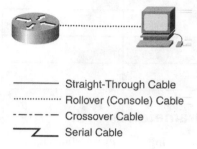

——————— Straight-Through Cable
···················· Rollover (Console) Cable
-·-·-·-· Crossover Cable
‾‾‾Z‾‾ Serial Cable

Objectives

- Connect a router and workstation using a console cable.

- Configure HyperTerminal to establish a console session with the router.

Background/Preparation

HyperTerminal is a simple Windows terminal-emulation program that you can use to connect to the router's console port. A PC with HyperTerminal provides a keyboard and monitor for the router. Connecting to the console port with a rollover cable and using HyperTerminal is the most basic way to access a router for checking or changing its configuration.

Cable a network as in Figure 2-2. You can use any router that meets the interface requirements (that is, 800, 1600, 1700, 2500, and 2600 routers or a combination). You need the following resources:

- A workstation with a serial interface and HyperTerminal

- A Cisco router

- A Console (rollover) cable for connecting the workstation to the router

Step 1. Connect a rollover cable to the console port.

Connect one end of the rollover cable to the console port on the router and the other end to the PC COM1 port (or COM2 if COM1 is not available) using a DB9 or DB25 adapter. Perform this step before you turn on any of the devices.

Step 2. Start HyperTerminal.

a. Turn on the computer and router.

b. From the Windows taskbar, locate the HyperTerminal program (**Start > Programs > Accessories > Communications > HyperTerminal**).

Step 3. Name the HyperTerminal session.

a. In the Connection Description window, enter a name in the connection Name field and select **OK**, as shown in Figure 2-3.

Figure 2-3 Entering a Connection Description in HyperTerminal

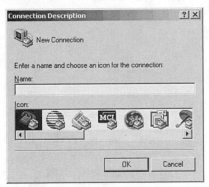

Step 4. Specify the computer's connecting interface.

In the Connect To window (see Figure 2-4), use the drop-down arrow in the **Connect Using** field to select **COM1** and click **OK**.

Figure 2-4 Selecting the Port to Connect to in HyperTerminal

Step 5. Specify the interface connection properties.

a. In the COM1 Properties window (see Figure 2-5), use the drop-down arrows to select the following properties:

Bits per second = **9600**

Data bits = **8**

Parity = **None**

Stop bits = **1**

Flow control = **none**

Then, click **OK**.

b. When the HyperTerminal session window opens, turn on the router; if router is already on, press the **Enter** key. You should see a response from the router.

If you do, then the connection was successfully completed. If there is no connection, troubleshoot as necessary. For example, verify that the router has power and that you are connected to the correct COM port on the PC and the console port on the router. If you still cannot connect, ask your instructor for assistance.

Figure 2-5 Specifying the Interface Connection Properties in HyperTerminal

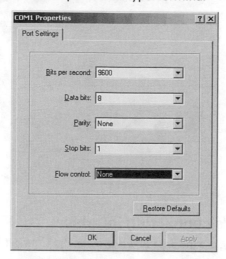

c. Record in the engineering journal the correct procedure for establishing a console session with the router.

Step 6. Close the session.

a. To end the console session from HyperTerminal, select **File > Exit**.

b. When the HyperTerminal disconnect warning window appears (see Figure 2-6), click **Yes**.

Figure 2-6 HyperTerminal Disconnect Warning

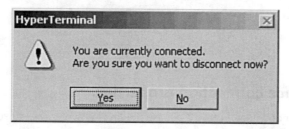

c. As Figure 2-7 shows, HyperTerminal will then ask whether you want to save the session. Click **Yes**.

Figure 2-7 Saving a HyperTerminal Session

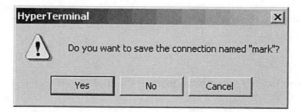

Step 7. Reopen the HyperTerminal connection, as shown in Step 2.

a. In the Connection Description window (see Figure 2-8), click **Cancel**.

Figure 2-8 Canceling the Connection in HyperTerminal

b. To open the saved console session from HyperTerminal, select **File > Open**.

The saved session appears. When you double-click the name, the connection opens without your needing to reconfigure it each time.

Step 8. Terminate the HyperTerminal session.

a. Close HyperTerminal.

b. Shut down the router.

Lab 2.2.9: Command-Line Fundamentals

Figure 2-9 Topology for Lab 2.2.9

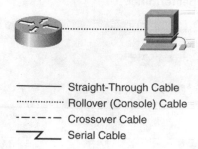

```
───────── Straight-Through Cable
············· Rollover (Console) Cable
─ ─ ─ ─ ─ Crossover Cable
───Z── Serial Cable
```

Objectives

- Log in to a router in both user and privileged modes.

- Use several basic router commands to determine how the router is configured.

- Use the router help facility.

- Use the command history and editing features.

- Log off of the router.

Background/Preparation

This lab focuses on basic command-line skills and the use of IOS help and command history features.

Cable a network as in Figure 2-9. You can use any router that meets the interface requirements (that is, 800, 1600, 1700, 2500, and 2600 routers or a combination). You should execute the following steps on each router unless specifically instructed otherwise. You need the following resources:

- A workstation with a serial interface and HyperTerminal

- A Cisco router

- A crossover (console) cable for connecting the workstation to the router

Step 1. Start HyperTerminal.

Start a HyperTerminal session as you did in Lab 2.2.4.

Step 2. Log in to the router.

a. Log into the router. If prompted to enter the initial setup mode, answer **no**. If prompted for a password, enter **cisco**.

b. By default, the prompt shows "Router." Something different might appear if this router has a name. What prompt did the router display? _____

c. What does the prompt symbol following a router name mean?

_____

Step 3. Use the help feature.

a. Enter the help command by typing the **?** at the EXEC router prompt.

`Router>?`

b. List eight available commands from the router response.

Step 4. Enter privileged EXEC mode.

a. Enter enable mode by using the **enable** command. If the router asks for a password, enter **class**.

`Router>`**`enable`**` [Enter]`

b. Was **enable** one of the commands available from Step 3?

c. What changed in the router prompt display, and what does it mean?

Step 5. Use the help feature.

a. Enter help mode by typing a question mark (**?**) at the router privileged EXEC prompt.

`Router#?`

b. List ten available commands from the router response.

Step 6. List the show commands.

a. List all **show** commands by entering **show ?** at the router privileged EXEC prompt.

`Router#`**`show`**` ?`

b. Is **running-config** one of the available commands in this mode?

Step 7. Examine the running configuration.

a. Display the running router configuration by using the command **show running-config** at the privileged EXEC router prompt.

```
Router#show running-config
```

b. List six key pieces of information displayed in the output of this command.

Step 8. Examine the configuration in more detail.

a. Continue looking at the configuration. When the word "more" appears, press the spacebar. The router will display the next page of information.

b. What happened when you pressed the spacebar?

_____

Step 9. Use the command history feature.

a. Use the command history to see and reuse the previously entered commands. Press the **up arrow** or **Ctrl-P** to see the last command you entered. Press it again to go to the command before that. Press the down arrow or (**Ctrl-N** to go back through the list. This function lets you view the command history.

b. What appeared at the router prompt as you pressed the up arrow?

_____

Step 10. Log off and turn off the router.

a. Close HyperTerminal.

b. Shut down the router.

Configuring a Router

The following labs are in this chapter:

Lab TI	Title
3.1.2	Command Modes and Router Identification
3.1.3	Configuring Router Passwords
3.1.4	Using Router **show** Commands
3.1.5	Configuring a Serial Interface
3.1.6	Making Configuration Changes
3.1.7	Configuring an Ethernet Interface
3.2.3	Configuring Interface Descriptions
3.2.5	Configuring Message-of-the-Day (MOTD)
3.2.7	Configuring Host Tables
3.2.9	Backing Up Configuration Files

Lab 3.1.2: Command Modes and Router Identification

Figure 3-1 Topology for Lab 3.1.2

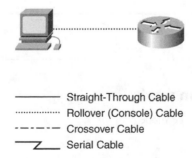

——— Straight-Through Cable
.... Rollover (Console) Cable
- - - - - Crossover Cable
⌐—Z— Serial Cable

Objectives

- Identify basic router modes of user EXEC and privileged EXEC.
- Use commands to enter specific modes.
- Become familiar with the router prompt for each mode.
- Assign a name to the router.

Background/Preparation

Cable a network similar to the topology in Figure 3-1. You can use any router that meets the interface requirements in Figure 3-1 (that is, 800, 1600, 1700, 2500, and 2600 routers or a combination). Please refer to the information in Appendix B, "Router Interface Summary Chart," to correctly specify the interface identifiers to be used based on the equipment in your lab. The 1721 series routers produced the configuration output in this lab. Any other router might produce slightly different output. You should execute the following steps on each router unless specifically instructed otherwise. Start a HyperTerminal session as you did in Lab 2.2.4, "Establishing a Console Session with HyperTerminal."

Please refer to and implement the procedure documented in Appendix C, "Erasing and Reloading the Router," before continuing with this lab.

Step 1. Log in to the router in user mode.

a. Connect to the router and log in.

b. What prompt did the router display?

_____

c. What does this prompt mean?

_____

Step 2. Log in to the router in privileged mode.

a. Enter enable at the user mode prompt.

```
Router>enable
```

b. If prompted for a password, enter the password **class**.

_____

c. What prompt did the router display?

_____

d. What does this prompt mean?

_____

Step 3. Enter global configuration mode.

a. Enter **configure terminal** at the privilege mode prompt.

```
Router#configure terminal
```

b. What prompt did the router display? _____

c. What does this prompt mean?

_____

Step 4. Enter router configuration mode.

a. Enter **router rip** at the global configuration mode prompt.

`Router(config)#router rip`

b. What prompt did the router display? _____

c. What does this prompt mean? _____

Step 5. Exit from router mode and go into interface configuration mode.

a. Enter **exit** at the prompt to return to global configuration mode.

`Router(config-router)#exit`

b. Enter **interface serial 0** (see chart for your interface identifier) at the global configuration mode prompt.

`Router(config)#interface serial 0`

c. What prompt did the router display? _____

d. What does this prompt mean? _____

e. Enter **exit** at the prompt to return to global configuration mode.

`Router(config-if)#exit`

Step 6. Assign a name to the router.

a. Enter **hostname GAD** at the prompt.

`Router(config)#hostname GAD`

b. What prompt did the router display? _____

c. What does this prompt mean? _____

d. What change occurred in the prompt?

_____

Step 7. Exit the router and global configuration mode.

`GAD(config)#exit`

After you finish the preceding steps, log off (by typing **exit**) and turn the router off.

Lab 3.1.3: Configuring Router Passwords

Figure 3-2 Topology for Lab 3.1.3

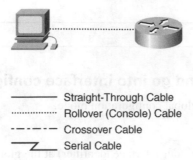

```
————————— Straight-Through Cable
·············· Rollover (Console) Cable
— — — — Crossover Cable
——Z—— Serial Cable
```

Objectives

- Configure a password for console login to user mode.
- Configure a password for virtual terminal (Telnet) sessions.
- Configure a secret password for privileged mode.

Background/Preparation

Cable a network similar to the one in Figure 3-2. You can use any router that meets the interface requirements in Figure 3-2 (that is, 800, 1600, 1700, 2500, and 2600 routers or a combination). Please refer to the information in Appendix B, "Router Interface Summary Chart," to correctly specify the interface identifiers to be used based on the equipment in your lab. The 1721 series routers produced the configuration output in this lab. Any other router might produce slightly different output. You should execute the following steps on each router unless specifically instructed otherwise.

Start a HyperTerminal session as you did in Lab 2.2.4.

Please refer to and implement the procedure documented in Appendix C, "Erasing and Reloading the Router," before continuing with this lab.

Step 1. Log in to the router in user EXEC mode.

a. Connect to the router and log in.

b. What prompt did the router display?

_____

c. What does this prompt mean?

_____

Step 2. Log in to the router in privileged EXEC mode.

a. Enter **enable** at the user mode prompt.

```
Router>enable
```

b. What prompt did the router display?

_____

c. What does this prompt mean?

_____

Step 3. Enter global configuration mode.

a. Enter **configure terminal** at the privilege mode prompt.

```
Router#configure terminal
```

b. What prompt did the router display? _____

c. What does this prompt mean?

_____

Step 4. Enter a host name of GAD for this router.

a. Enter **hostname GAD** at the prompt.

```
Router(config)#hostname GAD
```

b. What prompt did the router display? _____

c. What does this prompt mean?

_____

Step 5. Configure the console password on the router and exit line mode.

```
GAD(config)#line console 0
GAD(config-line)#password cisco
GAD(config-line)#login
GAD(config-line)#exit
GAD(config)#
```

Step 6. Configure the password on the virtual terminal lines and exit line mode.

```
GAD(config)#line vty 0 4
GAD(config-line)#password cisco
GAD(config-line)#login
GAD(config-line)#exit
GAD(config)#
```

Step 7. Configure the enable password and exit.

```
GAD(config)#enable password cisco
GAD(config)#exit
```

Step 8. Return to user EXEC mode by entering the disable command.

```
GAD#disable
```

Step 9. Enter privileged EXEC mode again.

This time, a prompt for a password will appear. Enter the password **cisco**, but you will not see the characters on the line.

```
GAD>enable
Password:cisco
```

Step 10. Return to configuration mode by entering configure terminal.

```
GAD#configure terminal
```

Step 11. Configure the enable secret password and exit global configuration mode.

```
GAD(config)#enable secret class
GAD(config)#exit
```

Note: Remember that the enable secret password is encrypted in the configuration view. Do not type **enable secret password class**, or your secret password will be password, not class.

Step 12. Return to user EXEC mode by entering the disable command.

```
GAD#disable
GAD>
```

Step 13. Enter privileged EXEC mode again.

This time, a prompt for a password will appear. Enter **cisco**, but you will not see the characters on the line. If it fails, keep trying until you see the **% Bad secrets** message.

```
GAD>enable
Password:cisco
Password:cisco
Password:cisco
% Bad secrets
```

Step 14. Enter privileged EXEC mode again.

A prompt for a password will appear. Enter class, but you will not see the characters on the line.

```
GAD>enable
Password:class
GAD#
```

Note: The enable secret password takes precedence over the enable password. After you enter an enable secret password, the router no longer accepts the enable password.

Step 15. Show the router's running configuration.

```
GAD#show running-config
```

    a. Do you see an encrypted password? _____

    b. Do you see any other passwords? _____

    c. Are any others encrypted? _____

Once you finish, log off (by typing **exit**) and turn the router off.

Lab 3.1.4: Using Router show Commands

Figure 3-3 Topology for Lab 3.1.4

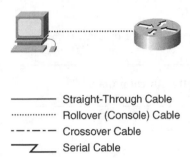

——————— Straight-Through Cable
················· Rollover (Console) Cable
- - — - - — Crossover Cable
⌐—z—— Serial Cable

Objectives

- Become familiar with the basic router **show** commands.
- Retrieve the current running configuration from RAM using **show running-config**.
- View the backup configuration file in non-volatile RAM (NVRAM) using **show startup-config**.
- View the IOS file information using **show flash** and **show version**.
- View the current status of the router interfaces using **show interface**.
- View the status of any configured Layer 3 protocol using **show protocols**.

Background/Preparation

This lab helps you become familiar with the router **show** commands. The **show** commands are the most important information-gathering commands available for the router:

- **show running-config** (or **show run**) is probably the single most valuable command to help determine the current status of a router because it displays the active configuration file running in RAM.
- **show startup-config** (or **show start**) displays the backup configuration file that is stored in NVRAM. You use this file to configure the router when you first start it or reboot it with the **reload** command. This file contains all the detailed router interface settings.
- **show flash** displays the available Flash memory and the amount used. Flash memory is where the router stores the Cisco IOS software file or image.
- **show arp** displays the router's address resolution table.
- **show interfaces** displays statistics for all interfaces configured on the router.
- **show protocols** displays global and interface-specific status of configured Layer 3 protocols (IP, IPX, etc.).

Cable a network similar to one in the diagram. You can use any router that meets the interface requirements in Figure 3-3 (that is, 800, 1600, 1700, 2500, and 2600 routers or a combination). The 1721 series routers produced the configuration output in this lab. Any other router might produce slightly different output. Please refer to the information in Appendix B, "Router Interface Summary," to correctly specify the interface identifiers to be used based on the equipment in your lab. You should execute the following steps on each router unless specifically instructed otherwise.

Start a HyperTerminal session as you did in Lab 2.2.4.

Step 1. Log in to the router.

a. Connect to the router and log in. If prompted, enter the password cisco.

Step 2. Enter the help command.

a. Enter the help command by typing **?** at the router prompt.

b. What did the router reply with? _____

c. Are all router commands available at the current prompt?

_____

d. Is **show** one of the options available? _____

Step 3. Display help for the show command.

a. Enter the **show ?** command. The router responds with the show subcommands available in user mode.

b. List three user-mode **show** subcommands.

show Subcommand	Description

Step 4. Display the IOS software version and other important information with the show version command.

a. Enter the **show version** command. The router will return information about the IOS that is running in RAM.

b. What is the IOS software version? _____

c. What is the name of the system image (IOS) file?

_____

d. Where was the router IOS image booted from?

_____

e. What type of processor (CPU) and how much RAM does this router have?

_____

f. How many Ethernet interfaces does this router have? _____ How many serial interfaces?

_____

g. The router backup configuration file is stored in NVRAM. How much NVRAM does this router have?

_____

h. The router operating system (IOS) is stored in Flash memory. How much Flash memory does this router have?

_____

i. What is the configuration register set to?

_____

Step 5. Display the router's time and date.

Enter the **show clock** command. What information is displayed?

Step 6. Display a cached list of host names and addresses.

Enter the **show hosts** command. What information is displayed?

Step 7. Display users who are connected to the router.

Enter the **show users** command. What information is displayed?

Step 8. Display the command buffer.

Enter the **show history** command. What information is displayed?

Step 9. Enter privileged mode.

a. From user EXEC mode, enter privileged EXEC mode using the **enable** command.

b. Enter the enable password **class**.

c. What command did you use to enter privileged mode?

d. How do you know whether you are in privileged mode?

Step 10. Enter the help command.

a. Enter the **show ?** command at the router prompt. What did the router reply with?

b. How is this output different from the one you got in user mode in Step 3?

Step 11. Display the router Address Resolution Protocol (ARP) table.

Enter the **show arp** command at the router prompt. What is the ARP table?

Step 12. Display information about the Flash memory device.

a. Enter **show flash** at the router prompt.

b. How much Flash memory is available and used?

c. What is the file that is stored in Flash memory?

d. What is the size in bytes of the Flash memory?

Step 13. Show information about the active configuration file.

Enter **show running-config** (or **show run**) at the router prompt. What important information is displayed?

_____

_____

Step 14. Display information about the backup configuration file.

Enter **show startup-config** (or **show start**) at the router prompt. What important information is displayed, and where is this information kept?

_____

_____

Step 15. Display statistics for all interfaces configured on the router.

a. Enter **show interfaces** at the router prompt.

b. Find the following information for interface FastEthernet 0. (Refer to Appendix B to correctly identify the interface based on equipment)

    1. What is MTU? _____

    2. What is rely? _____

    3. What is load? _____

c. Find the following information for interface Serial 0.

    1. What is the IP address and subnet mask?

    _____

    2. What data link layer encapsulation does the interface use?

    _____

Step 16. Display the protocols configured on the router.

Enter show protocols at the router prompt. What important information is displayed?

_____

Once you finish, log off (by typing **exit**) and turn the router off.

Lab 3.1.5: Configuring a Serial Interface

Figure 3-4 Topology for Lab 3.1.5

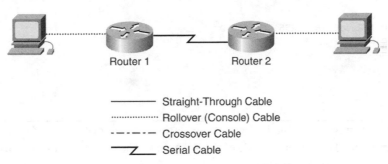

Use the information in Table 3-1 to configure the equipment for this lab.

Table 3-1 Lab Equipment Configuration

Router Designation	Router Name	Interface Type	Serial 0 Address	Subnet Mask	Enable Secret Password	Enable/vty/ Console Passwords
Router 1	GAD	DCE	192.168.15.1	255.255.255.0	class	cisco
Router 2	BHM	DTE	192.168.15.2	255.255.255.0	class	cisco

Objective

- Configure a serial interface on each of two routers so they can communicate.

Background/Preparation

Cable a network similar to the one in Figure 3-4. You can use any router that meets the interface requirements on this diagram (that is, 800, 1600, 1700, 2500, and 2600 routers or a combination). Please refer to the information in Appendix B, "Router Interface Summary Chart," to correctly specify the interface identifiers to be used based on the equipment in your lab. The 1721 series routers produced the configuration output in this lab. Any other router might produce slightly different output. You should execute the following steps on each router unless specifically instructed otherwise. Start a HyperTerminal session as you did in Lab 2.2.4.

Please refer to and implement the procedure documented in Appendix C, "Erasing and Reloading the Router," before continuing with this lab.

Step 1. Connect the router and workstation cabling.

Connect the routers as shown in Figure 3-4. This lab requires a null serial cable (a DTE and DCE cable connected together) and two rollover (console) cables.

Step 2. Configure the name and passwords for Router 1.

a. On Router 1, enter the global configuration mode and configure the host name as shown in the chart in Table 3-1.

b. Configure the console, virtual terminal, and enable passwords. If you have trouble doing this, refer to Lab 3.1.3.

Step 3. Configure serial interface Serial 0

From global configuration mode, configure serial interface Serial 0 (refer to Appendix B, "Router Interface Summary") on Router GAD.

```
GAD(config)#interface serial 0
GAD(config-if)#ip address 192.168.15.1 255.255.255.0
GAD(config-if)#clock rate 56000
GAD(config-if)#no shutdown
GAD(config-if)#exit
GAD(config)#exit
```

Note: Once you enter interface configuration mode, you must enter the IP address of the interface as well as the subnet mask. You enter the clock rate only on the DCE interface side of the WAN link. The command **no shutdown** turns on the interface. Shutdown is the name of the state when the interface is off.

Step 4. Save the running configuration to the startup configuration in privileged EXEC mode.

```
GAD#copy running-config startup-config
```

Note: If you do not save the running configuration, the next time that you restart the router, either with a software **reload** command or a power recycle, the running configuration will be lost. The router uses the startup configuration when the router is started.

Step 5. Display information about Serial interface 0 on GAD.

a. Enter the command **show interface serial 0** (refer to the "Router Interface Summary") on GAD.

```
GAD#show interface serial 0
```

This command shows the details of interface serial 0.

b. List at least the following three details you discovered from issuing this command.

c. Serial0 is _____. Line protocol is_____.

d. Internet address is _____.

e. Encapsulation is _____.

f. To what OSI layer is "Encapsulation" referring? _____

g. If the serial interface was configured, why did the show interface serial 0 say that the interface is down?

_____

Step 6. Configure the name and passwords for Router 2.

On the BHM router, enter the global configuration mode and configure the router name, console, virtual terminal, and enable passwords as shown in Table 3-1.

Step 7. Configure serial interface Serial 0

From global configuration mode, configure serial interface Serial 0 (refer to "Router Interface Summary") on Router BHM.

```
BHM(config)#interface serial 0
BHM(config-if)#ip address 192.168.15.2 255.255.255.0
BHM(config-if)#no shutdown
BHM(config-if)#exit
BHM(config)#exit
```

Step 8. Save the running configuration to the startup configuration in privileged EXEC mode.

```
BHM#copy running-config startup-config
```

Step 9. Display information about Serial interface 0 on BHM.

a. Enter the command **show interface serial 0** (refer to the "Router Interface Summary") on BHM.

```
BHM#show interface serial 0
```

This command shows the details of interface Serial 0.

b. List at least the following three details you discovered from issuing this command.

c. Serial 0 is _____. Line protocol is_____.

d. Internet address is _____.

e. Encapsulation is _____.

What is the difference in the Line Protocol Status recorded on GAD earlier? Why?

_____

Step 10. Verify that the serial connection is functioning.

a. Ping the serial interface of the other router.

```
BHM#ping 192.168.15.1
GAD#ping 192.168.15.2
```

b. From GAD, can you ping the BHM router's serial interface? _____

c. From BHM, can you ping the GAD router's serial interface? _____

d. If the answer is no for either question, troubleshoot the router configurations to find the error. Then, do the pings again until the answer to both questions is yes.

When you finish the preceding steps, log off (by typing **exit**) and turn the router off. Remove and store the cables and adapter.

Lab 3.1.6: Making Configuration Changes

Figure 3-5 Topology for Lab 3.1.6

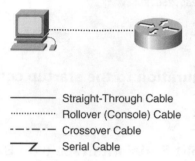

——— Straight-Through Cable
··············· Rollover (Console) Cable
—·—·—· Crossover Cable
╲╱ Serial Cable

Table 3-2 Lab Equipment Configuration

Router Name	Router Type	Serial 0 Address	Subnet Mask
GAD		192.168.14.1	255.255.255.0

The enable secret password is **class**.

The enable/vty/Console password is **cisco**.

Objectives

- Configure some basic router settings.
- Bring interfaces up and down.
- Make changes to the router configuration.

Background/Preparation

Cable a network similar to the one in Figure 3-5. You can use any router that meets the interface requirements in the diagram (that is, 800, 1600, 1700, 2500, and 2600 routers or a combination). Please refer to the information in Appendix B, "Router Interface Summary Chart," to correctly specify the interface identifiers to be used based on the equipment in your lab. The 1721 series routers produced the configuration output in this lab. Any other router might produce slightly different output. You should execute the following steps on each router unless specifically instructed otherwise.

Start a HyperTerminal session as you did in Lab 2.2.4.

Please refer to and implement the procedure documented in Appendix C, "Erasing and Reloading the Router," before continuing with this lab.

Step 1. Connect the router and workstation cabling.

Connect the router as shown in Figure 3-5. This lab requires a console (rollover) cable.

Step 2. Configure host name and passwords.

On the GAD router, enter global configuration mode and configure the router name as shown in Table 3-2. Then, configure the console, virtual terminal, and enable passwords.

Step 3. Configure the Serial 0 interface.

From global configuration mode, configure interface serial 0 (refer to the interface chart in Table 3-2) on Router GAD.

```
GAD(config)#interface Serial 0
GAD(config-if)#ip address 192.168.14.1 255.255.255.0
GAD(config-if)#no shutdown
GAD(config-if)#description Connection to the host
GAD(config-if)#exit
GAD(config)#exit
```

Step 4. Save the configuration.

Save the running configuration to the startup configuration in privileged EXEC mode.

```
GAD#copy running-config startup-config
```

Note: If you do not save the running configuration, the next time that you restart the router, either with a software **reload** command or a power recycle, the running configuration will be lost. The router uses the startup configuration when the router is started.

Step 5. Verify the configuration.

a. Enter the **show running-config** command from privileged EXEC mode.

b. If the configuration is not correct, re-enter any incorrect commands.

Step 6. Modify the configuration.

Based on the information in Table 3-3, reconfigure the GAD router. This step includes changing the router host name, changing the enable/vty/console passwords, and removing the secret password and interface description. You also need to change the interface address and subnet mask.

To change the information, go to the proper command mode and retype the command with the new information. To remove an old command, go to the proper command mode and retype the command exactly as it was entered with the word **no** in front of it:

```
GAD(config-if)#description Connection to location XYZ
GAD(config-if)#no description Connection to location XYZ
```

Note: Before making changes to the interface IP address and subnet mask, bring the interface down as shown in Step 7.

Table 3-3 Lab Equipment Configuration: Modified

Router Name	Serial 0 Address	Subnet Mask	Enable Secret Password	Enable/vty/Console Passwords
Gadsden	172.16.0.1	255.255.0.0		Cisco1

Step 7. Bring down Serial interface 0.

a. Bring the interface down for maintenance by entering the following:

```
Gadsden(config)# interface Serial 0
Gadsden(config-if)# shutdown
Gadsden(config-if)# exit
Gadsden(config)# exit
Gadsden#
```

b. Enter the command **show interface Serial 0** and note the interface status:

Serial 0 is _____. Line protocol is _____.

c. Issue the **show running-config** command and note the status of interface Serial 0:

_____

Step 8. Bring up the Serial 0 interface.

a. To make the interface operational, enable the interface by entering the following:

```
Gadsden(config)# interface Serial 0
Gadsden(config-if)# no shutdown
Gadsden(config-if)# exit
Gadsden (config)# exit
```

b. Enter the command **show interface Serial 0** and note the interface status:

Serial 0 is _____. Line protocol is _____.

Note: If the serial interface has been brought down with the **shutdown** command, it shows a status of "Administratively Down." Since there is no cable attached, it will show a status of "Down" even if brought up with the **no shutdown** command.

Step 9. Verify the configuration.

Enter a **show running-config** command from privileged EXEC mode to see whether the modifications took effect. If the configuration is not correct, re-enter any incorrect commands and verify again.

When you finish the preceding steps, log off (by typing **exit**) and turn the router off.

Lab 3.1.7: Configuring an Ethernet Interface

Figure 3-6 Topology for Lab 3.1.7

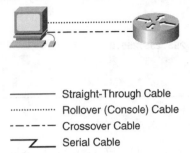

———— Straight-Through Cable
·············· Rollover (Console) Cable
– – – – – Crossover Cable
——Z—— Serial Cable

Table 3-4 Lab Equipment Configuration

Router Designation	Router Name	Ethernet 0 Address	Subnet Mask
Router 1	GAD	192.168.14.1	255.255.255.0

The enable secret password is **class**.

The enable/vty/Console password is **cisco**.

Objective

- Configure an Ethernet interface on the router with an IP address and a subnet mask.

Background/Preparation

In this lab, you will configure an Ethernet interface on the router with an IP address and a subnet mask. Cable a network similar to the one in Figure 3-6. You can use any router that meets the interface requirements in the diagram (that is, 800, 1600, 1700, 2500, and 2600 routers or a combination). Please refer to the information in Appendix B, "Router Interface Summary Chart," to correctly specify the interface identifiers to be used based on the equipment in your lab. The 1721 series routers produced the configuration output in this lab is. Any other router might produce slightly different output. You should execute the following steps on each router unless specifically instructed otherwise.

Start a HyperTerminal session as you did in Lab 2.2.4.

Please refer to and implement the procedure documented in Appendix C, "Erasing and Reloading the Router," before continuing with this lab.

Step 1. Configure the host name and passwords on the GAD router.

On the GAD router, enter global configuration mode and configure the router name as shown in Table 3-4. Then, configure the console, virtual terminal, and enable passwords.

Step 2. Configure the FastEthernet 0 interface.

Note: The designation for the first Ethernet interface on the router will vary. It might be ethernet 0, fastethernet 0, or fastethernet 0/0 depending on the type of router:

```
GAD(config)# interface fastethernet 0
GAD(config-if)# ip address 192.168.14.1 255.255.255.0
GAD(config-if)# no shutdown
GAD(config-if)# exit
GAD(config)# exit
```

Step 3. Save the configuration.

Save the configuration information from the privileged EXEC command mode.

```
GAD# copy running-config startup-config
```

Step 4. Display the FastEthernet 0 configuration information.

```
GAD#show interface fastethernet 0
```

This command shows the details of the Ethernet interface.

    a. List at least the following three details discovered from issuing this command:

        FastEthernet0 is _____. Line protocol is_____.

        Internet address is _____.

        Encapsulation is _____.

    b. To what OSI layer is "Encapsulation" referring? _____

        When you finish the preceding steps, log off (by typing **exit**) and turn the router off.

Lab 3.2.3: Configuring Interface Descriptions

Figure 3-7 Topology for Lab 3.2.3

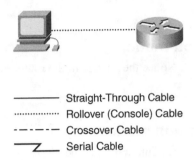

——————— Straight-Through Cable
················· Rollover (Console) Cable
– – – – – Crossover Cable
——⏗—— Serial Cable

Table 3-5 Lab Equipment Configuration

Router Designation	Router Name	FastEthernet0 Address	Serial 0 Address	Subnet Mask for Both Interfaces
Router 1	GAD	192.168.14.1	192.168.15.1	255.255.255.0

The enable secret password is **class**.

The enable/vty/Console password is **cisco**.

Objective

- Choose a description for an interface and use interface configuration mode to enter that description.

Background/Preparation

Interface descriptions are an important part of network documentation. They help you understand how a network is built and provide information for troubleshooting purposes.

Cable a network similar to the one in Figure 3-7. You can use any router that meets the interface requirements in the diagram (that is 800, 1600, 1700, 2500, and 2600 routers or a combination). Please refer to the information in Appendix B, "Router Interface Summary Chart," to correctly specify the interface identifiers to be used based on the equipment in your lab. The 1721 series routers produced the configuration output in this lab. Any other router might produce slightly different output. You should execute the following steps on each router unless specifically instructed otherwise.

Start a HyperTerminal session as you did in Lab 2.2.4.

Please refer to and implement the procedure documented in Appendix C, "Erasing and Reloading the Router," before continuing with this lab.

Step 1. Configure the host name and passwords on the router.

a. On the router, enter global configuration mode and configure the host name as shown in Table 3-5. Then, configure the console, virtual terminal, and enable passwords. If you have trouble doing this, refer to Lab 3.1.3.

b. What is the router command to view the current running configuration?

c. What command mode must you use to enter the command in the last question?

_____

d. Enter the command to verify the configuration that you just entered. If the configuration is not correct, fix the errors, and verify it again until it is correct.

Step 2. Enter global configuration mode.

Enter **configure terminal** at the router prompt. Notice the change in the router prompt.

What did the router prompt change to? _____

Step 3. Enter interface configuration mode.

Enter **interface serial 0** (refer to "Router Interface Summary") at the global configuration prompt.

What does the router prompt look like in interface configuration mode?

_____

Step 4. Display help for the description command.

Enter **description ?** at the router prompt.

What is the maximum number of characters in an interface description?

_____

Step 5. Choose a description for the interface.

a. An interface description includes the purpose and location of the interface, other devices or locations connected to the interface, and circuit identifiers. Descriptions help the support personnel better understand the problems related to an interface and allow for a faster resolution to those problems.

b. Given the following circuit information, choose a description for the Serial 0 interfaces for both GAD and BHM. Use the following form to document your choice.

Link	Carrier	Circuit ID	Speed
GAD to BHM	BellSouth	10DHDG551170	1.544 Mbps

Step 6. Enter a description for interface Serial 0.

From interface configuration mode for Serial 0, enter **description** *text* where *text* is the description from the previous step. Then, enter **Ctrl-Z** or type **end** to return to privileged EXEC mode.

Note: Typing **Ctrl-Z** is the same as typing **exit** to leave interface configuration mode and **exit** again to leave global configuration mode. It is a keyboard shortcut.

Step 7. Examine the active configuration file.

a. From enable mode (another name for privileged EXEC mode), enter the command that will show the running configuration. The router will display information on how it is currently configured.

b. What command did you enter? _____

c. What is the description for interface Serial 0?

_____

Step 8. Confirm that the interface description is correct.

From enable mode, enter the **show interfaces serial 0** command. The router will display information about the interface. Examine this output to confirm that the description you entered is the correct description.

When you finish the preceding steps, log off (by typing **exit**) and turn the router off.

Lab 3.2.5: Configuring Message-of-the-Day (MOTD)

Figure 3-8 Topology for Lab 3.2.5

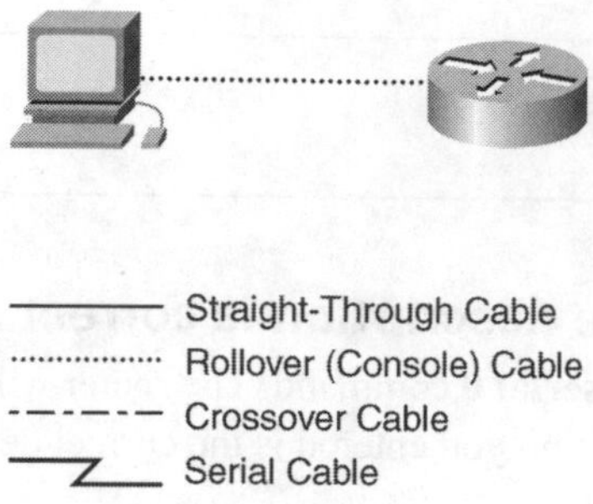
Straight-Through Cable
Rollover (Console) Cable
Crossover Cable
Serial Cable

Table 3-6 Lab Equipment Configuration

Router Name	Fa0	S0 Address	Subnet Mask
GAD	172.16.0.1	192.168.15.1	255.255.255.0

The enable secret password is **class**.

The enable/vty/Console password is **cisco**.

Objective

- Enter a message of the day (MOTD) on the router, which will allow all users to view the message upon entering the router.

Background/Preparation

In this lab a message-of-the-day banner will be configured. A message of the day or "login banner" can be useful as a warning to unauthorized users and can assist with security measures.

Cable a network similar to the one in Figure 3-8. You can use any router that meets the interface requirements in the diagram (that is, 800, 1600, 1700, 2500, and 2600 routers or a combination). Please refer to the information in Appendix B, "Router Interface Summary Chart," to correctly specify the interface identifiers to be used based on the equipment in your lab. The 1721 series routers produced the configuration output in this lab. Any other router might produce slightly different output. You should execute the following steps on each router unless specifically instructed otherwise.

Start a HyperTerminal session as you did in Lab 2.2.4.

Please refer to and implement the procedure documented in Appendix C, "Erasing and Reloading the Router," before continuing with this lab.

Step 1. Configure basic router information.

    a. On the router, enter global configuration mode and configure the router name as shown in Table 3-6. Then, configure the console, virtual terminal, and enable passwords. If you have trouble doing this, refer to Lab 3.1.3.

    b. Enter the **show running-config** command to verify the configuration that you just entered.

    c. Save the configuration information in privileged EXEC mode.

       `GAD#copy running-config startup-config`

Step 2. Enter global configuration mode.

Enter **configure terminal** at the router prompt. Notice the change in the router prompt.

Step 3. Display help for the banner motd command.

Enter **banner motd ?** at the router prompt.

What is the character called that indicates the beginning and end of the banner?

_____

Step 4. Choose a the text for MOTD.

The login banner should be a warning to users to not attempt login unless they are authorized. In the following space, enter an appropriate warning banner. The message can contain any printable character, other than the delimiting character, as well as spaces and carriage returns.

_____

Step 5. Enter the desired banner message.

From global configuration mode, enter **banner motd** # *message* #, where the # are delimiters and *message* is the banner message from the previous step.

Step 6. Test the MOTD display.

Exit the console session. Re-enter the router to display the message of the day by pressing the **Enter** key.

Step 7. Verify the MOTD by looking at the router configuration.

    a. Enter the **show running-config** command,

    b. How does the banner MOTD appear in the configuration listing?

_____

    c. Save the configuration information in privileged EXEC mode.

When you finish the steps, log off (by typing **exit**) and turn the router off.

Lab 3.2.7: Configuring Host Tables

Figure 3-9 Topology for Lab 3.2.7

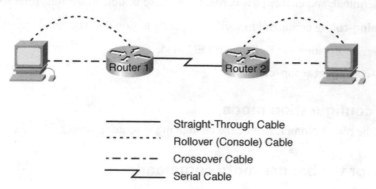

Straight-Through Cable
Rollover (Console) Cable
Crossover Cable
Serial Cable

Table 3-7 Lab Equipment Configuration

Router Designation	Router Name	FastEthernet 0 Address	Interface Type	Serial 0 Address
Router 1	GAD	172.16.0.1	DCE	172.17.0.1
Router 2	BHM	172.18.0.1	DTE	172.17.0.2

The enable secret password for both routers is **class**.

The enable/vty/Console password for both routers is **cisco**.

The subnet mask for both interfaces on both routers is 255.255.0.0.

Objective

- Create IP host tables associating router names with IP addresses.

Background/Preparation

IP host tables allow a router to use names to identify all of the attached interfaces on that router. You can use these names in place of IP addresses in commands that use IP addresses to identify a location such as ping or telnet.

Cable a network similar to the one in Figure 3-9. You can use any router that meets the interface requirements in the diagram (that is, 800, 1600, 1700, 2500, and 2600 routers or a combination). Please refer to the information in Appendix B, "Router Interface Summary Chart," to correctly specify the interface identifiers to be used based on the equipment in your lab. The 1721 series routers produced the configuration output in this lab. Any other router might produce slightly different output. You should execute the following steps on each router unless specifically instructed otherwise.

Start a HyperTerminal session as performed in Lab 2.2.4.

Please refer to and implement the procedure documented in Appendix C, "Erasing and Reloading the Router," before continuing with this lab.

Step 1. Configure the host name and passwords on the GAD router.

On the GAD router, enter global configuration mode and configure the router name as shown in Table 3-7. Then, configure the console, virtual terminal, and enable passwords. If you have trouble doing this, refer to Lab 3.1.3.

Step 2. Configure the interfaces and routing protocol on the GAD router.

Go to the proper command mode and enter the following:

```
GAD(config)#interface fastethernet 0
GAD(config-if)#ip address 172.16.0.1 255.255.0.0
GAD(config-if)#no shutdown
GAD(config-if)#exit
GAD(config)#interface serial 0
GAD(config-if)#ip address 172.17.0.1 255.255.0.0
GAD(config-if)#clock rate 56000
GAD(config-if)#no shutdown
GAD(config-if)#exit
GAD(config)#router rip
GAD(config-router)#network 172.16.0.0
GAD(config-router)#network 172.17.0.0
GAD(config-router)#exit
GAD(config)#exit
```

Step 3. Save the GAD router configuration.

```
GAD# copy running-config startup-config
```

Step 4. Configure the host name and passwords on the BHM router.

On the BHM router, enter global configuration mode and configure the router name as shown in Table 3-7. Then, configure the console, virtual terminal, and enable passwords. If you have trouble doing this, refer to Lab 3.1.3.

Step 5. Configure the interfaces and routing protocol on the BHM router.

Go to the proper command mode and enter the following:

```
BHM(config)# interface fastethernet 0
BHM(config-if)# ip address 172.18.0.1 255.255.0.0
BHM(config-if)# no shutdown
BHM(config-if)# exit
BHM(config)# interface serial 0
BHM(config-if)# ip address 172.17.0.2 255.255.0.0
BHM(config-if)# no shutdown
BHM(config-if)# exit
BHM(config)# router rip
BHM(config-router)# network 172.17.0.0
BHM(config-router)# network 172.18.0.0
BHM(config-router)# exit
BHM(config)# exit
```

Step 6. Save the BHM router configuration.

```
BHM# copy running-config startup-config
```

Step 7. Verify that the internetwork is functioning by pinging the FastEthernet interface of the other router.

a. From GAD, can you ping the BHM router's FastEthernet interface?

b. From BHM, can you ping the GAD router's FastEthernet interface?

_____

c. If the answer is no for either question, troubleshoot the router configurations to find the error. Then, do the pings again until the answer to both questions is yes.

Step 8. Configure the IP host table for the network.

a. Create a name for each router in the network lab. Enter that name along with the IP addresses of the router's interfaces in the table that follows. This local name can be anything that you want. Although the name does not have to match the configured host name of the router, that is a logical choice.

Router Name	IP Address Ethernet 0	IP Address Interface Serial 0

b. From global configuration mode, enter the command **ip host** followed by the name of each router in the network and all the IP addresses of the interfaces for each router.

For example, to name the GAD router accessible from BHM with the name G, enter the following:

```
BHM(conf)#ip host G 172.16.0.1 172.17.0.1
```

c. What commands did you enter on GAD?

_____

d. What commands did you enter on BHM?

_____

Step 9. Exit configuration mode and test.

a. From enable (privileged EXEC) mode, examine the host table entries using the command **show ip hosts** command on each router.

b. Do you see the host entries that were configured in the previous steps?

GAD _____   BHM _____

c. If there are no IP host entries, repeat Step 8.

d. Now ping the other router by host name. From the enable prompt, type **ping** _host_, where _host_ is the IP host name that you configured in the previous steps. For example, for a host name G, enter the following:

```
BHM#ping G
```

e. Was the ping successful? _____

If not, check the accuracy of the IP host table entries.

f. From the enable prompt, enter the host name and press **Enter**. For example, for a host name G, enter the following:

```
BHM#G
```

g. What happened? _____

When you finish the steps, log off (by typing **exit**) and turn the router off.

Lab 3.2.9: Backing Up Configuration Files

Figure 3-10 Topology for Lab 3.2.9

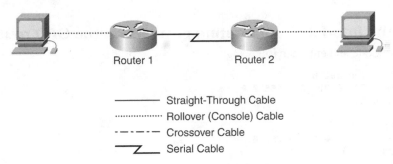

- Straight-Through Cable
- Rollover (Console) Cable
- Crossover Cable
- Serial Cable

Table 3-8 Lab Equipment Configuration

Router Designation	Router Name	FastEthernet 0 Address	Interface Type	Serial 0 Address
Router 1	GAD	172.16.0.1	DCE	172.17.0.1
Router 2	BHM	172.18.0.1	DTE	172.17.0.2

The enable secret password for this router is **class**.

The enable, vty, and console password for this router is **cisco**.

The subnet mask for all addresses is 255.255.255.0.

Objectives

- Capture the running configuration of a router to an ASCII text file with HyperTerminal.
- Edit the configuration with a text editor such as Notepad.
- Use the edited text file to configure another router using HyperTerminal.

Background/Preparation

The HyperTerminal capture option can be useful not only for saving configuration files but also for capturing command output and for documenting changes. It provides a simple way to save whatever is displayed on the screen of the PC acting as a console to the router.

Cable a network similar to the one in Figure 3-10. You can use any router that meets the interface requirements in Figure 3-10 (that is, 800, 1600, 1700, 2500, and 2600 routers or a combination). Refer to the information in Appendix B, "Router Interface Summary," to correctly specify the interface identifiers based on the equipment in your lab. The 1721 series routers produced the configuration output in this lab. Any other router might produce slightly different output. You should execute the following steps on each router unless specifically instructed otherwise.

Start a HyperTerminal session as you did in Lab 2.2.4.

Implement the procedure documented in Appendix C, "Erasing and Reloading the Router," before continuing with this lab.

Step 1. Configure the host name and passwords on the GAD router.

On the GAD router, enter global configuration mode and configure the router name as shown in Table 3-8. Then configure the console, vty, and enable passwords.

Step 2. Configure the interfaces and routing protocol on the GAD router.

Go to the proper command mode and enter the following:

```
GAD(config)#interface fastethernet 0
GAD(config-if)#ip address 172.16.0.1 255.255.0.0
GAD(config-if)#no shutdown
GAD(config-if)#exit
GAD(config)#interface serial 0
GAD(config-if)#ip address 172.17.0.1 255.255.0.0
GAD(config-if)#clock rate 56000
GAD(config-if)#no shutdown
GAD(config-if)#exit
GAD(config)#router rip
GAD(config-router)#network 172.16.0.0
GAD(config-router)#network 172.17.0.0
GAD(config-router)#exit
GAD(config)#exit
```

Step 3. Save the GAD router configuration.

```
GAD# copy running-config startup-config
Destination filename [startup-config]? [Enter]
```

Step 4. Configure the host name and passwords on the BHM router.

On the BHM router, enter global configuration mode and configure the router name as shown in Table 3-8. Then, configure the console, vty, and enable passwords.

Step 5. Configure the interfaces and routing protocol on the BHM router.

Go to the proper command mode and enter the following:

```
BHM(config)# interface fastethernet 0
BHM(config-if)# ip address 172.18.0.1 255.255.0.0
BHM(config-if)# no shutdown
BHM(config-if)# exit
BHM(config)# interface serial 0
BHM(config-if)# ip address 172.17.0.2 255.255.0.0
BHM(config-if)# no shutdown
BHM(config-if)# exit
BHM(config)# router rip
BHM(config-router)# network 172.17.0.0
BHM(config-router)# network 172.18.0.0
BHM(config-router)# exit
BHM(config)# exit
```

Step 6. Save the BHM router configuration.

```
BHM# copy running-config startup-config
Destination filename [startup-config]? [Enter]
```

Step 7. Verify that the internetwork is functioning by pinging the FastEthernet interface of the other router.

a. From GAD, can you reach the BHM router FastEthernet interface?

b. From BHM, can you reach the GAD router FastEthernet interface?

_____

c. If the answer is no for either question, troubleshoot the router configurations to find the error. Then, do the pings again until the answer to both questions is yes.

Step 8. Start capturing the configuration file.

a. Now, start the process of copying the router configuration to a text file.

Use HyperTerminal to capture all text displayed on its screen to a text file.

1. In HyperTerminal, click **Transfer**.

2. Specify the name of the router for the filename, and use .txt for the extension. Browse to find a location to store the text file on the computer. This file will be edited and used in later steps of this lab.

3. Click the **Start** button to start capturing text.

b. Write down the name and location of this file:

_____

c. Enter the **show running-config** command. Press the spacebar when the "-More -" prompt is displayed. You use the **show running-config** command to display the active configuration file for the router that is stored in RAM.

Step 9. Stop capturing the configuration file.

a. To discontinue capturing the output of the router configuration to a text file, do the following:

On the HyperTerminal menu bar, select the following, in this order:

1. Transfer

2. Capture Text

3. Stop

Step 10. Clean up the captured configuration file.

a. The captured text file will have information that is not required for configuring a router, such as the "- More -" prompts. To put this text in a form to be "pasted" back in the router, remove any unnecessary information from the captured configuration.

b. You might also want to add comments in the configuration to explain the various parts. You do so using the exclamation mark "!". Starting a line with ! creates a comment; the router will ignore this line. You can therefore write any kind of comment that helps you or other network associates understand the configuration.

c. First, start Notepad:

1. Choose **Start > Run**.

2. Type **Notepad**.

3. Press the **Enter** key.

d. In Notepad, choose **File > Open**. Find the file you created and click Open.

e. Delete the lines that contain the following:

- **show running-config**
- Building configuration

■ Current configuration:

■ - More -

■ Any lines that appear after the word "End"

f. At the end of each interface section, add the following line:

```
no shutdown
```

The following is an example:

```
interface Serial 0
ip address 199.6.13.1 255.255.255.0
 no shutdown
```

The next step is very important!

g. The last line to edit is as follows:

```
enable secret 5 $1$prts$Rbf8hxlss.ZrufvI7rMVy/
```

Change this line to the following:

```
enable secret class
```

You must enter this password in clear text, or the encryption algorithm will re-encrypt the current password and entry from the user prompt will be impossible.

h. Save the clean version of the configuration by clicking **File > Save**, and exit Notepad.

Step 11. Test your backup configuration.

a. Any form of backup that you do not test could be a liability in a failure situation. This rule includes backup configurations. You must test the backup configuration. Put your router out of service for a while. You should schedule the test during low network usage periods because you must take the router offline. You should notify all users who might be affected well in advance to ensure that the downtime will not be an inconvenience.

b. Before testing the backup configuration, erase the startup configuration. From the HyperTerminal session, enter the command erase startup-config at the enable router prompt. This command deletes the configuration file from NVRAM.

Confirm that startup configuration was deleted. Enter **show startup-config** at the router prompt.

c. What does the router show after you enter this command?

_____

Step 12. Restart the router to remove the running configuration.

a. Enter **reload** at the privileged EXEC mode prompt to reboot the router.

1. If prompted that the configuration has been modified. Save, type **N**, and press **Enter**.

2. When asked to proceed with the reload, enter **Y** and press the **Enter** key or just press the **Enter** key to confirm.

3. When the router restarts, note that the router may display the following message:

```
"Notice: NVRAM invalid, possibly due to write erase."
```

4. When prompted to enter the initial configuration dialog, type **N** and press **Enter**.

5. When prompted to terminate autoinstall, type **Y** and press **Enter**.

6. Press **Enter** an additional time.

b. What does the prompt look like?

_____

Step 13. Reconfigure the router from the saved text file.

a. Use the **send text file** command in HyperTerminal to restore the new configuration. The edited version of the router configuration file from the previous step will be copied into the area of memory known as the Clipboard.

b. Change to privileged EXEC mode.

c. Why did you not need a password?

_____

d. Enter global config mode by entering the command **configure terminal**.

e. In Hyperterminal:

   1. Click **Transfer/Send Text File**.

   2. Select the file.

   3. Each line of the text file will be entered at the router prompt.

f. Observe any errors on the router as commands are transferred.

g. What is the most obvious indication that the router was restored?

_____

   Press **Ctrl-Z** to exit global configuration mode.

h. Save the new configuration file as the startup configuration (in NVRAM).

   Use the command **copy running-config startup-config** (abbreviated **copy run start**) to save the newly created router configuration. This command copies the active router configuration from RAM into NVRAM.

   Verify that the running configuration is correct by using the **show running-config** command (abbreviated **show run**).

Step 14. Verify that the internetwork is functioning again by pinging the FastEthernet interface of the other router.

a. Use the **reload** command to restart the router. Verify that the new configuration was saved to NVRAM by restarting the router.

   When prompted to confirm, press **Y** to restart the router.

b. Once the router restarts, press the **Enter** key again.

c. From GAD, can you ping the BHM FastEthernet interface? _____

d. From BHM, can you ping the GAD FastEthernet interface? _____

e. If the answer is no for either question, troubleshoot the router configurations to find the error. Then, perform the pings again until the answer to both questions is yes.

When you finish these steps, log off (by typing **exit**) and turn off the router.

Learning About Other Devices

The following labs are in this chapter:

Lab TI	Title
4.1.4	Creating a Network Map Using CDP
4.1.6	Using CDP Commands
4.2.2	Establishing and Verifying a Telnet Connection
4.2.3	Suspending and Disconnecting Telnet Sessions
4.2.4	Advanced Telnet Operations
4.2.5a	Connectivity Tests – Ping
4.2.5b	Connectivity Tests – Traceroute
4.2.6	Troubleshooting IP Address Issues

Lab 4.1.4: Creating a Network Map Using CDP

Figure 4-1 Topology for Lab 4.1.4

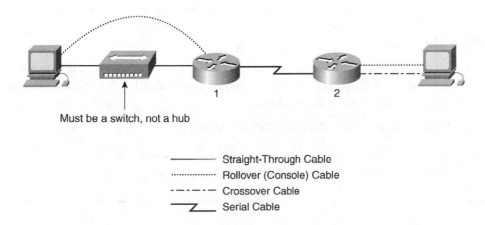

Must be a switch, not a hub

———— Straight-Through Cable
················ Rollover (Console) Cable
– – – – – Crossover Cable
⌐⌐ Serial Cable

Table 4-1 Lab Equipment Configuration

Router Designation	Router Name	Interface Type	Serial 0 Clock	Serial 0 Address	Ethernet 0 Address
Router 1	GAD	DCE	56000	192.168.15.1	192.168.14.1
Router 2	BHM	DTE	Not set	192.168.15.2	192.168.16.1

The subnet mask for all interfaces on both routers is 255.255.255.0.

Objective

- Use CDP commands to get information about neighboring network devices

Background/Preparation

In this lab the Cisco Discovery Protocol (CDP) commands will be used. CDP discovers and shows information about directly connected Cisco devices (routers and switches).

Cable a network similar to the one in Figure 4-1. Be sure to use a switch and not a hub as a hub will not be discovered by CDP. You can use any router that meets the interface requirements displayed in the diagram (that is, 800, 1600, 1700, 2500 and 2600 routers or a combination). Please refer to the information in Appendix B, "Router Interface Summary Chart," to correctly specify the interface identifiers to be used based on the equipment in your lab. The configuration output used in this lab is produced from 1721 series routers. Any other router used may produce slightly different output. The following steps are intended to be executed on each router unless specifically instructed otherwise.

Start a HyperTerminal session as performed in Lab 2.2.4.

Please refer to and implement the procedure documented in Appendix C, "Erasing and Reloading the Router," before continuing with this lab.

Step 1. Log on to Router 1 (GAD).

Why is it necessary to log on to Router 1 in order to see all of the devices (routers and switches) in the network shown in Figure 4-1?

_____

Step 2. Configure the routers.

a. Configure the routers according to the information in Table 4-1 in order for CDP to be able to collect information about them. Refer to Lab 3.1.5, "Configuring a Serial Interface," and Lab 3.1.7, "Configuring an Ethernet Interface," if you need help making changes to the configurations.

b. What is the clock rate to be set to and which interface is it set on?

_____

c. Why is it necessary to use the **no shutdown** command on all interfaces?

_____

Step 3. Gather information about GADs interfaces.

a. Enter **show interface** command at either the user EXEC or the privileged EXEC router prompt.

b. How many interfaces are present_____

c. What type are they? _____

Step 4. Display the CDP updates received on the local router.

a. Enter **show cdp neighbors** command at the router prompt.

b. Fill in Table 4-2.

Table 4-2 Entering CDP Neighbor Information

Device Port ID	Local Interface	Hold Time	Capability	Platform

Upon completion of the previous steps, log off (by typing **exit**) and turn the router off.

Lab 4.1.6: Using CDP Commands

Figure 4-2 Topology for Lab 4.1.6

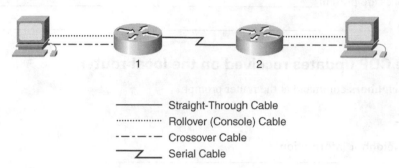

———————— Straight-Through Cable
···················· Rollover (Console) Cable
— — — — — Crossover Cable
——Z— Serial Cable

Table 4-3 Lab Equipment IP Address Information

Router Designation	Router Name	Interface Type	Serial 0 Clock	Serial 0 Address	Ethernet 0 Address
Router 1	GAD	DCE	56000	192.168.15.1	192.168.14.1
Router 2	BHM	DTE	Not set	192.168.15.2	192.168.16.1

The subnet mask for all interfaces on both routers is 255.255.255.0.

Objectives

- Use CDP commands to obtain information about neighboring networks and devices
- Display information on how CDP is configured for its advertisement and discovery frame transmission.
- Display CDP updates received on the local router.

Background/Preparation

In this lab, various Cisco Discovery Protocol (CDP) commands will be used. CDP discovers and shows information about directly connected Cisco devices (routers and switches). CDP is a Cisco proprietary protocol that runs at the data link layer (Layer 2) of the OSI model. This allows devices that may be running different network layer (Layer 3) protocols such as IP or IPX to learn about each other. CDP begins automatically upon a device's system startup, however if Cisco IOS Software Release 10.3 or a newer version is used, CDP must be enabled on each of the device's interfaces by using the **cdp enable** command. Using the command **show cdp interface** gathers information that CDP uses for its advertisement and discovery frame transmission. Use **show cdp neighbors** and **show cdp neighbors detail** to display the CDP updates received on the local router.

Cable a network similar to the one in Figure 4-2. You can use any router that meets the interface requirements displayed in the diagram (that is, 800, 1600, 1700, 2500 and 2600 routers or a combination). Please refer to the information in Appendix B, "Router Interface Summary Chart," to correctly specify the interface identifiers to be used based on the equipment in your lab. The configuration output used in this lab is produced from 1721 series routers. Any other router used may produce slightly different output. The following steps are intended to be executed on each router unless specifically instructed otherwise.

Start a HyperTerminal session as performed in Lab 2.2.4.

Please refer to and implement the procedure documented in Appendix C, "Erasing and Reloading the Router," before continuing with this lab.

Step 1. Configure the routers.

a. Configure the routers according to the information in Table 4-3 in order for CDP to be able to collect information about them. Refer to Lab 3.1.5, "Configuring a Serial Interface," and Lab 3.1.7, "Configuring an Ethernet Interface," if you need help making changes to the configurations.

Note: Do not use the **no shutdown** command on either of the router's interfaces at this time.

---

b. What is the clock rate to be set to and which interface is it set on?

_____

Step 2. Gather information about the GAD router's interfaces.

a. Enter **show interface** command at either the user EXEC or the privileged EXEC router prompt.

Document the following information about the router:

b. What is the name of the router? _____

c. List the operational status of each interface in Table 4-4.

Table 4-4 Router Interface Operational Status

Interface	Interface Up or Down? (Carrier Detect Signal)	Line Protocol Up or Down? (Keepalives Being Received)

Step 3. Enable the interfaces on GAD.

```
GAD(config)#interface serial 0
GAD(config-if)#no shutdown
GAD(config-if)#exit
GAD(config)#interface FastEthernet 0
GAD(config-if)#no shutdown
GAD(config-if)#exit
GAD(config)#exit
```

Step 4. Gather information about the GAD routers interfaces.

a. Enter **show interface** command at either the user EXEC or the privileged EXEC router prompt.

b. Document the following information about the router:

c. What is the name of the router? _____

d. List the operational status of each interface in Table 4-5.

Table 4-5 Router Interface Operational Status

Interface	Interface Up or Down? (Carrier Detect Signal)	Line Protocol Up or Down? (Keepalives Being Received)

Step 5. Display the values of the CDP timers, the interface status, and encapsulation used.

a. Enter **show cdp interface** command at the router prompt.

b. How often is the router sending CDP packets? _____

c. What is the holdtime value? _____

d. Global CDP settings can be seen using the **show cdp** command by itself.

e. What information is not displayed in the **show cdp** command?

_____

Step 6. Display the CDP updates received on the local router.

a. Enter **show cdp neighbors** command at the router prompt.

b. Fill in the information in Table 4-6.

Table 4-6 CDP Neighbor Information

Device and Port ID	Local Interface	Hold Time	Capability	Platform

Step 7. Enable Serial 0 interface on BHM.

Enter the **no shutdown** command on the Serial 0 interface of Router 2. Return to Router 1 and repeat step 4. Notice how the router now appears in the **cdp neighbor** command display.

Step 8. Display details about CDP updates received on the local router.

a. Enter **show cdp neighbors detail** from the router prompt.

b. Fill in the information in Table 4-7.

Table 4-7 CDP Neighbor Detail

Information Gathered	Device 1	Device 2
Neighbor Device Name		
Neighbor Device Type		
IP Address of Interface Attached to Your Router		
Port ID of Your Router That the Neighbor Is On		
Port ID of Neighbor Router That Your Router Is On		
IOS Version of Neighbor Router		

Step 9. Observe cdp packets being sent and received on the router.

a. Enter the **debug cdp packets** command from the privileged EXEC mode.

b. What is the output? (Wait for at least two minutes.)

_____

c. After observing the output, enter the **undebug all** command to stop debugging activity.

Step 10. Observe CDP packet traffic.

Enter the following commands at the privileged EXEC mode prompt and record the results:

show cdp traffic

_____

clear cdp counters

_____

show cdp traffic

_____

Lab 4.2.2: Establishing and Verifying a Telnet Connection

Figure 4-3 Topology for Lab 4.2.2

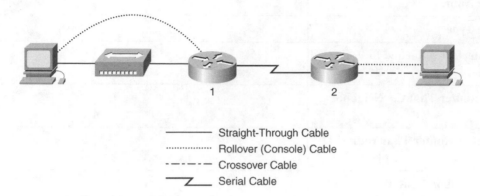

Straight-Through Cable
Rollover (Console) Cable
Crossover Cable
Serial Cable

Table 4-8 Lab Equipment Configuration

Router Designation	Router Name	Ethernet 0 Address	Interface Type	Serial 0 Address
Router 1	GAD	192.168.14.1	DCE	192.168.15.1
Router 2	BHM	192.168.16.1	DTE	192.168.15.2

The routing protocol on both routers is RIP.

The enable secret password for both routers is **class**.

The enable, vty, and console password for both routers is **cisco**.

The subnet mask for all interfaces on both routers is 255.255.255.0.

Objectives

- Establish a Telnet connection to a remote router
- Verify that the application layer between source and destination is working properly
- Retrieve information about remote routers using show commands
- Retrieve CDP information from routers not directly connected to you

Background/Preparation

This lab focuses on the Telnet (remote terminal) utility to access routers remotely. Telnet is used to connect from a local router to another remote router in order to simulate being at the console on the remote router. The local router acts as a Telnet client and the remote router acts as a Telnet server. Telnet is a good testing or troubleshooting tool since it is an application layer utility. A successful Telnet demonstrates that the entire TCP/IP protocol stack on both the client and server are functioning properly. You can Telnet from your workstation as a client into any router with IP connectivity on your network. In addition, you can Telnet into an Ethernet switch if an IP address has been assigned.

Cable a network similar to the one in Figure 4-3. You can use any router that meets the interface requirements displayed in the diagram (that is, 800, 1600, 1700, 2500 and 2600 routers or a combination). Please refer to the information in Appendix B, "Router Interface Summary Chart," to correctly specify the interface

identifiers to be used based on the equipment in your lab. The configuration output used in this lab is produced from 1721 series routers. Any other router used may produce slightly different output. The following steps are intended to be executed on each router unless specifically instructed otherwise.

Start a HyperTerminal session as performed in Lab 2.2.4.

Please refer to and implement the procedure documented in Appendix C, "Erasing and Reloading the Router," before continuing with this lab.

Step 1. Configure the routers.

a. If you have trouble configuring hostname or passwords, refer to Lab 3.1.3, "Configuring Router Passwords." If you have trouble configuring interfaces or the routing protocol, refer to Lab 3.1.5, "Configuring a Serial Interface," Lab 3.1.7, "Configuring an Ethernet Interface," and Lab 3.2.7, "Configuring Hosts Tables."

b. Verify the routers configurations by performing a **show running-config** on each router. If not correct, fix any configuration errors and verify.

Step 2. Log in to Router 1 and verify the connection to Router 2.

a. Login to the GAD router in user mode

b. Verify the connection between the two routers by pinging the Serial 0 interface of the BHM router. If the ping is not successful return to Step 1 and troubleshoot your configuration.

Step 3. Use help with the telnet command.

a. Enter **telnet ?** at either the user EXEC or the privileged EXEC router prompt.

b. What did the router reply with?

_____

Step 4. Telnet to a remote router.

a. Enter **telnet** *router-name* (if IP host tables were configured) or **telnet** *ip-address* at the router prompt to connect to a remote router. Enter the password **cisco** to enter the remote router.

b. What prompt did the router display? _____

Step 5. Look at the interfaces on the remote router.

a. Enter **show interface** at the router prompt.

b. List the interfaces, their IP address and subnet masks in Table 4-9.

Table 4-9 Remote Router Interface Information

Interface	IP Address	Subnet Mask

Step 6. Display the protocols on the remote router.

a. Enter **show protocols** at the router prompt.

b. Fill in Table 4-10 with the information that was generated by the remote access router.

Table 4-10 Remote Router Interface Information Determined from **show protocols**

Interface	Is There a Carrier Signal?	Are the Keepalive Messages Being Received?

Step 7. Enter privileged EXEC mode.

a. Enter **enable** at the command prompt. Enter the password **class**.

b. What prompt did the router display? What mode is this?

_____

Step 8. Look at the running configuration.

a. Enter **show running-config** at the remote router prompt.

b. What file is being viewing on the remote router? Where is this file stored?

_____

Step 9. Look at the saved configuration.

a. Enter **show startup-config** at the router prompt.

b. What file is being viewed on the remote router? Where is this file stored?

_____

c. What information is seen concerning the line vty connections?

_____

Step 10. Look at the neighbor configuration.

a. Enter **show cdp neighbors** command at the router prompt.

b. List all device IDs that are connected to the remote router with a Telnet session.

_____

Upon completion of the previous steps, log off (by typing **exit**) and turn the router off.

Lab 4.2.3: Suspending and Disconnecting Telnet Sessions

Figure 4-4 Topology for Lab 4.2.3

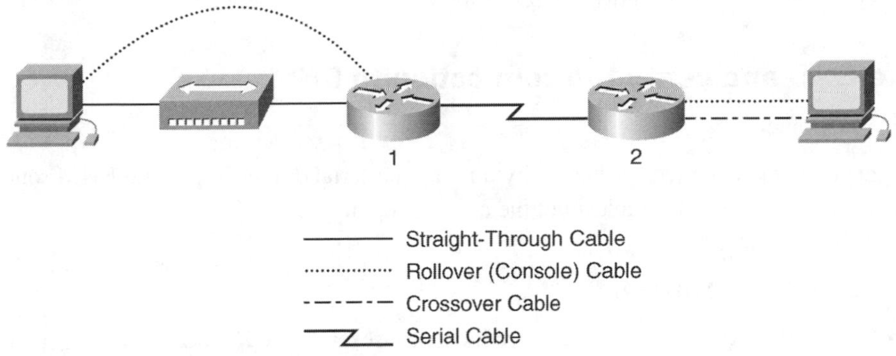
1
2
Straight-Through Cable
Rollover (Console) Cable
Crossover Cable
Serial Cable

Table 4-11 Lab Equipment Configuration

Router Designation	Router Name	Ethernet 0 Address	Interface Type	Serial 0 Address
Router 1	GAD	192.168.14.1	DCE	192.168.15.1
Router 2	BHM	192.168.16.1	DTE	192.168.15.2

The routing protocol on both routers is RIP.

The enable secret password for both routers is **class**.

The enable, vty, and console password for both routers is **cisco**.

The subnet mask for all interfaces on both routers is 255.255.255.0.

Objectives

- Establish a Telnet session with a remote router.
- Suspend and re-establish a Telnet session.
- Display active Telnet sessions.
- Disconnect a Telnet session.

Background/Preparation

This lab focuses on the ability to Telnet to a router, suspend that session, return to the local router console, and then re-establish the previous connection.

Cable a network similar to the one in Figure 4-4. You can use any router that meets the interface requirements displayed in the diagram (that is, 800, 1600, 1700, 2500 and 2600 routers or a combination). Please refer to the information in Appendix B, "Router Interface Summary Chart," to correctly specify the interface identifiers to be used based on the equipment in your lab. The configuration output used in this lab is produced from 1721 series routers. Any other router used may produce slightly different output. The following steps are intended to be executed on each router unless specifically instructed otherwise.

Start a HyperTerminal session as performed in Lab 2.2.4.

Please refer to and implement the procedure documented in Appendix C, "Erasing and Reloading the Router," before continuing with this lab.

Step 1. Configure the routers.

If you have trouble configuring hostname or passwords, refer to Lab 3.1.3, "Configuring Router Passwords.". If you have trouble configuring interfaces or the routing protocol, refer to Lab 3.1.5, "Configuring a Serial Interface," Lab 3.1.7, "Configuring an Ethernet Interface," and Lab 3.2.7, "Configuring Hosts Tables."

Step 2. Log in to GAD and verify the connection to BHM.

a. Log in to the GAD router.

b. Verify the connection between the two routers by pinging the serial 0 interface of the BHM router. If the ping is not successful return to step one and troubleshoot the configuration.

Step 3. Telnet to a remote router.

a. Enter **telnet BHM** if IP host tables were configured. Otherwise, enter the IP address at the router prompt to connect to the remote router.

Enter the password **cisco** to enter the router.

b. What prompt did the router display? _____

Step 4. Look at the interfaces on the remote router.

a. Enter **show interface** at the router prompt.

b. Are both the Serial 0 and the FastEthernet 0 interfaces up?

_____

Step 5. Suspend the current Telnet session.

a. Press **Ctrl-Shift-6** followed by the **x** key. This suspends the remote session only and returns to the previous router. It does not disconnect from this router.

b. What prompt did the router display? _____

Step 6. Resume a Telnet session.

a. Press the **Enter** key at the router prompt. The router will respond with

```
[Resuming connection 1 to 192.168.15.2 ... ]
```

b. Press the **Enter** key. This resumes the telnet session that was previously suspended in Step 5.

c. What prompt did the router display? _____

Step 7. Close a Telnet session.

a. Enter the command **exit** while in a telnet session. This terminates the telnet session.

b. What prompt did the router display?

_____

Note: To disconnect from a suspended telnet session, type **disconnect** and press **Enter**.

Upon completion of the previous steps, log off (by typing **exit**) and turn the router off.

Lab 4.2.4: Advanced Telnet Operations

Figure 4-5 Topology for Lab 4.2.4

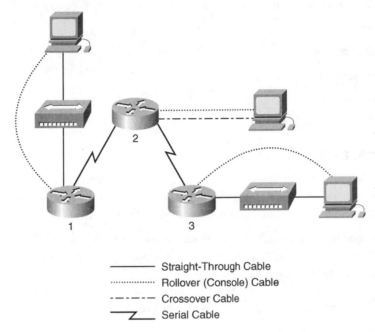

Straight-Through Cable
Rollover (Console) Cable
Crossover Cable
Serial Cable

Table 4-12 Lab Equipment Configuration: Part I

Router Designation	Router Name	RIP Network Statements
Router 1	GAD	192.168.14.0 192.168.15.0
Router 2	BHM	192.168.15.0 192.168.13.0 192.168.16.0
Router 3	PHX	192.168.13.0 192.168.17.0

The routing protocol on both routers is RIP.

The enable secret password for both routers is **class**.

The enable, vty, and console password for both routers is **cisco**.

Table 4-13 Lab Equipment Configuration: Part II

Router Designation	Router Name	FastEthernet 0 Address	Interface Type	Serial 0 Address	Interface Type	Serial 1 Address
Router 1	GAD	192.168.14.1	DCE	192.168.15.1	N/A	No Address
Router 2	BHM	192.168.16.1	DTE	192.168.15.2	DCE	192.168.13.1
Router 3	PHX	192.168.17.1	N/A	No Address	DTE	192.168.13.2

The subnet mask for all addresses on all routers is 255.255.255.0.

Objectives

- Use the **telnet** command to remotely access other routers.

- Verify that the application layer between source and destination is working properly.

- Suspend a Telnet session

- Engage in multiple Telnet sessions

- Return to the suspended session

- Disconnect from the Telnet session

Background/Preparation

It is often desirable to have Telnet sessions to multiple routers simultaneously in order to check and compare configuration information. This lab focuses on the ability the Telnet to a multiple routers, suspend those sessions and then switch between the active sessions. A list of active connections can also be displayed in the process.

Cable a network similar to the one in Figure 4-5. You can use any router that meets the interface requirements displayed in the diagram (that is, 800, 1600, 1700, 2500 and 2600 routers or a combination). Please refer to the information in Appendix B, "Router Interface Summary Chart," to correctly specify the interface identifiers to be used based on the equipment in your lab. The configuration output used in this lab is produced from 1721 series routers. Any other router used may produce slightly different output. The following steps are intended to be executed on each router unless specifically instructed otherwise.

Start a HyperTerminal session as performed in Lab 2.2.4.

Please refer to and implement the procedure documented in Appendix C, "Erasing and Reloading the Router," before continuing with this lab.

Step 1. Configure the GAD, BHM and PHX routers using the tables.

a. Configure the three routers as indicated in Tables 4-12 and 4-13.

If you have trouble configuring hostname or passwords, refer to Lab 3.1.3, "Configuring Router Passwords." If you have trouble configuring interfaces or the routing protocol, refer to Lab 3.1.5, "Configuring a Serial Interface," Lab 3.1.7, "Configuring an Ethernet Interface," and Lab 3.2.7, "Configuring Host Tables."

b. Verify the routers configurations by performing a **show running-config** on each router. If not correct, fix any configuration errors and verify.

Step 2. Log in to Router 1 and verify the connection to Routers 2 and 3.

a. Log in to the GAD router.

b. Verify the connection between the two routers by pinging the serial 0 interface of the BHM and PHX routers. If the pings are not successful, return to Step 1 and troubleshoot the configuration.

Step 3. Telnet to a remote router.

a. Enter **telnet BHM** if IP host tables were configured. Otherwise, enter **telnet** *ip-address* at the router prompt to connect to the BHM router.

Enter the password **cisco** to enter the router.

b. What prompt did the router display? _____

Step 4. Look at the interfaces on the remote router.

a. Enter **show interface** at the router prompt.

b. Are both the Serial 0 and the FastEthernet 0 interfaces up?

_____

Step 5. Suspend the current Telnet session.

a. Press **Ctrl-Shift-6** followed by the **x** key. This suspends the session only and returns to the previous router. It does not disconnect from this router.

b. What prompt did the router display?

_____

Step 6. Establish another telnet session.

a. Enter **telnet** *router-name* (if IP host tables were configured) or **telnet** *ip-address* at the router prompt to connect to the PHX router. Enter the password **cisco** to enter the router.

b. What prompt did the router display?

_____

Step 7. Suspend the current Telnet session.

a. Press **Ctrl-Shift-6** followed by the **x** key. This suspends the session only and returns to the previous router. It does not disconnect from this router.

b. What prompt did the router display?

_____

Step 8. Use the show sessions command to see the connections.

Enter **show sessions** at the command prompt.

This reveals that two sessions are in use.

Step 9. Resume the previously suspended telnet session.

a. Type **resume** and the number of the session that is to be resumed followed by the **Enter** key at the router prompt. You can also just type the number of the session and press **Enter**. The router responds with

```
[Resuming connection 1 to 192.168.X.X ... ]
```

b. Press the **Enter** key.

Pressing the **Enter** key also resumes a Telnet session that was previously suspended.

c. What prompt did the router display?

_____

Step 10. Use the show sessions command to see the connections.

a. Enter **show sessions** at the command prompt.

b. How many sessions are shown? _____

c. There were two the last time what is the difference?

_____

Step 11. Close a telnet session.

a. Enter the command **exit** while in a Telnet session. This terminates the Telnet session.

b. What prompt did the router display? _____

_____

Note: (Do not do this now.) To disconnect from a suspended Telnet session, type **disconnect** and press **Enter**.

_____

Step 12. Use the show session command to see the connections.

a. Enter **show sessions** at the command prompt.

b. How many sessions are shown? _____

c. There were two on this router the last time, what is the difference?

_____

Step 13. Resume the previously suspended telnet session.

a. Press the **Enter** key. The router will respond with

```
[Resuming connection 1 to 192.168.X.X ... ]
```

Press the **Enter** key. This resumes a Telnet session that was previously suspended.

b. What prompt did the router display?

_____

Step 14. Close a Telnet session.

Enter the command **exit** while in a Telnet session. This terminates the Telnet session.

Step 15. Problems with linked Telnet sessions on multiple routers.

a. When working with Telnet, one of the most common problems is remembering the focus of the session. *Focus* means "the device (router) that is the focus of the commands that you are issuing". Many times people Telnet to a router, and then Telnet from that router to another and so on. Without host names, or if the routers have similar hostnames, confusion can occur. This is an example of this:

b. Telnet to the PHX router. From the configuration prompt, type **no hostname**.

Step 16. Telnet to the BHM router.

From the configuration prompt type **no hostname**.

Step 17. Telnet back to the PHX router.

By looking at the prompt, it is not evident whether your Telnet worked or not.

Step 18. Telnet to the GAD router.

From the configuration prompt, type **no hostname**.

Step 19. Telnet to the BHM router.

    a. Type **show sessions**.

    b. How many sessions are there running? _____

    c. Why are there that many? _____

    d. Now, type **exit** three times.

    e. What router are you on? _____

    f. How many Telnet sessions are still open? _____

Step 20. Exiting from all sessions.

    a. Keep typing **exit** until the following prompt appears.

```
Router con0 is now available.
```

    Press **Return** to get started.

    b. Scroll back up the HyperTerminal listing.

    c. How many session closed messages were displayed? _____

    d. Is that the number listed in the "How many Telnet sessions are still open" question?

    _____

    Upon completion of the previous steps, log off (by typing **exit**) and turn the router off.

Lab 4.2.5a: Connectivity Tests—Ping

Figure 4-6 Topology for Lab 4.2.5a

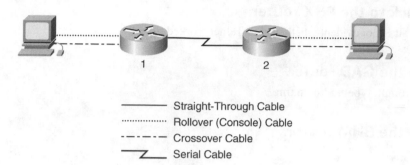

Straight-Through Cable

Rollover (Console) Cable

Crossover Cable

Serial Cable

Table 4-14 Lab Equipment Configuration: Part I

Router Designation	Router Name	RIP Network Statements
Router 1	GAD	192.168.14.0 192.168.15.0
Router 2	BHM	192.168.15.0 192.168.16.0

The routing protocol on both routers is RIP.

The enable secret password for both routers is **class**.

The enable, vty, and console password for both routers is **cisco**.

Table 4-15 Lab Equipment Configuration: Part II

Router Designation	Router Name	FastEthernet 0 Address	Interface Type Serial 0	Serial 0 Address
Router 1	GAD	192.168.14.1	DCE	192.168.15.1
Router 2	BHM	192.168.16.1	DTE	192.168.15.2

The subnet mask for all addresses on all routers is 255.255.255.0.

The Serial 1 interface is inactive on both routers.

Objectives

- Use the **ping** command to send ICMP datagrams to target host.
- Verify that the network layer between source and destination is working properly.
- Retrieve information to evaluate the path-to-host reliability.
- Determine delays over the path and whether the host can be reached or is functioning.
- Use **extended ping** command to increase number of packets.

Background/Preparation

The **ping** command is a good tool for troubleshooting Layers 1 though 3 of the OSI model and diagnosing basic network connectivity. Using **ping** sends an ICMP packet to the specified device (workstation, server, router or switch) and then waits for a reply. The IP address or host name can be pinged. In order to ping the host name of a router, there must be a static host lookup table in the router or a DNS server for name resolution to IP addresses.

Cable a network similar to the one in Figure 4-6. You can use any router that meets the interface requirements displayed in the diagram (that is, 800, 1600, 1700, 2500 and 2600 routers or a combination). Please refer to the information in Appendix B, "Router Interface Summary Chart," to correctly specify the interface identifiers to be used based on the equipment in your lab. The configuration output used in this lab is produced from 1721 series routers. Any other router used may produce slightly different output. The following steps are intended to be executed on each router unless specifically instructed otherwise.

Start a HyperTerminal session as performed in Lab 2.2.4.

Please refer to and implement the procedure documented in Appendix C, "Erasing and Reloading the Router," before continuing with this lab.

Step 1. Configure the GAD and BHM routers.

a. If you have trouble configuring hostname or passwords, refer to Lab 3.1.3, "Configuring Router Passwords." If you have trouble configuring interfaces or the routing protocol, refer to Lab 3.1.5, "Configuring a Serial Interface," Lab 3.1.7, "Configuring an Ethernet Interface," and Lab 3.2.7, "Configuring Host Tables."

b. This lab requires that IP hostnames be configured.

c. Verify the routers configurations by performing a **show running-config** on each router. If not correct, fix any configuration errors and verify.

Step 2. Log in to GAD and verify the connection to BHM.

a. Login to the GAD router.

b. Verify the connection between the two routers by pinging the Serial 0 interface of the BHM router. If the ping is not successful return to Step 1 and troubleshoot your configuration.

Step 3. Display information about host to Layer 3 address mappings.

a. Enter **show host** at the router prompt.

The router displays information about host to Layer 3 (IP) address mappings, how this information was acquired and the age of the entry.

b. List host names and the IP addresses listed for each one and record the information in Table 4-16.

Table 4-16 Host Name/IP Address Information

Host Name	IP Address

Step 4. Use the ping command.

a. Enter **ping** *xxx.xxx.xxx.xxx* where *xxx.xxx.xxx.xxx* is a listed IP address listed.

b. Repeat with all IP addresses listed.

c. The router sends an Internet Control Message Protocol (ICMP) packet to verify the hardware connection and network layer address. The PC is acting as the console to the router, pinging from one router to another router is taking place.

d. Did all the IP addresses **ping**? _____

e. List four (4) important pieces of information received back from issuing the **ping** command.

_____   _____

_____   _____

Step 5. Examine the results of the ping command.

a. Look at the example of the **ping** command generated by a router:

```
lab-b# ping 192.168.3.1
Type escape sequence to abort.
Sending 5, 100-byte ICMP Echoes to 210.93.105.1, timeout is 2 seconds: .!!!!
Success rate is 80 percent (4/5), round-trip min/avg/max = 68/68/168 ms
```

b. What does the exclamation point (!) indicate?

_____

c. What does the period (.) indicate? _____

d. What does the **ping** command test for?

_____

Step 6. Configure the workstations.

a. The configuration for the host connected to the GAD router is

```
IP address: 192.168.14.2
IP subnet mask: 255.255.255.0
Default gateway: 192.168.14.1
```

b. The configuration for the host connected to the BHM router is

```
IP address: 192.168.16.2
IP subnet mask: 255.255.255.0
Default gateway: 192.168.16.1
```

Step 7. Ping from the workstation.

a. From Windows go to **Start>Programs>Accessories>Command Prompt**. This will open a Command Prompt window.

b. To test that the TCP/IP stack and default gateway on the workstation are configured and working properly, use the MS-DOS window to ping the routers by issuing the following commands:

```
C:\> ping 192.168.14.1
```

The ping should respond with successful results. If not, check the configurations on the host and directly connected router.

Step 8. Test Layer 3 connectivity.

a. Using the command prompt, enter **ping** and the IP address of all routers interfaces.

This tests Layer 3 connectivity between the workstation and the routers.

b. Is the output from the workstation's **ping** command the same as the output from the **ping** command from a router?

Step 9. From the Host telnet to the directly connected router.

a. Telnet to the connected router by typing telnet and the default gateway IP address of the router.

```
C:\> telnet 192.168.14.1
```

b. The password prompt will appear, enter **cisco**.

Step 10. Perform an extended ping.

a. Enter privileged EXEC mode by typing **enable** and then the password **class**.

Type **ping** and press **Enter**. Fill out the rest of the prompts as you see them.

```
Protocol [ip]:
Target IP address: 192.168.16.1
Repeat count [5]: 50
Datagram size [100]:
Timeout in seconds [2]:
Extended commands [n]:
Sweep range of sizes [n]:
Type escape sequence to abort.
Sending 50, 100-byte ICMP Echos to 192.168.16.1, timeout is 2 seconds:
!!!!!!!!!!!!!!!!!!!!!!!!!!!!!!!!!!!!!!!!!!!!!!!!!!!!
Success rate is 100 percent (50/50), round-trip min/avg/max = 32/32/40 ms
GAD#
```

b. Notice how fast the ping response is. What was the average response time?

Step 11. Perform another extended ping.

a. Type **ping** and press **Enter,** fill out the rest of the prompts as you see them.

This time, during the ping, remove the crossover cable from BHM's FastEthernet port after 10 pings have responded.

```
Protocol [ip]:
Target IP address: 192.168.16.1
Repeat count [5]: 50
Datagram size [100]: 1500
Timeout in seconds [2]:
Extended commands [n]:
Sweep range of sizes [n]:
Type escape sequence to abort.
Sending 50, 1500-byte ICMP Echos to 192.168.16.1, timeout is 2 seconds:
!!!!!!!!!!!!!!!!!U.U..........!!!!!!!!!!!!!!!!!!!!!!
Success rate is 72 percent (36/50), round-trip min/avg/max = 432/434/464 ms
GAD#
```

b. What does the output from this extended ping say?

---

c. Try doing this with a standard ping. Can the cable be removed before the ping is over?

_____

d. What was the result of increasing the datagram size in the extended ping?

_____

Step 12. Perform an extended ping from the host.

a. Exit the Telnet session and return to the host MS-dos prompt. Type **ping** and hit **Enter**.

b. Does the extended ping work the same way on the router as on the host?

_____

At the MS-dos prompt,

```
C:\>ping 192.168.16.1-n 25
```

You should see 25 responses from the command.

c. Experiment with other combinations of the extended ping commands on both the router and the host.

Upon completion of the previous steps, log off (by typing **exit**) and turn the router off.

Lab 4.2.5b: Connectivity Tests—Traceroute

Figure 4-7 Topology for Lab 4.2.5b

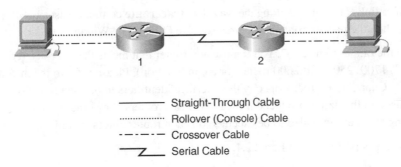

Straight-Through Cable
.... Rollover (Console) Cable
– – – – – Crossover Cable
‾‾‾⁄‾‾‾ Serial Cable

Table 4-17 Lab Equipment Configuration: Part I

Router Designation	Router Name	RIP Network Statements
Router 1	GAD	192.168.14.0 192.168.15.0
Router 2	BHM	192.168.15.0 192.168.16.0

The routing protocol on both routers is RIP.

The enable secret password for both routers is **class**.

The enable, vty, and console password for both routers is **cisco**.

Table 4-18 Lab Equipment Configuration: Part II

Router Designation	Router Name	FastEthernet 0 Address	Interface Type Serial 0	Serial 0 Address
Router 1	GAD	192.168.14.1	DCE	192.168.15.1
Router 2	BHM	192.168.16.1	DTE	192.168.15.2

The subnet mask for all addresses on all routers is 255.255.255.0.

The Serial 1 interface is inactive on both routers.

Objectives

- Use the **traceroute** Cisco IOS Software command from the source router to the destination router.
- Use the **tracert** MS-DOS command from the source workstation to the destination router. Verify that the network-layer between source, destination and each router along the way is working properly.
- Retrieve information to evaluate the end-to-end path reliability.
- Determine delays at each point over the path and whether the host can be reached.

Background/Preparation

The **traceroute** IOS command, abbreviated as **trace**, is excellent utility for troubleshooting the path that a packet takes through an internetwork of routers.

It can help to isolate problem links and routers along the way. The **traceroute** command uses ICMP packets and the error message generated by routers when the packet exceeds its Time-To-Live (TTL). The Windows version of this command is **tracert**.

Cable a network similar to the one in Figure 4-7. You can use any router that meets the interface requirements displayed in the diagram (that is, 800, 1600, 1700, 2500 and 2600 routers or a combination). Please refer to the information in Appendix B, "Router Interface Summary Chart," to correctly specify the interface identifiers to be used based on the equipment in your lab. The configuration output used in this lab is produced from 1721 series routers. Any other router used may produce slightly different output. The following steps are intended to be executed on each router unless specifically instructed otherwise.

Start a HyperTerminal session as performed in Lab 2.2.4.

Please refer to and implement the procedure documented in Appendix C, "Erasing and Reloading the Router," on all routers before continuing with this lab.

Step 1. Configure the routers.

a. If you have trouble configuring hostname or passwords, refer to Lab 3.1.3, "Configuring Router Passwords." If you have trouble configuring interfaces or the routing protocol, refer to Lab 3.1.5, "Configuring a Serial Interface," Lab 3.1.7, "Configuring an Ethernet Interface," and Lab 3.2.7, "Configuring Host Tables."

b. This lab requires that IP hostnames be configured.

c. Verify the routers configurations by performing a **show running-config** on each router. If not correct, fix any configuration errors and re-verify.

Step 2. Configure the workstations.

a. The configuration for the host connected to the GAD router is

```
IP address: 192.168.14.2
IP subnet mask: 255.255.255.0
Default gateway: 192.168.14.1
```

b. The configuration for the host connected to the BHM Router is

```
IP address: 192.168.16.2
IP subnet mask: 255.255.255.0
Default gateway: 192.168.16.1
```

Step 3. Ping from the workstation

a. From a Windows host, click **Start > Programs > Accessories > Command Prompt**. This opens a Command Prompt window.

b. To test that the TCP/IP stack and default gateway on the workstation are configured and working properly, use the MS DOS window to ping the routers by issuing the following command:

```
C:\> ping 192.168.14.1
```

c. The ping should respond with successful results. If not, check the configurations on the host and directly connected router.

Step 4. Test Layer 3 connectivity.

a. Using the command prompt, enter **ping** and the IP address of all routers interfaces.

This tests Layer 3 connectivity between the workstation and the routers.

b. Is the output from the workstation's **ping** command the same as the output from the **ping** command from a router?

_____

Step 5. Log in to the router in user mode.

Log in to the GAD user EXEC prompt.

Step 6. Discover the traceroute options.

a. Type **traceroute** at the router prompt and press **Enter**.

b. With what did the router respond? _____

Step 7. Use the help function with traceroute.

a. Enter **traceroute ?** at the router prompt.

b. What did the router respond with? _____

Step 8. Continue discovering of the traceroute options.

a. Enter into the privileged EXEC mode and type **traceroute ?**.

b. What did the router respond with? _____

c. Was there anything different between the two traceroute outputs? _____

d. If you noticed that there was an added option of <cr>, good. This allows an extended ping at the privileged EXEC mode, unavailable at the user EXEC mode.

Step 9. Use the traceroute command.

a. Enter **traceroute ip** *xxx.xxx.xxx.xxx* where *xxx.xxx.xxx.xxx* is the IP address of the target destination. *Note*: Use one of the end routers and **traceroute** to the other end host. The **ip** keyword may be omitted if tracing to an IP address because it is the default.

```
GAD#traceroute 192.168.16.2
The router responds with
Type the escape sequence to abort.
Tracing the route to 192.168.16.2
 1 BHM (192.168.15.2) 16 msec 16 msec 16 msec
   2 192.168.16.2 16 msec 16 msec 12 msec
GAD#
```

b. If the output is not successful, check your router and host configurations.

Step 10. Continue using trace.

Log in to the other routers and repeat the **traceroute** command.

Step 11. Use the tracert command from a workstation.

a. From the console workstation click on **Start > Programs > Accessories > Command Prompt**. An MS-DOS Command Prompt window will open up.

Enter **tracert** and the same IP address used in Step 5.

b. The first hop is the default gateway or the near side router interface on the LAN that the workstation is connected to. List the host names and IP addresses of the routers that the ICMP packet was routed through, as well as any other entries displayed, in Table 4-19.

Table 4-19 Host Name/IP Address Information

Host Name	IP Address

c. There is one more entry in the output of the **tracert** command when the trace is from the computer command prompt to the target host.

Why? _____

_____

Step 12. Trace to Cisco and other common websites.

a. From a Windows host that has Internet access, click **Start> Programs> Accessories> Command Prompt**. An MS-DOS Command Prompt window opens up.

```
C:\>tracert www.cisco.com
C:\>tracert www.yahoo.com
C:\>tracert www.aol.com
```

b. This procedure will show the IP address and the route of the destination.

c. What is the IP address of Cisco.com? _____

d. How many hops did it take to get to Cisco.com? _____

If a packet passes through a router it is considered one (1) hop and the TTL of the packet is decremented by one (1).

Step 13. Compare the IP route traces to Cisco, Yahoo, and AOL.

a. Where are the differences in the traces?

_____

_____

_____

b. Why are they always the same in the beginning?

_____

Upon completion of the previous steps, log off (by typing **exit**) and turn the router off.

Lab 4.2.6: Troubleshooting IP Address Issues

Figure 4-8 Topology for Lab 4.2.6

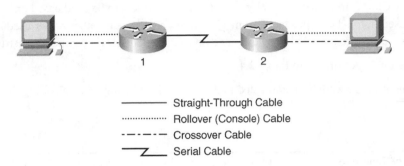

Straight-Through Cable
Rollover (Console) Cable
Crossover Cable
Serial Cable

Table 4-20 Lab Equipment Configuration: Part I

Router Designation	Router Name	RIP Network Statements
Router 1	GAD	192.168.14.0 192.168.15.0
Router 2	BHM	192.168.15.0 192.168.16.0

The routing protocol on both routers is RIP.

The enable secret password for both routers is **class**.

The enable, vty, and console password for both routers is **cisco**.

Table 4-21 Lab Equipment Configuration: Part II

Router Designation	Router Name	FastEthernet 0 Address	Interface Type Serial 0	Serial 0 Address
Router 1	GAD	192.168.14.1	DCE	192.168.16.1
Router 2	BHM	192.168.16.1	DTE	192.168.15.2

The subnet mask for all addresses on all routers is 255.255.255.0.

The Serial 1 interface is inactive on both routers.

Objectives

- Configure two routers and two workstations in a small WAN.
- Troubleshoot problems introduced by incorrect configurations.

Background/Preparation

Cable a network similar to the one in Figure 4-8. You can use any router that meets the interface requirements displayed in the diagram (that is, 800, 1600, 1700, 2500 and 2600 routers or a combination). Please refer to the information in Appendix B, "Router Interface Summary Chart," to correctly specify the interface identifiers to be used based on the equipment in your lab. The configuration output used in this lab is produced from 1721 series routers. Any other router used may produce slightly different output. The following steps are intended to be executed on each router unless specifically instructed otherwise.

Start a HyperTerminal session as performed in Lab 2.2.4.

Please refer to and implement the procedure documented in Appendix C, "Erasing and Reloading the Router," on all routers before continuing with this lab.

Note: Work in teams of two. Team member 1 should configure the GAD router according to Table 4-21 and its attached workstation according to the instructions below. Team member 2 should configure the BHM router and its workstation. Both configurations have errors and will result in IP-related communications problems. Team member 1 will then troubleshoot problems with the BHM router and workstations and Team member 2 will troubleshoot problems with the GAD router and workstations.

Step 1. Configure the routers.

a. If you have trouble configuring hostname or passwords, refer to Lab 3.1.3, "Configuring Router Passwords." If you have trouble configuring interfaces or the routing protocol, refer to Lab 3.1.5, "Configuring a Serial Interface," Lab 3.1.7, "Configuring an Ethernet Interface," and Lab 3.2.7, "Configuring Host Tables."

b. This lab requires that IP host names be configured.

c. Verify the routers configurations by performing a **show running-config** on each router. If not correct, fix any configuration errors and reverify.

Step 2. Configure the workstations.

a. The configuration for the host connected to the GAD Router is

```
IP Address: 192.168.14.2
IP subnet mask: 255.255.255.0
Default gateway: 192.168.14.2
```

b. The configuration for the host connected to the BHM Router is

```
IP Address: 192.168.16.2
IP subnet mask: 255.255.255.0
Default gateway: 192.168.16.1
```

Step 3. Ping from the workstation.

a. From Windows host, click **Start> Programs> Accessories> Command Prompt**. This opens a Command Prompt window.

b. To test that the TCP/IP stack and default gateway on the workstation are configured and working properly, use the MS-DOS window to ping the router by issuing the following command:

```
C:\> ping 192.168.14.1
```

The ping should respond with unsuccessful results. So check configurations on the host and routers.

c. Two problems were introduced into the configurations. Correct the configurations to allow pinging of all the interfaces on the hosts and routers.

What was problem 1? _____

What was problem 2? _____

Upon completion of the previous steps, log off (by typing **exit**) and turn the router off.

Managing Cisco IOS Software

The following labs are in this chapter:

Lab TI	Title
5.1.3	Using the **boot system** Command
5.1.5	Troubleshooting Configuration Register Boot Problems
5.2.3	Managing Configuration Files with TFTP
5.2.5	Managing IOS Images with TFTP
5.2.6a	Password Recovery Procedures
5.2.6b	Managing IOS Images with ROMmon and Xmodem

Lab 5.1.3: Using the boot system Command

Figure 5-1 Topology for Lab 5.1.3

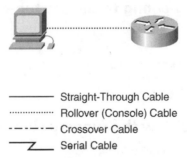

———— Straight-Through Cable
················· Rollover (Console) Cable
— · — · — Crossover Cable
—Z— Serial Cable

Table 5-1 Lab Equipment Configuration

Router Designation	Router Name	Enable Secret Password	Enable/vty/Console Password
Router 1	GAD	class	cisco

Objectives

- Display information about the Cisco IOS Software image that is currently running.

- Determine where the IOS image is booting from.

- Check the amount of RAM, Flash memory, and nonvolatile RAM (NVRAM) memory the router has.

- Check the IOS image and Flash memory for space used and availability.

- Document the parts of the IOS image filename.

- Check and document the configuration register settings related to the boot method.

- Document a fallback boot sequence.

Background/Preparation

Cable a network similar to the one in Figure 5-1. You can use any router that meets the interface requirements in Figure 5-1 (that is, 800, 1600, 1700, 2500, and 2600 routers or a combination). Refer to the information in Appendix B, "Router Interface Summary," to correctly specify the interface identifiers based on the equipment in your lab. The 1721 series routers produced the configuration output in this lab. Any other router might produce slightly different output.

Start a HyperTerminal session as you did in Lab 2.2.4, "Establishing a Console Session with HyperTerminal." Implement the procedure documented in Appendix C, "Erasing and Reloading the Router," before continuing with this lab.

Step 1. Log in to the router.

Connect to the router and log in.

Step 2. Enter privileged EXEC mode.

Type **enable** at the command prompt.

Step 3. Save the existing running-config to the startup-config.

At the privileged EXEC command prompt, enter the following:

```
Router#copy running-config startup-config
Destination filename [startup-config]? Enter
```

This step saves the current blank configuration.

Step 4. Configure the router and view the running configuration file.

a. Configure the router with the information in Table 5-1.

b. Enter **show running-config** at the router prompt. The router displays information on the running configuration file stored in RAM.

c. Do you see the configuration that you just entered? _____

Step 5. Show information about the backup configuration file.

a. Enter **show startup-config** at the router prompt. The router displays information on the backup configuration file stored in NVRAM.

b. Do you see the configuration that you just entered?

c. If not, why? _____

d. What command would make the running-config file and startup-config file identical?

_____

e. Why is the startup-config file so important?

_____

f. Is there any indication of the configuration register setting?

_____

Step 6. Display the IOS version and other important information.

a. Enter **show version** at the router prompt.

The router returns information about the IOS image that is running in RAM.

b. What is the IOS version and rev level? _____

c. What is the name of the system image (IOS) file? _____

d. Where was the router IOS image booted from? _____

e. What type of processor and how much RAM does this router have?

_____

f. What kind of router (platform type) is this? _____

g. The router backup configuration file is stored in NVRAM. How much NVRAM does this router have?

_____

h. The router operating system (IOS) is stored in Flash memory. How much Flash memory does this router have?

_____

i. What is the configuration register set to? What boot type does this setting specify?

_____

Step 7. Create the statements to perform the following functions.

a. Assuming that in the previous step, the configuration register was set to 0x2102, write the configuration mode commands to specify that the IOS image should be loaded from the following:

ROM monitor: _____

Flash (without checking for **boot system** commands):

_____

Flash (checks for **boot system** commands first):

_____

ROM IOS: _____

Note: ROM IOS is the default on older platforms.

b. If the router were in ROM monitor (ROMmon) mode, what command would boot the IOS?

_____

Step 8. Show information about the Flash memory device.

a. Enter **show flash** at the router prompt.

The router responds with information about the Flash memory and what IOS image files are stored there.

b. Document the following information:

How much Flash memory is available and used? _____

What is the file that is stored in Flash memory? _____

What is the size in bytes of the Flash memory? _____

Step 9. Specify a fallback boot sequence.

a. Write the **boot system** command to specify that the IOS image should be loaded from the following:

Flash memory: _____

A Trivial File Transfer Protocol (TFTP) server:

_____

ROM: _____

Will this be a full IOS image? _____

e. To ensure that these commands are available for the router to use the next time you restart it, which task would need to be completed before reloading or power cycling the router?

When you finish the preceding steps, log off (by typing **exit**) and turn off the router.

Lab 5.1.5: Troubleshooting Configuration Register Boot Problems

Figure 5-2 Topology for Lab 5.1.5

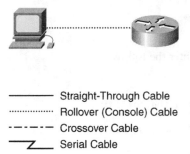

—————— Straight-Through Cable
··············· Rollover (Console) Cable
– – – – – Crossover Cable
⌐‾Z_ Serial Cable

Table 5-2 Lab Equipment Configuration

Router Designation	Router Name	Enable Secret Password	Enable/vty/Console Password
Router 1	GAD	class	cisco

Objectives

- Check and document the configuration register settings related to the boot method.
- Configure the router to boot using the configuration file in NVRAM, and reload the router.

Background/Preparation

Cable a network similar to the one in Figure 5-2. You can use any router that meets the interface requirements in Figure 5-2 (that is, 800, 1600, 1700, 2500, and 2600 routers or a combination). Refer to the information in Appendix B, "Router Interface Summary," to correctly specify the interface identifiers based on the equipment in your lab. The 1721 series routers produced the configuration output in this lab. Any other router might produce slightly different output.

Start a HyperTerminal session as you did in Lab 2.2.4.

Implement the procedure documented in Appendix C, "Erasing and Reloading the Router," before continuing with this lab.

Step 1. Log in to the router.

Connect to the router and log in.

Step 2. Configure the router name and configuration register setting.

Enter the following commands:

```
Router>enable
Router#configure terminal
Router(config)#hostname GAD
GAD(config)#config-register 0x2142
GAD(config)#exit
```

Step 3. Save the existing running-config to the startup-config.

At the privileged EXEC command prompt, enter the following:

```
GAD#copy running-config startup-config
Destination filename [startup-config]? Enter
```

Step 4. Restart the router.

At the privileged EXEC command prompt, enter the following:

```
GAD#reload
Proceed with reload? [confirm] Enter
After the reload, the router responds with the following:
--- System Configuration Dialog ---
Would you like to enter the initial configuration dialog? [yes/no]: n
Type n and press Enter.
```

Step 5. View the running configuration file.

a. Enter **show running-config** at the privileged EXEC mode prompt. The router displays information on the running configuration file stored in RAM.

b. Do you see the configuration that you just entered? _____

Step 6. Reload the saved configuration.

At the privileged EXEC command prompt, enter the following:

```
Router#copy startup-config running-config
Destination filename [running-config]? Enter
```

Step 7. Display the IOS version and other important information.

a. Enter **show version** at the router prompt.

The router will display information about the IOS image that is running in RAM.

b. Notice that the end of the output shows a configuration register setting of 0x2142. This setting is the problem. The setting configures the router to ignore the Startup configuration file on bootup. The setting will be useful to boot up in the password recovery mode.

Step 8. Change the configuration register to load the Startup Configuration file from NVRAM, save, and reload the router.

Enter global configuration mode and enter the following commands:

```
Router>enable
GAD#configure terminal
GAD(config)#config-register 0x2102
GAD(config)#exit
GAD#copy running-config startup-config
Destination filename [startup-config]? Enter
GAD#reload
Proceed with reload? [confirm]Enter
```

Step 9. Verify the configuration register setting and log out of the router.

Once the router reboots, it should look to NVRAM for the Startup Configuration. Verify it by issuing the command **show version**.

```
GAD#show version
```

The results will be shown. You should be able to see the config-register 0x2102.

When you finish these steps, log off (by typing **exit**) and turn off the router.

Lab 5.2.3: Managing Configuration Files with TFTP

Figure 5-3 Topology for Lab 5.2.3

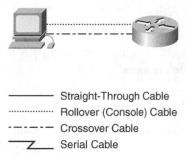

———————— Straight-Through Cable
················· Rollover (Console) Cable
—·—·—· Crossover Cable
——Z—— Serial Cable

Table 5-3 Lab Equipment Configuration

Router Designation	Router Name	FastEthernet 0 Address	Subnet Mask
Router 1	GAD	192.168.14.1	255.255.255.0

The enable secret password for this router is **class**.

The enable, vty, and console password for this router is **cisco**.

Objectives

- Back up a copy of a router's configuration file.
- Reload the backup configuration file from a TFTP server into RAM on a router.
- Save the new running-config to NVRAM.

Background/Preparation

For documentation and recovery purposes, it is important to keep backup copies of router configuration files. You can store them in a central location such as a TFTP server for reference and retrieval if necessary.

Cable a network similar to the one in Figure 5-3. You can use any router that meets the interface requirements in Figure 5-3 (that is, 800, 1600, 1700, 2500, and 2600 routers or a combination). Refer to the information in Appendix B, "Router Interface Summary," to correctly specify the interface identifiers based on the equipment in your lab. The 1721 series routers produced the configuration output in this lab. Any other router might produce slightly different output.

Start a HyperTerminal session as you did in Lab 2.2.4.

Implement the procedure documented in Appendix C, "Erasing and Reloading the Router," before continuing with this lab.

Step 1. Configure the GAD router.

a. If you have trouble configuring the host name, refer to Lab 3.1.3, "Configuring Router Passwords." If you have trouble configuring interfaces, refer to Lab 3.2.7, "Configuring Host Tables."

b. Verify the router's configuration by performing a **show running-config**. If it is not correct, fix any configuration errors and verify.

Step 2. Configure the workstation.

A workstation with the TFTP server software must be available for this lab. Verify that the software is available. If not, ask your instructor for assistance. The configuration for the TFTP server host connected to the GAD router is as follows:

```
IP address: 192.168.14.2
IP subnet mask: 255.255.255.0
Default gateway: 192.168.14.1
```

Confirm that the host has accepted the new IP settings with the **winipcfg** command (Windows 9x) or the **ipconfig /all** command (Windows NT/200/XP) at the workstation command prompt.

Step 3. Start and configure the Cisco TFTP server.

Start the TFTP server. If the computer is properly connected, there is no configuration for the Cisco TFTP server needed (see Figure 5-4). An alternative freeware TFTP server can also be used, such as tftpd32, which can be downloaded from http://tftpd32.jounin.net/.

Figure 5-4 Cisco TFTP Server Setup

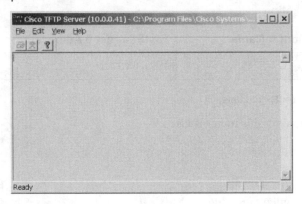

Step 4. Verify connectivity by pinging the TFTP server.

Ping the TFTP server from the GAD router.

If the ping fails, review the host and router configurations to resolve the problem.

Step 5. Copy the running-config to the TFTP server.

a. Before copying the files, verify that the TFTP server is running.

b. Record the IP address of the TFTP server.

_____

c. Start the process by issuing the **copy running-config tftp** command from the privileged EXEC prompt, and then follow the prompts:

```
GAD#copy running-config tftp
Address or name of remote host []? 192.168.14.2
Destination filename [gad-confg]? startup-config
!!
667 bytes copied in 0.036 secs (18528 bytes/sec)
```

Step 6. Verify the transfer to the TFTP server.

Check the TFTP server log file by clicking **View > Log File.** The output should be similar to the following:

```
Mon Sep 16 14:10:08 2003: Receiving 'startup-config' file from 192.168.14.1 in binary mode
Mon Sep 16 14:11:14 2003: Successful.
```

Step 7. Copy the startup-config from the TFTP server.

a. Now that you have backed up the startup-config, you need to test this image by restoring the file to the router. First, verify that the TFTP server is running, that it is sharing a network with the router, and that the router can reach it by pinging its IP address.

Assume that the configuration on the GAD router has become corrupt. To simulate this, change the hostname of the router from GAD to "Router".

```
GAD(config)# hostname  Router
```

b. What is the IP address of the TFTP server? _____

c. Complete the following to copy the startup-config file from the TFTP server to the router.

```
Router#copy tftp running-config
Address or name of remote host []? 192.168.14.2
Source filename []? startup-config
Destination filename [running-config]? [Enter]
Accessing tftp://192.168.14.2/startup-config...
Loading startup-config from 192.168.14.2 (via FastEthernet0): !
[OK - 667 bytes]
667 bytes copied in 9.584 secs (70 bytes/sec)
GAD#
```

Step 8. Save the new running-config.

Save the new running config to NVRAM using the following command:

```
GAD#copy running-config startup-config
Destination filename [startup-config]?[Enter]
Building configuration...
[OK]
```

Step 9. Test the restored file.

Issue the **show startup-config** command to verify the entire configuration.

When you finish these steps, log off (by typing **exit**) and turn off the router.

Lab 5.2.5: Managing IOS Images with TFTP

Figure 5-5 Topology for Lab 5.2.5

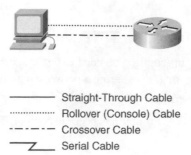

——————— Straight-Through Cable
·················· Rollover (Console) Cable
— · — · — · — Crossover Cable
⎯⎯Ζ⎯⎯ Serial Cable

Table 5-4 Lab Equipment Configuration

Router Designation	Router Name	FastEthernet 0 Address	Subnet Mask
Router 1	GAD	192.168.14.1	255.255.255.0

Objectives

- Back up a copy of a router's IOS from Flash memory to a TFTP server.

- Reload the backup IOS image from a TFTP server into Flash memory on a router.

Background/Preparation

For recovery purposes, it is important to keep backup copies of router IOS images. You can store them in a central location such as a TFTP server and retrieve them if necessary.

Cable a network similar to the one in Figure 5-5. You can use any router that meets the interface requirements in Figure 5-5 (that is, 800, 1600, 1700, 2500, and 2600 routers or a combination). Refer to the information in Appendix B, "Router Interface Summary," to correctly specify the interface identifiers based on the equipment in your lab. The 1721 series routers produced the configuration output in this lab. Any other router might produce slightly different output.

Start a HyperTerminal session as you did in Lab 2.2.4.

Step 1. Configure the GAD router.

a. If you have trouble configuring the host name, refer to Lab 3.1.3. If you have trouble configuring interfaces, refer to Lab 3.2.7.

b. Verify the router's configuration by performing a **show running-config** on the router. If it is not correct, fix any configuration errors and re-verify.

Step 2. Configure the workstation.

A workstation with the TFTP server software must be available for this lab. Verify that the software is available. If not, ask your instructor for assistance. The configuration for the TFTP server host connected to the GAD router is as follows:

```
IP address: 192.168.14.2
IP subnet mask: 255.255.255.0
Default gateway: 192.168.14.1
```

Confirm that the host has accepted the new IP settings with the **ipconfig /all** command at the workstation command prompt.

Step 3. Collect information to document the router.

a. Issue the **show version** command.

b. What is the current value of the config register? _____0x _____

c. How much Flash memory does this router have? _____

d. Is there at least 4 MB (4096 KB) of Flash memory? _____
   (This lab requires at least 4 MB of Flash memory.)

e. What is the version number of boot ROM? _____

f. Is the boot ROM version 5.2 or later? _____
   (This lab requires 5.2 or later.)

Step 4. Collect more information to document the router.

a. Issue the **show flash** command.

b. Is there a file already stored in Flash memory?

_____

c. If so, what is the exact name of that file? _____

d. How much Flash memory is available (unused)?

_____

Step 5. Start and configure the Cisco TFTP server.

Check with your instructor about the IP address of the Cisco TFTP server (see Figure 5-6). An alternative freeware TFTP server can also be used such as tftpd32 which can be downloaded from http://tftpd32.jounin.net/.

Figure 5-6 Cisco TFTP Server

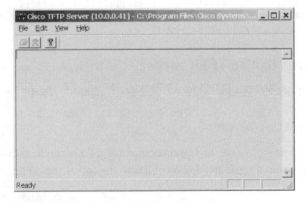

Step 6. Verify connectivity by pinging the TFTP server.

Ping the TFTP server from the GAD router.

If the ping fails, review the host and router configurations to resolve the problem.

Step 7. Prepare for copying the IOS to the TFTP server.

a. Before copying the files, verify that the TFTP server is running.

b. What is the IP address of the TFTP server? _____

c. From the console session, enter **show flash**.

d. What is the name and length of the IOS image stored in Flash memory?

_____

e. What attributes can you identify from codes in the IOS filename?

_____

Step 8. Write the configuration mode commands to specify that the IOS image should be loaded from the following:

Flash memory: _____

TFTP server: _____

ROM: _____

Will it be a full IOS image? _____

Step 9. Copy the IOS image to the TFTP server.

From the console session in privileged EXEC mode, enter the **copy flash tftp** command. At the prompt, enter the IP address of the TFTP server.

```
GAD#copy flash tftp
Source filename [ ]? flash:c1700-y-mz.122-11.T.bin
Address or name of remote host [ ]? 192.168.14.2
Destination filename [c1700-y-mz.122-11.T.bin]? y
```

After entering this command and answering the process requests, you should see the following output on the console. The process may take a few minutes depending on the size of the image. Do *not* interrupt this process!

```
!!!!!!!!!!!!!!!!!!!!!!!!!!!!!!!!!!!!!!!!!!!!!!!!!!!!!!!!!!!!!!!!!!!!!!!!!!!!!!!!
!!!!!!!!!!!!!!!!!!!!!!!!!!!!!!!!!!!!!!!!!!!!!!!!!!!!!!!!!!!!!!!!!!!!!!!!!!!!!!!!
!!!!!!!!!!!!!!!!!!!!!!!!!!!!!!!!!!!!!!!!!!!!!!!!!!!!!!!!!!!!!!!!!!!!!!!!!!!!!!!!
!!!!!!!!!!!!!!!!!!!!!!!!!!!!!!!!!!!!!!!!!!!!
4284648 bytes copied in 34.012 secs (125975 bytes/sec)
```

Step 10. Verify the transfer to the TFTP server.

a. Check the TFTP server log file by clicking **View > Log File.** The output should look something like the following:

```
Mon Sep 16 14:10:08 2003: Receiving 'c1700-y-mz.122-11.T.bin' in binary mode
Mon Sep 16 14:11:14 2003: Successful.
```

b. Verify the Flash memory image size in the TFTP server directory. To locate it, choose **View > Options**. This command shows the TFTP server root directory. It should be similar to the following, unless the default directories were changed:

```
C:\Program Files\Cisco Systems\Cisco TFTP Server
```

c. Locate this directory using Windows Explorer or My Computer and look at the detail listing of the file. The file length in the **show flash** command should be the same file size as the file stored on the TFTP server. If the file sizes are not identical, check with your instructor.

Step 11. Copy the IOS image from the TFTP server.

a. Now that the IOS image is backed up, you must test it and restore IOS to the router. Verify again that the TFTP server is running, that it is sharing a network with the router, and that the router can reach it by pinging the TFTP server IP address.

b. Record the IP address of the TFTP server: _____

c. To start the actual copying, from the privileged EXEC prompt, type the following:

```
GAD#copy tftp flash
Address or name of remote host [ ]?192.168.14.2
Source filename []?c1700-y-mz.122-11.T.bin
Destination filename [c1700-y-mz.122-11.T.bin]? Enter
%Warning:There is a file already existing with this name
Do you want to over write? [confirm] Enter
Accessing tftp://192.168.14.2/c1700-y-mz.122-11.T.bin...
Erase flash: before copying? [confirm] Enter
Erasing the flash filesystem will remove all files! Continue? [confirm] Enter
Erasing device... eeeeeeeeeeeeeeeeeeeeeeeeeeeeeeeeeeeeeeeeeeeeeeeeeeeeeeeeeeeee
eeeeeeeeeeeeeeeeeeeeeeeeeeeeeeeeeeeeeeeeeeeeeeeeeeeeeeeeeeeeeeee ...erased
Erase of flash: complete
Loading c1700-y-mz.122-11.T.bin from 192.168.14.2 (via FastEthernet0):!!!!!!!!!!!
!!!!!!!!!!!!!!!!!!!!!!!!!!!!!!!!!!!!!!!!!!!!!!!!!!!!!!!!!!!!!!!!!!!!!!!!!!!!!!!!!!!!!
!!!!!!!!!!!!!!!!!!!!!!!!!!!!!!!!!!!!!!!!!!!!!!!!!!!!!!!!!!!!!!!!!!!!!!!!!!!!!!!!!!!!!
!!!!!!!!!!!!!!!!!!!!!!!!!!!!!!!!!!
[OK - 4284648 bytes]
Verifying checksum...  OK (0x9C8A)
4284648 bytes copied in 26.584 secs (555739 bytes/sec)
```

d. The router might prompt you to erase Flash memory. Will the image fit in the available Flash memory?

_____

e. If you erased the Flash memory, what happened on the router console screen as it was doing so?

_____

f. What is the size of the file being loaded? _____

g. What happened on the router console screen as the file was being downloaded? _____

h. Was the verification successful? _____

i. Was the whole operation successful? _____

Step 12. Test the restored IOS image.

a. To verify that the router image is correct, cycle the router power and observe the startup process to confirm that there were no Flash-memory errors. If there are no errors, then the router's IOS should start correctly.

b. Further verify the IOS image in Flash memory by issuing the **show version** command, which will show output similar to the following:

```
System image file is "flash:c1700-y-mz.122-11.T.bin"
```

When you finish these steps, log off (by typing **exit**) and turn off the router.

Lab 5.2.6a: Password Recovery Procedures

Figure 5-7 Topology for Lab 5.2.6a

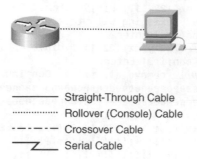

———— Straight-Through Cable
············ Rollover (Console) Cable
--·--·-- Crossover Cable
——Z— Serial Cable

Table 5-5 Lab Equipment Configuration

Router Designation	Router Name	Enable Secret Password	Enable/vty/Console Passwords
Router 1	GAD	class	cisco

Objective

- Gain access to a router with an unknown privileged EXEC mode (enable) password.

Background/Preparation

This lab demonstrates how you gain access to a router with an unknown privileged EXEC mode (enable) password. Anyone with this procedure and access to a console port on a router can change the password and take control of the router. That is why routers must also have physical security to prevent unauthorized access.

Cable a network similar to the one in Figure 5-7. You can use any router that meets the interface requirements in the diagram (that is, 800, 1600, 1700, 2500, and 2600 routers or a combination). Please refer to the information in Appendix B, "Router Interface Summary Chart," to correctly specify the interface identifiers to be used based on the equipment in your lab. The 1721 series routers produced the configuration output in this lab. Any other router might produce slightly different output.

Start a HyperTerminal session as you did in Lab 2.2.4.

Note: Configure the host name and passwords on the router. Let an instructor, lab assistant, or other student configure a basic configuration change the enable secret password, perform **copy running-config startup-config**, and reload the router.

Note: The version of HyperTerminal with Windows 95, 98, NT, and 2000 was developed for Microsoft by Hilgraeve, and some versions might not issue a "break" sequence as required for the Cisco router password-recovery technique. If you have this version, upgrade to HyperTerminal Private Edition (PE), which is free for personal and educational use. You can download the program at http://www.hilgraeve.com.

Step 1. Attempt to log in to the router.

Make the necessary console connections and establish a HyperTerminal session with the router. Attempt to log in to the router using the privileged mode password **class**. Your output should look something like the following:

```
Router>enable
Password:
Password:
Password:
% Bad secrets
Router>
```

Step 2. Document the current configuration register setting.

a. At the user EXEC prompt, type **show ver**.

b. Record the value displayed for configuration register: _____ (for example, 0x2102).

Step 3. Enter ROM monitor mode.

Turn the router off, wait a few seconds, and turn it back on. When the router starts displaying "System Bootstrap, Version …" on the HyperTerminal screen, press the **Ctrl** key and the **Break** key together. The router will boot in ROM monitor mode. Depending on the router hardware, you get one of several prompts, such as **rommon 1 >** or simply **>**.

Step 4. Examine the ROM monitor mode help.

Type **?** at the prompt. The output should be similar to the following:

```
rommon 1 >?
alias            set and display aliases command
boot             boot up an external process
break            set/show/clear the breakpoint
confreg          configuration register utility
context          display the context of a loaded image
dev              list the device table
dir              list files in file system
dis              display instruction stream
help             monitor builtin command help
history          monitor command history
meminfo          main memory information
repeat           repeat a monitor command
reset            system reset
set              display the monitor variables
sysret           print out info from last system return
tftpdnld         tftp image download
xmodem           x/ymodem image download
```

Step 5. Change the configuration register setting to boot without loading the configuration file.

From ROM monitor mode, type **confreg 0x2142** to change the configuration register.

```
rommon 2 > confreg 0x2142
```

Step 6. Restart the router.

a. From ROM monitor mode, type **reset** or power cycle the router.

```
rommon 2 > reset
```

b. Because of the new configuration register setting, the router will not load the configuration file. When the system prompts, "Would you like to enter the initial configuration dialog? [yes]," enter **no** and press **Enter**.

Step 7. Enter privilege EXEC mode and change the password.

a. At the user EXEC mode prompt, type **enable** and press **Enter** to go to privileged EXEC mode without a password.

b. Use the command **copy startup-config running-config** to restore the existing configuration. Because you are already in privileged EXEC mode, you do not need a password.

c. Type **configure terminal** to enter global configuration mode.

d. In global configuration mode, type **enable secret class** to change the secret password.

e. While still in global configuration mode, type **config-register** *xxxxxx*, where *xxxxxx* is the original configuration register value recorded in Step 2, and press **Enter**.

f. Type **Ctrl-Z** to return to privileged EXEC mode.

g. Use the **copy running-config startup-config** command to save the new configuration.

h. Before restarting the router, verify the new configuration setting. From the privileged EXEC prompt, enter the **show version** command and press **Enter**.

i. Verify that the last line of output is the following:

Configuration register is 0x2142 (will be 0x2102 at next reload)

j. Use the **reload** command to restart the router.

Step 8. Verify the new password and configuration.

When the router reloads, the enable password will be **class**.

When you finish these steps, log off (by typing **exit**) and turn the router off.

Lab 5.2.6b: Managing IOS Images with ROMmon and Xmodem

Figure 5-8 Topology for Lab 5.2.6b

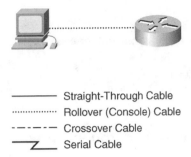

——————— Straight-Through Cable
················· Rollover (Console) Cable
– – – – – Crossover Cable
⌐‾‾z‾ Serial Cable

Objective

- Recover a Cisco router stuck in ROM monitor (ROMmon) mode due to a missing or corrupt IOS or boot Flash memory image.

- Learn how to avoid having to use Xmodem to restore an IOS file

Background/Preparation

You will only need this process in an emergency when a user deletes or erases the IOS and there is no possibility of uploading a new version of the IOS from a TFTP server. The first steps will show you how to avoid needing this procedure.

In case you cannot avoid the procedure, this lab will explain how to use the **xmodem** command at the console to download IOS using ROMmon. You can use Xmodem on a group of routers and in disaster-recovery situations where the router has no valid IOS or boot Flash memory image to boot from. (Hence, it only boots up in ROMmon.) You can also use this procedure where there are no TFTP servers or network connections and a direct PC connection (or a modem connection) to the router's console is the only viable option. Because this procedure relies on the console speed of the router and the serial port of the PC, it can take a long time to download an image. Downloading Cisco IOS Software Release 12.1(16) IP Plus image to a Cisco 1600 series router using a speed of 38,400bps takes approximately 25 minutes. This process is valid for the Cisco 827, 1600, 1700, 2600, 3600, and 3700 series routers.

Cable a network similar to the one in Figure 5-8. You can use any router that meets the interface requirements in Figure 5-8 (that is, 800, 1600, 1700, 2500, and 2600 routers or a combination). Refer to the information in Appendix B, "Router Interface Summary," to correctly specify the interface identifiers based on the equipment in your lab. The 1721 series routers produced the configuration output in this lab. Any other router might produce slightly different output.

Start a HyperTerminal session as you did in Lab 2.2.4.

Implement the procedure documented in Appendix C, "Erasing and Reloading the Router," before continuing with this lab.

Note: To complete this lab, a copy of the recommended Cisco IOS software image (for example, **c1700-y-mz.122-11.T.bin**) must be available on your PC.

Step 1. Enter the ROM Monitor mode

To simulate this, power cycle the router and press **Ctrl-Break** to enter ROM monitor mode. Depending on the router hardware, one of several prompts, such as rommon 1 > or simply >, may appear.

Step 2. Find a valid image in Flash memory.

From the ROM Monitor prompt, issue the **dir flash:** command for each available device, and look for a valid IOS image.

```
rommon 3 > dir flash:
        File size        Checksum    File name
 3307884 bytes (0x804b4c)0x6ba0   c1700-ny-mz.121-6.bin
rommon 4 >
```

Step 3. Recover from the listed images if you see any.

Try to boot from any image that is listed in Step 1. If the image is valid, you will return to normal operation mode:

```
rommon 5 > boot flash:c1700-ny-mz.121-6.bin
program load complete, entry point: 0x80008000, size: 0x804a30
Self decompressing the image : #################################
########...
```

Step 4. Record information using show version.

a. If none of the files are valid, you must download a new one using one of the following procedures. The first step is to record the **show version** information at initial setup. It will provide the information you need about the IOS image name.

```
Cisco Internetwork Operating System Software
IOS (tm) C1700 Software (C1700-Y-M), Version 12.2(11)T,  RELEASE SOFTWARE (fc1)
TAC Support: http://www.cisco.com/tac
Copyright  1986-2002 by cisco Systems, Inc.
Compiled Wed 31-Jul-02 09:08 by ccai
Image text-base: 0x80008124, data-base: 0x807E332C
ROM: System Bootstrap, Version 12.2(7r)XM1, RELEASE SOFTWARE (fc1)
Router uptime is 15 minutes
System returned to ROM by reload
System image file is "flash:c1700-y-mz.122-11.T.bin"
cisco 1721 (MPC860P) processor (revision 0x100) with 29492K/3276K bytes of memory.
Processor board ID FOC06380F0T (479701011), with hardware revision 0000
MPC860P processor: part number 5, mask 2
Bridging software.
X.25 software, Version 3.0.0.
1 FastEthernet/IEEE 802.3 interface(s)
2 Serial(sync/async) network interface(s)
32K bytes of non-volatile configuration memory.
16384K bytes of processor board System flash (Read/Write)
  --More--
Configuration register is 0x2102
```

b. Record the highlighted information in case you need to perform this procedure.

Step 5. Configure the boot register to enter ROMmon mode.

Configure HyperTerminal for 8-N-1 at 9600 bps and connect your PC's serial port to the console port of the router. Once connected, you need to get to the ROMmon prompt (rommon 1>). Typically, if the router's IOS image and boot Flash memory image are both corrupt, the router only comes up in ROMmon mode. If you need to get to the ROMmon prompt, change the configuration register (typically 0x2102, as given by **show version**) to 0x0 as follows:

```
Router>ena
Router#configure terminal
```

Enter configuration commands, one per line. End with **Ctrl-Z**.

```
Router(config)#config-register 0x0
Router(config)#exit
Router#
*Mar  1 00:29:21.023: %SYS-5-CONFIG_I: Configured from console by console
Router#reload
System configuration has been modified. Save? [yes/no]: n
Proceed with reload? [confirm][Enter]
*Mar  1 00:30:32.235: %SYS-5-RELOAD: Reload requested by console.
System Bootstrap, Version 12.2(7r)XM1, RELEASE SOFTWARE (fc1)
TAC Support: http://www.cisco.com/tac
Copyright  2001 by cisco Systems, Inc.
C1700 platform with 32768 Kbytes of main memory
rommon 1 >
```

Step 6. View available commands from the ROMmon prompt.

a. Enter the following at the ROMmon prompt:

```
rommon 1 >?
alias            set and display aliases command
boot             boot up an external process
break            set/show/clear the breakpoint
confreg          configuration register utility
context          display the context of a loaded image
dev              list the device table
dir              list files in file system
dis              display instruction stream
help             monitor builtin command help
history          monitor command history
meminfo          main memory information
repeat           repeat a monitor command
reset            system reset
set              display the monitor variables
sync             write monitor environment to NVRAM
sysret           print out info from last system return
tftpdnld         tftp image download
unalias          unset an alias
unset            unset a monitor variable
xmodem           x/ymodem image download
```

b. This lab uses **confreg** to reset the console speed and **xmodem** to transfer the file.

Step 7. Reset the terminal speed for a faster download.

By specifying a data rate of 115,200bps, for example, you can increase the download rate, reducing download time. Follow these steps to reset the speed on the router:

```
rommon 2 >confreg
Configuration Summary
(Virtual Configuration Register: 0x1820)
enabled are:
break/abort has effect
console baud: 9600
boot: the ROM Monitor
do you wish to change the configuration? y/n  [n]:  y
enable  "diagnostic mode"? y/n  [n]:[Enter]
enable  "use net in IP bcast address"? y/n  [n]: [Enter]
enable  "load rom after netboot fails"? y/n  [n]: [Enter]
enable  "use all zero broadcast"? y/n  [n]: [Enter]
disable "break/abort has effect"? y/n  [n]:  y
enable  "ignore system config info"? y/n  [n]: [Enter]
change console baud rate? y/n  [n]:  y
enter rate: 0 = 9600,  1 = 4800,  2 = 1200,  3 = 2400
```

```
4 = 19200, 5 = 38400, 6 = 57600, 7 = 115200  [0]:  7
change the boot characteristics? y/n  [n]: [Enter]
Configuration Summary
(Virtual Configuration Register: 0x1920)
enabled are:
console baud: 115200
boot: the ROM Monitor
do you wish to change the configuration? y/n  [n]:  y
```

You must reset or power cycle for new config to take effect

```
rommon 3 > reset
```

Note: You must change the HyperTerminal setting to reflect the new console speed of 115,200 instead of 9600. Otherwise, you will see garbled output until you change the settings.

```
System Bootstrap, Version 12.2(7r)XM1, RELEASE SOFTWARE (fc1)
TAC Support: http://www.cisco.com/tac
Copyright  2001 by cisco Systems, Inc.
C1700 platform with 32768 Kbytes of main memory
```

Step 8. Use the xmodem command to request a file from the host.

From the ROMmon prompt, issue the **xmodem** command. However, before issuing the **xmodem** command, *ensure that you have the new IOS image on your PC.*

```
rommon 2 > xmodem
usage: xmodem [-cyrx] <destination filename>
-c  CRC-16
-y  ymodem-batch protocol
-r  copy image to dram for launch
-x  do not launch on download completion
rommon 3 > xmodem c1700-y-mz.122-11.T.bin
Do not start the sending program yet...
   File size       Checksum           File name
   4284648 bytes (0x4160e8)   0x9c8a  c1700-y-mz.122-11.T.bin
WARNING: All existing data in bootflash will be lost!
Invoke this application only for disaster recovery.
Do you wish to continue? y/n  [n]:  y
Ready to receive file c1700-y-mz.122-11.T.bin ...
```

Step 9. Send the file from the HyperTerminal program.

a. From the HyperTerminal program, send the IOS file using the steps outlined in Figure 5-9.

b. Select **Transfer > Send File** and specify the location of the IOS file on the host hard drive, as shown in Figure 5-10.

Figure 5-9 Sending the IOS file using HyperTerminal

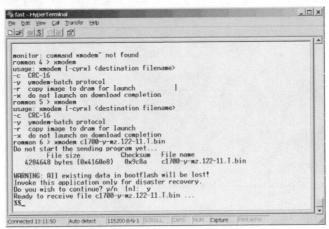

Figure 5-10 Specifying the IOS File Location

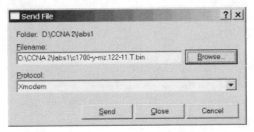

c. Next click **Send** to initiate the file transfer to the router (see Figure 5-11).

Figure 5-11 IOS File Transfer Initiated

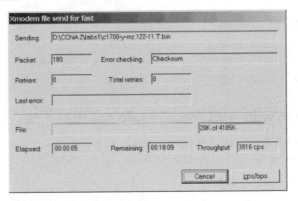

d. As the transfer progresses, it will look like Figure 5-12.

e. When finished, the transfer will look like Figure 5-13.

Figure 5-12 IOS File Transfer Progress

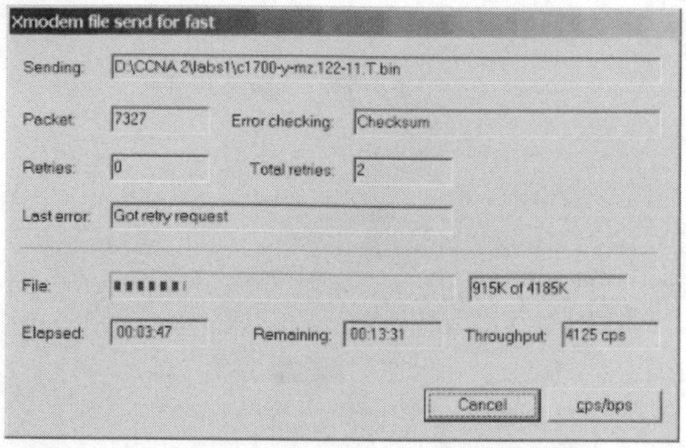

Figure 5-13 IOS File Transfer Complete

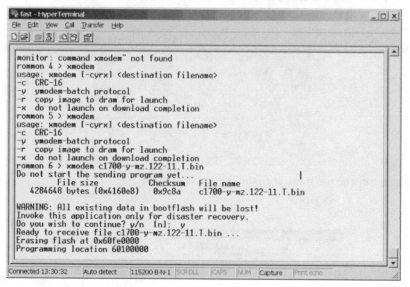

f. When the process is finished, the router reloads.

Step 10. Reset the boot register and the console speed.

a. From the configuration prompt, set the boot register back to 0x2102 or the original setting before the IOS transfer. Use the **config-register** command at the global configuration prompt:

```
Router(config)#config-register 0x2102
Router(config)#exit
Router#show flash

System flash directory:
File  Length   Name/status
  1   4284648  c1700-y-mz.122-11.T.bin
[4285452 bytes used, 12491764 available, 16777216 total]
16384K bytes of processor board System flash (Read/Write)
Reset the console speed in HyperTerminal to 9600.
Router(config)#line con 0
Router(config-line)#speed 9600
Router(config-line)#^Z
```

b. HyperTerminal will stop responding. Reconnect to the router with HyperTerminal using 9600 bps, 8-N-1.

c. Save the configuration to NVRAM on the router.

```
Router#copy running-config startup-config
```

Step 11. Review the new settings.

Reload the router and review the new settings using the **show version** command:

```
Router#show version
Cisco Internetwork Operating System Software
IOS (tm) C1700 Software (C1700-Y-M), Version 12.2(11)T,  RELEASE SOFTWARE (fc1)
TAC Support: http://www.cisco.com/tac
Copyright  1986-2002 by cisco Systems, Inc.
Compiled Wed 31-Jul-02 09:08 by ccai
Image text-base: 0x80008124, data-base: 0x807E332C
ROM: System Bootstrap, Version 12.2(7r)XM1, RELEASE SOFTWARE (fc1)
Router uptime is 12 minutes
System returned to ROM by power-on
System image file is "flash:c1700-y-mz.122-11.T.bin"
cisco 1721 (MPC860P) processor (revision 0x100) with 29492K/3276K bytes of memory
Processor board ID FOC06380F95 (3103823619), with hardware revision 0000
MPC860P processor: part number 5, mask 2
Bridging software.
X.25 software, Version 3.0.0.
1 FastEthernet/IEEE 802.3 interface(s)
2 Serial(sync/async) network interface(s)
32K bytes of non-volatile configuration memory.
16384K bytes of processor board System flash (Read/Write)
 --More—
Configuration register is 0x2102
```

Routing and Routing Protocols

The following labs are in this chapter:

Lab TI	Title
6.1.6	Configuring Static Routes

Lab 6.1.6: Configuring Static Routes

Figure 6-1 Topology for Lab 6.1.6

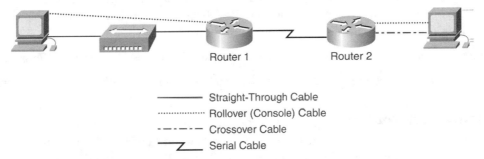

——————— Straight-Through Cable
···················· Rollover (Console) Cable
— · — · — · — Crossover Cable
——Z—— Serial Cable

Table 6-1 Lab Equipment Configuration: Part I

Router Designation	Router Name	Routing Protocol	RIP Network Statements
Router 1	GAD	None	None
Router 2	BHM	None	None

The enable secret password for both routers is **class**.

The enable/vty/console password for both routers is **cisco**.

Table 6-2 Lab Equipment Configuration: Part II

Router Designation	FastEthernet 0 Address	Interface Type Serial 0	Serial 0 Address	IP Host Table Entry
Router 1	192.168.14.1	DCE	192.168.15.1	BHM
Router 2	192.168.16.1	DTE	192.168.15.2	GAD

No Serial 1 address exists for either router.

The subnet mask for all addresses on both routers is 255.255.255.0.

The IP Host Table Entry column contents indicate the name(s) of the other router(s) in the IP host table.

Objective

- Configure static routes between routers to allow data transfer between networks without using dynamic routing protocols.

Background/Preparation

Cable a network similar to the one in Figure 6-1. You can use any router that meets the interface requirements in Figure 6-1 (that is, 800, 1600, 1700, 2500, and 2600 routers or a combination). Refer to the information in Appendix B, "Router Interface Summary," to correctly specify the interface identifiers based on the equipment in your lab. The 1721 series routers produced the configuration output in this lab. Any other router might produce slightly different output. You should execute the following steps on each router unless specifically instructed otherwise.

Start a HyperTerminal session as you did in Lab 2.2.4, "Establishing a Console Session with HyperTerminal."

Implement the procedure documented in Appendix C, "Erasing and Reloading the Router," before continuing with this lab.

Step 1. Configure both routers.

Enter the global configuration mode and configure the host name as shown in Table 6-1. Then, configure the console, virtual terminal, and enable passwords. If you have trouble doing this, refer to Lab 3.1.3, "Configuring Router Passwords." Then, configure the interfaces and IP host tables. If you have trouble doing this, refer to Lab 3.1.3. Do not configure a routing protocol.

Step 2. Configure the workstations with the proper IP address, subnet mask, and default gateway.

a. The configuration for the host connected to the GAD Router is:

```
IP Address 192.168.14.2
IP subnet mask 255.255.255.0
Default gateway 192.168.14.1
```

b. The configuration for the host connected to the BHM Router is:

```
IP Address 192.168.16.2
IP subnet mask 255.255.255.0
Default gateway 192.168.16.1
```

c. Check connectivity between the workstations using **ping**. From the workstation attached to the GAD router, ping the workstation attached to the BHM router.

```
C:\>ping 192.168.16.2

Pinging 192.168.16.2 with 32 bytes of data:

Request timed out.
Request timed out.
Request timed out.
```

```
Request timed out.
Ping statistics for 192.168.16.2:
Packets: Sent = 4, Received = 0, Lost = 4 (100% loss),
Approximate round trip times in milli-seconds:
Minimum = 0ms, Maximum = 0ms, Average = 0ms
```

d. Was it successful? _____

e. Why did the ping fail? _____

Step 3. Check the interface status.

a. Check the interfaces on both routers with the command **show ip interface brief**.

b. Are all the necessary interfaces up?

_____

Step 4. Check the routing table entries.

a. Using the command **show ip route**, view the IP routing table for GAD.

```
GAD>show ip route
output eliminated
Gateway of last resort is not set
C    192.168.14.0/24 is directly connected, FastEthernet0
C    192.168.15.0/24 is directly connected, Serial0
```

b. Using the command **show ip route**, view the IP routing table for BHM.

```
BHM>show ip route
output eliminated
Gateway of last resort is not set
C    192.168.15.0/24 is directly connected, Serial0
C    192.168.16.0/24 is directly connected, FastEthernet0
```

c. Do all the routes you need appear in the routing tables of each router?

_____

d. Based on the output from the **show ip route** command on the GAD and BHM routers, can a host on network 192.168.16.0 connect to a host on network 192.168.14.0?

_____

e. If a route does not appear in the routing table of the router to which the host is connected, the host cannot reach the other host.

Step 5. Add static routes.

a. How can you remedy this situation so that the hosts can ping each other?

Add static routes to each router or run a routing protocol.

b. In global configuration mode, add a static route on Router1 to network 192.168.16.0.

```
GAD(config)#ip route 192.168.16.0 255.255.255.0 192.168.15.2
BHM(config)#ip route 192.168.14.0 255.255.255.0 192.168.15.1
```

c. Why do you need a static route on both routers?

_____

Step 6. Verify the new routes.

a. Using the command **show ip route**, view the IP routing table for GAD.

```
GAD>show ip route
output eliminated
Gateway of last resort is not set
C    192.168.14.0/24 is directly connected, FastEthernet0
C    192.168.15.0/24 is directly connected, Serial0
S    192.168.16.0/24 [1/0] via 192.168.15.2
```

b. Using the command **show ip route**, view the IP routing table for BHM.

```
BHM>show ip route
output eliminated
Gateway of last resort is not set
C    192.168.16.0/24 is directly connected, FastEthernet0
C    192.168.15.0/24 is directly connected, Serial0
S    192.168.14.0/24 [1/0] via 192.168.15.1
```

c. Do all the routes you need appear in the routing tables of each router? _____

d. Based on the output from the **show ip route** command on the GAD and BHM routers, can a host on network 192.168.16.0 connect to a host on network 192.168.14.0 now? _____

Step 7. Try to ping host to host again.

a. Check connectivity between the workstations using **ping**. From the workstation attached to the GAD router, ping the workstation attached to the BHM router.

```
C:\>ping 192.168.16.2
Pinging 192.168.16.2 with 32 bytes of data:
Reply from 192.168.16.2: bytes=32 time=20ms TTL=254
Reply from 192.168.16.2: bytes=32 time=20ms TTL=254
Reply from 192.168.16.2: bytes=32 time=20ms TTL=254
Reply from 192.168.16.2: bytes=32 time=20ms TTL=254
Ping statistics for 192.168.16.2:
Packets: Sent = 4, Received = 4, Lost = 0 (0% loss),
Approximate round trip times in milli-seconds:
Minimum = 20ms, Maximum = 20ms, Average = 20ms
```

b. If the ping was not successful, check the routing table to make sure the static routes are entered correctly.

When you finish the preceding steps, log off (by typing **exit**) and turn the router off.

Distance Vector Routing Protocols

The following labs are in this chapter:

Lab 7.2.2: Configuring RIP

Figure 7-1 Topology for Lab 7.2.2

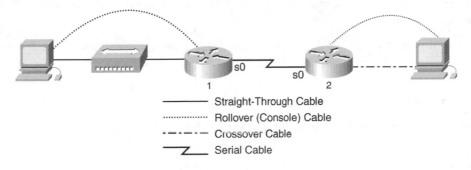

Table 7-1 Lab Equipment Configuration

Router Designation	Router Name	FastEthernet 0 Address	Interface Type	Serial 0 Address
Router 1	GAD	172.16.0.1	DCE	172.17.0.1
Router 2	BHM	172.18.0.1	DTE	172.17.0.2

The enable secret password for both routers is **class**.

The enable, vty, and console passwords for both routers is **cisco**.

The subnet mask for both interfaces on both routers is 255.255.0.0.

Objective

- Set up an IP addressing scheme using Class B networks.
- Configure the dynamic Routing Information Protocol (RIP) on routers.

Background/Preparation

Cable a network similar to the one in Figure 7-1. You can use any router that meets the interface requirements in Figure 7-1 (that is, 800, 1600, 1700, 2500, and 2600 routers or a combination). Refer to the information in Appendix B, "Router Interface Summary," to correctly specify the interface identifiers based on the equipment in your lab. The 1721 series routers produced the configuration output in this lab. Any other router might produce slightly different output. You should execute the following steps on each router unless specifically instructed otherwise.

Start a HyperTerminal session as you did in Lab 2.2.4, "Establishing a Console Session with HyperTerminal."

Implement the procedure documented in Appendix C, "Erasing and Reloading the Router," before continuing with this lab.

Step 1. Configure the routers.

On the routers, enter the global configuration mode and configure the router name as shown in Table 7-1. Then, configure the console, vty, and enable passwords.

If you have trouble doing this, refer to Lab 3.1.3, "Configuring Router Passwords." Next, configure the interfaces according to Table 7-1. If you have problems doing this, refer to Lab 3.2.7, "Configuring Host Tables."

Step 2. Check the routing table entries.

a. Using the command **show ip route**, view the IP routing table for GAD.

```
GAD>show ip route
output eliminated
Gateway of last resort is not set
C    172.16.0.0/16 is directly connected, FastEthernet0
C    172.17.0.0/16 is directly connected, Serial0
```

b. Using the command **show ip route**, view the IP routing table for BHM.

```
BHM>show ip route
output eliminated
Gateway of last resort is not set
C    172.17.0.0/24 is directly connected, Serial0
C    172.18.0.0/24 is directly connected, FastEthernet0
```

Step 3. Configure the routing protocol on the GAD router.

From the global configuration mode, enter the following:

```
GAD(config)#router rip
GAD(config-router)#network 172.16.0.0
GAD(config-router)#network 172.17.0.0
GAD(config-router)#exit
GAD(config)# exit
```

Step 4. Save the GAD router configuration.

```
GAD# copy running-config startup-config
```

Step 5. Configure the routing protocol on the BHM router.

From global configuration mode, enter the following:

```
BHM(config)# router rip
BHM(config-router)# network 172.17.0.0
BHM(config-router)# network 172.18.0.0
BHM(config-router)# exit
BHM(config)# exit
```

Step 6. Save the BHM router configuration.

```
BHM# copy running-config startup-config
```

Step 7. Configure the hosts with the proper IP addresses, subnet masks, and default gateways.

Step 8. Verify that the internetwork is functioning by pinging the FastEthernet interface of the other router.

a. From the host attached to GAD, can you ping the BHM router's FastEthernet interface? _____

b. From the host attached to BHM, can you ping the GAD router's FastEthernet interface? _____

c. If the answer is no for either question, troubleshoot the router configurations to find the error. Then, do the pings again until the answer to both questions is yes.

Step 9. Show the routing tables for each router.

a. From enable (privileged EXEC) mode, examine the routing table entries, using **show ip route** on each router.

b. What are the entries in the GAD routing table?

_____

c. What are the entries in the BHM routing table?

_____

When you finish the preceding steps, log off (by typing **exit**) and turn off the router.

Lab 7.2.6: Troubleshooting RIP

Figure 7-2 Topology for Lab 7.2.6

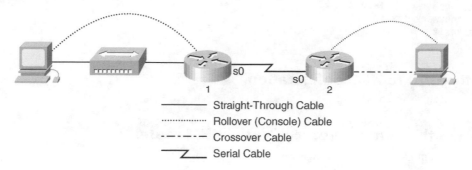

Table 7-2 Lab Equipment Configuration

Router Designation	Router Name	FastEthernet 0 Address	Interface Type	Serial 0 Address
Router 1	GAD	172.16.0.1	DCE	172.17.0.1
Router 2	BHM	172.18.0.1	DTE	172.17.0.2

The enable secret password for both routers is **class**.

The enable, vty, and console passwords for both routers is **cisco**.

The subnet mask for both interfaces on both routers is 255.255.0.0.

Objectives

- Set up an IP addressing scheme using Class B networks.
- Configure RIP on both routers.
- Observe routing activity using the **debug ip rip** command.
- Examine routes using the **show ip route** command.

Background/Preparation

Cable a network similar to the one in Figure 7-2. You can use any router that meets the interface requirements in Figure 7-2 (that is, 800, 1600, 1700, 2500, and 2600 routers or a combination). Refer to the information in Appendix B, "Router Interface Summary," to correctly specify the interface identifiers based on the equipment in your lab. The 1721 series routers produced the configuration output in this lab. Any other router might produce slightly different output. You should execute the following steps on each router unless specifically instructed otherwise.

Start a HyperTerminal session as you did in Lab 2.2.4.

Implement the procedure documented in Appendix C, "Erasing and Reloading the Router," before continuing with this lab.

Step 1. Configure the routers.

On the routers, enter global configuration mode and configure the router name as shown in Table 7-2. Then, configure the console, vty, and enable passwords. If you have problems doing so, refer to Lab 3.1.3. Next, configure the interfaces according to Table 7-2. If you have problems doing so, refer to Lab 3.2.7. "Finally, configure the RIP routing. Refer to Lab 7.2.2, "Configuring RIP," if you need help. Don't forget to save the configurations to the startup configuration file.

Step 2. Configure the hosts with the proper IP addresses, subnet masks, and default gateways.

Step 3. Make sure that routing updates are being sent.

    a. Type the command **debug ip rip** at the privileged EXEC mode prompt. Wait for at least 45 seconds.

    b. Was there any output from the **debug** command? _____

    c. What did the output show? _____

    d. To turn off specific **debug** commands, type the **no** option, as in **no debug ip rip events.** To turn off all **debug** commands, type **undebug all.**

Step 4. Show the routing tables for each router.

    a. From enable (privileged EXEC) mode, examine the routing table entries, using **show ip route** on each router.

    b. What are the entries in the GAD routing table?

    _____

    c. What are the entries in the BHM routing table?

    _____

Step 5. Show the RIP routing table entries for each router.

    a. Enter **show ip route rip**.

    b. List the routes listed in the routing table:

    _____

    c. What is the administrative distance?

    _____

Step 6. Verify that the internetwork is functioning by pinging the FastEthernet interface of the other router.

    a. From the host attached to GAD, can you ping the BHM router's FastEthernet interface?

    _____

    b. From the host attached to BHM, can you ping the GAD router's FastEthernet interface?

    _____

    c. If the answer is no for either question, troubleshoot the router configurations using **show ip route** to find the error. Also, check the workstation IP settings. Then, do the pings again until the answer to both questions is yes.

When you finish these steps, log off (by typing **exit**) and turn off the router.

Lab 7.2.7: Preventing Routing Updates Through an Interface

Figure 7-3 Topology for Lab 7.2.7

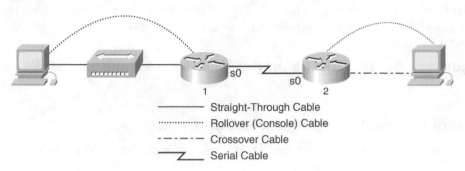

Straight-Through Cable
.... Rollover (Console) Cable
– – – – – Crossover Cable
Serial Cable

Table 7-3 Lab Equipment Configuration

Router Designation	Router Name	Routing Protocol	RIP Network Statements
Router 1	GAD	RIP	192.168.14.0 192.168.15.0
Router 2	BHM	RIP	192.168.15.0 192.168.16.0

The enable secret password for both routers is **class**.

The enable, vty, and console passwords for both routers is **cisco**.

Table 7-4 Lab Equipment IP Address and Interface Configuration

Router Designation	FastEthernet 0 Address	Interface Type Serial 0	Serial 0 Address	IP Host Table Entry
Router 1	192.168.14.1	DCE	192.168.15.1	BHM
Router 2	192.168.16.1	DTE	192.168.15.2	GAD

The subnet mask on all addresses for both routers is 255.255.255.0.

The IP Host Table Entry column contents indicate the name(s) of the other router(s) in the IP host table.

Objectives

- Prevent routing updates through an interface to regulate advertised routes.
- Use the **passive-interface** command and add a default route.

Background/Preparation

This lab will focus on preventing routing updates through an interface to regulate advertised routes and observing the results. To make this work, you must use the **passive-interface** command and add a default route.

Cable a network similar to the one in Figure 7-3. You can use any router that meets the interface requirements in Figure 7-3 (that is, 800, 1600, 1700, 2500, and 2600 routers or a combination). Refer to the information in Appendix B, "Router Interface

Summary," to correctly specify the interface identifiers based on the equipment in your lab. The 1721 series routers produced the configuration output in this lab. Any other router might produce slightly different output. You should execute the following steps on each router unless specifically instructed otherwise. Start a HyperTerminal session as you did in Lab 2.2.4. Implement the procedure documented in Appendix C, "Erasing and Reloading the Router," before continuing with this lab.

Step 1. Configure the routers.

On the routers, enter global configuration mode and configure the router name as shown in Table 7-3. Then, configure the console, vty, and enable passwords. If you have problems doing so, refer to Lab 3.1.3. Next, configure the interfaces according to Table 7-4. If you have problems doing so, refer to Lab 3.2.7. Finally, configure the RIP routing. Refer to Lab 7.2.2 if you need help. Make sure to copy the **running-config** to the **startup-config** on each router.

Step 2. Configure the hosts with the proper IP addresses, subnet masks, and default gateways.

Test your configuration by pinging all interfaces from each host. If the pinging is not successful, troubleshoot your configuration.

Step 3. Check the basic routing configuration.

a. Enter **show ip protocol** on each router.

b. In the configuration, is "Routing protocol is RIP" displayed?

_____

c. Enter the command **show ip route** on both routers. List how the route is connected (directly, RIP), the IP address, and the network or interface in Table 7-5.

Table 7-5 Lab Equipment IP Address and Interface Configuration

GAD	Route Connected	IP Address	Through Network/Interface
BHM	**Route Connected**	**IP Address**	**Through Network/Interface**

Step 4. Observe RIP routing updates.

a. From the GAD router, use the **debug ip rip** command to verify that the router is sending updates out the interface to the BHM router. Look for a section in the output that looks something like the following:

```
GAD#debug ip rip
RIP protocol debugging is on
GAD#
*Mar 1 03:12:17.555: RIP: sending v1 update to 255.255.255.255 via FastEthernet 0 (192.168.14.1)
*Mar 1 03:12:17.555: RIP: build update entries
*Mar 1 03:12:17.555:   network 192.168.15.0 metric 1
*Mar 1 03:12:17.555:   network 192.168.16.0 metric 2
*Mar 1 03:12:17.555: RIP: sending v1 update to 255.255.255.255 via Serial0 (192.168.15.1)
```

```
*Mar 1 03:12:17.555: RIP: build update entries
*Mar 1 03:12:17.555:   network 192.168.14.0 metric 1
*Mar 1 03:12:22.671: RIP: received v1 update from 192.168.15.2 on Serial0
*Mar 1 03:12:22.671:   192.168.16.0 in 1 hops
```

b. Other debug commands that function with RIP are as follows:

```
debug ip rip events
debug ip rip trigger
debug ip rip database
```

c. To turn off specific **debug** commands, type the **no** option, as in **no debug ip rip events.** To turn off all **debug** commands, type **undebug all.**

Step 5. Stop routing updates from GAD to BHM.

a. On the console session for the GAD router, enter global configuration mode and then enter router mode with the command **router rip**. Enter the command **passive-interface serial 0** (refer to Appendix B for your model or router). This step prevents the GAD router from advertising its routes to the BHM router.

b. To confirm this change, use the **debug ip rip events** command on the GAD router. Verify from the output that the router is not sending updates out the interface to the BHM router.

c. Disable the debug output with the **no debug all** command.

d. Also from the BHM router, issue **show ip route** to verify that you have removed the route to the GAD LAN.

e. Attempt to ping from the computers in GAD to the computers in BHM.

f. What response do you get? _____

g. Confirm that the BHM router is still sending updates to GAD. To do this, use the **debug ip rip events** command on the BHM router. Verify from the output that the router is sending updates out the interface to the GAD router.

h. How many routes are being sent? _____

i. Disable the debug output with the **no debug all** command.

Step 6. Add a default route to BHM.

a. Because BHM is not getting routing updates, it does not have a route to the outside world. You must provide it with a default route. A *default route* is the route by which the router sends data if the routing table does not have a specific route to use.

b. From global configuration mode on the BHM router, enter the following:

BHM(config)#**ip route 0.0.0.0 0.0.0.0 192.168.15.1**

c. Verify that the default route is in the BHM routing table by issuing the **show ip route** command.

You should see an output similar to the following:

```
BHM#show ip route
Codes: C - connected, S - static, I - IGRP, R - RIP, M - mobile, B - BGP
    D - EIGRP, EX - EIGRP external, O - OSPF, IA - OSPF inter area
    N1 - OSPF NSSA external type 1, N2 - OSPF NSSA external type 2
    E1 - OSPF external type 1, E2 - OSPF external type 2, E - EGP
    i - IS-IS, L1 - IS-IS level-1, * - candidate default
    U - per-user static route, o - ODR
```

```
Gateway of last resort is 192.168.15.1 to network 0.0.0.0

C  192.168.15.0/24 is directly connected, Serial0
C  192.168.16.0/24 is directly connected, Ethernet0
S*  0.0.0.0/0 [1/0] via 192.168.15.1
BHM#
```

d. Ensure that you can ping from the computers in GAD to the computers in BHM. If not, check the routing tables and interfaces.

When you finish these steps, log off (by typing **exit**) and turn off the router.

Lab 7.2.9: Load Balancing Across Multiple Paths

Figure 7-4 Topology for Lab 7.2.9

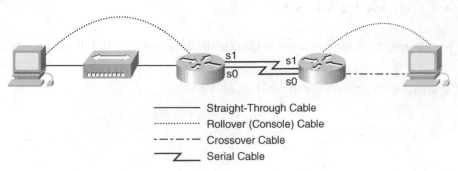

```
                                          s1            s1
                                  ┌─────┐               ┌─────┐
                                        s0            s0
```

——————— Straight-Through Cable
·············· Rollover (Console) Cable
— — — — Crossover Cable
~~z~~ Serial Cable

Table 7-6 Lab Equipment Configuration

Router Designation	Router Name	Routing Protocol	RIP Network Statements
Router 1	GAD	RIP	192.168.14.0 192.168.15.0 192.168.13.0
Router 2	BHM	RIP	192.168.15.0 192.168.16.0 192.168.13.0

The enable secret password for both routers is **class**.

The enable, vty, and console passwords for both routers is **cisco**.

Table 7-7 Lab Equipment IP Address and Interface Configuration

Router Designation	FastEthernet 0 Address	Interface Type Serial 0	Serial 0 Address	Interface Type Serial 1	Serial 1 Address	IP Host Table Entry
Router 1	192.168.14.1	DCE	192.168.15.1	DCE	192.168.13.1	BHM
Router 2	192.168.16.1	DTE	192.168.15.2	DTE	192.168.13.2	GAD

The subnet mask on all addresses for both routers is 255.255.255.0.

The IP Host Table Entry column contents indicate the name(s) of the other router(s) in the IP host table.

Objectives

- Configure load balancing across multiple paths.
- Observe the load-balancing process.

Background/Preparation

Cable a network similar to the one in Figure 7-4. You can use any router that meets the interface requirements in Figure 7-4 (that is, 800, 1600, 1700, 2500, and 2600 routers or a combination). Refer to the information in Appendix B, "Router Interface Summary," to correctly specify the interface identifiers based on the equipment in your lab. The 1721 series routers produced the configuration output in this lab. Any other router might produce slightly different output. You should execute the following steps on each router unless specifically instructed otherwise.

Start a HyperTerminal session as you did in Lab 2.2.4.

Implement the procedure documented in Appendix C, "Erasing and Reloading the Router," before continuing with this lab.

Step 1. Configure the routers.

On the routers, enter global configuration mode and configure the router name as shown in Table 7-6. Then, configure the console, vty, and enable passwords. If you have problems doing so, refer to Lab 3.1.3. Next, configure the interfaces and routing according to Table 7-7. If you have problems doing so, refer to Labs 3.2.7 and 7.2.2. Make sure to copy the **running-config** to the **startup-config** on each router so you won't lose the configuration if the router is power-cycled.

Step 2. Configure the hosts with the proper IP addresses, subnet masks, and default gateways.

Test your configuration by pinging all the interfaces from each host. If the pinging is not successful, troubleshoot your configuration.

Step 3. Check the basic routing configuration.

a. Enter **show ip protocol** on each router.

b. In the configuration, is "Routing protocol is RIP" displayed?

_____

c. Enter the command **show ip route** on both routers . List how the route is connected (directly, RIP), the IP address, and through what network interface. You should list four routes for each. Record the information in Table 7-8.

Table 7-8 IP Route Information for GAD and BHM

GAD	Route Connected	IP Address	Through Network/Interface
BHM	Route Connected	IP Address	Through Network/Interface

d. Circle the evidence of load balancing in the output from **show ip route**.

Step 4. Make sure that the router load-balances on a per-packet basis.

a. Configure the router to load-balance on a per-packet basis. Both serial interfaces must use process switching. *Process switching* forces the router to look in the routing table for the destination network of each routed packet. In contrast, fast switching (the default) stores the initial table lookup in a high-speed cache and uses the information to route packets to the same destination.

b. Enable process switching on both serial interfaces.

```
GAD(config-if)# no ip route-cache

BHM(config-if)# no ip route-cache
```

c. Verify that fast switching is disabled by using **show ip interface** command.

d. Was fast switching disabled? _____

Step 5. Verify per-packet load balancing.

a. Because there are two routes to the destination network, half the packets are sent along one path and half travel over the other. The path selection alternates with each packet.

b. Observe this process by using the **debug ip packet** command on the GAD router.

c. Send 30 ping packets across the network from the host attached to the BHM router to the host attached to the GAD router. This can be done with the with the **ping 192.168.16.2 – n 30** command on the host. As the pings are responded to, the router generates IP packet information. Stop the debug by using the command **undebug all** on the GAD router.

d. Examine and record part of the debug output.

e. What is the evidence of load balancing in the output? _____

Step 6. Verify per-destination load balancing.

a. After verifying per-packet load balancing, configure the router to use per-destination load balancing. Both serial interfaces must use fast switching so that the they can use the route cache after the initial table lookup.

b. Use the command GAD(config-if)# **ip route-cache**.

c. Use **show ip interface** to verify that fast switching is enabled.

d. Is fast switching enabled? _____

e. The router consults the routing table only once per destination; therefore, packets that are part of a packet train to a specific host all follow the same path. Only when a second destination forces another table lookup or when the cached entry expires does the router use the alternate path.

Use the **debug ip packet** command and **ping** across the network. Note which serial interface the router sent the packet on.

f. Examine and record part of the debug output. Which serial interface did the router send the packet on?_____

When you finish these steps, log off (by typing **exit**) and turn off the router.

Lab 7.3.5: Configuring IGRP

Figure 7-5 Topology for Lab 7.3.5

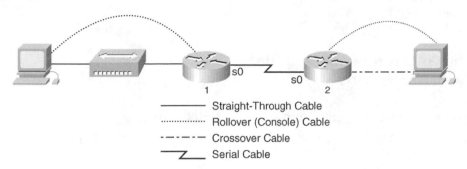

——————— Straight-Through Cable
.... Rollover (Console) Cable
– – – – – Crossover Cable
——ʒ—— Serial Cable

Table 7-9 Lab Equipment Configuration

Router Designation	Router Name	FastEthernet 0 Address	Interface Type	Serial 0 Address
Router 1	GAD	192.168.20.1	DCE	192.168.22.1
Router 2	BHM	192.168.25.1	DTE	192.168.22.2

The subnet mask for both interfaces on both router is 255.255.255.0.

The enable secret password for both routers is **class**.

The enable, vty, and console passwords for both routers is **cisco**.

Objectives

- Set up an IP addressing scheme using Class C networks.
- Configure the Interior Gateway Routing Protocol (IGRP) on the routers.

Background/Preparation

Cable a network similar to the one in Figure 7-5. You can use any router that meets the interface requirements in Figure 7-5 (that is, 800, 1600, 1700, 2500, and 2600 routers or a combination). Refer to the information in Appendix B, "Router Interface Summary," to correctly specify the interface identifiers based on the equipment in your lab. The 1721 series routers produced the configuration output in this lab. Any other router might produce slightly different output. You should execute the following steps on each router unless specifically instructed otherwise.

Start a HyperTerminal session as you did in Lab 2.2.4.

Implement the procedure documented in Appendix C, "Erasing and Reloading the Router," before continuing with this lab.

Step 1. Configure the routers.

On the routers, enter global configuration mode and configure the router name as shown in Table 7-9. Then, configure the console, vty, and enable passwords. If you have problems doing so, refer to Lab 3.1.3. Next, configure the interfaces according to Table 7-9. If you have problems doing so, refer to Lab 3.2.7.

Step 2. Configure the routing protocol on the GAD router.

Configure IGRP using autonomous system (AS) 101 on GAD. Go to the proper command mode and enter the following:

```
GAD(config)#router igrp 101
GAD(config-router)#network 192.168.22.0
GAD(config-router)#network 192.168.20.0
```

Step 3. Save the GAD router configuration.

```
GAD#copy running-config startup-config
```

Step 4. Configure the routing protocol on the BHM router.

Configure IGRP using AS 101 on BHM. Go to the proper command mode and enter the following:

```
BHM(config)#router igrp 101
BHM(config-router)#network 192.168.25.0
BHM(config-router)#network 192.168.22.0
```

Step 5. Save the BHM router configuration.

```
BHM#copy running-config startup-config
```

Step 6. Configure the hosts with the proper IP addresses, subnet masks, and default gateways.

Step 7. Verify that the internetwork is functioning by pinging the FastEthernet interface of the other router.

a. From the host attached to GAD, can you ping the BHM host?

_____

b. From the host attached to BHM, can you ping the GAD host?

_____

c. If the answer is no for either question, troubleshoot the router configurations to find the error. Then, do the pings again until the answer to both questions is yes.

Step 8. Show the routing tables for each router.

a. From enable (privileged EXEC) mode, examine the routing table entries using **show ip route** on each router.

b. What are the entries in the GAD routing table?

_____

_____

c. What are the entries in the BHM routing table?

_____

_____

Step 9. Verify the routing protocol.

a. Type **show ip protocol** on both routers to verify IGRP is running and that it is the only protocol running.

b. Is IGRP the only protocol running on GAD? _____

c. Is IGRP the only protocol running on BHM? _____

Step 10. Verify the IGRP statements in the running configuration of both routers.

a. Use the **show run | begin igrp** command on both routers.

b. List the IGRP part of the configuration for GAD:

_____

_____

_____

Step 11. Verify the IGRP routing updates using the debug ip igrp events command.

a. Type **debug ip igrp events** on the GAD router in privileged EXEC mode.

b. Do the routing updates appear? _____

c. Where are the updates being sent to?

_____

d. Where are the updates being received from?

_____

e. Turn off debugging.

Step 12. Verify the IGRP routing updates using the debug ip igrp transactions command.

a. Type **debug ip igrp transactions** on the GAD router in privileged exec mode.

b. How are the outputs of the two **debug** commands **debug ip igrp events** and **debug ip igrp transactions** different?

_____

_____

c. Turn off debugging.

Step 13. Analyze specific routes.

a. Type **show ip route 192.168.25.0** on the GAD router to see more detail on the route to the 192.168.25.0 network on BHM.

b. What is the total delay for this route?

_____

c. What is the minimum bandwidth? _____

d. What is the reliability of this route?

_____

e. What is the minimum maximum transmission unit (MTU) size for this route?

_____

f. Type **show ip route 192.168.20.0** on the BHM router to see more detail on the route to the 192.168.20.0 network on GAD.

g. What is the total delay for this route?

_____

h. What is the minimum bandwidth? _____

i. What is the reliability of this route? _____

j. What is the minimum MTU size for this route?

_____

When you finish these steps, log off (by typing **exit**) and turn off the router.

Lab 7.3.6: Default Routing with RIP and IGRP

Figure 7-6 Topology for Lab 7.3.6

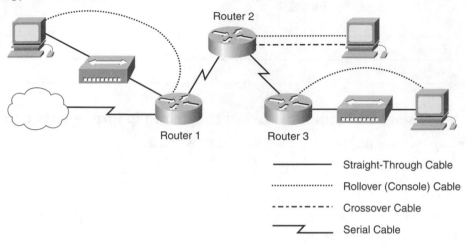

————	Straight-Through Cable
··············	Rollover (Console) Cable
- - - - - - - -	Crossover Cable
—‾Z‾—	Serial Cable

Table 7-10 Lab Equipment Configuration: Part I

Router Designation	Router Name	Routing Protocol	RIP Network Statements
Router 1	Centre	RIP	192.168.2.0 192.168.3.0
Router 2	Boaz	RIP	192.168.1.0 192.168.2.0 192.168.4.0
Router 3	Mobile	RIP	192.168.1.0 192.168.5.0

The enable secret password for all routers is **class**.

The enable, vty, and console passwords for all routers is **cisco**.

Table 7-11 Lab Equipment Configuration: Part II

Router Designation	FastEthernet 0 Address	Interface Type Serial 0	Serial 0 Address	Interface Type Serial 1	Serial 1 Address	IP Host Table Entry
Router 1	192.168.3.1	DTE	192.168.2.2	N/A	No address	Boaz Mobile
Router 2	192.168.4.1	DCE	192.168.1.1	DCE	192.168.2.1	Centre Mobile
Router 3	192.168.5.1	DTE	192.168.1.2	N/A	No address	Boaz Centre

The subnet mask on all addresses for all routers is 255.255.255.0.

The IP Host Table Entry column contents indicate the name(s) of the other router(s) in the IP host table.

Objective

- Configure a default route and use RIP to propagate this default information to other routers.
- Migrate the network from RIP to IGRP.
- Configure default routing to work with IGRP.

Background/Preparation

In this lab, you will configure a default route and use RIP to propagate this default information to other routers. When this configuration is working properly, you will migrate the network from RIP to IGRP and configure default routing to work with that protocol as well.

Cable a network similar to the one in Figure 7-6. You can use any router that meets the interface requirements in Figure 7-6 (that is, 800, 1600, 1700, 2500, and 2600 routers or a combination). Refer to the information in Appendix B, "Router Interface Summary," to correctly specify the interface identifiers based on the equipment in your lab. The 1721 series routers produced the configuration output in this lab. Any other router might produce slightly different output. You should execute the following steps on each router unless specifically instructed otherwise.

Start a HyperTerminal session as you did in Lab 2.2.4.

Implement the procedure documented in Appendix C, "Erasing and Reloading the Router," before continuing with this lab.

Step 1. Configure the routers.

On the routers, enter global configuration mode and configure the router name as shown in Table 7-10. Then, configure the console, vty, and enable passwords. If you have problems doing so, refer to Lab 3.1.3. Next, configure the interfaces and routing according to Tables 7-10 and 7-11. If you have problems doing so, refer to Labs 3.2.7 and 7.2.2. Make sure to copy the **running-config** to the **startup-config** on each router so you won't lose the configuration if the router is power-cycled.

Step 2. Configure the hosts with the proper IP addresses, subnet masks, and default gateways.

Test your configuration by pinging all the interfaces from each host. If the pinging is not successful, troubleshoot your configuration.

Step 3. Check the basic routing configuration.

a. Enter **show ip protocol** on each router.

b. In the configuration, does the Router RIP appear?

Step 4. Verify connectivity.

To verify connectivity of the network you just set up, ping all the interfaces from each of the attached hosts. If you cannot ping all the interfaces, correct the configuration until you can.

Step 5. Configure Centre as the connection to the Internet service provider (ISP).

a. Configure Centre to simulate the existence of an outside network. You simulate the link between the company and its ISP by configuring a loopback interface with an IP address. Enter the following commands on the Centre router:

```
Centre(config)# interface loopback0
Centre(config-if)# ip address 172.16.1.1 255.255.255.255
```

Note: If you ping 172.16.1.1 from Centre's console, the loopback interface replies.

b. From the Boaz console, attempt to ping 172.16.1.1. This ping should fail because the 172.16.0.0/16 network is not in the Boaz routing table.

c. If no default route exists, what does a router do with a packet destined for a network that is not in its table?

_____

Step 6. Set up a default route on the Centre router.

a. You must create a default route on the Centre router pointed at the simulated ISP. Issue the following command on the Centre router in configuration mode:

```
Centre(config)#ip route 0.0.0.0 0.0.0.0 loopback0
```

b. This command statically configures the default route. The default route directs traffic destined for networks that are not in the routing table to the ISP WAN link (loopback 0).

c. Unless you use Cisco IOS Software Release 12.1, RIP automatically propagates statically defined default routes. Depending on the IOS version, you might need to explicitly configure RIP to propagate this 0.0.0.0/0 route. Enter these commands on the Centre router in the proper command mode:

```
Centre(config)#router rip
Centre(config-router)#default-information originate
```

Step 7. Verify the routing tables.

a. Check the routing tables of Mobile and Boaz using the **show ip route** command. Verify that they both have received and installed a route to 0.0.0.0/0 in their tables.

b. On Boaz, what is the metric of this route?

_____

c. On Mobile, what is the metric of this route?

_____

d. Mobile and Boaz still don't have routes to 172.16.0.0/16 in their tables. From Boaz, **ping 172.16.1.1**. This ping should be successful.

e. Why does the ping to 172.16.1.1 work, even though there is no route to 172.16.0.0/16 in the Boaz routing table?

_____

f. Ensure that Mobile can also ping 172.16.1.1. Troubleshoot if necessary.

Step 8. Migrate the network from RIP to IGRP.

a. With default routing now working, you must migrate the network from RIP to IGRP for testing purposes. Issue the following command on all three routers:

```
Mobile(config)#no router rip
```

Note: With a normal migration, the IGRP routing protocol would be configured prior to removing the RIP routing protocol. IGRP routes would then replace the RIP routes in the routing table since they have a lower administrative distance and RIP could then be safely removed.

b. With RIP removed from each router's configuration, configure IGRP on all three routers using AS 24, as shown:

```
Mobile(config)#router igrp 24
Mobile(config-router)#network 192.168.1.0
Mobile(config-router)#network 192.168.5.0
...
Boaz(config)#router igrp 24
Boaz(config-router)#network 192.168.1.0
Boaz(config-router)#network 192.168.2.0
Boaz(config-router)#network 192.168.4.0
...
Centre(config)#router igrp 24
Centre(config-router)#network 192.168.2.0
Centre(config-router)#network 192.168.3.0
```

c. Use **ping** and **show ip route** to verify that IGRP is working properly. Don't worry about the 172.16.1.1 loopback address on Centre yet.

Step 9. Check Centre's routing table for the static default route.

a. Check Centre's routing table. The static default route to 0.0.0.0/0 should still be there. To propagate this route with RIP, you issued the **default-information originate** command. (Depending on your IOS version, you might not have needed to do that.) The **default-information originate** command is not available in an IGRP configuration. Thus, you must use a different method to propagate default information in IGRP.

On Centre, issue the following commands:

```
Centre(config)#router igrp 24
Centre(config-router)#network 172.16.0.0
Centre(config-router)#exit
Centre(config)#ip default-network 172.16.0.0
```

b. These commands configure IGRP to update its neighbor routers about the network 172.16.0.0/16, which includes your simulated ISP link (loopback 0). Not only will IGRP advertise this network, but the **ip default-network** command also will flag this network as a candidate default route (denoted by an asterisk in the routing table). When a network is flagged as a default, that flag stays with the route as it passed from neighbor to neighbor by IGRP.

c. Check the routing tables of Mobile and Boaz. If they don't yet have the 172.16.0.0/16 route with an asterisk, you might need to wait for another IGRP update (90 seconds). You can also issue the **clear ip route *** command on all three routers if you want to force them to immediately send new updates.

d. When the 172.16.0.0/16 route appears as a candidate default in all three routing tables, proceed to the next step.

Step 10. Create a second loopback interface on Centre to test the default route.

a. Because the 172.16.0.0/16 network is known explicitly by Mobile and Boaz, you need to create a second loopback interface on Centre to test your default route. Issue the following commands on Centre:

```
Centre(config)#interface loopback1
Centre(config-if)#ip address 10.0.0.1 255.0.0.0
```

This loopback interface simulates another external network.

b. Return to Mobile and check its routing table using the **show ip route** command.

c. Is there a route to the 10.0.0.0/8 network?

From Mobile, ping 10.0.0.1. This ping should be successful.

d. If there is no route to 10.0.0.0/8 and no route to 0.0.0.0/0, why does this ping succeed?

Lab 7.3.8: Unequal Cost Load Balancing with IGRP

Figure 7-7 Topology for Lab 7.3.8

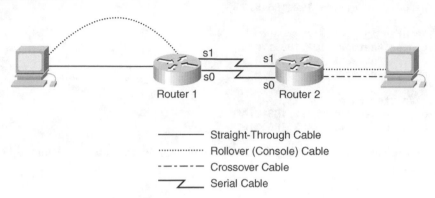

Table 7-12 Lab Equipment Configuration: Part I

Router Designation	Router Name	Routing Protocol	RIP Network Statements
Router 1	MAD	IGRP	192.168.41.0 192.168.50.0 192.168.52.0
Router 2	MIL	IGRP	192.168.50.0 192.168.52.0 192.168.33.0

The enable secret password for all routers is **class**.

The enable, vty, and console passwords for all routers is **cisco**.

Table 7-13 Lab Equipment Configuration: Part II

Router Designation	FastEthernet 0 Address	Interface Type Serial 0	Serial 0 Address	Interface Type Serial 1	Serial 1 Address	IP Host Table Entry
Router 1	192.168.41.1	DCE	192.168.50.1	DCE	192.168.52.1	MIL
Router 2	192.168.33.1	DTE	192.168.50.2	DTE	192.168.52.2	MAD

The subnet mask on all addresses for all routers is 255.255.255.0.

The IP Host Table Entry column contents indicate the name(s) of the other router(s) in the IP host table.

Objectives

- Observe unequal-cost load balancing.
- Tune IGRP networks by using advanced debug commands.

Background/Preparation

Cable a network similar to the one in Figure 7-7. You can use any router that meets the interface requirements in Figure 7-7 (that is, 800, 1600, 1700, 2500, and 2600 routers or a combination). Refer to the information in Appendix B, "Router Interface Summary," to correctly specify the interface identifiers based on the equipment in your lab. The 1721 series routers produced the configuration output in this lab. Any other router might produce slightly different output. You should execute the following steps on each router unless specifically instructed otherwise.

Start a HyperTerminal session as you did in Lab 2.2.4.

Implement the procedure documented in Appendix C, "Erasing and Reloading the Router," before continuing with this lab.

Step 1. Configure the routers.

On the routers, enter global configuration mode and configure the router name as shown in Table 7-12. Then, configure the console, vty, and enable passwords. If you have problems doing so, refer to Lab 3.1.3. Next, configure the interfaces according to Table 7-13. If you have problems doing so, refer to Lab 3.2.7. Finally, configure IGRP routing on the routers using AS 34. If you have problems doing sp, refer to Lab 7.3.5, "Configuring Interior Gateway Routing Protocol." Make sure to copy the **running-config** to the **startup-config** on each router.

Step 2. Configure bandwidth on the MAD router interfaces.

a. To make unequal-cost load balancing work, you need to establish different metrics for the IGRP routes. You use the **bandwidth** command. Set the Serial 0 interface to a bandwidth of 56Kbps and the Serial 1 interface to a value of 384Kbps. You must also turn off the route cache for load balancing. Both serial interfaces must use process switching. Process switching forces the router to look in the routing table for the destination network of each routed packet. In contrast, fast switching (the default) stores the initial table lookup in a high-speed cache and uses the information to route packets to the same destination. Enter the following statements on the MAD router.

```
MAD(config)#interface serial 0/0
MAD(config-if)#bandwidth 56
MAD(config-if)#no ip route-cache
MAD(config-if)#interface serial 0/1
MAD(config-if)#bandwidth 384
MAD(config-if)#no ip route-cache
```

b. Because the IGRP metric includes bandwidth in its calculation, you must manually configure bandwidth on the serial interfaces to ensure accuracy. (For the purposes of this lab, the alternative paths to network 192.168.41.0 from the MAD router are not of unequal cost until you set the appropriate bandwidths.)

c. Use the **show interface** command output to verify the correct bandwidth settings and the **show ip interface** command to ensure that fast switching is disabled.

d. Can you set the bandwidth of Ethernet interfaces manually?

Step 3. Configure the hosts with the proper IP addresses, subnet masks, and default gateways.

Test your configuration by pinging all the interfaces from each host. If the pinging is not successful, troubleshoot your configuration.

Step 4. Use the variance command to configure unequal-cost load balancing.

a. The variance value determines whether IGRP will accept unequal-cost routes. An IGRP router will only accept routes equal to the local best metric for the destination multiplied by the variance value. If an IGRP router's local best metric for a network is 10476 and the variance is 3, the router will accept unequal-cost routes with any metric up to 31428 (10,476 * 3), as long as the advertising router is closer to the destination. An IGRP router accepts only up to four paths to the same network.

Note: An alternate route is added to the route table only if the next-hop router in that path is closer to the destination (has a lower metric value) than the current route.

---

b. By default, IGRP's variance is set to 1, which means that only routes that are exactly 1 times the local best metric are installed. Thus, a variance of 1 disables unequal-cost load balancing.

c. Configure the MAD router to enable unequal-cost load balancing using the following commands:

```
MAD(config)#router igrp 34
MAD(config-router)#variance 10
```

d. According to the help feature, what is the maximum variance value?

_____

e. Check the MAD routing table. It should have two routes to network 192.168.33.0 with unequal metrics.

f. What is the IGRP metric for the route to 192.168.33.0 through Serial 0?

_____

g. What is the IGRP metric for the route to 192.168.33.0 through Serial 1?

_____

Step 5. Check the basic routing configuration.

a. Enter **show ip protocol** on each router.

b. Enter the command **show ip route** on each router. List how the route is connected (directly, IGRP), the IP address, and the network. Each table should have four routes.

Table 7-14 IP Route Information for MAD and MIL

MAD	Route Connected	IP Address	Through Network/Interface

c. Circle the evidence of load balancing in the output from **show ip route**.

Step 6. Verify per-packet load balancing.

a. Because there are two routes to the destination network, half the packets are sent along one path and half travel over the other. The path selection alternates with each packet.

b. Observe this process by using the **debug ip packet** command on the MAD router.

c. Send 30 ping packets across the network from the host attached to MIL router to the host attached to the MAD router. This can be done with the with the "ping 192.168.41.2 – n 30" command on the host. As the pings are responded to, the router outputs IP packet information. Stop the debug after the pings by using the command **undebug all**.

d. Examine and record part of the debug output.

e. What is the evidence of load balancing in the output?

_____

Step 7. Verify per-destination load balancing.

a. After verifying per-packet load balancing, configure the router to use per-destination load balancing. Both serial interfaces must use fast switching so that the routers can use the route cache after the initial table lookup.

b. Use the command **ip route-cache** on both serial interfaces of the MAD router.

c. Use the command **show ip interface** to verify that fast switching is enabled.

d. Is fast switching enabled? _____

e. The routers consult the routing table only once per destination; therefore, packets that are part of a packet train to a specific host all follow the same path. Only when a second destination forces another table lookup or when the cached entry expires does the router use the alternate path.

f. Use the **debug ip packet** command and **ping** across the network. Note which serial interface the router sent the packet on.

g. Examine and record part of the debug output.

h. Which serial interface did the router send the packet on?_____

When you finish these steps, log off (by typing **exit**) and turn off the router.

TCP/IP Suite Error and Control Messages

There are no labs in this module. Please review the information in Chapter 8 of CCNA 2 in the *Cisco Networking Program CCNA 1 and 2 Companion Guide*, Revised Third Edition, to ensure that you can answer the following questions:

- What are important uses of ICMP?
- What are some of the ICMP error message types and how are they identified?
- What are potential causes of specific ICMP error messages and how are they identified?
- What are some of the kinds of ICMP control messages used in networks today?
- What are some of the possible event that can cause ICMP control messages?

Basic Router Troubleshooting

The following labs are in this chapter:

Lab TI	Title
9.1.1	Using **show ip route** to Examine Routing Tables
9.1.2	Gateway of Last Resort
9.1.8	Last Route Update
9.2.6	Troubleshooting Using **ping** and **telnet**
9.3.4	Troubleshooting Using **traceroute**
9.3.5	Troubleshooting Routing Issues with **show ip route** and **show ip protocols**
9.3.7	Troubleshooting Routing Issues with **debug**

Lab 9.1.1: Using show ip route to Examine Routing Tables

Figure 9-1 Topology for Lab 9.1.1

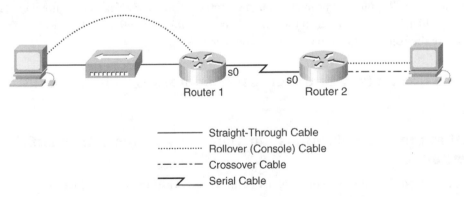

Straight-Through Cable
Rollover (Console) Cable
Crossover Cable
Serial Cable

Table 9-1 Lab Equipment Configuration

Router Designation	Router Name	FastEthernet 0 Address	Interface Type Serial 0	Serial 0 Address
Router 1	BHM	172.16.0.1	DCE	172.17.0.1
Router 2	GAD	172.18.0.1	DTE	172.17.0.2

The enable secret password for both routers is **class**.

The enable, vty, and console passwords for both routers is **cisco**.

The subnet mask for both interfaces on both routers is 255.255.0.0.

Objectives

- Set up IP an addressing scheme using Class B networks.

- Configure the Routing Information Protocol (RIP) and Interior Gateway Routing Protocol (IGRP) on routers.

- Examine the impact on the routing table of multiple routing protocols using the **show ip route** command.

Background/Preparation

Cable a network similar to the one in Figure 9-1. You can use any router that meets the interface requirements in Figure 9-1 (that is, 800, 1600, 1700, 2500, and 2600 routers or a combination). Refer to the information in Appendix B, "Router Interface Summary," to correctly specify the interface identifiers based on the equipment in your lab. The 1721 series routers produced the configuration output in this lab. Any other router might produce slightly different output. You should execute the following steps on each router unless specifically instructed otherwise. Start a HyperTerminal session as you did in Lab 2.2.4.

Implement the procedure documented in Appendix C, "Erasing and Reloading the Router," before continuing with this lab.

Step 1. Configure the routers.

On the routers, enter global configuration mode and configure the router name as shown in Table 9-1. Then, configure the console, vty, and enable passwords. If you have problems doing so, refer to Lab 3.1.3. Next, configure the interfaces according to Table 9-1. If you have problems doing so, refer to Lab 3.2.7. Finally, configure the RIP routing. Refer to Lab 7.2.2 if you need help. Don't forget to save the configurations to the startup configuration file.

Step 2. Configure the hosts with the proper IP addresses, subnet masks, and default gateways.

Step 3. Verify that the internetwork is functioning by pinging the FastEthernet interface of the other router.

a. From the host attached to GAD, can you ping the BHM router's FastEthernet interface?

_____

b. From the host attached to BHM, can you ping the GAD router's FastEthernet interface?

_____

c. If the answer is no for either question, troubleshoot the router configurations to find the error. Then, do the pings again until the answer to both questions is yes.

Step 4. Make sure that routing updates are being sent.

a. Type the command **debug ip rip** at the privileged EXEC mode prompt. Wait for at least 45 seconds.

b. Was there any output from the debug command? _____

c. What did the output display? _____

d. Stop the debug with **no debug ip rip**.

Step 5. Show the routing tables for each router.

a. Examine the routing table entries using **show ip route** on each router.

b. What are the entries in the GAD routing table?

_____

c. What are the entries in the BHM routing table?

_____

Step 6. Enable IGRP routing on both routers.

a. Leave RIP enabled, but enter **router igrp 25** on both routers at the configuration prompt. Enter the appropriate **network** statements for each router.

```
GAD(config)#router igrp 25
GAD(config-router)#network 172.16.0.0
GAD(config-router)#network 172.17.0.0
BHM(config)# router igrp 25
BHM(config-router)#network 172.18.0.0
BHM(config-router)#network 172.17.0.0
```

b. On the router where you entered **debug ip rip**, enter **debug ip igrp events**. Then, wait at least 2 minutes.

c. What type of routing updates is being sent?

_____

d. Why are both protocols sending updates?

_____

Step 7. Show the routing tables for each router again.

a. Examine the routing table entries using **show ip route** on each router.

b. What are the entries in the GAD routing table?

_____

c. What are the entries in the BHM routing table?

_____

d. Why are the RIP routes not in the tables?

_____

e. What should you do for this network to be more efficient?

_____

Step 8. Add a second serial cable between routers.

a. Add a second serial cable between Interface S1 on GAD and Serial S1 on BHM. GAD is the DCE.

b. Configure the GAD router with the following additional statements:

```
GAD(config)#interface Serial1
GAD(config-if)#ip address 172.22.0.2 255.255.0.0
GAD(config-if)#clockrate 56000
GAD(config-if)#no shutdown
```

c. Configure the BHM router with the following additional statements:

```
BHM(config)#interface Serial1
BHM(config-if)#ip address 172.22.0.1 255.255.0.0
BHM(config-if)#no shutdown
```

d. On the BHM router, remove the IGRP network statement **network 172.18.0.0** so your **router IGRP 25** contains only the **network 172.17.0.0** statement.

Step 9. Clear the routing tables on both routers.

a. Type the command **clear ip route *** at the privileged EXEC prompt on both routers. Wait at least 90 seconds and then type the command **show ip route** on both routers.

b. What types of routes appear on GAD? _____

c. What types of routes appear on BHM? _____

d. Why is this? _____

Step 10. Use show ip route to see different routes by type.

a. Enter **show ip route** while connected to the GAD router.

b. What networks appear? _____

c. What interface is directly connected?

_____

d. Enter **show ip route rip**.

e. List the routes in the routing table: _____

f. What is the administrative distance?

_____

g. Enter **show ip route** while connected to the BHM router.

h. What networks appear? _____

i. What interface is directly connected?

_____

j. Enter **show ip route rip**.

k. List the routes in the routing table: _____

l. If you saw none, that is correct, why?

_____

    m. Enter **show ip route igrp**.

    n. List the routes in the routing table: _____

    o. What is the administrative distance?

    _____

When you finish these steps, log off (by typing **exit**) and turn off the router.

Lab 9.1.2: Gateway of Last Resort

Figure 9-2 Topology for Lab 18-4

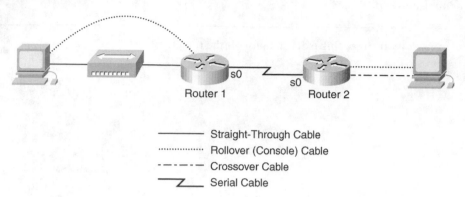

Table 9-2 Lab Equipment Configuration

Router Designation	Router Name	FastEthernet 0 Address	Interface Type Serial 0	Serial 0 Address
Router 1	GAD	172.16.0.1	DCE	172.17.0.1
Router 2	BHM	172.18.0.1	DTE	172.17.0.2

The enable secret password for both routers is **class**.

The enable, vty, and console passwords for both routers is **cisco**.

The subnet mask for both interfaces on both routers is 255.255.0.0.

Objectives

- Configure RIP routing and add default routes (gateways) to the routers.
- Remove RIP and the default routes.
- Configure IGRP routing and add default routes (gateways) to the routers.

Background/Preparation

This lab shows the purpose of the gateway of last resort, also known as the default gateway. Cable a network similar to the one in Figure 9-2. You can use any router that meets the interface requirements in Figure 9-2 (that is, 800, 1600, 1700, 2500, and 2600 routers or a combination). Refer to the information in Appendix B, "Router Interface Summary," to correctly specify the interface identifiers based on the equipment in your lab. The 1721 series routers produced the configuration output in this lab. Any other router might produce slightly different output. You should execute the following steps on each router unless specifically instructed otherwise.

Start a HyperTerminal session as you did in Lab 2.2.4.

Implement the procedure documented in Appendix C, "Erasing and Reloading the Router," before continuing with this lab.

Step 1. Configure the routers.

On the routers, enter global configuration mode and configure the router name as shown in Table 9-2. Then, configure the console, vty, and enable passwords. If you have trouble doing so, refer to Lab 3.1.3. Next, configure the interfaces according to Table 9-2. If you have trouble doing so, refer to Lab 3.2.7. Finally, configure the RIP routing, which is covered in Lab 7.2.2 in case you need help. Don't forget to save the configurations to the startup configuration file.

Step 2. Configure the hosts with the proper IP addresses, subnet masks, and default gateways.

Step 3. Verify that the internetwork is functioning by pinging the FastEthernet interface of the other router.

a. From the host attached to GAD, can you ping the BHM router's FastEthernet interface?

b. From the host attached to BHM, can you ping the GAD router's FastEthernet interface?

c. If the answer is no for either question, troubleshoot the router configurations to find the error. Then, do the pings again until the answer to both questions is yes.

Step 4. Make sure that routing updates are being sent.

a. Type the command **debug ip rip** at the privileged EXEC mode prompt. Wait for at least 45 seconds.

b. Was there any output from the **debug** command? _____

c. What did the output display? _____

d. Type **undebug all** to turn off debugging.

Step 5. Show the routing tables for each router.

a. Examine the routing table entries using **show ip route** on each router.

b. What are the entries in the GAD routing table?

c. What are the entries in the BHM routing table?

Step 6. Add the default route to the BHM router.

a. Enter the command **ip route 0.0.0.0 0.0.0.0 172.17.0.1** at the configuration mode prompt.

b. Type **show ip route** at privileged EXEC mode.

c. What is the gateway of last resort? _____

d. What does the gateway of last resort mean?

Step 7. Add the default route to the GAD router.

a. Enter the command **ip route 0.0.0.0 0.0.0.0 172.17.0.2** at the configuration prompt.

b. Type **show ip route** at privileged EXEC mode.

c. What is the gateway of last resort? _____

d. Are there any other new entries in the routing table?

_____

Step 8. Remove RIP routing from both routers.

a. To remove RIP routing, type the **no router rip** command at the configuration mode prompt. Then, ping the FastEthernet 0 interface on the GAD router from the BHM router.

b. What were the results of the ping? _____

c. Why was the ping successful? _____

Step 9. Remove the default route from only the GAD router.

a. Remove the gateway of last resort on the GAD router by typing **no ip route 0.0.0.0 0.0.0.0 172.17.0.2** at the configuration mode prompt on the GAD router.

b. Type **show ip route** at privileged EXEC mode.

c. What is the gateway of last resort? _____

d. Why is the gateway gone? _____

e. Ping the FastEthernet 0 interface on the GAD router from the BHM router.

f. What were the results of the ping? _____

g. Why was the ping successful? _____

h. Ping the FastEthernet 0 interface on the BHM router from the GAD router.

i. What were the results of the pings? _____

j. Why was the ping unsuccessful? _____

k. Remove the gateway of last resort from the BHM router.

Step 10. Remove RIP routing from the routers and use IGRP instead.

a. Remove RIP routing by using the **no** form of the **rip routing** command. Then, set up IGRP routing using 30 as the autonomous system (AS) number. Remember to wait for the routes to propagate to the other router.

b. Check the new routing protocol by typing **show ip route** at the privileged EXEC mode prompt. There should be two connected routes and two IGRP routes in **show ip route** output.

Step 11. Enter a default network entry on the BHM router.

a. Enter the command **ip default-network 172.17.0.0** at the configuration mode prompt

b. Type the **show ip route** command at privileged EXEC mode.

c. Is there a default route listed? _____

When you finish these steps, log off (by typing **exit**) and turn off the router.

Lab 9.1.8: Last Route Update

Figure 9-3 Topology for Lab 9.1.8

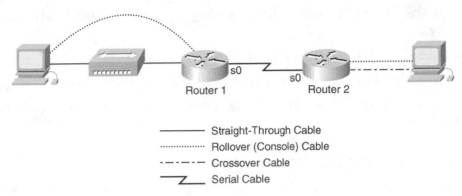

Straight-Through Cable
Rollover (Console) Cable
Crossover Cable
Serial Cable

Table 9-3 Lab Equipment Configuration

Router Designation	Router Name	FastEthernet 0 Address	Interface Type Serial 0	Serial 0 Address
Router 1	GAD	172.16.0.1	DCE	172.17.0.1
Router 2	BHM	172.18.0.1	DTE	172.17.0.2

The enable secret password for both routers is **class**.

The enable, vty, and console passwords for both routers is **cisco**.

The subnet mask for both interfaces on both routers is 255.255.0.0.

Objective

- Gather information about routing updates and routing protocols.

Background/Preparation

Cable a network similar to the one in Figure 9-3. You can use any router that meets the interface requirements in Figure 9-3 (that is, 800, 1600, 1700, 2500, and 2600 routers or a combination). Refer to the information in Appendix B, "Router Interface Summary," to correctly specify the interface identifiers based on the equipment in your lab. The 1721 series routers produced the configuration output in this lab. Any other router might produce slightly different output. You should execute the following steps on each router unless specifically instructed otherwise.

Start a HyperTerminal session as you did in Lab 2.2.4.

Implement the procedure documented in Appendix C, "Erasing and Reloading the Router," before continuing with this lab.

Step 1. Configure the routers.

On the routers, enter global configuration mode and configure the router name as shown in Table 9-3. Then, configure the console, vty, and enable passwords. If you have trouble doing so, refer to Lab 3.1.3. Next, configure the interfaces according to Table 9-3. If you have trouble doing so, refer to Lab 3.2.7. Finally, configure the RIP routing, which is covered in Lab 7.2.2 in case you need help. Don't forget to save the configurations to the startup configuration file.

Step 2. Configure the hosts with the proper IP addresses, subnet masks, and default gateways.

Step 3. Verify that the internetwork is functioning by pinging the FastEthernet interface of the other router.

a. From the host attached to GAD, can you ping the BHM router's FastEthernet interface? _____

b. From the host attached to BHM, can you ping the GAD router's FastEthernet interface? _____

c. If the answer is no for either question, troubleshoot the router configurations to find the error. Then, do the pings again until the answer to both questions is yes.

Step 4. Make sure that routing updates are being sent.

a. Type the command **debug ip rip** at the privileged EXEC mode prompt. Wait for at least 45 seconds.

b. Was there any output from the **debug** command? _____

c. Type **undebug all** to turn off debugging.

Step 5. Show the routing tables for each router.

Examine the routing table entries using **show ip route** on each router.

Step 6. Check the routing table for a specific route.

a. From the privileged EXEC mode prompt on BHM, enter **show ip route 172.16.0.0**.

b. When was the last update? _____

c. When did BHM receive the last RIP update? _____

   Wait 5 seconds and enter **show ip route 172.16.0.0** a second time.

d. What has changed from the first time?

   _____

   Wait 5 seconds and enter **show ip route 172.16.0.0** a third time.

e. What has changed from the second time?

   _____

f. What is the default update time for RIP? _____

Step 7. Check the IP RIP database on the BHM router (router must use Cisco IOS Software Release 12.0 or later).

a. Type **show ip rip database** from the privileged EXEC mode prompt.

b. When was the last update? _____

   Wait 5 seconds and enter **show ip rip database**.

c. What has changed from the first time? _____

   Wait 5 seconds and enter **show ip rip database**.

d. What has changed from the second time? _____

Step 8. Configure IGRP using AS number 101 on all routers. Leave RIP on all routers.

Step 9. From BHM, enter show ip route.

a. List the routes displayed in the routing table:

   _____

b. When did BHM receive the last IGRP update? _____

   Wait 5 seconds and enter **show ip route**.

c. What has changed from the first time? _____

   Wait 5 seconds and enter **show ip route**.

d. What has changed from the second time?

   _____

e. What is the default update time for IGRP? _____

Step 10. Check the routing protocol on router BHM.

a. From privileged EXEC mode on BHM, enter **show ip protocols**.

b. What protocols appear? _____

c. In how many seconds is the next update due for each protocol? _____

When you finish these steps, log off (by typing **exit**) and turn off the router.

Lab 9.2.6: Troubleshooting Using ping and telnet

Figure 9-4 Topology for Lab 9.2.6

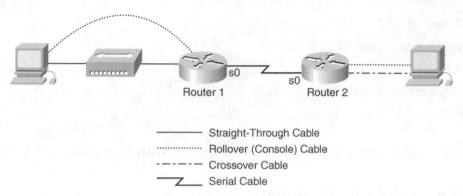

Straight-Through Cable
Rollover (Console) Cable
Crossover Cable
Serial Cable

Table 9-4 Lab Equipment Configuration: Part I

Router Designation	Router Name	Routing Protocol	RIP Network Statements
Router 1	GAD	RIP	192.168.14.0 192.168.15.0
Router 2	BHM	RIP	192.168.16.0 192.168.13.0

The enable secret password for both routers is **class**.

The enable, vty, and console passwords for both routers is **cisco**.

Table 9-5 Lab Equipment Configuration: Part II

Router Designation	FastEthernet 0 Address	Interface Type Serial 0	Serial 0 Address	Interface Type Serial 1	Serial 1 Address	IP Host Table Entry
Router 1	192.168.14.1	DCE	192.168.15.1	DCE	192.168.15.2	BHM
Router 2	192.168.16.1	DTE	192.168.13.1	DTE	192.168.13.2	GAD

The subnet mask for all address on both routers is 255.255.255.0.

The IP Host Table Entry column contents indicate the name(s) of the other router(s) in the IP host table.

Objectives

- Use your knowledge of the Open System Interconnection (OSI) model Layers 1, 2, and 3 to diagnose network configuration errors.

- Use the Ping and Telnet utilities in testing.

Background/Preparation

Cable a network similar to the one in Figure 9-4. You can use any router that meets the interface requirements in Figure 9-4 (that is, 800, 1600, 1700, 2500, and 2600 routers or a combination). Refer to the information in Appendix B, "Router Interface Summary," to correctly specify the interface identifiers based on the equipment in your lab. The 1721 series routers produced the configuration output in this lab. Any other router might produce slightly different output. You should execute the following steps on each router unless specifically instructed otherwise.

Start a HyperTerminal session as you did in Lab 2.2.4, "Establishing a Console Session with HyperTerminal."

Note: Work in teams of two. Team Member 1 should cable and configure the routers and workstations according to the information in Tables 9-4 and 9-5. Using this information will introduce some errors. Team Member 2 should test the configuration using physical inspection, ping, and Telnet.

Implement the procedure documented in Appendix C, "Erasing and Reloading the Router," before continuing with this lab.

Step 1. Configure the routers.

There are intentional configuration errors in Tables 9-4 and 9-5. Configure the routers using these parameters to introduce errors for troubleshooting practice. On the routers, enter global configuration mode and configure the router name as shown in Table 9-4. Then, configure the console, vty, and enable passwords. If you have problems doing so, refer to Lab 3.1.3, "Configuring Router Passwords." Next, configure the interfaces and routing according to the chart. If you have problems doing so, refer to Lab 3.2.7, "Configuring Host Tables," and Lab 7.2.2, "Configuring RIP." Make sure to copy the **running-config** to the **startup-config** on each router so you won't lose the configuration if the router is power-recycled.

Step 2. Configure the hosts with the proper IP addresses, subnet masks, and default gateways.

a. Test the configuration by pinging all the interfaces from each host. If the pinging is not successful, go on to Step 3.

b. If the pinging is successful, advise the instructor that the configuration is operational. The instructor will introduce fault(s) in the configuration to diagnose and repair.

Step 3. Check the connections.

a. Review the physical connections on the standard lab setup.

b. Check all physical devices, cables, and connections.

Step 4. Troubleshoot.

a. Troubleshoot the network problems.

b. Use the commands **ping** and **telnet** to discover problems.

Step 5. List the findings.

a. Write down the problems as you encounter them.

b. Write down what you did to correct the problems.

c. Have the instructor verify that you corrected all the problems.

Use Table 9-6 to record the information.

Table 9-6 Troubleshooting Documentation Table

Problem #	Problem Discovered	Solution	Instructor Verification
1			
2			
3			
4			
5			

Step 6. Perform the lab again with Team Members 1 and 2 switching roles.

When you finish the preceding steps, log off (by typing **exit**) and turn off the router.

Lab 9.3.4: Troubleshooting Using traceroute

Figure 9-5 Topology for Lab 9.3.4

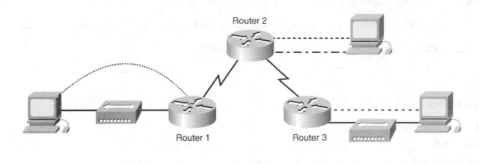

Straight-Through Cable

· · · · · · · · · · Rollover (Console) Cable

— · — · — Crossover Cable

Serial Cable

Table 9-7 Lab Equipment Configuration: Part I

Router Designation	Router Name	Routing Protocol	RIP Network Statements
Router 1	GAD	RIP	192.168.14.0 192.168.15.0
Router 2	BHM	RIP	192.168.15.0 192.168.13.0 192.168.16.0
Router 3	PHX	RIP	192.168.13.0 192.168.17.0

The enable secret password for all routers is **class**.

The enable, vty, and console passwords for all routers is **cisco**.

Table 9-8 Lab Equipment Configuration: Part II

Router Designation	FastEthernet 0 Address	Interface Type Serial 0	Serial 0 Address	Interface Type Serial 1	Serial 1 Address	IP Host Table Entries
Router 1	192.168.14.1	DCE	192.168.15.1	N/A	No address	BHM PHX
Router 2	192.168.16.1	DTE	192.168.15.2	DCE	192.168.13.1	GAD PHX
Router 3	192.168.17.1	N/A	No address	DTE	192.168.13.2	GAD BHM

The subnet mask for all address on both routers is 255.255.255.0.

Objectives

- Use the **traceroute** Cisco IOS Software command from source router to destination router.

- Use the **tracert** MS-DOS command from source workstation to destination router.

- Verify that the network layer between source, destination, and each router along the way is working properly.

- Retrieve information to evaluate the end-to-end path reliability.

Background/Preparation

Cable a network similar to the one in Figure 9-5. You can use any router that meets the interface requirements in Figure 9-5 (that is, 800, 1600, 1700, 2500, and 2600 routers or a combination). Refer to the information in Appendix B to correctly specify the interface identifiers based on the equipment in your lab. The 1721 series routers produced the configuration output in this lab. Any other router might produce slightly different output. You should execute the following steps on each router unless specifically instructed otherwise.

Start a HyperTerminal session as you did in Lab 2.2.4.

Implement the procedure documented in Appendix C on all routers before continuing with this lab.

Step 1. Configure the routers.

a. On the routers, enter global configuration mode and configure the router name as shown in the tables. Then, configure the console, vty, and enable passwords. If you have problems doing so, refer to Lab 3.1.3. "Next, configure the interfaces and routing according to the chart. If you have problems doing so, refer to Labs 3.2.7 and 7.2.2. Make sure to copy the **running-config** to the **startup-config** on each router so you won't lose the configuration if the router is power-recycled.

This lab requires that the routers have IP host names configured.

b. Verify the routers' configurations by performing a show running-config on each router. If they are not correct, fix any configuration errors and reverify.

Step 2. Configure the workstations with the appropriate IP address subnet masks and default gateways.

Step 3. Ping from the workstations.

a. From a Windows host, choose **Start > Programs > Accessories > MS-DOS**. This step opens a command-prompt window. (If this not the correct location, see the instructor for the proper location on this computer.)

b. To test that the TCP/IP stack and default gateway on the workstation are configured and working properly, use the MS-DOS window to ping the routers by issuing the following command:

```
C:\> ping 192.168.14.1
```

c. The ping should respond with successful results. If not, check the configurations on the host and directly connected router.

Step 4. Test Layer 3 connectivity.

a. Using the command prompt, enter **ping** and the IP addresses of all routers' interfaces.

This step tests Layer 3 connectivity between the workstation and the routers.

b. Is the output from the workstation's **ping** command the same as the output from the **ping** command from a router?

_____

Step 5. Log in to the router in user mode.

Log in to the GAD router and stay at the user EXEC prompt.

Step 6. Discover the trace options.

a. Enter **traceroute** at the router prompt.

b. What did the router respond with? _____

Step 7. Use the traceroute command.

a. Enter **traceroute ip** *xxx.xxx.xxx.xxx* where *xxx.xxx.xxx.xxx* is the IP address of the target destination. *Note*: Use one of the end routers and **traceroute ip** to the other end host. The router will respond with the following:

```
GAD#traceroute ip 192.168.16.2

Type escape sequence to abort.

Tracing the route to 192.168.16.2

  1 BHM (192.168.15.2) 16 msec 16 msec 16 msec
  2 192.168.16.2 16 msec 16 msec 12 msec
GAD#
```

b. If the output is not successful, check the router and host configurations.

_____

Note: If the **ip** keyword is omitted, traceroute will default to IP.

_____

Step 8. Continue using traceroute.

Repeat Steps 5 through 7 with all other routers on the network.

Step 9. Use the tracert command from a workstation.

a. From the console workstation, choose **Start > Programs > Command Prompt**. An MS-DOS command-prompt window will open.

b. Enter **tracert** and the same IP address you used in Step 5.

c. The first hop is the default gateway or the near-side router interface on the LAN that the workstation is connected to. List the host name and IP address of the router that the ICMP packet was routed through in Table 9-9.

Table 9-9 Recording Host Names and IP Addresses of Routed ICMP Packets

Host Name	IP Address

d. There is one more entry in the output of the tracert command when the trace is from the computer command prompt to the target host. Why?

_____

When you finish the preceding steps, log off (by typing **exit**) and turn off the router.

Lab 9.3.5: Troubleshooting Routing Issues with show ip route and show ip protocols

Figure 9-6 Topology for Lab 9.3.5

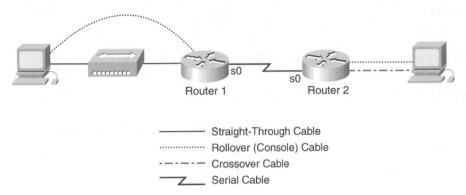

```
——————  Straight-Through Cable
·············  Rollover (Console) Cable
— — — —  Crossover Cable
⎯Ζ⎯  Serial Cable
```

Table 9-10 Lab Equipment Configuration

Router Designation	Router Name	FastEthernet 0 Address	Interface Type Serial 0	Serial 0 Address
Router 1	GAD	192.168.1.1	DCE	192.168.2.1
Router 2	BHM	192.168.3.1	DTE	192.168.2.2

The enable secret password for both routers is **class**.

The enable, vty, and console passwords for both routers is **cisco**.

The subnet mask for both interfaces on both routers is 255.255.255.0.

Objective

- Use the **show ip route** and **show ip protocol** commands to diagnose a routing configuration problem.

Background/Preparation

Cable a network similar to the one in Figure 9-6. You can use any router that meets the interface requirements in Figure 9-6 (that is, 800, 1600, 1700, 2500, and 2600 routers or a combination). Refer to the information in Appendix B, "Router Interface Summary," to correctly specify the interface identifiers based on the equipment in your lab. The 1721 series routers produced the configuration output in this lab. Any other router might produce slightly different output. You should execute the following steps on each router unless specifically instructed otherwise.

Start a HyperTerminal session as you did in Lab 2.2.4.

Implement the procedure documented in Appendix C, "Erasing and Reloading the Router," before continuing with this lab.

Step 1. Configure the host name, passwords, and interfaces on the GAD router.

On the GAD router, enter global configuration mode and configure the router name as shown in Table 9-10. Then, configure the console, vty, and enable passwords. If you have trouble doing so, refer to Lab 3.1.3. Configure interfaces as shown in Table 9-10.

Step 2. Configure the routing protocol on the GAD router.

Go to the proper command mode and enter the following:

```
GAD(config)#router rip
GAD(config-router)#network 192.168.1.0
GAD(config-router)#network 192.168.2.0
GAD(config-router)#exit
GAD(config)#exit
```

Step 3. Save the GAD router configuration.

```
GAD# copy running-config startup-config
Destination filename [startup-config]? [Enter]
```

Step 4. Configure the host name, passwords, and interfaces on the BHM router.

On the BHM router, enter global configuration mode and configure the host name as shown in Table 9-10. Then, configure the console, vty, and enable passwords. Finally, configure the interfaces.

Step 5. Configure the routing protocol on the BHM router.

Go to the proper command mode and enter the following:

```
BHM(config)# router rip
BHM(config-router)# network 192.168.2.0
BHM(config-router)# network 192.168.1.0
BHM(config-router)# exit
BHM(config)# exit
```

Step 6. Save the BHM router configuration.

```
BHM# copy running-config startup-config
    Destination filename [startup-config]? [Enter]
```

Step 7. Verify that the internetwork is functioning by pinging the FastEthernet interface of the other router.

a. From GAD, can you ping the BHM router's FastEthernet interface?

_____

b. From BHM, can you ping the GAD router's FastEthernet interface?

_____

Step 8. Examine the routing table.

a. After an unsuccessful ping, you need to check the routing table with the **show ip route** command. From the GAD router, type the following:

```
GAD#show ip route
```

b. Is there a route to the BHM Ethernet LAN? _____

Step 9. Examine the routing protocol status.

a. After examining the routing tables, you discover that there is no route to the BHM Ethernet LAN. So you use the **show ip protocols** command to view the routing protocol status. From the BHM router, type the following:

```
BHM#show ip protocols
```

b. What networks is RIP routing? _____

c. Are these the correct networks? _____

Step 10. Change the configuration to route the correct networks.

After examining the **show ip protocols** command results, you notice that the network on the Ethernet LAN is not being routed. After examining it further, you also find that a network that does not belong has been configured to be advertised. You decide this is a typo and you need to correct it. You enter the router RIP configuration mode and make the appropriate changes. From the BHM router, type the following:

```
BHM#configure terminal
BHM(config)#router rip
BHM(config-router)#no network 192.168.1.0
BHM(config-router)#network 192.168.3.0
BHM(config-router)#^Z
```

Step 11. Confirm that RIP is routing the correct networks.

a. Confirm that the new statement corrected the RIP configuration problem. Again type the **show ip protocols** command to observe what networks are being routed.

b. From the BHM router, type the following:

```
BHM#show ip protocols
```

c. What networks is RIP routing? _____

d. Are these the correct networks? _____

Step 12. Verify the routing table.

a. Having confirmed that you corrected the configuration problem, verify that the proper routes are now in the routing table. Again issue the **show ip route** command to verify that the router now has the proper route.

b. From the GAD router, type the following:

```
GAD#show ip route
```

c. Is there a route to the BHM LAN? _____

Step 13. Verify connectivity between the GAD router and the host in BHM.

a. Use the **ping** command to verify connectivity from GAD router to a host in BHM.

b. From the GAD router, type the following:

```
GAD#ping host-ip
```

For example, for host with an IP address, type the following:

```
GAD#ping 192.168.3.2
```

c. Was the ping successful? _____

When you finish these steps, log off (by typing **exit**) and turn off the router.

Lab 9.3.7: Troubleshooting Routing Issues with debug

Figure 9-7 Topology for Lab 9.3.7

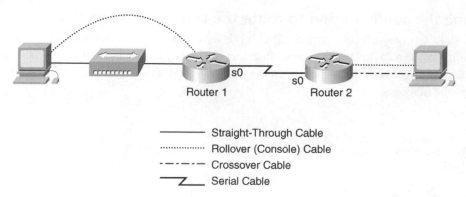

Straight-Through Cable
Rollover (Console) Cable
Crossover Cable
Serial Cable

Table 9-11 Lab Equipment Configuration

Router Designation	Router Name	FastEthernet 0 Address	Interface Type Serial 0	Serial 0 Address
Router 1	GAD	192.168.1.1	DCE	192.168.2.1
Router 2	BHM	192.168.3.1	DTE	192.168.2.2

The enable secret password for both routers is **class**.

The enable, vty, and console passwords for both routers is **cisco**.

The subnet mask for both interfaces on both routers is 255.255.255.0.

Objectives

- Use a systematic OSI troubleshooting process to diagnose routing problems.
- Use various **show** commands to gather information.
- Use **debug** commands and logging.

Background/Preparation

Cable a network similar to the one in Figure 9-7. You can use any router that meets the interface requirements in Figure 9-7 (that is, 800, 1600, 1700, 2500, and 2600 routers or a combination). Refer to the information in Appendix B, "Router Interface Summary," to correctly specify the interface identifiers based on the equipment in your lab. The 1721 series routers produced the configuration output in this lab. Any other router might produce slightly different output. You should execute the following steps on each router unless specifically instructed otherwise.

Start a HyperTerminal session as you did in Lab 2.2.4.

Implement the procedure documented in Appendix C, "Erasing and Reloading the Router," before continuing with this lab.

Step 1. Configure the host name, passwords, and interfaces on the GAD router.

On the GAD router, enter global configuration mode and configure the router name as shown in Table 9-11. Then, configure the console, vty, and enable passwords. If you have trouble doing so, refer to Lab 3.1.3. Configure the interfaces as shown in Table 9-11.

Step 2. Configure the routing protocol on the GAD router.

Go to the proper command mode and enter the following:

```
GAD(config)#router rip
GAD(config-router)#network 192.168.1.0
GAD(config-router)#network 192.168.2.0
GAD(config-router)#version 2
GAD(config-router)#exit
GAD(config)#exit
```

Step 3. Save the GAD router configuration.

```
GAD#copy running-config startup-config
Destination filename [startup-config]? [Enter]
```

Step 4. Configure the host name, passwords, and interfaces on the BHM router.

On the BHM router, enter global configuration mode and configure the host name as shown in Table 9-11. Then, configure the console, vty, and enable passwords. Finally, configure the interfaces.

Step 5. Configure the routing protocol on the BHM router.

Go to the proper command mode and enter the following:

```
BHM(config)#router rip
BHM(config-router)#network 192.168.2.0
BHM(config-router)#network 192.168.1.0
BHM(config-router)#version 1
BHM(config-router)#exit
BHM(config)#exit
```

Step 6. Save the BHM router configuration.

```
BHM# copy running-config startup-config
Destination filename [startup-config]? [Enter]
```

Step 7. Gather facts. (Ask and listen.)

After asking around, you are told that a network associate on the night shift changed some of the routing parameters on the routers for a circuit between the GAD office and the BHM office. Unfortunately, he did not follow the proper procedure and there is no documentation on these changes.

Step 8. Gather facts (test basic functionality).

Verify that the internetwork is not functioning by pinging the LAN interfaces.

a. From GAD, can you ping the BHM router's FastEthernet interface?

_____

b. From BHM, can you ping the GAD router's FastEthernet interface?

_____

Step 9. Gather facts. (Start testing to isolate the problem.)

a. You know that there is no communication between GAD and BHM. Even though you suspect a routing issue, you resist the temptation to directly begin testing the routing. Instead, you follow a scientific troubleshooting method.

b. First, start at the physical layer; confirm that the WAN link circuit is up. From the GAD router, issue the **show interfaces serial 0** command to confirm that the line and protocol is up.

c. Are they both up? _____

d. Now that you know that the line and protocol are both up, test the data link layer. From the GAD router, issue the **show CDP neighbors** command to confirm that the BHM router is a neighbor to the GAD router Serial 0 interface.

e. Do you see BHM as a neighbor on interface Serial 0? _____

Step 10. Examine the routing table.

a. It looks like the data-link layer is good. Time to move up and examine the network layer. Check the GAD routing table to see whether there is a route to the BHM LAN. To do this, issue the **show ip route** command on the GAD router.

b. Is the route there? _____

c. Are there any RIP routes? _____

Step 11. Examine the routing protocol status.

a. After examining the routing tables, you discover that there is no route to the BHM Ethernet LAN. You use the **show ip protocols** command to view the routing protocol status. From the GAD router, type the following:

```
GAD#show ip protocols
```

b. What networks is RIP routing? _____

c. Are these the correct networks? _____

Step 12. Gather facts. (Identify the exact problem.)

a. Now that you have confirmed a routing issue, you must discover the exact source of the routing problem so that you can correct it. To observe the routing exchange between the routers, you will use the **debug ip rip** command.

b. From a GAD console, type the **debug ip packet** command and watch the output for a minute or two.

c. Record a sample of output from GAD or BHM.

_____

d. Are routing updates being passed? _____

e. What is happening to the routing updates from BHM?

_____

f. Type **undebug all** to stop the output.

Step 13. Consider the possibilities.

From the information you have discovered through the troubleshooting process, what are the possible problems?

_____

Step 14. Create an action plan.

How are you going to correct the problem?

_____

Step 15. Implement the action plan.

Try the solution that you proposed in the preceding step.

Step 16. Observe the results.

a. You need to confirm that your plan has solved the problem. You do so by reversing the tests that you previously performed.

b. Observe the routing exchange between the routers using the **debug ip rip** command and watch the output for a minute or two.

c. Type **undebug all** to stop the output.

d. Check the GAD routing table to see if there is a route to BHM by using **show ip route**.

e. Are there any IP routes? _____

f. Is the route to BHM there? _____

g. To confirm that everything is working, from the GAD router ping the LAN interface of the BHM router. Was it successful? _____

h. If your plan did not correct the problem, then you need to repeat the process.

i. If the tests were successful, you need to document the changes and back up the configuration.

When you finish these steps, log off (by typing **exit**) and turn off the router.

Intermediate TCP/IP

The following labs are in this chapter:

Lab TI	Title
10.1.6	Multiple Active Host Sessions
10.2.5	Well-Known Port Numbers and Multiple Sessions

Lab 10.1.6: Multiple Active Host Sessions

Figure 10-1 Topology for Lab 10.1.6

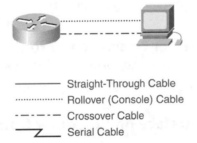

——————— Straight-Through Cable
················· Rollover (Console) Cable
— — — — Crossover Cable
———∿—— Serial Cable

Table 10-1 Lab Equipment Configuration

Router Designation	Router Name	FA0/0 Address	Subnet Mask
Router 1	GAD	192.168.14.1	255.255.255.0

The enable secret password is **class**.

The enable/vty/console password is **cisco**.

Objectives

- Enable HTTP services on a router.
- Observe multiple HTTP and Telnet sessions on a single host using **netstat**.

Background/Preparation

Cable a network similar to the one in Figure 10-1. You can use any router that meets the interface requirements in Figure 10-1 (that is, 800, 1600, 1700, 2500, and 2600 routers or a combination). Refer to the information in Appendix B, "Router Interface Summary," to correctly specify the interface identifiers based on the equipment in your lab. The 1721 series routers produced the configuration output in this lab. Any other router might produce slightly different output. You should execute the following steps on each router unless specifically instructed otherwise.

Start a HyperTerminal session as you did in Lab 2.2.4, "Establishing a Console Session with HyperTerminal."

Implement the procedure documented in Appendix C, "Erasing and Reloading the Router," before continuing with this lab.

Step 1. Configure the host name, passwords, and interface on the GAD router.

On the GAD router, enter global configuration mode and configure the router name as shown in Table 10-1. Then, configure the console, virtual terminal, and enable passwords. Configure the Ethernet interface.

Step 2. Save the configuration information from privileged EXEC command mode.

```
GAD# copy running-config startup-config
```

Step 3. Configure the host with the proper IP address, subnet mask, and default gateway.

Step 4. Allow HTTP access to the router.

Allow HTTP access by issuing the **ip http server** command in global configuration mode.

Step 5. Use the workstation browser to access the router.

Open a browser on Host 1 and type **http://**ip-address-of-Router-GAD. You will be prompted for a username and the enable password of the router. The username can be left blank; only the password is required.

Step 6. Telnet to the Ethernet interface on the router from the host.

Step 7. Start a second Telnet session to the router.

Step 8. Check the sessions on the host.

a. Enter the **netstat** command from the command or MS-DOS prompt.

b. How many sessions are running on the host?

_____

c. Why isn't the web browser listed as an active session?

_____

When you finish these steps, log off (by typing **exit**) and turn off the router.

Lab 10.2.5: Well-Known Port Numbers and Multiple Sessions

Figure 10-2 Topology for Lab 10.2.5

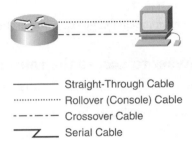

————— Straight-Through Cable
················· Rollover (Console) Cable
– – – – – Crossover Cable
———Z— Serial Cable

Table 10-2 Lab Equipment Configuration

Router Designation	Router Name	FA0/0 Address	Subnet Mask
Router 1	GAD	192.168.14.1	255.255.255.0

The enable secret password is **class**.

The enable/vty/console password is **cisco**.

Objectives

- Enable HTTP services on a router.
- Show multiple HTTP and Telnet sessions on a single host.
- Observe well-known TCP port numbers on the host and router.

Background/Preparation

Cable a network similar to the one in Figure 10-2. You can use any router that meets the interface requirements in Figure 10-2 (that is, 800, 1600, 1700, 2500, and 2600 routers or a combination). Refer to the information in Appendix B, "Router Interface Summary," to correctly specify the interface identifiers based on the equipment in your lab. The 1721 series routers produced the configuration output in this lab. Any other router might produce slightly different output. You should execute the following steps on each router unless specifically instructed otherwise.

Start a HyperTerminal session as you did in Lab 2.2.4.

Implement the procedure documented in Appendix C, "Erasing and Reloading the Router," before continuing with this lab.

Step 1. Configure the host name, passwords, and interface on the GAD router.

On the GAD router, enter global configuration mode and configure the router name as shown in Table 10-2. Then, configure the console, virtual terminal, and enable passwords. Configure the Ethernet interface.

Step 2. Save the configuration information from privileged EXEC command mode.

```
GAD# copy running-config startup-config
```

Step 3. Configure the host with the proper IP address, subnet mask, and default gateway.

Step 4. Allow HTTP access to the router.

Allow HTTP access by issuing the **ip http server** command in global configuration mode.

Step 5. Use the workstation browser to access the router.

a. Open a browser on Host 1 and type **http://***ip-address-of-Router-GAD*.

b. You will be prompted for a username and the enable password of the router. The username can be left blank; only the password is required.

Step 6. Telnet to the Ethernet interface on the router from the host.

Step 7. Start a second Telnet session to the router by opening another command prompt.

Step 8. Start a third Telnet session to router by opening another command prompt.

Step 9. Start a fourth Telnet session to router by opening another command prompt.

Step 10. Check the number of sessions on the host.

a. Open another command prompt on the host and type **netstat /?** at the DOS prompt.

b. What options are available for the **netstat** command? _____

_____

c. Type **netstat -n**.

d. How many open sessions are there? _____

e. What are the open sessions? _____

f. What are the port numbers? _____

Step 11. Check the number of sessions on the router.

a. In privileged EXEC mode, type **show tcp**.

b. How many open sessions are there? _____

c. What are the open sessions? _____

d. What are the port numbers on the sessions? _____

e. Why can all the sessions use port 23 (under Foreign Address)?

_____

f. List some of the Local Address port numbers (number after the colon following the IP address).

_____

g. Why are all the Local Address port numbers different?

When you finish these steps, log off (by typing **exit**) and turn off the router.

Access Control Lists (ACLs)

The following labs are in this chapter:

Lab TI	Title
11.2.1a	Configuring Standard Access Lists
11.2.1b	Standard ACLs
11.2.2a	Configuring Extended Access Lists
11.2.2b	Simple Extended Access Lists
11.2.3a	Configuring a Named Access List
11.2.3b	Simple DMZ Extended Access Lists
11.2.3c	Multiple Access Lists Functions (Challenge Lab)
11.2.6	VTY Restriction

Lab 11.2.1a: Configuring Standard Access Lists

Figure 11-1 Topology for Lab 11.2.1a

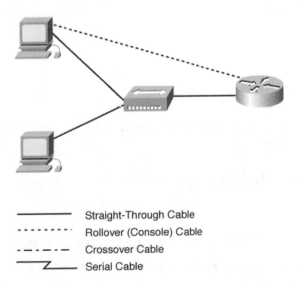

Straight-Through Cable

Rollover (Console) Cable

Crossover Cable

Serial Cable

Table 11-1 Lab Equipment Configuration

Router Designation	Router Name	FA0/0 Address	Subnet Mask	Enable Secret Password	Enable/vty/ Console Passwords
Router 1	GAD	192.168.14.1	255.255.255.0	class	cisco

Objectives

- Configure and apply a standard access control list (ACL) to permit or deny specific traffic.
- Test the ACL to determine whether you achieved the desired results.

Background/Preparation

Cable a network similar to the one in Figure 11-1. You can use any router that meets the interface requirements in Figure 11-1 (that is, 800, 1600, 1700, 2500, and 2600 routers or a combination). Refer to the information in Appendix B, "Router Interface Summary," correctly specify the interface identifiers based on the equipment in your lab. The 1721 series routers produced the configuration output in this lab. Any other router might produce slightly different output. You should execute the following steps on each router unless specifically instructed otherwise. Start a HyperTerminal session as you did in Lab 2.2.4, "Establishing a Console Session with HyperTerminal."

Implement the procedure documented in Appendix C, "Erasing and Reloading the Router," before continuing with this lab.

Step 1. Configure the host name and passwords on the GAD router.

On the GAD router, enter global configuration mode and configure the router name as shown in Table 11-1. Then, configure the console, virtual terminal, and enable passwords. Configure the FastEthernet interface on the router according to Table 11-1.

Step 2. Configure the hosts on the Ethernet segment.

a. **Host 1:**

```
IP address: 192.168.14.2
Subnet mask: 255.255.255.0
Default gateway: 192.168.14.1
```

b. **Host 2:**

```
IP address: 192.168.14.3
Subnet mask: 255.255.255.0
Default gateway: 192.168.14.1
```

Step 3. Save the configuration information from privileged EXEC command mode.

```
GAD# copy running-config startup-config
```

Step 4. Confirm connectivity by pinging the default gateway from both hosts.

If the pings are not successful, correct your configuration and repeat until they are successful.

Step 5. Prevent access to the Ethernet interface from the hosts.

a. Create an ACL that will prevent access to FastEthernet 0 from the 192.168.14.0 network.

b. At the router configuration prompt, type the following command:

```
GAD(config)#access-list 1 deny 192.168.14.0  0.0.0.255
GAD(config)#access-list 1 permit any
```

c. Why do you need the second statement?

_____

Step 6. Ping the router from the hosts.

a. Were these pings successful? _____

b. Why or why not? _____

Step 7. Apply the ACL to the interface.

At the FastEthernet 0 interface mode prompt, type the following:

```
GAD(config-if)#ip access-group 1 in
```

Step 8. Ping the router from the hosts.

a. Were these pings successful? _____

b. Why or why not? _____

Step 9. Create a new ACL.

a. Create an ACL that will not allow the even-numbered hosts to ping but that permits the odd-numbered hosts to ping.

b. What does that ACL look like? Finish this command with an appropriate comparison IP address (*aaa.aaa.aaa.aaa*) and wildcard mask (*www.www.www.www*):

```
access-list 2 permit aaa.aaa.aaa.aaa   www.www.www.www
```

c. Why didn't you need the **permit any** statement at the end this time?

_____

Step 10. Apply the ACL to the proper router interface.

a. First, remove the old ACL application by typing **no ip access-group 1 in** in interface configuration mode.

b. Apply the new ACL by typing **ip access-group 2 in**.

Step 11. Ping the router from each host.

a. Was the ping from Host 1 successful? _____

b. Why or why not? _____

c. Was the ping from Host 2 successful? _____

d. Why or why not? _____

When you finish the preceding steps, log off (by typing **exit**) and turn off the router.

Lab 11.2.1b: Standard ACLs

Figure 11-2 Topology for Lab 11.2.1b

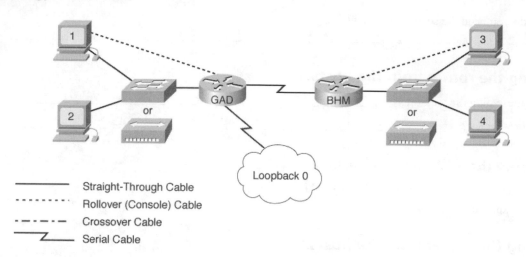

Straight-Through Cable
Rollover (Console) Cable
Crossover Cable
Serial Cable

Table 11-2 Lab Equipment Configuration

Router Name	FA0/0 Address	S0/0 Address	LO0 Address
GAD	192.168.1.1/24	192.168.2.1/24	172.16.1.1/24
BHM	192.168.3.1/24	192.168.2.2/24	N/A

The enable password for both routers is **cisco**.

The vty password for both routers is **class**.

The routing protocol for both routers is RIP.

Table 11-3 Host IP Address, Subnet Mask, and Gateway Configuration

Host	IP Address	Subnet Mask	Gateway
1	192.168.1.2	255.255.255.0	192.168.1.1
2	192.168.1.3	255.255.255.0	192.168.1.1
3	192.168.3.2	255.255.255.0	192.168.3.1
4	192.168.3.3	255.255.255.0	192.168.3.1

Objectives

- Plan, configure, and apply a standard ACL to permit or deny specific traffic.
- Test the ACL to determine whether it achieved the desired results.

Background/Preparation

The company's home office in Gadsden (GAD) provides services to branch offices such as the Birmingham (BHM) office. These offices have some minor security and performance concerns. You will implement standard ACLs as a simple and effective tool to control traffic based on the following assumptions:

Host 3 represents the kiosk station that needs its access limited to the local network.

Host 4 represents another host in the BHM office and the Loopback 0 interface on the GAD router represents the Internet.

Step 1. Perform basic router interconnection.

Interconnect the routers as shown in Figure 11-2.

Step 2. Perform basic configuration.

a. The router might contain configurations from a previous use. Implement the procedure documented in Appendix C on all routers before continuing with this lab. Using the information in Tables 11-2 and 11-3, set up the router and host configurations and verify communications by pinging all systems and routers from each system.

b. To simulate the Internet, add the following configuration to the GAD router:

```
GAD(config)#interface loopback0
GAD(config-if)#address 172.16.1.1 255.255.255.0
GAD(config-if)#exit
GAD(config)#router rip
GAD(config-router)#network 172.16.0.0
GAD(config-if)#^z
```

Step 3. Establish access list requirements.

a. The kiosk station (Host 3) needs its access limited to the local network. You must create a standard access list to prevent traffic from this host from reaching any other networks. The ACL should block traffic from this host and not affect other traffic from this network. A standard IP ACL satisfies this requirement as it filters based on the source address to any destination.

b. What is the source address of the kiosk? _____

Step 4. Plan the access list requirements.

As with any project, the most important part of the process is the planning. First, you must define the information you need to create the ACL. An access list consists a series of ACL statements. Because the list will consist of more than one statement, you must carefully plan the order of the statements. Each of these statements is performed in sequence as the ACL is processed.

a. This ACL requires two logical steps. You can accomplish these steps with one statement each. For a planning tool, you can use a text editor such as Notepad to organize the logic and then write the list. In the text editor, enter the logic by typing the following:

```
! stop traffic from host 3
! permit all other traffic
```

From this logic, you will write the actual ACL.

b. Using Table 11-4, document the information for each statement.

Table 11-4 Recording Information to Deny or Permit Traffic

Stop Traffic from Host 3			
List #	Permit or Deny	Source Address	Wildcard Mask
Permit All Other Traffic			
List #	Permit or Deny	Source Address	Wildcard Mask

c. What would be the result of not including a statement to permit all other source addresses?

_____

d. What would be the result of reversing the order of the two statements in the list?

_____

e. Why do both statements use the same ACL number?

_____

f. The final step in the planning process is to determine the best location (interface) for the access list and the direction in which you should apply the list. Examine the internetwork diagram and choose the appropriate interface and direction. Document this information in Table 11-5.

Table 11-5 Selecting an Interface and Direction for Applying an ACL

Router	Interface	Direction

Step 5. Write and apply the ACL.

a. Using the previously constructed logic and information, complete the commands in the text editor. Comments are entered into the ACL by using an exclamation mark as the first character of a line. This makes it easier to understand the function of the statements. The list syntax should look similar to the following:

```
! stop traffic from host 3
   access-list # deny address wildcard
! permit all other traffic
   access-list # permit address wildcard
```

b. Add to this text file the configuration statements to apply the list.

The configuration statements take the following form:

```
interface type #/#
ip access-group # {in, out}
```

c. Now you must apply the text-file configuration to the router. Enter configuration mode on the appropriate router, and copy and paste the configuration. Observe the command-line interface (CLI) display to ensure that no errors appeared.

Step 6. Verify the ACL.

a. Now you must confirm and test the ACL.

The first step is to check the list to see whether it was configured properly in the router. To check the ACL logic, use the **show access-lists** command. Record the output:

_____

_____

_____

b. Next, verify that the access list was applied to the proper interface and in the correct direction. To do so, examine the interface with the **show ip interface** command. Look at the output from each interface, and record the lists applied to the interface.

Interface: _____

Outgoing access list is _____

Inbound access list is _____

c. Finally, test the functionality of the ACL by trying to send packets from the source host, and verify that the packet is permitted or denied as appropriate. In this case, you use ping for the test.

d. Verify that Host 3 can ping Host 4.

e. Verify that Host 3 cannot ping Host 1.

f. Verify that Host 3 cannot ping Host 2.

g. Verify that Host 3 cannot ping GAD Fa0/0.

h. Verify that Host 3 cannot ping GAD LO0.

i. Verify that Host 4 can ping Host 1.

j. Verify that Host 4 can ping Host 2.

k. Verify that Host 4 can ping GAD Fa0/0.

l. Verify that Host 4 can ping GAD LO0.

Step 7. Document the ACL.

a. As a part of all network management, you need to create documentation. The first step in documentation is to add comments to ACL as shown in Step 5. Using the text file created for the configuration, add additional comments as necessary to describe the purpose and application of the ACL. This file should also contain output from the **show access-lists** and the **show ip interface** commands.

b. Save the file with other network documentation. The file-naming convention should reflect the function of the file and the date of implementation.

When you finish the preceding steps, log off (by typing **exit**) and turn off the routers.

Lab 11.2.2a: Configuring Extended Access Lists

Figure 11-3 Topology for Lab 11.2.2a

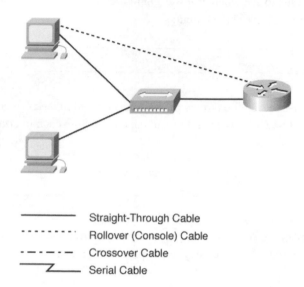

	Straight-Through Cable
	Rollover (Console) Cable
	Crossover Cable
	Serial Cable

Table 11-6 Lab Equipment Configuration

Router Designation	Router Name	FA0/0 Address	Subnet Mask	Enable Secret Password	Enable/vty/Console Passwords
Router 1	GAD	192.168.14.1	255.255.255.0	class	cisco

Objectives

- Configure and apply an extended ACL to permit or deny specific traffic.
- Test the ACL to determine whether you achieved the desired results.

Background/Preparation

Cable a network similar to the one in Figure 11-3. You can use any router that meets the interface requirements in Figure 11-3 (that is, 800, 1600, 1700, 2500, and 2600 routers or a combination). Refer to the information in Appendix B, "Router Interface Summary," correctly specify the interface identifiers based on the equipment in your lab. The 1721 series routers produced the configuration output in this lab. Any other router might produce slightly different output. You should execute the following steps on each router unless specifically instructed otherwise. Start a HyperTerminal session as you did in Lab 11-2.

Implement the procedure documented in Appendix C, "Erasing and Reloading the Router," before continuing with this lab.

Step 1. Configure the host name and passwords on the GAD router.

a. On the GAD router, enter global configuration mode and configure the router name as shown in Table 11-6. Then, configure the console, virtual terminal, and enable passwords. Configure the FastEthernet interface on the router according to the Table.

b. Allow HTTP access by issuing the **ip http server** command in global configuration mode.

Step 2. Configure the hosts on the Ethernet segment.

a. **Host 1:**

```
IP address: 192.168.14.2
Subnet mask: 255.255.255.0
Default gateway: 192.168.14.1
```

b. **Host 2:**

```
IP address: 192.168.14.3
Subnet mask: 255.255.255.0
Default gateway: 192.168.14.1
```

Step 3. Save the configuration information from privileged EXEC command mode.

GAD# `copy running-config startup-config`

Step 4. Confirm connectivity by pinging the default gateway from both hosts.

If the pings are not successful, correct your configuration and repeat until they are successful.

Step 5. Connect to the router using the web browser.

From a host, Connect to the router using a web browser to ensure that the web server function is active.

Step 6. Prevent access to HTTP (port 80) from the Ethernet interface hosts.

a. Create an ACL that prevents web-browsing access to FastEthernet 0 from the 192.168.14.0 network.

b. At the router configuration prompt, type the following command:

```
GAD(config)#access-list 101 deny tcp 192.168.14.0 0.0.0.255 any eq 80
GAD(config)#access-list 101 permit ip any any
```

c. Why do you need the second statement? _____

Step 7. Apply the ACL to the interface.

At the FastEthernet 0 interface mode prompt, type the following:

GAD(config-if)#`ip access-group 101 in`

Step 8. Ping the router from the hosts.

a. Were these pings successful? _____

b. If they were, why? _____

Step 9. Connect to the router using the web browser.

Was the browser able to connect? _____

Step 10. Telnet to the router from the hosts.

a. Were you able to Telnet successfully? _____

b. Why or why not? _____

When you finish these steps, log off (by typing **exit**) and turn off the router.

Lab 11.2.2b: Simple Extended Access Lists

Figure 11-4 Topology for Lab 11.2.2b

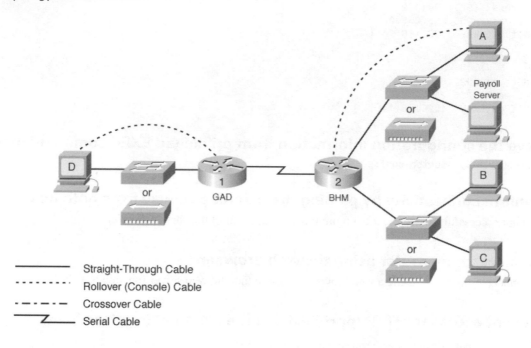

Table 11-7 Lab Equipment Configuration: Part I

Router Designation	Router Name	Routing Protocol	RIP Network Statements
Router 1	GAD	RIP	172.16.0.0
Router 2	BHM	RIP	192.168.1.0 172.16.0.0

The enable secret password for both routers is **class**.

The enable, vty, and console passwords for both routers is **cisco**.

Table 11-8 Lab Equipment Configuration: Part II

Router Designation	FastEthernet 0 Address	Interface Type Serial 0	Serial 0 Address	FastEthernet 1 Address	IP Host Table Entry
Router 1	172.16.2.1/24	DTE	172.16.1.1/24	N/A	BHM
Router 2	192.168.1.17/28	DCE	172.16.1.2/24	192.168.1.33/28	GAD

Table 11-9 Host IP Address, Subnet Mask, and Gateway Configuration

Host	IP Address	Subnet Mask	Gateway
Payroll server	192.168.1.18	255.255.255.240	192.168.1.17
A	192.168.1.19	255.255.255.240	192.168.1.17

Table 11-9 Host IP Address, Subnet Mask, and Gateway Configuration (Continued)

Host	IP Address	Subnet Mask	Gateway
B	192.168.1.34	255.255.255.240	192.168.1.33
C	192.168.1.35	255.255.255.240	192.168.1.33
D	172.16.2.2	255.255.255.0	172.16.2.1

Objectives

- Configure extended access lists to filter network-to-network traffic.

- Configure extended access lists to filter host-to-network traffic.

- Configure extended access lists to filter network-to-host traffic.

Background/Preparation

A marketing company has two locations. The main site is in Birmingham (BHM) and the branch site is in Gadsden (GAD). The telecommunication administrator for both sites needs to plan and implement ACLs for security and performance. The Birmingham site has two groups of network users, an Administrative group and a Production group, and each is on separate networks. The networks are connected by routers.

The Gadsden site is a stub network and has only a small LAN connected to it.

Step 1. Perform basic router and host configurations.

a. Connect the routers and hosts as shown in Figure 11-4. Then, configure the console, vty, and enable passwords. If you have problems doing so, refer to Lab 3.1.3, "Configuring Router Passwords." Next, configure the interfaces and routing according to Tables 11-7 and 11-8. If you have problems doing so, refer to Lab 3.2.7, "Configuring Host Tables," and Lab 7.2.2, "Configuring RIP."

Note: The BHM router requires two Ethernet interfaces.

---

b. Configure each router as follows:

```
BHM#show running-config

<Output Omitted>

hostname BHM
!
enable secret class
!
interface FastEthernet0
 ip address 192.168.1.17 255.255.255.240
!
interface Serial0
 ip address 172.16.1.2 255.255.255.0
 clock rate 56000
!
interface FastEthernet0/1
 ip address 192.168.1.33 255.255.255.240
!
```

```
router rip
 network 172.16.0.0
 network 192.168.1.0
!
line vty 0 4
 password cisco
 login
!
end

BHM#


GAD#show running-config

<Output Omitted>

!
hostname GAD
!
enable password class
!
interface FastEthernet0
 ip address 172.16.2.1 255.255.255.0
!
interface Serial0
 ip address 172.16.1.1 255.255.255.0
!
router rip
 network 172.16.0.0
!
line vty 0 4
 password cisco
 login
!
no scheduler allocate
end

GAD#
```

c. Configure each host IP Address, Subnet Mask, and Gateway according to Table 11-9.

d. Before applying any type of access list, it is important to verify communications by pinging all systems and routers from each system.

All hosts should be able to ping each other and the router interfaces. If the pings to some interfaces are not successful, you must locate and correct the problem.

e. Always verify the physical layer connections because they are a common source of connectivity problems.

f. Next, verify the router interfaces. Make sure that they are not shut down or improperly configured and that RIP is correctly configured.

g. Remember that along with valid IP addresses, hosts must also have default gateways specified.

Now that the infrastructure is in place, it is time to begin securing the internetwork.

Step 2. Prevent the production users from accessing the Gadsden network.

a. Company policy specifies that only the Administrative group should have access to the Gadsden site. You should restrict the Production group from accessing that network.

Configure an extended access list to allow the Administrative group access to the Gadsden site. The Production group should not have access to the Gadsden site.

b. Careful analysis dictates it would be best to use an extended access list and apply it to the outgoing Serial 0 interface on the BHM router.

Note: Remember when you configure the access list that the router processes each statement in the list in the order you create it. It is not possible to reorder an access list, skip statements, edit statements, or delete statements from a numbered access list. For this reason, create the access list in a text editor such as Notepad and then paste the commands to the router, instead of typing them directly on a router.

Enter the following:

```
BHM#conf terminal
```

Enter configuration commands, one per line. End with **Crtl-Z**.

```
BHM(config)#access-list 100 deny ip 192.168.1.32 0.0.0.15 172.16.2.0 0.0.0.255
```

This statement defines an extended access list called **100**. It will deny **ip** access for any users on the 192.168.1.32/28 network who are trying to access network 172.16.2.0/24. Although you could define a less specific access list, this access list could allow the Production users to access other sites (if available) through the Serial 0 interface.

Remember that there is an implicit deny all at the end of every access list.

c. You must now make sure to let the Administrative group access the Gadsden network. Although you could be more restrictive, you will simply let any other traffic through. Enter the following statement:

```
BHM(config)#access-list 100 permit ip any any
```

d. Now you need to apply the access list to an interface. You could apply the list to any incoming traffic going to the Production network's Fa0/1 interface. However, for traffic between the Administrative network and the Production network, the router must check every packet. You can avoid adding this unwanted overhead to the router. Apply the access list to the any outgoing traffic through the BHM router's S0 interface.

Enter the following:

```
BHM(config)#interface s0
BHM(config-if)#ip access-group 100 out
```

e. Verify the syntax of the access list with the **show running-config** command. The following lists the valid statements that should appear in the configuration:

```
interface Serial0
 ip access-group 100 out

<Output Omitted>

access-list 100 deny   ip 192.168.1.32 0.0.0.15 172.16.2.0 0.0.0.255
access-list 100 permit ip any any
```

Another valuable command is the **show access-lists** command. The following is a sample output:

```
BHM#show access-lists
Extended IP access list 100
    deny ip 192.168.1.32 0.0.0.15 172.16.2.0 0.0.0.255
    permit ip any any
```

The **show access-lists** command also displays counters indicating how many times the router used the list. No counters appear here because you haven't attempted to verify the list yet.

Note: Use the **clear access-list counters** command to restart the access list counters.

---

f. Now, test the access list by verifying communications with the Gadsden network on the Administrative and Production hosts.

g. Can the Production Host B ping the Gadsden Host D? _____

h. Can the Production Host C ping the Gadsden Host D? _____

i. Can the Administrative Host A ping the Gadsden Host D? _____

j. Can the Production Host B ping the Administrative Host A? _____

k. Can the Production Host B ping the Gadsden router's serial interface?

_____

l. The Production Hosts B and C should be able to ping the Administrative Host A and Gadsden router's serial interface. However, they should not be able to ping the Gadsden Host D. The router should return a reply message to the host, "Destination net unreachable."

m. Issue the **show access-lists** command. How many matches are there? _____

Note: The **show access-lists** command displays the number of matches per line. Therefore, the number of deny matches might seem odd until you realize that the pings match the deny statement and the permit statement.

---

n. To understand how the access list is operating, keep periodically issuing the **show access-lists** command.

Step 3. Allow a production user access to the Gadsden network.

a. A user in the Production Group B because he is responsible for exchanging certain files between the Production network and the Gadsden network. You must alter the extended access list to give him access to the Gadsden network while denying everyone else on the production network.

Configure an extended access-list to give that user access to Gadsden.

b. Unfortunately, it is not possible to reorder an access list, skip statements, edit statements, or delete statements from a numbered access list. With numbered access lists, any attempt to delete a single statement results in the entire list's deletion.

You must delete the initial extended access list and create a new one. To delete **access-list 100**, enter the following:

BHM#`conf t`

Enter configuration commands, one per line. End with **Ctrl-Z**.

BHM(config)#`no access-list 100`

c. Verify that it has been deleted with the **show access-lists** command.

d. Now, create a new extended access list. Always filter from the most specific to the most generic. The first line of the access list should allow the Production Host B access to the Gadsden network. The remainder of the access list should be the same as the previous you entered.

To filter the Production Host B, the first line of the access list should appear as follows:

BHM(config)#`access-list 100 permit ip host 192.168.1.34 172.16.2.0 0.0.0.255`

e. Now, deny all the remaining Production hosts access to the Gadsden network and permit anyone else. Refer to the Step 2 for the next two lines of the configuration.

f. The **show access-list** command will display output similar to the following:

```
BHM#show access-lists
Extended IP access list 100
    permit ip host 192.168.1.34 172.16.2.0 0.0.0.255
    deny ip 192.168.1.32 0.0.0.15 172.16.2.0 0.0.0.255
    permit ip any any
BHM#
```

g. Test the access list by verifying communications with the Gadsden network on the Administrative and Production hosts.

h. Can the Production Host B ping the Gadsden Host D? _____

i. Can the Production Host C ping the Gadsden Host D? _____

j. The Production Host B should now be able to ping the Gadsden Host D. However, all other Production hosts should not be able to ping the Gadsden Host D. Again, the router should return a reply message to the host, "Destination net unreachable," for Host C.

Step 4. Allow Gadsden users access to the administration payroll server.

a. The Administrative group houses the payroll server. Users from the Gadsden site need FTP and HTTP access to the payroll server from time to time to upload and download payroll reports.

Configure an extended access list to give users from the Gadsden site FTP and HTTP access to the payroll server only. Also allow Internet Control Message Protocol (ICMP) access so they can ping the server. Gadsden users should not be able to ping any other host on the Administrative network.

You do not want unnecessary traffic between the sites so configure an extended access list on the Gadsden router.

b. Because someone anticipated that you might need privileged EXEC access to the Gadsden router, she configured Telnet access to it. Otherwise, you would have to travel to the Gadsden site to configure it.

Telnet to the Gadsden router from the Birmingham router and enter enable mode. Troubleshoot as necessary.

Note: A common pitfall when configuring access lists on remote routers is inadvertently "locking" yourself out. This pitfall is not a big problem when the router is local. However, it can be a huge problem if the router is physically located in another geographical area.

For this reason, we strongly suggest that you issue the **reload in 30** command on the remote router. This command would automatically reload the remote router within 30 minutes. Therefore, if you get locked out, the router eventually reloads to the previous configuration, allowing access again. Use the **reload cancel** command to deactivate the pending reload.

c. Configure an extended access list to allow FTP access to the payroll server. The access list statement should be similar to the following:

```
GAD(config)#access-list 110 permit tcp any host 192.168.1.18 eq ftp
```

This line will give any host from the Gadsden network FTP access to the payroll server at address 192.168.1.18.

d. What could you define instead of using the keyword **any**?

---

e. What could you define instead of using the keyword **host**?

_____

f. What could you define instead of using the keyword **ftp**?

_____

g. Now, configure the next line of the access list to permit HTTP access to the payroll server. The access list statement should be similar to the following:

```
GAD(config)#access-list 110 permit tcp any host 192.168.1.18 eq www
```

This line will give any host from the Gadsden network HTTP access to the payroll server at address 192.168.1.18.

h. What else could you define instead of using the keyword **www?**

_____

i. Configure the next line of the access list to permit ICMP access to the payroll server. The access list statement should be similar to the following:

```
GAD(config)#access-list 110 permit icmp any host 192.168.1.18
```

This line will permit any host from the Gadsden network to ping the payroll server at address 192.168.1.18.

j. Finally, no Gadsden user should be able to access any other host on the Administrative network. Although it is not required, it is always a good idea to include a **deny** statement. The statement serves as a reminder and makes it easier to "read" the access list. The access-list statement should be similar to the following:

```
GAD(config)#access-list 110 deny ip any 192.168.1.16 0.0.0.15
```

k. Now, you need to apply the access list to an interface. To reduce unwanted WAN traffic, apply the access list to the any outgoing traffic through the Gadsden router's S0 interface.

Enter the following:

```
GAD(config)#interface s0
GAD(config-if)#ip access-group 110 out
```

l. Test the access list by verifying communications with the payroll server on Gadsden Host D.

m. Can the Gadsden Host D ping the payroll server? _____

n. Can the Gadsden Host D ping Host A? _____

The Gadsden host should be able to ping the payroll server only. The router should return "Destination net unreachable" when it tries to ping the Administrative Host D.

Step 5. Document the ACL.

a. As a part of all network management, you should create documentation. Using the text file created for the configuration, add your comments. This file should also contain output from the **show access-lists** and the **show ip interface** commands.

b. Save the file with other network documentation. The file-naming convention should reflect the function of the file and the date of implementation.

When you finish the preceding steps, log off (by typing **exit**) and turn off the routers.

Lab 11.2.3a: Configuring a Named Access List

Figure 11-5 Topology for Lab 11.2.3a

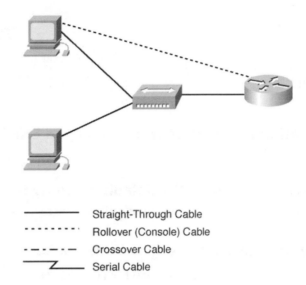

Straight-Through Cable
Rollover (Console) Cable
Crossover Cable
Serial Cable

Table 11-10 Lab Equipment Configuration

Router Designation	Router Name	FA0/0 Address	Subnet Mask	Enable Secret Password	Enable/vty/ Console Passwords
Router 1	GAD	192.168.14.1	255.255.255.0	class	cisco

Objectives

- Create a named ACL to permit or deny specific traffic.
- Test the ACL to determine whether you achieved the desired results.

Background/Preparation

Cable a network similar to the one in Figure 11-5. You can use any router that meets the interface requirements in Figure 11-5 (that is, 800, 1600, 1700, 2500, and 2600 routers or a combination). Refer to the information in Appendix B, "Router Interface Summary," correctly specify the interface identifiers based on the equipment in your lab. The 1721 series routers produced the configuration output in this lab. Any other router might produce slightly different output. You should execute the following steps on each router unless specifically instructed otherwise. Start a HyperTerminal session as you did in Lab 2.2.4.

Implement the procedure documented in Appendix C, "Erasing and Reloading the Router," before continuing with this lab.

Step 1. Configure the host name and passwords on the GAD router.

On the GAD router, enter global configuration mode and configure the router name as shown in Table 11-10. Then, configure the console, virtual terminal, and enable passwords. Configure the FastEthernet interface on the router according to Table 11-10.

Step 2. Configure the hosts on the Ethernet segment.

a. **Host 1:**

```
IP address: 192.168.14.2
Subnet mask: 255.255.255.0
Default gateway: 192.168.14.1
```

b. **Host 2:**

```
IP address: 192.168.14.3
Subnet mask: 255.255.255.0
Default gateway: 192.168.14.1
```

Step 3. Save the configuration information from privileged EXEC command mode.

GAD# `copy running-config startup-config`

Step 4. Confirm connectivity by pinging the default gateway from both hosts.

If the pings are not successful, correct your configuration and repeat until they are successful.

Step 5. Prevent access to the Ethernet interface from the hosts.

a. Create a named ACL that prevents access to FastEthernet 0 from the 192.168.14.0 network.

b. At the configuration prompt, type the following command:

```
GAD(config)#ip access-list standard no_access
GAD(config-std-nacl)#deny 192.168.14.0 0.0.0.255
GAD(config-std-nacl)#permit any
```

c. Why do you need the third statement?

_____

Step 6. Ping the router from the hosts.

a. Were these pings successful? _____

b. If they were, why? _____

Step 7. Apply the ACL to the interface.

At the FastEthernet interface mode prompt, type the following:

GAD(config-if)# `ip access-group no_access in`

Step 8. Ping the router from the hosts.

a. Were these pings successful? _____

b. Why or why not? _____

When you finish these steps, log off (by typing **exit**) and turn off the router.

Lab 11.2.3b: Simple DMZ Extended Access Lists

Figure 11-6 Topology for Lab 11.2.3c

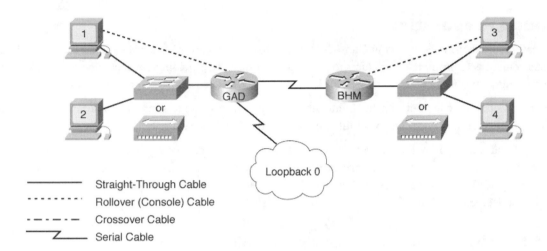

Table 11-11 Lab Equipment Configuration: Part I

Router Designation	Router Name	Routing Protocol	RIP Network Statements
Router 1	ISP	RIP	172.16.0.0
Router 2	GAD	RIP	10.0.0.0 172.16.0.0

The enable secret password for both routers is **class**.

The enable, vty, and console passwords for both routers is **cisco**.

Table 11-12 Lab Equipment Configuration: Part II

Router Designation	FastEthernet 0 Address	Interface Type Serial 0	Serial 0 Address	FastEthernet 1 Address	IP Host Names
Router 1	172.16.2.1/24	DTE	172.16.1.1/24	N/A	ISP
Router 2	10.1.1.1/24	DCE	172.16.1.2/24	10.10.10.1/24	GAD

Table 11-13 Host IP Address, Subnet Mask, and Gateway Configuration

Host	IP Address	Subnet Mask	Gateway
Web server	10.1.1.10	255.255.255.0	10.1.1.1
A	10.10.10.10	255.255.255.0	10.10.10.1
B	172.16.2.10	255.255.255.0	172.16.2.1

Objective

■ Use extended access lists to create a simple demilitarized zone (DMZ).

Background/Preparation

BMTC is a small manufacturing company in Gadsden. It wants to create an awareness of its products over the Internet. The immediate requirement is to promote its products to potential customers by providing product overviews, reports, and testimonials. Future requirements could include e-mail, FTP, Domain Name System (DNS), and online e-commerce services.

The company has contracted you to design and configure a secure infrastructure to support its internal and external network requirements while maintaining fiscal responsibility—which means, "Make it secure but keep costs down."

Careful analysis dictates that you will create a two-tier security architecture consisting of a corporate network zone and a DMZ. The corporate network zone will house private servers and internal clients. The DMZ will house only one external server to provide World Wide Web services. Although the one server creates a single point of failure, the service is only informational and is not deemed mission-critical.

Step 1. Perform basic router and host configurations.

a. Connect the routers and hosts as shown in Figure 11-7.

b. Configure all router basics such as host name, router interfaces, and routing protocol using the preceding tables for reference. The configurations on each router should be similar to the following:

```
GAD#show running-config

<Output Omitted>

!
hostname GAD
!
interface FastEthernet0
 ip address 10.1.1.1 255.255.255.0
!
interface Serial0
 ip address 172.16.1.2 255.255.255.0
!
interface FastEthernet1
 ip address 10.10.10.1 255.255.255.0
!
router rip
 network 10.0.0.0
 network 172.16.0.0
!
GAD#
```

```
ISP#show running-config

<Output Omitted>

!
hostname ISP
!
interface FastEthernet0
 ip address 172.16.2.1 255.255.255.0
!
interface Serial0
```

```
 ip address 172.16.1.1 255.255.255.0
 !
router rip
 network 172.16.0.0
 !

 ISP#
```

c. Configure the hosts IP Address, Subnet Mask, and Gateway according to Table 11-15 with the appropriate information.

d. To make the lab more realistic, install web-server software on the web-server host. Examples include Microsoft IIS or Microsoft Personal Web Server (Windows 98). You can use third-party software such as TinyWeb Server (http://www.ritlabs.com/tinyweb/). If you use TinyWeb Server, also install TinyBox (http://people.freenet.de/ralph.becker/tinybox/), which is a GUI front end for TinyWeb Server.

e. Create a default index.html page. The web page should include a message such as "Hello World." Save the page as instructed by the web-server software.

f. Before applying any type of access list, verify communications between the systems by pinging all the systems and routers from each system.

g. Can Host A ping Host B? _____

h. Can Host A ping the web server? _____

i. Can Host B ping Host A? _____

j. Can Host B ping the web server? _____

All hosts should be able to ping each other. Troubleshoot if ping is not successful to some interfaces.

k. Always verify the physical layer connections because they are a common source of connectivity problems.

l. Verify the router interfaces. Make sure that they are not shut down or improperly configured and that RIP is correctly configured.

m. Along with valid IP addresses, hosts must also have default gateways specified.

n. On Host A, open a web browser such as Windows Explorer or Netscape Navigator. Enter the address of the web server to verify that each host has web access to the web server.

o. Can Host A view the index.html page? _____

p. Can Host B view the index.html page? _____

q. Both hosts should be able to view the index.html page in the web browser. Troubleshoot as necessary.

Now that the infrastructure is in place, it is time to begin securing the internetwork.

Step 2. Protect the corporate network.

The corporate network zone houses private servers and internal clients. No other network should be able to access it.

a. Configure an extended access list to protect the corporate network. Protecting a corporate network begins by specifying which traffic can exit the network. Although this step might initially sound strange, realize that the most damage results from hackers who are internal employees. The first access list will specify which traffic can exit the network.

Enter the following:

```
GAD#conf terminal
```

Enter configuration commands, one per line. End with CNTL/Z.

```
GAD(config)#access-list 101 permit ip 10.10.10.0 0.0.0.255 any
GAD(config)#access-list 101 deny ip any any
```

The first line defines that access list **101** will only let valid corporate users on network 10.10.10.0 into the router. The second line is not really required because of the implicit **deny all** but improves code readability.

b. Now, you need to apply the access list to the corporate network interface. Enter the following:

```
GAD(config)#interface fa1
GAD(config-if)#ip access-group 101 in
```

c. Test the access lists by pinging all the systems and routers from each system.

d. Can Host A ping the web server? _____

e. Can Host A ping Host B? _____

f. Can Host B ping the web server? _____

g. Can Host B ping Host A? _____

All hosts should be able to ping any location.

h. Next, configure an outbound extended access list on the corporate network interface. Traffic entering the corporate network will be coming from either the Internet or the DMZ. For this reason, you must limit which traffic is allowed into the corporate network.

First, make sure that only traffic which originates from the corporate network can return to that network. Enter the following:

```
GAD(config)#access-list 102 permit tcp any any established
```

The keyword **established** in this line permits only TCP traffic that originates from the 10.10.10.0 network.

i. To make network management and troubleshooting easier, you will permit ICMP traffic into the network. This step will allow the internal hosts to receive ICMP messages (ping messages).

Enter the following:

```
GAD(config)#access-list 102 permit icmp any any echo-reply
GAD(config)#access-list 102 permit icmp any any unreachable
```

The first line allows only successful pings back into the corporate network. The second line allows unsuccessful ping messages to appear.

j. At this time, you want to allow no other traffic into the corporate network. Therefore, enter the following:

```
GAD(config)#access-list 102 deny ip any any
```

k. Finally, you must apply the access list to the corporate network FastEthernet port:

```
GAD(config)#interface fa1
GAD(config-if)#ip access-group 102 out
```

Remember that an interface can support one incoming and one outgoing access list. The **show ip interface fa1** command can be used to confirm that the outgoing access list is 102 and that the inbound access list is 101.

l. Use the **show access-lists** command to verify the syntax of the access lists. The output should be similar to the following:

```
GAD#show access-lists
Extended IP access list 101
    permit ip 10.10.10.0 0.0.0.255 any
    deny ip any any

Extended IP access list 102
```

```
permit tcp any any established
permit icmp any any echo-reply
permit icmp any any unreachable
deny ip any any
```

m. You might have to delete and re-enter access lists if you spot any discrepancy between the preceding output and the configuration.

Now, it's time to test the access lists.

n. Verify communications by pinging all the systems and routers from each system.

o. Can Host A ping the web server? _____

p. Can Host A ping Host B? _____

q. Can Host B ping the web server? _____

r. Can Host B ping Host A? _____

Host A should be able to ping all locations. However, no external host should be able to ping Host A.

s. On Host A, open a web browser and enter the address of the web server.

Can Host A view the index.html page? _____

Host A should still be able to view the index.html page in the web browser. Troubleshoot as necessary.

The internal corporate network is now secure. Next, you need to secure the DMZ network.

Step 3. Protect the DMZ network.

The DMZ network will house only one external server, which will provide World Wide Web services. The company will add other services such as e-mail, FTP, and DNS at a later time. Although the one server creates a single point of failure, the service is only informational and not considered mission critical.

a. Configure an extended access list to protect the DMZ network. As with the corporate network, specify which traffic can exit the network and apply it to the interface.

Enter the following:

```
GAD#conf terminal
```

Enter configuration commands, one per line. End with CNTL/Z.

```
GAD(config)#access-list 111 permit ip 10.1.1.0 0.0.0.255 any
GAD(config)#access-list 111 deny ip any any

GAD(config)#interface fa0
GAD(config-if)#ip access-group 111 in
```

b. Test the new access lists by pinging all the systems and routers from each system.

c. Can Host A ping the web server? _____

d. Can Host A ping Host B? _____

e. Can Host B ping the web server? _____

f. Can Host B ping Host A? _____

Host A should be able to ping all locations. However, no external host should be able to ping Host A.

g. Next, you need an outbound extended access list to specify which traffic can enter the DMZ network. Traffic entering the DMZ network will come from either the Internet or the corporate network requesting World Wide Web services.

Configure an outbound extended access list specifying that World Wide Web requests be allowed into the network.

Enter the following:

```
GAD(config)#access-list 112 permit tcp any host 10.1.1.10 eq www
```

This line will allow World Wide Web (HTTP) service requests destined for the web server into the DMZ network.

h. What command would you enter to allow DNS requests into the DMZ?

_____

i. What command would you enter to allow e-mail requests into the DMZ?

_____

j. What command would you enter to allow FTP requests into the DMZ?

_____

k. For management purposes, it would be useful to let corporate users ping the web server. However, Internet users should not get the same privilege. Add a line to the access list to give only corporate users ICMP access into the DMZ network.

Enter the following:

```
GAD(config)#access-list 112 permit icmp 10.10.10.0 0.0.0.255 host 10.1.1.10
```

This line allows only hosts on the corporate network to ping the web server. Although the configuration could be more restrictive with the ICMP options, the company does not view it as necessary.

l. You could permit other services into the DMZ network in the future. However, at this time, you want no other traffic permitted into the DMZ network. Therefore, enter the following:

```
GAD(config)#access-list 112 deny ip any any
```

m. Apply the outbound access list to the DMZ network FastEthernet port.

```
GAD(config)#interface fa0
GAD(config-if)#ip access-group 112 out
```

n. To verify the syntax of the access lists, use the **show-access-lists** command. The output should be similar to the following:

```
GAD#show access-lists
Extended IP access list 101
    permit ip 10.10.10.0 0.0.0.255 any (70 matches)
    deny ip any any
Extended IP access list 102
    permit tcp any any established (8 matches)
    permit icmp any any echo-reply (12 matches)
    permit icmp any any unreachable
    deny ip any any (4 matches)
Extended IP access list 111
    permit ip 10.1.1.0 0.0.0.255 any (59 matches)
    deny ip any any
Extended IP access list 112
    permit tcp any host 10.1.1.10 eq www (29 matches)
    permit icmp 10.10.10.0 0.0.0.255 host 10.1.1.10 (4 matches)
    deny ip any any (14 matches)
```

You might have to delete and re-enter the access lists if you spot any discrepancy between the preceding output and the configuration.

o. Test the access lists by verify communications by pinging all the systems and routers from each system.

p. Can Host A ping the web server? _____

q. Can Host A ping Host B? _____

r. Can Host B ping the web server? _____

s. Can Host B ping Host A? _____

Only Host A should be able to ping all locations.

t. Use a web browser on each host and enter the address of the web server to verify that the hosts still have web access to the web server.

u. Can Host A view the index.html page? _____

v. Can Host B view the index.html page? _____

Both hosts should still be able to view the index.html page in the web browser. Troubleshoot as necessary.

The DMZ network is now secure. Next, you need to configure your external interface to deter spoofing and hacking practices.

Step 4. Deter spoofing.

Networks are prone to attacks from outside users. Hackers, crackers, and script kiddies are titles for various individuals who maliciously break into networks or render networks incapable of responding to legitimate requests (denial-of-service (DoS) attacks). Such attacks are troublesome for the Internet community.

You are well aware of the practices that some of these hackers use. A common method they employ is to forge a valid internal source IP addresses, a practice commonly known as *spoofing*.

To deter spoofing, you will configure an access list so that Internet hosts cannot easily spoof an internal network addresses. Three common source IP addresses that hackers attempt to forge are valid internal addresses (e.g., 10.10.10.0), loopback addresses (i.e., 127.$x.x.x$), and multicast addresses (i.e., 224.$x.x.x$ through 239.$x.x.x$).

a. Configure an inbound access list that will make it difficult for outside users to spoof internal addresses and apply it to the Serial 0 interface.

Enter the following:

```
GAD(config)#access-list 121 deny ip 10.10.10.0 0.0.0.255 any
GAD(config)#access-list 121 deny ip 127.0.0.0 0.255.255.255 any
GAD(config)#access-list 121 deny ip 224.0.0.0 31.255.255.255 any
GAD(config)#access-list 121 permit ip any any

GAD(config)#interface serial 0
GAD(config-if)#ip access-group 121 in
```

The first line will stop outside users from forging a valid source IP address. The second line stops them from using the loopback address range. The third line stops hackers from using the multicast range of addresses (i.e., 224.0.0.0 through 239.255.255.255) to create unnecessary internal traffic.

b. Verify the syntax of the access lists with the **show-access-lists** command. The output should be similar to the following:

```
GAD#show access-lists
Extended IP access list 101
    permit ip 10.10.10.0 0.0.0.255 any (168 matches)
    deny ip any any
Extended IP access list 102
    permit tcp any any established (24 matches)
    permit icmp any any echo-reply (28 matches)
    permit icmp any any unreachable
    deny ip any any (12 matches)
Extended IP access list 111
    permit ip 10.1.1.0 0.0.0.255 any (122 matches)
    deny ip any any
Extended IP access list 112
```

```
        permit tcp any host 10.1.1.10 eq www (69 matches)
        permit icmp 10.10.10.0 0.0.0.255 host 10.1.1.10 (12 matches)
        deny ip any any (22 matches)
Extended IP access list 121
        deny ip 10.10.10.0 0.0.0.255 any
        deny ip 127.0.0.0 0.255.255.255 any
        deny ip 224.0.0.0 31.255.255.255 any
        permit ip any any (47 matches)
```

You might have to delete and re-enter the access lists if you spot any discrepancy between the preceding output and the configuration.

c. Test whether connectivity still exists by pinging all the systems and routers from each system.

d. Can Host A ping the web server? _____

e. Can Host A ping Host B? _____

f. Can Host B ping the web server? _____

g. Can Host B ping Host A? _____

Only Host A should be able to ping all locations.

h. Use a web browser on each host and enter the address of the web server to verify that the hosts still have web access to the web server.

i. Can Host A view the index.html page? _____

j. Can Host B view the index.html page? _____

Both hosts should still be able to view the index.html page in the web browser.

Troubleshoot as necessary.

The BMTC network is now secure.

Note: The preceding lab is a basic solution to providing a secure network. It is by no means a complete solution.

To properly protect enterprise networks, you should implement dedicated network devices such as Cisco PIX devices. As well, we strongly recommend you use advanced features such as Network Address Translation (NAT) and advanced access-list options such as reflexive access lists and Context Based Access Control (CBAC). These topics are beyond the scope of CCNA certification. Finally, we recommend that network administrators maintain strong relationships with their service providers to help when network security is compromised.

Step 5. Document the ACL.

As a part of all network management, you should create documentation. Using the text file you created for the configuration, add your comments. This file should also contain output from the **show access-list** and the **show ip interface** commands.

Save the file with other network documentation. The file-naming convention should reflect the function of the file and the date of implementation.

When you finish the preceding steps, log off (by typing **exit**) and turn off the routers.

Lab 11.2.3c: Multiple Access Lists Functions (Challenge Lab)

Figure 11-7 Topology for Lab 11.2.3d

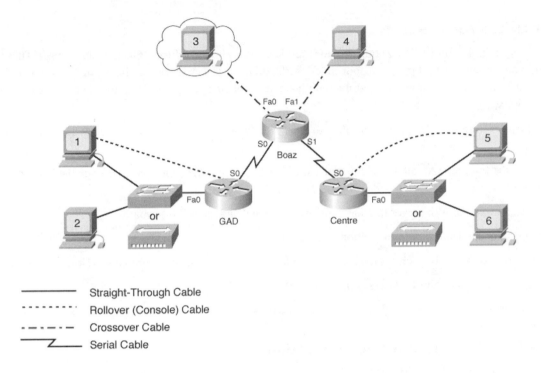

Straight-Through Cable
Rollover (Console) Cable
Crossover Cable
Serial Cable

Table 11-14 Lab Equipment Configuration

Router Name	Router Type	FA0 Address	FA1 Address	S0 Address	S1 Address	Subnet Mask	Routing	Enable Password	vty Password

Table 11-15 Host IP Address, Subnet Mask, and Gateway Configuration

Host	IP Address	Subnet Mask	Gateway

Objective

- Configure and apply an extended ACL to control Internet traffic using one or more routers.

Background/Preparation

The company has a regional office (Boaz) that provides services to two branch offices (Gaston and Centre). These offices each have a branch manager and several people responsible for providing customer services. The service department has experienced a significant amount of turnover. A security audit it revealed that the computers that the service personnel use have no network restrictions.

The network infrastructure team leader wants a plan to enforce network security to prevent access. The criteria for this infrastructure follow:

Host 3 represents the Internet. (An alternative is to use the Loopback 0 interface on Boaz and issue the Boaz(config)#**ip http server** command.)

Host 4 represents an internal web server that has sensitive personnel and payroll information.

Host 4 also represents the network administration computer.

The lowest four host addresses in each subnet are reserved for the branch managers' computers (Hosts 1 and 5).

The router interfaces use the highest addresses in the subnets.

The service personnel computers (Hosts 2 and 6) will use the remaining addresses in each branch's subnet.

Step 1. Perform basic router interconnection.

Connect the routers as shown in Figure 11-8.

Step 2. Design the internetwork addressing scheme .

Using a private Class C IP address for the internal network, design and document the network. Complete the preceding charts and include the interface type and number, IP address, subnet mask, and cable type. The "Internet" (cloud) network can be any private space address. Be sure that the address ranges assigned to the routers and hosts meet the criteria described in the infrastructure section.

Step 3. Perform basic router configuration.

The router might contain configurations from previous use. Implement the procedure in Appendix C on all routers before continuing with this lab. Using the information previously created, set up the router configurations using RIP or Interior Gateway Routing Protocol (IGRP) and verify communications by pinging all the systems and routers from each system.

To simulate specific locations on the Internet, add the following configuration to the Boaz router:

```
Boaz(config)#interface loopback 1
Boaz(config-if)#ip address 192.168.255.1 255.255.255.255
Boaz(config-if)#exit
Boaz(config)#interface loopback 2
Boaz(config-if)#ip address 192.168.255.2 255.255.255.255
Boaz(config-if)#exit
Boaz(config)#interface loopback 3
Boaz(config-if)#ip address 192.168.255.3 255.255.255.255
Boaz(config-if)#exit
Boaz(config)#interface loopback 4
Boaz(config-if)#ip address 192.168.255.4 255.255.255.255
Boaz(config-if)#exit
Boaz(config)#interface loopback 5
Boaz(config-if)#ip address 192.168.255.5 255.255.255.255
```

```
Boaz(config-if)#exit
Boaz(config)#interface loopback 6
Boaz(config-if)#ip address 192.168.255.6 255.255.255.255
Boaz(config-if)#exit
Boaz(config)#interface loopback 7
Boaz(config-if)#ip address 192.168.255.7 255.255.255.255
Boaz(config-if)#exit
Boaz(config)#interface loopback 8
Boaz(config-if)#ip address 192.168.255.8 255.255.255.255
Boaz(config-if)#exit
Boaz(config)#interface loopback 9
Boaz(config-if)#ip address 192.168.255.9 255.255.255.255
Boaz(config-if)#exit
Boaz(config)#interface loopback 10
Boaz(config-if)#ip address 192.168.255.10 255.255.255.255
Boaz(config-if)#exit
```

Add a network statement to the Boaz routing protocol to advertise this network:

```
Boaz(config-router)#network 192.168.255.0
```

Step 4. Configuration the clients.

Configure the hosts with the appropriate information using the information previously defined.

 a. Verify communications by pinging all the systems and routers from each system.

 b. On Hosts 3 and 4, install and configure a web server such as TinyWeb (http://www.simtel.net/pub/pd/13103.html). (Host 3 represents the Internet. Host 4 represents an internal web server that has sensitive personnel and payroll information. Host 4 can be the loopback of the Boaz router.)

 c. Verify that all systems can use a web browser to access the web pages of both the intranet server (Host 4) and the Internet server (Host 3).

 d. On Host 3, install and configure a Telnet server such as TelnetXQ (http://www.datawizard.net/Free_Software/ TelnetXQ_Free/telnetxq_free.htm).

 e. Verify that all systems can Telnet to the Internet (Host 3).

Now that the infrastructure is in place, it is time to begin securing the internetwork.

Step 5. Secure the intranet server.

Host 4 represents an internal web server that has sensitive personnel and payroll information. The information on this server should be accessible only to the branch managers. Create ACLs to secure this server so that only branch managers' machines have web access (HTTP) to this internal server.

 a. How many ACLs will you use? _____

 b. Where will you apply the ACLs? _____

 c. In which direction will you apply the ACLs? _____

 d. For what reasons might it be better to use multiple ACLs?

 _____

 _____

 _____

 e. For what reasons might it be better to use a single ACL?

 _____

 _____

f. Using a text editor, such as Notepad, construct the logic of the access lists and then type the proper commands. Once you properly construct the list, paste it into the router's configuration and apply it to the appropriate interface(s).

Confirm that the ACL is functioning properly.

g. Verify communications by pinging all the systems and routers from each system.

h. Verify that all the computers systems can use a web browser to access the web pages on the Internet (anywhere except the internal web server).

i. Verify that the service personnel computers cannot use a web browser to access (HTTP) the intranet server.

j. Verify that the computers from the Internet (Host 3) cannot use a web browser to access (HTTP) the intranet server.

Step 6. Secure the intranet documents.

There is concern that internal policy and procedures documents are available outside of the company. To ensure that users in the internetwork cannot forward these documents, do not allow any Telnet or FTP access to the Internet.

a. Will you create new ACLs or modify the current lists? _____

If you create new lists:

b. How many new ACLs will you create? _____

c. Where will you apply the new ACLs?

_____

d. In which direction will you apply the new ACLs? _____

e. Again, use a text editor, such as Notepad, to construct the logic of the access lists and type the proper commands. Once you properly construct the list, paste it into the routers and apply it to the appropriate interfaces.

Confirm that the ACL is functioning properly.

f. Verify communications by pinging all the systems and routers from each system.

g. Verify that all computers systems can use a web browser to access the web pages on the Internet (anywhere except the internal web server).

h. Verify that the service personnel computers cannot use a web browser to access (HTTP) the intranet server.

i. Verify computers from the Internet (Host 3) cannot use a web browser to access (HTTP) the intranet server.

j. Verify that the computers cannot Telnet to the Internet (Host 3 and loopback interfaces on Boaz) but can Telnet to the routers.

Step 7. Deter Internet abuse.

There have also been some complaints that employees are abusing Internet access. They have been accessing sites with questionable content. To help stop this practice, do not allow any IP traffic from the internetwork to the following sites:

192.168.255.1

192.168.255.4

192.168.255.8

192.168.255.9

a. Will you create new ACLs or modify the current lists? _____

If you create new lists:

b. How many new ACLs will you create? _____

c. Where will you apply the new ACLs?

_____

d. In which direction will you apply the new ACLs? _____

e. Again, use a text editor, such as Notepad, to construct the logic of the access lists and type the proper commands. Once you properly construct the list, paste it into the routers and apply it to the appropriate interfaces.

   Confirm that the ACL is functioning properly.

f. Verify that the service personnel computers cannot use a web browser to access (HTTP) the intranet server.

g. Verify that the computers from the Internet (Host 3) cannot use a web browser to access (HTTP) the intranet server.

h. Verify that the computers cannot Telnet to the Internet (Host 3 and loopback interfaces on Boaz) but can Telnet to the routers.

i. Verify that the computers cannot Telnet, use a web browser to access, nor ping 192.168.255.1.

j. Verify that the computers cannot Telnet, use a web browser to access, nor ping 192.168.255.4.

k. Verify that the computers cannot Telnet, use a web browser to access, nor ping 192.168.255.8.

l. Verify that the computers cannot Telnet, use a web browser to access, nor ping 192.168.255.9.

m. Verify communications by pinging all the other systems and routers from each system.

n. Verify that all the computer systems can use a web browser to access the other web pages on the Internet (Host 3 and loopback interfaces on Boaz).

Step 8. Deter DoS attacks.

In the last few weeks, the company's internetwork has been the subject of numerous Denial of Service (DoS) attacks. Most have had the form of the "ping of death" (oversized ICMP echo packets) or directed broadcasts (*x.x.x*.255). To help stop the ping-of-death attacks, do not allow any ICMP echo packets into the internetwork. To stop the directed broadcast, stop all IP packets addressed to the directed broadcast address from entering the internetwork.

a. Will you create new ACLs or modify the current lists? _____

   If new list(s):

b. How many new ACLs will you create? _____

c. Where will you apply the new ACLs?

_____

d. In which direction will you apply the new ACLs? _____

e. Use a text editor, such as Notepad, to construct the logic of the access lists and type the proper commands. Once you properly construct the list, paste it into the routers and apply it to the appropriate interfaces.

   Confirm that the ACL is functioning properly.

f. Verify that the service personnel computers cannot use a web browser to access (HTTP) the intranet server.

g. Verify that the computers from the Internet (Host 3) cannot use a web browser to access (HTTP) the intranet server.

h. Verify that the computers cannot Telnet to the Internet (Host 3 and loopback interfaces on Boaz) but can Telnet to the routers.

i. Verify that the computers cannot Telnet, use a web browser to access, nor ping 192.168.255.1.

j. Verify that the computers cannot Telnet, use a web browser to access, nor ping 192.168.255.4.

k. Verify that the computers cannot Telnet, use a web browser to access, nor ping 192.168.255.8.

l. Verify that the computers cannot Telnet, use a web browser to access, nor ping 192.168.255.9.

m. Verify that all the computer systems can use a web browser to access the other web pages on the Internet (Host 3 and loopback interfaces on Boaz).

n. Verify that Host 3 cannot successfully ping anything in the internetwork.

o. Verify that the systems can successfully ping the other Internet hosts.

p. Verify communications by pinging all the other systems and routers from each system.

Step 9. Stop Telnet into the routers.

There have been some attempts to Telnet into the routers both inside and outside the internetwork. The only host that should have Telnet access to the routers is the network administration computer. To stop Telnet access to the routers, create an ACL and apply it to the vty lines of the routers that will permit only the network administration computer to Telnet.

a. What type of access list will you use? _____

b. What command will you use to apply the list to the vty lines?

_____

c. Use a text editor, such as Notepad, to construct the logic of the access lists and type the proper commands. After you properly construct the list, paste it to the routers and apply it to the vty lines.

Confirm that the ACL is functioning properly.

d. Verify that the service personnel computers cannot use a web browser to access (HTTP) the intranet server.

e. Verify that the computers from the Internet (Host 3) cannot use a web browser to access (HTTP) the intranet server.

f. Verify that the computers cannot Telnet to the Internet (Host 3 and loopback interfaces on Boaz) but can Telnet to the routers.

g. Verify that the computers cannot Telnet, use a web browser to access, nor ping 192.168.255.1.

h. Verify that the computers cannot Telnet, use a web browser to access, nor ping 192.168.255.4.

i. Verify that the computers cannot Telnet, use a web browser to access, nor ping 192.168.255.8.

j. Verify that the computers cannot Telnet, use a web browser to access, nor ping 192.168.255.9.

k. Verify that all the computer systems can use a web browser to access the other web pages on the Internet (Host 3 and loopback interfaces on Boaz).

l. Verify that Host 3 cannot successfully ping anything in the internetwork.

m. Verify that the systems can successfully ping to the other Internet hosts.

n. Verify that the systems can successfully ping Host 3.

o. Verify that the network administration computer (Host 4) can Telnet to all the routers.

p. Verify that the other internal computers cannot Telnet to any of the routers.

q. Verify that the other external computers (Host 3) cannot Telnet to any of the routers.

Step 10. Verify the access lists.

Once you apply the access lists, you need to verify them.

a. First, verify what lists you have defined. From a CLI session on one of the routers with access lists, display the access lists with the Boaz#**show ip access-lists** command. Record the information about one of the access lists:

_____

_____

_____

_____

_____

b. What does the (**# matches**) in the output represent?

_____

c. Next, confirm which access list is applied to each interface. You do so from the terminal session of one of the routers with access lists, with the Boaz#**show ip interface** command. Look at the output from each interface and record the lists applied to each interface:

Interface: _____

Outgoing access list is _____

Inbound access list is _____

Interface: _____

Outgoing access list is _____

Inbound access list is _____

Interface: _____

Outgoing access list is _____

Inbound access list is _____

Interface: _____

Outgoing access list is _____

Inbound access list is _____

When you finish the preceding steps, log off (by typing **exit**) and turn off the routers.

Lab 11.2.6: VTY Restriction

Figure 11-8 Topology for Lab 11.2.3b

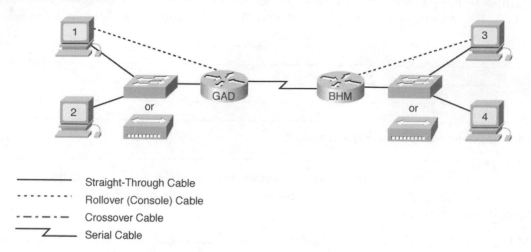

```
Straight-Through Cable
Rollover (Console) Cable
Crossover Cable
Serial Cable
```

Table 11-16 Lab Equipment Configuration

Router Name	FA0 Address	S0 Address
GAD	192.168.1.1/24	192.168.2.1/24
BHM	192.168.3.1/24	192.168.2.2/24

The enable password for both routers is **cisco**.

The vty password for both routers is **class**.

The routing protocol for both routers is RIP.

Table 11-17 Host IP Address, Subnet Mask, and Gateway Configuration

Host	IP Address	Subnet Mask	Gateway
1	192.168.1.2	255.255.255.0	192.168.1.1
2	192.168.1.3	255.255.255.0	192.168.1.1
3	192.168.3.2	255.255.255.0	192.168.3.1
4	192.168.3.3	255.255.255.0	192.168.3.1

Objective

- Use the **access-class** and **line** commands to control Telnet access to the router.

Background/Preparation

The company's home office in Gadsden (GAD) provides services to branch offices such as the Birmingham (BHM) office. Only systems within the local network should be able to Telnet to the router. You will create a standard access list that will permit users on the local network to Telnet to the local router. You will then apply the access list to the virtual terminal lines (vty).

Step 1. Perform basic router interconnection.

Connect the routers as shown in Figure 11-6.

Step 2. Perform basic configuration.

a. The router might contain configurations from a previous use. Implement the procedure in Appendix C on all routers before continuing with this lab. Using the information in Tables 11-11 and 11-12, set up the router and host configurations and verify communications by pinging all systems and routers from each system.

b. Telnet from the hosts to both the local router and the remote router.

Step 3. Create the access list that represents the Gadsden LAN.

The LAN in Gadsden has a network address of 192.168.1.0 /24. To create the access list, use the following commands:

```
GAD(config)#access-list 1 permit 192.168.1.0 0.0.0.255
```

Step 4. Apply the access list to permit only the Gadsden LAN.

After you create the list to represent traffic, you must apply it to the vty lines. This will restrict any Telnet access to the router. Although you could apply it separately to each interface, it is easier to apply the list to all vty lines in one statement. Enter interface mode for all five lines with the global configuration command **line vty 0 4.**

For the GAD router, type the following:

```
GAD(config)#line vty 0 4
        GAD(config-line)#access-class 1 in
        GAD(config-line)#^Z
```

Step 5. Test the restriction.

Test the functionality of the ACL by trying to Telnet from the hosts, and verify that the access list is working correctly.

a. Verify that Host 1 can Telnet to GAD.

b. Verify that Host 2 can Telnet to GAD.

c. Verify that Host 3 cannot Telnet to GAD.

d. Verify that Host 4 cannot Telnet to GAD.

Step 6. Create the restrictions for the BHM Router.

a. Repeat the preceding process in Steps 3, 4, and 5 to restrict the Telnet access to BHM. The restriction should allow only hosts in the Birmingham LAN to Telnet to BHM.

b. Test the functionality of the ACL by trying to Telnet from the hosts, and verify that the access list is working correctly.

c. Verify that Host 1 cannot Telnet to BHM.

d. Verify that Host 2 cannot Telnet to BHM.

e. Verify that Host 3 can Telnet to BHM.

f. Verify that Host 4 can Telnet to BHM.

Step 7. Document the ACL.

As a part of all network management, you should create documentation. Capture a copy of the configuration and add your comments to explain the purpose of the ACL code.

Save the file with other network documentation. The file-naming convention should reflect the function of the file and the date of implementation.

When you finish the preceding steps, log off (by typing **exit**) and turn off the routers.

PART III

Appendixes

Appendix A: Structured Cabling Case Study Labs

Appendix B: Router Interface Summary

Appendix C: Erasing and Reloading the Router

Structured Cabling Case Study Labs

The labs in this appendix appear as a supplement at the end of the CCNA 1 modules in the online curriculum. Although the actual CCNA exam might not cover this material, you should definitely be familiar with the content as a CCNA candidate. The following labs are in this chapter:

Lab Number	Title
Lab A-1	Examination of Termination Types
Lab A-2	Terminating a Category 5e Cable on a Category 5e Patch Panel
Lab A-3	Tool Usage and Safety
Lab A-4	Identification of Cables
Lab A-5	Category 5e Outlet Termination
Lab A-6	Terminating Category 5e to a 110 Block
Lab A-7	Category 6 Jack Termination

Lab A-1: Examination of Termination Types

Objectives

- Review wiring standards T-568A, T-568B, and RJ-45 USOC.
- Terminate the ends of a Category (CAT) 5e cable.

Background/Preparation

Bell Telephone established the technique for terminating twisted-pair cabling. This technique, called the Bell Telephone Universal Service Order Code (USOC), logically organizes the wires into a modular plug. Basically, the first pair goes into the center two pins and the other pairs follow from left to right, splitting each pair down the middle. This technique separates the data wire pairs, which if not separated can lead to crosstalk.

In this lab, you will learn the identification, preparation, and termination of CAT 5e cable by using the two most popular wiring schemes in the American National Standards Institute, Telecommunications Industry Association, and Electronic Industries Association (ANSI/TIA/EIA) standards: T-568A and T-568B.

Work in teams of two to four. Each team will need four CAT 5e cables with a minimum length of 1 m (3 ft) each. Each team will need the following resources:

- 4–5 m (12–15 ft) CAT 5e cable
- Pan-Plug modular plugs

- Pan-Plug crimp tool
- Wire-stripper tool
- Scissors
- Wire-snipping tool
- Wire-prep tool
- Safety glasses

Additional Materials

- USOC wiring schematic

URLs

- http://www.panduit.com
- http://www.tiaonline.org

Safety

Wear safety glasses at all times during this lab. Working with sharp tools can cause deep cuts. Ensure that the lab has a first-aid kit available for emergencies.

Step 1. Remove the cable sheath.

a. Using a ruler, measure 8 cm (3 in) from the end of the cable and put a mark on the cable.

b. Use the wire-stripper tool to carefully score the outer sheathing of the cable without fully cutting through to the conductors. Cut off as close as possible to the marked length and remove the cut sheathing.

Do not nick any of the insulators.

Note: On the stripping tool is a minimum or maximum cutting direction. Use the minimum cutting direction. Do not make more than two 360-degree turns with this tool.

Step 2. Fan the four pairs.

a. Untwist each of the cable pairs. Take care not to untwist more than is needed because the twisting provides noise cancellation (see Figure A-1).

Figure A-1 Fanning Four Pairs: Step 1

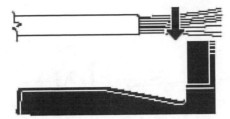

b. Keep the individual pairs grouped together for ease of identification. Some tip wires might not have any visible trace of color and might appear to be solid wires.

c. Using the wire-prep tool, insert the conductors individually in the proper sequence by using the T-568A wiring scheme (see Figure A-2).

Figure A-2 Fanning Four Pairs: Step 2

Note: The top of the arrow in the preceding diagram will be Pin 1 and 2 (white/orange and orange).

d. Pull the conductors until the cable jacket is at the conductor retention slot.

e. Trim the conductors flush with the wire-snipping tool (see Figure A-3).

Figure A-3 Fanning Four Pairs: Step 3

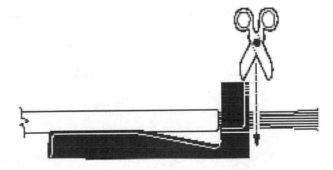

f. Remove the cable from the conductor retention slot, keeping the conductors held in position by placing your thumb and forefinger at the cable jacket end (see Figure A-4).

Figure A-4 Fanning Four Pairs: Step 4

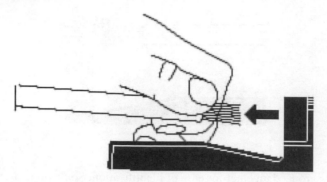

Step 3. Terminate a plug with the T-568A wiring standard.

Pin#	Pair#	Function	Wire Color
1	3	Transmit	White/green
2	3	Transmit	Green
3	2	Receive	White/orange
4	1	Not used	Blue
5	1	Not used	White/blue
6	2	Receive	Orange
7	4	Not used	White/brown
8	4	Not used	Brown

Note: Shown here is a diagram of an RJ-45 jack. The plug will fit with the key toward the bottom of the jack. Positioning the plug with the key pointed away from you when inserting the conductors will ensure that Pin 1 will start on the left and proceed to Pin 8 on the right.

a. Terminate one side of the cable using the T-568A standard (see Figure A-5).

Figure A-5 T-568A

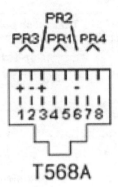

T568A

b. Apply a slight downward pressure as you insert the conductors. Apply slight pressure until they are fully inserted and under the plug contacts at the top of the plug (see Figure A-6).

Figure A-6 Conductor Insertion

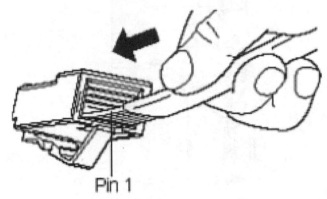

c. Place the plug into the die until it clicks.

d. Complete the termination by closing the handles fully and then releasing them (see Figure A-7).

Figure A-7 Termination

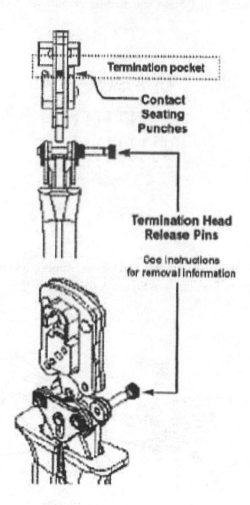

Step 4. Repeat Steps 1 through 3.

Table 5-1 T-568B Standard

Pin#	Pair#	Function	Wire Color
1	3	Transmit	White/orange
2	3	Transmit	Orange
3	2	Receive	White/green
4	1	Not used	Blue
5	1	Not used	White/blue
6	2	Receive	Green
7	4	Not used	White/brown
8	4	Not used	Brown

Use the T-568B standard on the other end of the cable. After you finish both ends of the cable, have a team member review the wiring standards to ensure that the plugs are correctly terminated (see Figure A-8).

Figure A-8 T-568B

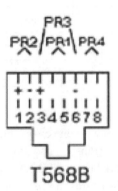

Step 5. Decide which wiring standard to use.

When deciding which wiring standard to use, ask the following questions:

- Does the job specification require a certain wiring standard?

- Has it already been established by the existing cabling?

- Does the new wiring match the existing wiring?

- Has the customer specified a wiring standard?

- Have patch panels already been purchased for the job? If so, they will probably be either T-568A or T-568B. The jacks should be wired to the same standard as the panels.

If none of the previous factors apply, you can use either T-568A or T-568B. It is important to ensure that the workstation connectors and the patch panels are wired to the same standard. In the United States, commercial installations commonly use T-568B, and T-568A is common in residential installations.

Step 6. Test.

Use the Fluke 620 CableMeter or LinkRunner to test the cable installation.

What are the results of the test?

_____

_____

Step 7. Clean up.

Ensure that you properly store all the tools and remove all trash and debris from the work area.

Table 5-2 RJ-45 USOC Schematic

Pin#	Pair#	Wire Color
1	4	White/brown
2	3	Green
3	2	White/orange
4	1	Blue
5	1	White/blue
6	2	Orange
7	3	White/green
8	4	Brown

USOC is an old standard for voice cabling. For phones with one or two lines (which use Pins 4/5 and 3/6), T-568A or T-568B will work just as well as USOC. However, for Ethernet (Pins 1/2 and 3/6), USOC will not work. An Ethernet network interface card (NIC) trying to transmit on Pins 1/2 will not work because 1/2 is not a pair. (They are not the same color and not twisted together.) The USOC code is not recognized by the standards; however, it is common in the termination of T1 circuits.

Lab A-2: Terminating a CAT 5e Cable on a CAT 5e Patch Panel

Objectives

- Terminate a CAT 5e cable on a CAT 5e patch panel.
- Use the 110 punch-down tool.
- Use the cable stripper.

Background/Preparation

To cross connect patch panels, you must properly punch down wires on a CAT 5e patch panel. It is important that you correctly execute each punch-down to ensure proper connectivity.

A CAT 5e patch panel is a device that terminates wires in a central location. One patch panel contains cables from local data and voice networks; a separate panel collects cables from the outside. These panels provide a way to connect the two collections of wires to supply connectivity from outside the building all the way to the desktop. This system of wire management lets you organize the wires and make quick changes.

In this lab, you will terminate a CAT 5e cable on a patch panel. You will terminate the other end of the cable on a 110 connection block and use a 110-to-RJ-45 adapter cable. You will test the cable you installed.

The instructor or lab assistant will designate the location of the punch-down for each student at the top of this sheet, which indicates the rack, row, and position on the patch panel. You need the following resources:

- CAT 5e patch panel
- 1.2 m (4 ft) of CAT 5e UTP cable
- Wire-stripper tool
- Wire-snipping tool
- Impact tool with 110 cutting blade
- C4 clips
- 110-to-RJ-45 adapter cable
- Fluke 620 LAN CableMeter or LinkRunner
- Safety glasses

URL

- http://www.panduit.com

Safety

Remember to always wear safety glasses when punching down wires. Remember that because the impact tools have sharp blades, you must always be conscious of the task you are performing to avoid accidental cuts.

Step 1. Prepare the cable.

Remove enough of the sheath to terminate the cable on the patch panel.

Step 2. Insert the conductors.

a. Fan out the conductor pairs without untwisting the wires at all.

b. Follow the label on the rear of the patch panel. You will terminate the cables as T-568B.

c. Make sure to have 8-10 cm (3-4 in) of extra wire past the termination point and split a twist on the colored tip. The tip color goes to the left and the ring color goes to the right. This step ensures that the twisting continues up to the point of termination. It is important that the twists in the wire remain as tight as possible up to the point of termination. The maximum untwist length for CAT 5e cable is 1 cm (0.5 in), but 3 mm (0.125 in) is preferable. It is also important to keep the end of the jacket as close as possible to the termination hardware. This step will help keep the pairs properly spaced to eliminate NEXT insertion and other electrical deficiencies.

d. To make sure that the termination of the cable looks professional, it is best to begin the insertion of the conductors with the center pairs and work towards the outside termination points, as shown in Figure A-9. This procedure provides the outside wire pairs a minimal and equal amount of exposure.

Figure A-9 Wire Insertions

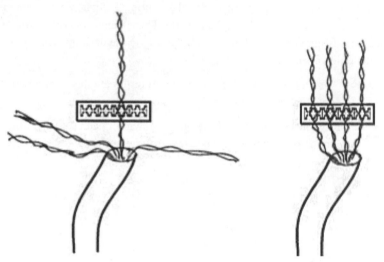

Step 3. Punch down.

Note: If you punch down on the patch panel too hard, you can damage the circuit board inside. You should only use the single-wire impact tool with the 110 blade for this application. Set the impact tool on the "lo" setting. Never use the multipunch tool when terminating on a patch panel.

---

a. Position the impact tool over the wire with the blade facing toward the end of the wire and press firmly on the impact tool until it clicks. Do not hit the tool with the hand to punch down the wires. With the impact tool set to "lo," it might be necessary to punch the wire two or three times to ensure a proper termination.

b. Follow Steps 2 and 3 for the other wire of the pair. Gently remove the excess wire.

c. Repeat this step for each pair of wires.

Step 4. Terminate the cable on the 110 panel.

a. Strip 7.5 cm (3 in) from the other end of the cable and then terminate it on the designated row and position of 110 connection block AA or BB-5. This block is located on the relay rack.

b. Install a C4 clip over the CAT 5e cable.

Step 5. Examine the RJ-45-to-110 adapter cable.

a. An RJ-45-to-110 adapter cable is a cable with an RJ-45 connector on one end and a connecter that plugs into a 110 panel on the other end. (See Figure A-10.)

Figure A-10 RJ-45-to-110 Adapter Cable

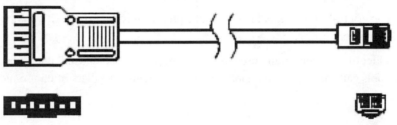

b. Will this cable test as a straight-through cable or a crossover cable?

_____

c. Explain why.

_____

_____

d. Snap the adapter over the installed C4 clip. Using the Fluke 620, test the cable between the patch panel and the 110 connection block.

e. What are the results of the test?

_____

f. Was your initial assumption correct?

_____

Step 6. Clean up.

Ensure that you properly store all the tools. Remove all trash and debris.

Lab A-3: Tool Usage and Safety

Objectives

- Identify the tools that are used in cable installations.
- Examine and handle the tools that are used in cable installations.

Background/Preparation

The type of cable that you install determines the tools that you need for a job. You must have proper tools to install cables correctly and safely. Although you will not use every tool in every cable installation job, it is important to know about most of the tools and supplies that can ensure quality installations and to complete the jobs in a safe and timely manner.

Safety is a consideration for every task. It is critical that you take precautions to ensure that you do the job safely. Knowing how to use the tools will help prevent injury.

The purpose of this lab is to identify the commonly used tools and supplies in cable installation jobs and learn how to use them safely. The names of some tools can vary between regions and countries, and installers often use nicknames for some tools.

Warning: The instructor *must* be present during this lab. Some of the tools introduced in this lab are dangerous. Before handling each tool, read the section in the lab that corresponds to the tool. The section will review how each tool works and any safety measures that you must follow.

You need the following resources:

- Cutting tools
- Terminating tools

URLs

- http://www.du.edu/risk/Tool_Safety.html
- http://siri.uvm.edu/ftp/ppt/handsafe/handsafety.ppt

Step 1. Examine the cutting tools.

Handle all the tools. Simulate how you would use them in the field.

Panduit Wire-Stripper Tool

The wire-stripper tool removes the outer sheath from CAT 5e cable and small coaxial cable. You pull the tool apart to retract the cutting blade (see Figure A-11). You insert cable into the hole and release the blade. Spin the tool around the cable one turn. It turns in a clockwise direction for cables with thinner jackets and counter clockwise for cables with thicker jackets. You then spread the tool apart to remove it. You can now easily pull off the jacket. Because this is a cutting tool, you should wear safety glasses when using this tool.

Figure A-11 Panduit Wire-Stripper Tool

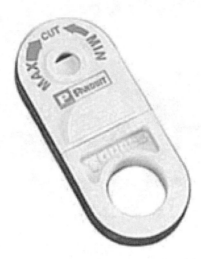

Electrician's Scissors

You can use electrician's scissors, also known as snips, for cutting CAT 5e cable and miscellaneous wire on an installation project (see Figure A-12). There are two notches on one of the blades. These notches skin insulation from individual conductors. The scissors can also score cable jackets. As with other cutting tools, you should take care not to pinch your fingers between the handles or cut your fingers. Always wear safety glasses when using snips.

Figure A-12 Electrician's Scissors

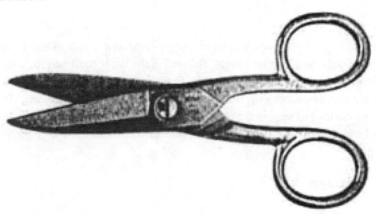

Panduit Wire-Snipping Tool

The wire-snipping tool cuts excess wire when you install a TX mini-jack (see Figure A-13). The tool cuts copper conductors flush with the termination cap. You should not use the wire-snipping tool for cutting CAT 5e cables. It is designed for cutting individual cable pairs only. This tool is sharp, and you should take care when using it. Remember to be careful of the sharp tips on the blades. As with all cutting tools, you should wear safety glasses when using this tool.

Figure A-13 Panduit Wire-Snipping Tool

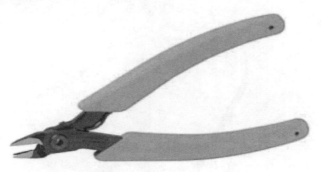

a. How many times do you rotate the cable-stripping tool to remove a cable jacket?

_____

b. Which tools require safety glasses during use?

_____

_____

Step 2. Examine the termination tools.

Handle all the tools. Simulate how they you would use them in the field.

Panduit Single-Pair Punch Tool

The single-pair punch tool terminates cable pairs on termination blocks and on the back of patch panels (see Figure A-14). The tool accepts blades from all the popular termination panels. The tool in the lab is equipped for terminating cable pairs on 110 blocks. The blade is reversible. It has a cut position on one side. In this configuration, the tool punches down a wire and cuts off the excess wire in a single motion. The other side of the blade punches down without cutting. The cutting side is marked on the body of the tool. You remove blades by twisting the blade counter-clockwise and pulling the blade out of the tool. To install the blade, insert it into the tool and twist clockwise. Be careful when using this tool or changing the blades because the small blade on the end can cause cuts.

Figure A-14 Panduit Single-Pair Punch Tool

Insert a wire into its slot in a termination panel. Grasp the tool by the handle. Keeping the tool perpendicular to the block, push the blade over the wire. This tool is an impact tool. As you push the handle, spring tension increases until the tool snaps and releases the energy of the compressed spring. The wire is completely seated into its position and the excess wire is cut off. The tool features an adjustable impact setting.

Panduit Multipair Punch Tool

The multipair punch tool inserts conductors on 110 blocks (see Figure A-15). The tool inserts and cuts five pairs at one time. The tool also terminates three, four, or five pairs of conductors at a time by seating C clips over them after they have been inserted. The multipair punch tool features reversible and replaceable cutting blades. By twisting the head of the tool, you release a detent and you can remove the head from the tool. You slide the cutting blades out from the side of the head. You install the blades facing forward for cutting or facing backward for seating C clips. Be careful with this tool because it has numerous small blades that can cause cuts. You use the tool in a fashion similar to the single-pair punch tool. You insert multiple pairs in the block, place the tool over the pairs, and push on the tool until the energy in the spring is released in a sharp impact. This tool is a high-impact tool and is not suitable for use on the back of patch panels.

Figure A-15 Panduit Multipair Punch Tool

TX Mini-Jack Termination Tool

The TX mini-jack termination tool presses the termination cap into a TX mini-jack (see Figure A-16). The termination tool ensures a proper and uniform installation of the termination cap into the jack.

Figure A-16 TX Mini-Jack Termination Tool

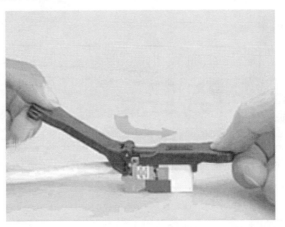

a. Describe the difference between the two ends of the blade on the 110 punch tool.

_____

_____

b. How do you remove the blade on the multipair punch tool?

_____

_____

c. How do you remove the blade on the 110 punch tool?

_____

_____

d. Why does the multipair punch tool have a reversible blade?

_____

_____

e. Why does the 110 punch tool have a reversible blade?

_____

_____

f. What tool terminates a mini-jack?

_____

g. Why can't you use the multipair punch tool at the back of a patch panel?

_____

_____

Step 3. Examine the crimp tools.

Panduit RJ-45 Crimp Tool

The RJ-45 crimp tool installs RJ-45 connectors on the end of a cable (see Figure A-17). You insert wires into the connector following the proper color code. Insert the connector into the tool until the connector clicks into place. Squeeze the handles of the tool completely until they release. This tool is a ratcheting tool, so the handles will not return to their full open position until the tool fully closes. Keep your fingers out of the open jaws of the tool. There is a release lever between the handles of the tool that lets you open the jaws without fully closing them. This lever is a safety feature.

Figure A-17 Panduit RJ-45 Crimp Tool

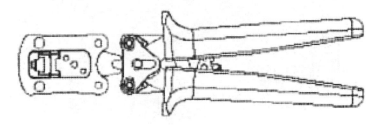

What are the two ways to open the RJ-45 crimp tool?

_____

_____

Lab A-4: Identification of Cables

Objective

Identify the different types of cables used in this course.

Background/Preparation

Category (CAT) is the term that distinguishes the grades of twisted-pair cables. Each grade is distinguished by the number of wires in the cable, the number of twists of the wires (to reduce interference from other wires), and the speed of data transmission it can accommodate. This lab will identify several categories of copper cables.

The instructor or lab assistant will prepare 0.3 m (1 ft) to 0.6 m (2 ft) lengths of each type of cable listed. Strip off 15 cm (6 in) of the outer sheathing at one end of the cable so that you can examine the construction of the cables.

There is a minimum and maximum cutting edge on the cable-stripping tool. Use the minimum cutting edge to ensure that you do not nick the conductors. Make sure that you use a maximum of two 360-degree turns with the cable-stripping tool to prevent nicking the conductors. Work in teams of four or five. You need the following resources:

- CAT 5e UTP stranded-conductor cable
- CAT 5e UTP solid-conductor cable
- CAT 6 UTP stranded-conductor cable
- CAT 6 UTP solid-conductor cable
- Cable-stripping tool
- Tape measure

URL

- http://www.panduit.com

Step 1. Examine the CAT 5e UTP solid-conductor cable.

a. Select the CAT 5e UTP solid-conductor cable by inspecting the cable jacket. It identifies the type of cable.

b. What is the marking on this cable? _____

c. Now look at the inside structure of the cable.

d. How many pairs are in the cable? _____

e. What helps to identify a particular wire?_____

f. Look at the individual wires.

g. How many strands of copper are within each wire?

_____

Step 2. Examine the CAT 5e UTP stranded-conductor cable.

a. Select the CAT 5e UTP stranded-core cable.

b. Does the outer jacket differ from that of the CAT 5e UTP solid-conductor cable?

_____

c. What is the marking on this cable? _____

d. Examine the internal construction of the cable.

e. How does it differ from the CAT 5e UTP solid-conductor cable?

_____

f. How many strands of copper are within each wire?

_____

Step 3. Examine the Category 6 UTP solid-conductor cable

a. Select the Category 6 UTP solid-conductor cable. Inspect the cable carefully, and note that the cable's jacket identifies the type of cable.

b. What is the marking on this cable? _____

c. Examine the internal construction of the cable.

d. How does it differ from a Category 5e UTP cable? _____

e. How many layers of shielding does it have? _____

f. How many strands of copper are within each wire? _____

Step 4. Examine the CAT 6 UTP stranded-conductor cable.

a. Select the CAT 6 UTP stranded-conductor cable.

b. What is the marking on this cable? _____

c. Examine the internal construction of the cable.

d. How many pairs are in the cable? _____

e. How does it differ from a CAT 5e UTP cable?

_____

f. How many layers of shielding does it have?

_____

g. How many strands of copper are within each wire?

_____

Question

Describe the differences between the CAT 5e and CAT 6 cables.

_____

_____

_____

Lab A-5: CAT 5e Outlet Termination

Objectives

- Practice proper safety procedures when using cabling tools.

- Use the T-568B standard when terminating CAT 5e cable on a modular jack at a wall outlet and at the patch panel.

Background/Preparation

Jacks terminate the CAT 5e cable, and the faceplate provides the finishing touch. A modular patch panel allows the termination of the cable with the same mini-jack module used in a wall outlet.

To provide connectivity in the structured cable system infrastructure, you must be able to terminate CAT 5e cable at wall outlets. During this lab, you will terminate one end of a CAT 5e cable with an RJ-45 mini-jack and insert it into a patch panel. Work in teams of two. You need the following resources:

- RJ-45 mini-jack

- 60 cm (2 ft) of CAT 5e UTP solid-core cable

- Safety glasses

- Wire-stripper tool

- Mini-jack module-termination tool

- Permanent marker pen

- Wire-snipping tool

- Electrician's scissors

- Fluke 620 LAN CableMeter or LinkRunner

URL

- http://www.panduit.com

Safety

You should always wear safety glasses when you use cutting tools.

Step 1. Label the cable.

Place a label on the cable approximately 15 cm (6 in) from the end. Each cable must have a unique identifier. For this exercise, you should use a permanent marking pen to write your first name on the cable. Follow the name with pp1 (patch panel 1) and the port number of the patch panel to which you will insert the jack.

Step 2. Remove the sheathing.

Now that the cable is the proper length and has a unique label, remove the sheathing without causing any damage to the conductors. Use the wire-stripper tool to ring the cable about 5 cm (2 in) from the end of the cable. Should there be any exposed copper on the conductors where you removed the cable jacket, cut off the end of the cable and remove 5 cm (2 in) of jacket again. If needed, repeat the labeling process.

Step 3. Prepare the cable and jack.

a. Separate the twisted pairs from each other without untwisting the pairs (see Figure A-18). Pull the wire pairs to set their positions. Use the T-568B wiring standard when terminating this jack.

Figure A-18 Separating Twisted Pairs

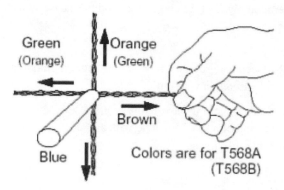

b. Gather the twisted pairs and insert them into the cap (see Figure A-19).

Figure A-19 Inserting Twisted Pairs

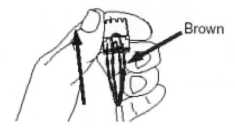

c. Push the cable jacket until the jacket end is located under the label (see Figure A-20).

Figure A-20 Pushing the Cable Jacket

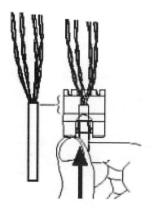

d. Untwist the pairs one at a time, starting with the outside pairs, and place them into the correct slots (see Figure A-21). It is very important to untwist each pair only as far as required to place the conductors in the correct slots.

Figure A-21 Untwisting Pairs

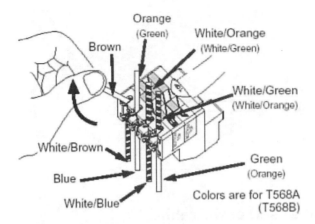

e. Trim each conductor flush with the cap with the wire-snipping tool (see Figure A-22). Make sure that all the conductors are still seated in their slots.

Figure A-22 Trimming Conductor Flush

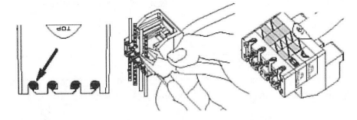

Step 4. Terminate the cable.

a. Slide the front of the mini-jack into the backing, making sure that it is straight (see Figure A-23).

Figure A-23 Terminating the cable

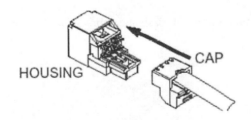

b. Use the mini-jack tool to press the two pieces together until they snap (see Figure A-24). You have now terminated the cable. From behind the panel, snap the jack module into a vacant position on the modular patch panel.

Figure A-24 Mini-Jack Tool

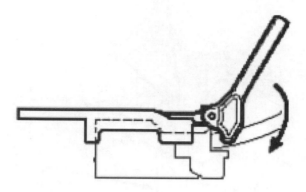

Step 5. Terminate the other end of the cable.

Install the other mini-jack module using the T-568B wiring standard to terminate the cable and insert this jack into the correct patch panel port.

Step 6. Test your work.

a. Use the Fluke 620 LAN CableMeter or LinkRunner to test the jack installation.

b. What are the results of the test?

_____

_____

c. Are the results exactly the same when you test the second jack?

_____

d. Why or why not?

_____

_____

Step 7. Clean up.

Ensure that you properly store all tools and remove all trash and debris from the work area.

Lab A-6: Terminating CAT 5e to a 110 Block

Objectives

- Terminate CAT 5e cable to a 110-type termination block.
- Properly use a 110 punch-down tool and 110 multipunch tool.

Background/Preparation

To prepare to cross-connect blocks, you must be able to properly punch down a 110 block. It is important that you execute each punch-down correctly to ensure proper connectivity.

A 110 punch-down block is a device that terminates wires in a common place. One block collects wires from internal data networks and telephones. A separate block collects wires from outside the building. These two blocks provide a way to connect the two collections of wires to supply connectivity from external sources to the desktop. This system of wire management keeps the wires organized and allows for quick changes.

The instructor or lab assistant will designate the location of the punch-down, indicating the row (1-4) and position (1-6) on the block. Work in teams of one to four. You need the following resources:

- 110 punch block
- 1 m (3 ft) of CAT 5e UTP cable
- C-4 clips
- Copper strip tool
- Impact tool with 110 cutting blade
- 110 multipunch tool
- Pliers

URL

- http://www.panduit.com

Safety

You should always wear safety glasses when using cutting tools. Use caution when using impact tools because they have sharp blades.

Step 1. Prepare the cable.

a. Determine the position on the 110 block that you will use to terminate the cable. Because you are using a four-pair cable, determine the positions by counting four pairs from the left end of the block (see Figure A-25). For example, Position 1 is the first four pairs, Position 2 is the second four pairs, and so on. Label the cable with respect to its position on the block. If the plan is to terminate the cable on Position 3, use the labeler and pen to number the cable #3.

Figure A-25 110 Block

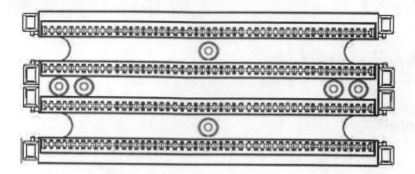

b. Now that the cable has a unique label, you need to remove the sheathing without causing any damage to the conductors.

Step 2. Fan the conductors.

a. Separate and fan out the conductor pairs without untwisting the wires.

b. Place the wires one pair at a time into the termination points 7-10 cm (2-3 in) from the end of the wires. This placement will put the two wires in the correct position to be punched down while ensuring that the twisting continues up to the point of termination. Use the proper color-coding scheme, which is white/blue, white/orange, white/green, and white/brown. Make sure that you place the tip colored wire to the left and the ring to the right.

Step 3. Punch down.

a. Place the single-wire punch-down tool over the wire that you will punch. Be sure that the blade will only cut off the end of the wire. The cutting edge of the blade should be facing the direction to be cut.

b. Press firmly on the impact tool until it clicks. This click ensures that you have punched the wire down all the way and that you have cut the excess wire. Do not hit the tool to punch down the wires.

c. Repeat this step for the other wire. Gently remove the excess wire.

Step 4. Punch down the rest of the pairs.

Repeat Steps 2 and 3 for each pair of wires.

Step 5. Place the C-4 connector.

a. Use a C-4 connector is used for four-pair cables (see Figure A-26). The C-4 connector makes the actual connection to the CAT 5e cable. Place the C-4 connector over the wires punched down, being sure to match the color-coding correctly.

Figure A-26 C-4 Connector

b. Position the 110 multipunch tool over the C-4 connector. The multipunch tool seats the C-4 connector.

c. Press firmly on the multipunch tool until it clicks. This click ensures that you have attached the C-4 connector correctly and properly terminated the wire.

Step 6. Perform an inspection.

a. Look carefully at the punched-down cable.

b. Approximate the length of the wires that are untwisted.

_____

c. What is the maximum allowable untwist length?

_____

d. How much of the pairs are exposed?

_____

e. How many CAT 5e cables can you terminate in a single row of a 110 block?

_____

Step 7. Clean up.

Remove the C-4 connector that you installed by using a pair of pliers to grasp the clip and pulling it straight back until it pops off. Make sure that you properly store all the tools and remove all trash and debris from the work area.

Lab A-7: Category 6 Jack Termination

Objectives

- Practice proper safety procedures when using cabling tools.
- Terminate a Category (CAT) 6 cable using proper techniques for high-bandwidth data cabling.

Background/Preparation

You must follow certain precautions when jacks terminate CAT 6 cable. The tolerances of dimensions increase in importance as the frequencies of voltages on the cables and the data rates increase.

The following instructions explain how to terminate Panduit Mini-Com TX-6 Plus modules. Although installation techniques will vary slightly, paying attention to these procedures will facilitate working with many CAT 6 terminations and devices.

During this lab, each student on the team will terminate one end of a CAT 6 cable with an RJ-45 mini-jack and insert it into a patch panel. You need the following resources to complete this lab:

- 2 RJ-45 Mini-Com TX-6 Plus modules
- 60 cm (2 ft) of CAT 6 UTP solid-core cable
- Safety glasses
- Wire-stripper tool
- Permanent marker pen
- Mini-jack module termination tool
- Wire-snipping tool
- Electrician's scissors
- Cable tester for verifying that the wires were connected correctly

URL

- http://www.panduit.com

Safety

Make sure to wear safety glasses or goggles during the entire lab.

Step 1. Label the cable.

Place a label on the cable approximately 15 cm (6 in) from the end. Each cable must have a unique identifier. For this exercise, use a permanent marking pen to write your first name on the end of the cable that you terminate. If you will insert the jack into a patch panel, follow your name with pp1 (patch panel 1) and the port number of the patch panel to which you will insert the jack.

Step 2. Remove the sheathing and order the pairs.

Now that the cable is the proper length and has a unique label, remove the sheathing without causing any damage to the conductors. Use the wire stripper tool to ring the cable about 5 cm (2 in) from the end of the cable. If there is any exposed copper on the conductors where you removed the cable jacket, cut off the end of the cable and remove 5 cm (2 in) of jacket again. If needed, repeat the labeling process.

Avoid damaging or disturbing the cable pairs any more than is necessary. Fan out the cable pairs as shown in Figure A-27, ordering the colors as shown in Figure A-28. Trim the pairs to length as shown in Figure A-27. Note that these instructions apply to solid, not stranded, conductors.

Figure A-27 Fanning Out the Cable Pairs

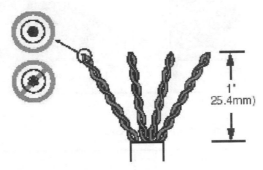

Figure A-28 T-568A and T-568B Cabling

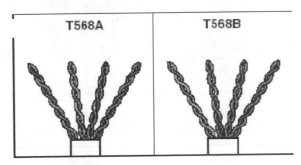

Step 3. Insert the cable into the jack.

Holding the module assembly with the correct side up as shown in Figure A-29, and with the cable oriented as shown in the previous step, gently push the ordered pairs through the holes in the module assembly. Insert the cable fully, making sure that the pairs go through the correct holes.

Figure A-29 How to Insert the Cable into the Jack

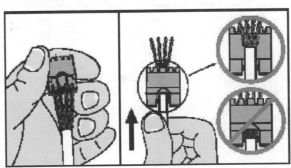

Step 4. Insert the wires into the notches.

Using Figures A-30, A-31, and A-32 as a guide, twist the pairs in the order shown, one at a time starting with the outside pairs, and place them into the correct slots. It is very important to untwist each pair only as far as required to place the conductors in the correct slots.

Figure A-30 Inserting T-568A and T-568B Wires into Notches: Step 1

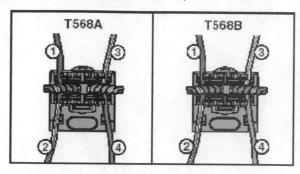

Figure A-31 Inserting T-568A and T-568B Wires into Notches: Step 2

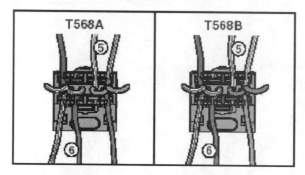

Figure A-32 Inserting T-568A and T-568B Wires into Notches: Step 3

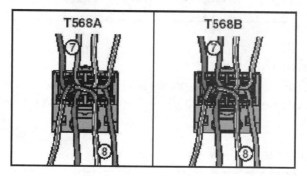

Step 5. Snip the wire ends flush.

As illustrated in Figure A-33, trim each conductor flush with the cap with the wire-snipping tool. Be sure that all the conductors are still seated in their slots.

Figure A-33 Snipping the Wire Ends Flush

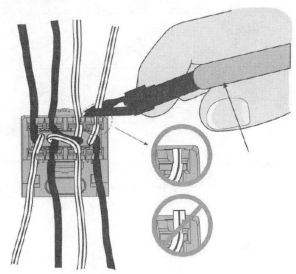

Step 6. Assemble the module.

As illustrated in Figure A-34, slide the front of the mini-jack into the backing, making sure that it is straight.

Use the mini-jack tool to press the two pieces together until they snap. You have now terminated the cable. Alternatively, use slip-jaw pliers with the jaws set to the distance of the finished jack. If the pliers consistently damage the modules, wrap a little electrical tape over each jaw before using.

Figure A-34 Assembling the Module

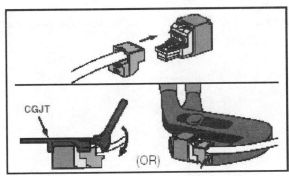

Step 7. Install the shielded cables.

For shielded cables, it will be necessary to install the metallic cover as shown in Figure A-35. Route the drain wire to the rear of the module and wrap it over the ground lug that extends to the rear of the cover. Secure it with the plastic crimp ring as shown. If you will use the module in a surface-mount fixture, use a nylon cable tie instead.

Figure A-35 Shielded Installation

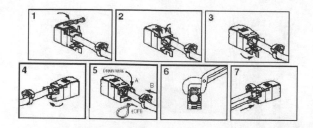

Step 8. Terminate the other end of the cable.

Install the other mini-jack module by using the same wiring pattern (T-568A or T-568B) to terminate the cable.

Step 9. Test.

Use the cable tester to test the jack installation.

What are the results of the test?

_____

Are the results exactly the same when you text the second jack?

_____

Why or why not?

_____

Step 10. Clean up.

Ensure that you properly store all tools and remove all trash and debris from the work area.

Router Interface Summary

For the majority of CCNA 2 labs, you need to examine the following chart to correctly reference the router interface identifiers to use in IOS commands. The correct identifier to use is based on the equipment in your lab.

Router Model	Ethernet Interface #1	Ethernet Interface #2	Serial Interface #1	Serial Interface #2
800 (806)	Ethernet 0 (E0)	Ethernet 1 (E1)		
1600	Ethernet 0 (E0)	Ethernet 1 (E1)	Serial 0 (S0)	Serial 1 (S1)
1700	FastEthernet 0 (FA0)	FastEthernet 1 (FA1)	Serial 0 (S0)	Serial 1 (S1)
2500	Ethernet 0 (E0)	Ethernet 1 (E1)	Serial 0 (S0)	Serial 1 (S1)
2600	FastEthernet 0/0 (FA0/0)	FastEthernet 0/1 (FA0/1)	Serial 0/0 (S0/0)	Serial 0/1 (S0/1)

To find out exactly how the router is configured, look at the interfaces and identify what type and how many interfaces the router has. There is no way to effectively list all of the combinations of configurations for each router class. What the chart provides are the identifiers for the possible combinations of interfaces in the device. This interface chart does not include any other type of interface even though a specific router might contain one. An example of this is an ISDN BRI interface. The string in parentheses is the legal abbreviation that you can use in Cisco IOS software commands to represent the interface.

Erasing and Reloading the Router

For the majority of CCNA2 labs, it is necessary to start with a basic unconfigured router; otherwise, the configuration parameters you enter might combine with previous ones and produce unpredictable results. The instructions here allow you to prepare the router prior to performing the lab so that previous configuration options do not interfere with your configurations.

The following is the procedure for clearing out previous configurations and starting with an unconfigured router.

1. Enter into privileged EXEC mode by typing **enable**.

   ```
   Router> enable
   ```

   If prompted for a password, enter **class**. (If that does not work, ask your instructor.)

2. In privileged EXEC mode, enter the command **erase startup-config**:

   ```
   Router# erase startup-config
   ```

   The response from the router will be

   ```
   Erasing the nvram filesystem will remove all files! Continue? [confirm]
   ```

3. Press **Enter** to confirm.

   The response will be

   ```
   Erase of nvram: complete
   ```

4. Now in privileged EXEC mode, enter the command **reload**:

   ```
   Router# reload
   response:
   System configuration has been modified. Save? [yes/no]:
   ```

   Type **n** and then **Enter**.

   The router will respond with

   ```
   Proceed with reload? [confirm]
   ```

5. Press **Enter** to confirm.

   The first line of the response will be

   ```
   Reload requested by console.
   ```

   After the router reloads, the prompt will be

   ```
   Would you like to enter the initial configuration dialog? [yes/no]:
   ```

6. Type **n** and then **Enter**.

   The responding prompt will be

   ```
   Press RETURN to get started!
   ```

7. Press **Enter**.

   Now, the router is ready for you to perform the assigned lab.